Creating the Old Testament

Creating the Old Testament

The Emergence of the Hebrew Bible

EDITED BY

Stephen Bigger

Basil Blackwell

Copyright © Basil Blackwell Ltd 1989

First published 1989

Basil Blackwell Ltd
108 Cowley Road, Oxford, OX4 1JF, UK

Basil Blackwell, Inc.
3 Cambridge Center
Cambridge, Massachusetts 02142, USA

British Library Cataloguing in Publication Data
A CIP catalogue record for this book is available from the British Library.

Library of Congress Cataloging in Publication Data
Creating the Old Testament : the emergence of the Hebrew Bible /
  edited by Stephen Bigger.
        p.   cm.
  Bibliography: p.
  Includes index.
  ISBN 0-631-15909-6 — ISBN 0-631-16249-6 (pbk.)
  1. Bible.   O.T.—Introductions.   I. Bigger, Stephen.
BS1140.2.C73   1989   89-30938
221.6'1—dc 19   CIP

Typeset in Garamond on 10/12 pt Garamond by Times Graphics.
Printed in Great Britain by T.J. Press Ltd., Padstow

Contents

List of Contributors   vii

Preface   xi

Introduction   xiii
Note on Texts and Transliteration   xviii
List of Abbreviations   xix

Part I   Introductory   1

1   The Hebrew World   *Adrian H. W. Curtis*   3

2   The Authority and Use of the Hebrew Bible   23

    The History of the Text   *Peter Robson*   23
    A Jewish Perspective   *Sybil Sheridan and Dan Cohn-Sherbok*   31
    A Christian Perspective   *Mervyn Tower*   37
    A Muslim Perspective   *Stephen Bigger*   43
    A Humanist Perspective   *Stephen Bigger*   47

3   Symbol and Metaphor in the Hebrew Bible   *Stephen Bigger*   51

Part II   The Torah   81

4   Genesis: History or Story?   83

    The Torah: Some Preliminary Remarks   *Stephen Bigger*   83
    Genesis: the Story   *Stephen Bigger*   86
    Genesis: the Evidence   *Alastair G. Hunter*   90

5   Moses   *Stephen Bigger*   117

6   Covenant and Law   *Dan Cohn-Sherbok and Stephen Bigger*   135

Part III   Nebi'im: the Prophets   149

7   The Former Prophets   *Keith W. Whitelam*   151

8 Jerusalem   *Philip Davies*   169

9 Stories of the Prophets   *Michael E. W. Thompson and Stephen*   185
   Bigger

10 Prophecy and the Prophets   *A. Graeme Auld*   203

Part IV   Kethubim: the Writings   227

11 After the Exile   *Richard J. Coggins*   229

12 The Psalms   *Roger Tomes*   251

13 The Wisdom Books   *David J. A. Clines*   269

14 The Five Megilloth   *Sybil Sheridan*   293

15 The Other Books   *Margaret Barker*   319

Glossary   345
References and Bibliography   351
Index   360

List of Contributors

Dr A. Graeme Auld is Senior Lecturer in Hebrew and Old Testament Studies, University of Edinburgh. He has been Assistant Director of the British School of Archaeology in Jerusalem, and is the current editor of the Society for Old Testament Study's *Book List*. His writings include *Joshua, Moses and the Land* (1980), *Joshua, Judges and Ruth* (1984), *Kings* (1986) and *Amos* (1986).

Margaret Barker, a teacher and diocesan lecturer, has written *The Older Testament* (1987) and *The Lost Prophet: The Book of Enoch and its Influence on Christianity* (1988).

Dr Stephen Bigger is Postgraduate Tutor at Westminster College, Oxford, and Principal Lecturer in World Religions and Religious Education.

Dr David J. A. Clines is Professor of Biblical Studies in the University of Sheffield, and a director and publisher of Sheffield Academic Press. His publications include *I, He, We, and They: a Literary Approach to Isaiah 53* (1976), *The Theme of the Pentateuch* (1978), *Midian, Moab and Edom* (with J. F. A. Sawyer, 1983), *Art and Meaning: Rhetoric in Biblical Literature* (edited with D. M. Gunn and A. J. Hauser, 1982), *The Esther Scroll: the Story of a Story* (1984), *Ezra, Nehemiah, Esther* (1984), and *Job 1–20* (1989).

Richard J. Coggins is Lecturer in Old Testament at King's College, London. His publications include *Samaritans and Jews* (1975), *Ezra and Nehemiah* (1976), *Chronicles* (1976), *Who's Who in the Bible?* (1981), *Israel's Prophetic Tradition: Essays in Honour of Peter Ackroyd* (edited with

A. Phillips and M. Knibb, 1982), *Israel among the Nations: a Commentary on the Books of Nahum, Obadiah, Esther* (with S. P. Re'emi, 1985) and *Haggai, Zechariah, Malachi* (1987).

Dan Cohn-Sherbok is a rabbi and Director of the Centre for the Study of Religion and Society, University of Kent at Canterbury. His writings include *The Jewish Community of Canterbury* (1984), *On Earth as it is in Heaven: Jews, Christians and Liberation Theology* (1987), *Exploring Reality* (with Michael Irwin, 1987), *The Jewish Heritage* (1988), and *Jewish Petitionary Prayer: a Theological Exploration* (1989).

Dr Adrian H. W. Curtis is Senior Lecturer in Old Testament at Manchester University. His writings include *Ugarit* (1985).

Dr Philip Davies is Senior Lecturer in Biblical Studies at the University of Sheffield and an editor of JSOT Press. His writings include *The Damascus Covenant: an Interpretation of the 'Damascus Document'* (1982), *Qumran* (1982), *Daniel* (1985), *A Word in Season* (with J. D. Martin, 1986), and *The Old Testament World* (with J. Rogerson, 1989).

Alastair G. Hunter is Lecturer in Biblical Studies at Glasgow University. His writings include *Christianity and Other Faiths in Britain* (1985).

Peter Robson was, before his retirement, Chaplain of Brasenose College, University of Oxford.

Sybil Sheridan is a lecturer at Leo Baeck College in London and author of *Stories from the Jewish World* (1987). She is a rabbi.

Dr Michael E. W. Thompson is minister of the Whaley Bridge Uniting Church, Derbyshire. He has written *Situation and Theology: Old Testament Interpretations of the Syro-Ephraimite War* (1982).

Roger Tomes is Lecturer in Old Testament at Northern College, Manchester. His writings include *The Fear of the Lord: an Introduction to Old Testament Religion* (1971).

Mervyn Tower is a lecturer at Oscott College, Birmingham.

Dr Keith W. Whitelam is Lecturer in Religious Studies at the University of Stirling. His writings include *The Just King: Monarchical Judicial Authority in Ancient Israel* (1979) and *The Emergence of Early Israel in Historical Perspective* (with R. B. Coote, 1987).

Preface

This volume is the result of collaboration between the contributors and began life during discussions in the Society for Old Testament Study about the need for an introductory book for students, teachers, churches and synagogue study groups, and general readers. There is now, in religious education in primary and secondary schools, a renewed interest in the Bible following the 1988 Education Act: this book will set the beginner on the road to understanding Old Testament texts, and to unravelling the tangled skein of views about the Bible.

Few other ancient books in our history and culture have been the centre of such wide-ranging and bitter controversies, or have so many diverse views held about them. This volume has two aims: to introduce readers to the biblical material; and to explore with them the major strategies used in biblical studies to reach a better understanding of how the text is best interpreted. These strategies may themselves be controversial, and readers will be encouraged to challenge established views, whether these are the 'assured results' of critical scholarship, or stem from doctrinal positions. To borrow a phrase from Dennis Nineham (1976, 25), in biblical inter-pretation there are many 'doctrines felt as facts' – assumptions about what is true which are never subjected to proper scrutiny because it has never occurred to the reader that they might not be true. We try in this book to start with what we can say reasonably certainly, and then examine the hypotheses which are used to make some sense of what we know. For the most part, what we can say for certain can be summed up in one sentence – *that the text reached its present form some time.* The present text is therefore the starting-point of our studies.

As editor, I should like to thank the contributors for their work, and for their patience during discussions about how the book's aims could best be met and how it might best be made to fit together smoothly. Their comments at the editorial stage were also invaluable. Without their efforts this book would not have been written. Without their good humour the editor's task would have been much more difficult. It is, however, with the editor that responsibility for the final form of the text must lie.

Particular thanks are also due to Enid Mellor and Margaret Barker for much of the initial impetus for this project; to the Society for Old Testament Study for support and encouragement; to Philip Budd and the contributors for comments on the typescript; to Farah Hamirani for comments on Muslim attitudes; to Stephan Chambers of Basil Blackwell for patience, encouragement and understanding; and to my wife Jean for her support and great tolerance.

Stephen Bigger
Westminster College, Oxford

Introduction

Stephen Bigger

The concept of 'Old Testament', the old covenant as contrasted to a newly emerging covenant, emerged before the Christian era. The prophet Jeremiah saw the possibility of a new covenant written on the heart, a spiritual faith in which all will know God. It would replace the Sinai covenant made after the exodus from Egypt, which had been broken so often and so completely. Greek translations preferred the word 'testament' (*diatheke*) to 'covenant' (*suntheke*), perhaps because 'testament' left the initiative in God's hand, while 'covenant' suggested a relationship of mutual influence.

Paul – a Jew, and a Pharisee turned Christian – spoke, in a vein similar to Jeremiah, of the Torah of Moses as the old 'testament' or covenant, a written code which kills, a 'dispensation of death, carved in letters on stone' (2 Corinthians 3.6–16). Its injunctions were so far-reaching that no one could hope to obey them perfectly, and all must live with their failure and its implications. The early Church regarded the Hebrew Bible as scripture, often quoting it as an authoritative text. Melito of Sardis (died *c*.190 CE[*]) and Tertullian (*c*.160–225 CE) are the first known writers to call the books 'Old Testament' – the first in Greek, and the second in Latin. By the third century CE, Christian writers had begun to *contrast* the Hebrew Bible with the New Testament writings, often with pejorative overtones, to create the impression of a group of archaic books, of little value except for Messianic prophecies foretelling Jesus' mission – that is, to create the idea of an Old Testament which looked forward to the coming of Jesus and Christianity, preparing the way for something better. The contributors to this volume wish to allow the Old Testament writings to speak for themselves, helping

---

[*] 'AD' and 'BC' derives from early Christian scholarship. This dating-system is in common use in most cultures but, in the interests of neutrality, CE (Common Era) is used in this book to replace the Christian designation AD (*Anno Domini*, 'in the year of the Lord'), in accordance with the common usage in religious studies. BCE (Before the Common Era) similarly replaces BC (Before Christ).

the reader to understand what they are trying to say, and to appreciate the books for what they really are.

The books of the Hebrew Bible were created by anonymous writers during the first millennium BCE. Their messages and concerns are the central theme of this book. Ours is the story of how the writings which make up the Hebrew Bible emerged from their mouths and from their pens as expressions of their great creativity, interpreting life as they saw it and conveying meanings they glimpsed. Others appreciated their ideas, preserved their words, and developed their teaching, sometimes in new directions. It is easy for readers to get lost in the minutiae of biblical criticism, interested for so long primarily in historical reconstruction; but this book encourages those who will, to listen to the words themselves with an open mind, and to allow the messages of the Hebrew Bible to emerge once again after centuries of Christian interpretation, which has been selective in its concerns and has obscured by reinterpretation some of the intrinsic value of the Hebrew books. The Christian dimension is not unimportant – but it is a secondary dimension, involving reinterpretation, and should not blind us to other perspectives.

This book is not an introduction to the books of the Hebrew Bible, nor yet another history of Israel. It is, in essence, an exploration, inviting the reader to set off on an expedition of discovery. It often perplexes the general reader that, on virtually every issue in the study of the Hebrew Bible, scholars disagree, often fundamentally. In this book, issues are raised and explored to enable the reader to observe how decisions are made, on what evidence, how hypotheses are formed and how the so-called 'assured results' of scholarship are constantly tested. In following this path, readers are encouraged to develop their skill in evaluating historical data, recognizing textual problems, interpreting symbolic language and exploring the deep concerns of the biblical writers. They will explore different and varied exegetical traditions. They will be stirred to reflect on what the biblical books have to say for life today, whether viewed from a Jewish, a Christian, a Muslim or a secular perspective.

The fundamental aim of this volume on the Hebrew Bible is encourage readers to *understand* the text and its implications. Since the text was handwritten, mostly in Hebrew (some portions are in Aramaic) we need to explore whether the text has been accurately transmitted. For example, 1 Samuel 13.1 notes that 'Saul was son of one year when he became king, and he ruled over Israel for two years.' The Revised Standard Version assumes that the numbers have dropped out and leaves a gap; the New English Bible somewhat cavalierly inserts numbers from guesswork; Saul becomes fifty years old, and reigned for twenty-two years! The early Greek translation, the

Septuagint, also had trouble with this verse, so the corruption had taken place at a very early stage. There seem also to have been different families of manuscripts with different readings. The 2000-year-old texts found near Qumran (the so-called Dead Sea Scrolls), differ in very many respects from the Hebrew text used as the basis of English translations – which is scarcely 1000 years old. Sometimes the New Testament, when quoting a passage from the Hebrew Bible, differs considerably from the Hebrew text that we know (compare, for example, Acts 15.17–18 and Amos 9.11–12).

Another question to be asked is whether we should understand passages *literally* or *symbolically*. Augustine of Hippo, writing in the fifth century CE, looked for solutions to problems raised for example by Genesis 1–11, where we find great ages, sons of God and giants. The Jewish philosopher Moses Maimonides (1138–1204) explained problem passages in the light of the world as he knew it: miracles and supernatural events must have rational explanations! Both writers recognized descriptions of God as metaphor – God has no body or emotions, and is beyond human understanding.

In studying the Hebrew Bible, we spend most of our time reflecting on a wide range of *interpretation*, rather than on the text itself. A translation is itself an interpretation which selects one line of thought: the original writer would have been acutely aware of the wide range of meanings in a word and intended these to interact. There are also traditions of modern interpretation which are hard to break through: notably the Hebrew Bible is viewed from the standpoint of Christian theology, which can blind the reader even to the obvious. Detailed interpretation of the text is called *exegesis* – drawing out meanings and interpretations. In the Jewish tradition the same general process of interpretation is called *midrash*.

No interpretation of any text is 'just a matter of opinion'. To reach an *informed* view, the reader has to develop a careful methodology. D. J. A. Clines describes these (in Rogerson, 1983, 26–43) as 'first-order methods', dealing with our understanding of the *text;* and 'second-order methods', using the text for other purposes, such as historical reconstructions. His first-order methods are

> *historical–grammatical criticism*: to discover the natural sense of a text, for the authors in their own time;
> *textual criticism*: to examine the original texts, and in so doing seek to resolve problems of detail;
> *redaction criticism*: to examine the literary artistry of the writers (called here *redactors* or editors), and to discover why a work has been constructed in the way it has been. (This is sometimes called *literary analysis* or *literary criticism*.)

His second-order methods are

> *historical criticism*: using the text to reconstruct, as far as possible, what actually happened.
> *source criticism*: examining sources *if known* and reconstructing hypothetical sources behind a work.
> *form criticism*: reconstructing the (now lost) oral process, and the hypothetical oral layer underlying a text.

Priority has often been given to these 'second-order' tasks, alongside historical-grammatical commentaries. The interest in literary questions – of a text's flow and artistry – is relatively recent. R. Alter (1981, 12f) argues that the major emphasis in biblical studies had been 'excavative' – searching the text for data about history – with astonishingly little interest in developing a disciplined way of studying the text itself, as one might with Shakespeare or Tolstoy. Literary studies have mushroomed over the past decade, and Alter's work is now viewed as 'pioneering'. R. Polzin (1980, 5), in agreeing with Alter, called the results of historical-critical analyses of biblical material 'disappointing and inadequate'. The present work strikes a balance between literary and historical methods, in the belief that each is essential to the task of developing our understanding and appreciation of the texts of the Hebrew Bible.

The divine name in the Hebrew Bible is written with four letters, YHWH, which Jewish readers have traditionally read as *Adonai* ('my Lord'), in case the divine name is uttered 'in vain' – so contravening the third commandment. Attention here is focused on the dangers of insincerity. In Hebrew YHWH is vocalized with the vowels *Adonai*, reminding readers to make the replacement: this produced in English the hybrid name 'Jehovah'. To find the appropriate vowels, scholars went to early translations and transliterations (e.g. writing Hebrew in Greek characters). Critical works normally refer to the Israelite god as Yahweh, or God if the reference is more general. This convention has been followed in this volume because of its wide audience; Jewish readers are asked to bear with this usage and make their own mental adjustments. English translations generally replace Yahweh with 'the LORD' and this too has been followed in biblical quotations.

FURTHER READING

This volume seeks to bridge the gap between the beginner and scholarly literature. Further reading is recommended at the end of individual contributions, and in the course of their text contributors supply references by author and date (and page where appropriate) to relevant discussions elsewhere. Full details of all works cited will be found in the References and Bibliography (pp. 351–9). Listed below are a number of books which could be usefully consulted in relation to most chapters.

Barton, J. 1984: *Reading the Old Testament: Method in Biblical Study.*
Boadt, L. 1984: *Reading the Old Testament: an Introduction.*
Childs, B. S. 1979: *Introduction to the Old Testament as Scripture.*
Eissfeldt, O. 1976: *The Old Testament: an Introduction,* rev edn.
Gottwald N. K. 1985: *The Hebrew Bible: a Socio-Literary Introduction.*
Hayes J. H. 1979: *An Introduction to Old Testament Study.*
Hayes, J. H. and Miller, J. M. 1977: *Israelite and Judaean History.*
Knight, D. A. and Tucker, G. M. (eds) 1985: *The Hebrew Bible and its Modern Interpreters.*
Lemche N. P. 1988: *Ancient Israel: A New History of Israelite Society.*
Miller, J. M. and Hayes, J. H. 1986: *A History of Ancient Israel and Judah.*
Rogerson J. (ed.) 1983: *Beginning Old Testament Study.*

Note on Texts and Transliteration

Quotations from the Bible and Apocrypha are, unless otherwise indicated, taken from the Revised Standard Version of the Bible, copyright 1946, 1952, 1971, and from the Revised Standard Edition Apocrypha, copyright 1957, by the Division of Christian Education of the National Council of the Churches of Christ in the USA, and used by permission. Citations by chapter and verse likewise correspond to this version.

This book does not assume any knowledge of Hebrew, but occasionally it is necessary or helpful to indicate the Hebrew original of a particular term or phrase. Where this happens, the Hebrew is transliterated approximately, without the diacritical marks used in exact transcriptions and thus without any indication of length of vowel. The aim has been to minimize the difficulty for the general reader while still affording some clue to pronunciation (the pronunciations indicated are based on the Sephardic scheme). The system of transliteration adopted is reasonably consistent on its own terms, but does not differentiate sounds that cannot be easily differentiated using the English alphabet (thus, for example, the letters *sin* and *samek* are both transcribed as *s*). There is also no distinction made between different sound values (for example, aspirated/non-aspirated) of the same letter, except in the case of *taw* (*t/th*) and *pe* (*p/ph*). Two letters are represented by varieties of raised comma:' (omitted at the beginning of a word) represents *aleph*, a consonant with no sound value of its own, and 'represents *ayin*, a type of guttural with a strong gulping sound.

The names of people and places mentioned in the Bible are generally spelt as in the RSV, while the spelling of names and terms that belong to the history and practice of Judaism takes into account existing preferences.

List of Abbreviations

The following abbreviations are used in parenthetical references to chapter and verse of Old Testament and Apocryphal books (e.g. Gen 1.26). The list omits books that are not cited or whose usual titles are not abbreviated.

OLD TESTAMENT

Gen	Genesis
Exod	Exodus
Lev	Leviticus
Num	Numbers
Deut	Deuteronomy
Josh	Joshua
Judg	Judges
1, 2 Sam	1, 2 Samuel
1, 2 Kgs	1, 2 Kings
1, 2 Chron	1, 2 Chronicles
Neh	Nehemiah
Esth	Esther
Job	Job
Ps(s)	Psalm(s)
Prov	Proverbs
Eccles	Ecclesiastes
Song	Song of Songs (or Solomon)
Isa	Isaiah
Jer	Jeremiah
Lam	Lamentations
Ezek	Ezekiel
Dan	Daniel
Hos	Hosea
Obad	Obadiah

Jon	Jonah
Mic	Micah
Hag	Haggai
Zech	Zechariah
Mal	Malachi

APOCRYPHA

1, 2 Esd	1, 2 Esdras (3, 4 Esdras in Roman Catholic Bibles)
Wisdom	The Wisdom of Solomon
Ecclus	Ecclesiasticus, or The Wisdom of Jesus ben Sirach
1, 2 Macc	1, 2 Maccabees

The following further abbreviations also occur.

ANET	*Ancient Near Eastern Texts Relating to the Old Testament*, ed. J. B. Pritchard, 3rd edn (Princeton, NJ: Princeton University Press, 1969).
BCE	Before the Common Era (see note, p.xiii)
CE	Common Era (see note, p.xiii)
NEB	New English Bible
RSV	Revised Standard Version (of the Bible)

Part I

Introductory

1

The Hebrew World

Adrian H. W. Curtis

The Hebrew Bible, which Christians were later to call the Old Testament, emerged from the creative genius of the Hebrew people in a period which began over 3000 years ago, and ended a thousand years later, before the Christian era began. How it emerged has long puzzled scholars – who the writers were, when it first appeared, what sources were used, and why the writings were selected as 'Scripture'. Scholars are often suspicious of traditional claims that Moses, David, Solomon and even Samuel were significant authors. Despite the claims of later manuscripts and versions, most works in the Hebrew Bible are anonymous, and their dates problematic. As historians, we can be sure of few things. We can be sure that the books existed, and can try to reconstruct a text from the available manuscripts; and we can read and interpret that text. It is, however, much more hazardous to attempt to reconstruct a historical sequence using this material, since much of our information is ambiguous, and our conclusions will therefore often be tentative.

Yet 'Old Testament history' is a popular genre, often telling us more about its writers than about the events of history. In general outline, the chronology is clear enough, and is set out later in this chapter – but even here there are unresolved problems and major uncertainties. This book starts from what we know: the books themselves. From this vantage point, the problems – and yet the fun – of interpreting the material is explored.

The Land

This book is about problems and their attempted solutions, not about dogma. The study of the Hebrew Bible can boast few certainties, even on major issues. The land of the Hebrew Bible is a case in point. Judaism, Christianity and modern scholarship have worked on the unchallenged assumption that the biblical story unfolded in what we now call Israel or Palestine – even though the geographical evidence is not overwhelming, and

3

detailed identifications are constantly challenged. The tourist learns to apply caution to supposed locations of biblical incidents, even where the identification has tradition on its side. In fact, much of what we take for granted in the biblical story's geography is at best uncertain and at worst dubious. We long for archaeological inscriptions that may help, and traditional place-names which still bear some resemblance to biblical names – but these are few; and where we find them we wonder just how early 'tourist make-believe' started. To discover that the archaeological inscriptions, place-names and geographical features *did* in fact fit another area entirely, would necessitate a major re-evaluation of the Hebrew Bible, and a rewriting of most commentaries. Such a reshaping of our assumptions is not beyond the bounds of feasibility – Asir, south of Mecca has been suggested (Salibi, 1985). The dominant view nevertheless identifies the land with Israel/Palestine.

Why should there be such interest in a relatively small area of land, not 150 miles (240 km) in length (according to the traditional limits 'from Dan to Beersheba') and only a little larger than Wales? Why did early map-makers make Jerusalem the *omphalos*, the 'navel' or centre of the world? This land is significant for three of the world's major religious traditions: Judaism, Christianity and Islam. It lies at what has been called the 'point of balance' between the continents of the Old World – Europe, Africa and Asia. Trade routes from Africa and the Arabian sub-continent to Anatolia (modern Turkey) or Mesopotamia passed through the narrow coastal strip of land at the eastern end of the Mediterranean. The international trade routes were also the routes of armies as conquering monarchs expanded their empires. Thus, control of this territory was of the utmost strategic importance.

Our land forms part of what has come to be known as the Fertile Crescent, a very approximately crescent-shaped swathe of territory comprising at its extremities the lands watered by the great rivers Nile (Egypt), Tigris and Euphrates (Lower Mesopotamia), and, in between, the areas of the east Mediterranean coast and of Upper Mesopotamia where the fertility of the soil depended largely on the rains. Travellers, whether commercial or military, must journey by way of the fertile land and avoid the desert. The east Mediterranean coastal strip forms a land bridge between Africa on the one hand, and Anatolia and Mesopotamia on the other: the area in which we are particularly interested is a very narrow section of the bridge.

To understand the body of literature which is known to Christians as the Old Testament, and to Jews as *Tenakh*, it is vital to know something of the people who produced the literature, and the land in which they lived. Geographical features have had a profound effect on the history of the land and its people. Internal features of the lie of the land – such as the location of important cities and fortresses, valleys and passes, roads and water supplies – also add to our understanding of history. The nature of the land and its varied regions, its climate and products, has left its mark upon the literature.

The Name

This land has been called by many names: the Holy Land, the Promised Land, Canaan, Palestine, Israel. None is without its problems. 'Holy Land' was particularly used by pilgrims. 'Promised Land' stems primarily from the Jewish religious tradition. 'Canaan' seems to refer to territory which extended considerably further north than that occupied at any time by the Israelites. 'Palestine' ironically derives ultimately from the Philistines, who gave their name to the southern coastal plain of Philistia; after the Jewish revolt (132–5 CE) the Romans adopted the name *Palaestina* as the name of the imperial province. Today 'Palestine' and 'Israel' have acquired sharp political overtones. In the Hebrew Bible 'Israel' referred to the northern kingdom (to distinguish it from 'Judah' in the south) but it was also used (as it is today) for a larger area from northern Galilee to the Negeb desert. The term Palestine tends to be preferred as a geographical designation.

General Features

The most notable feature of the region is the rift valley, formed as the result of a geological fault which begins in northern Syria (the Orontes valley), continues south between the Lebanon and Antilebanon mountains, then through Palestine, the Red Sea and into Africa. Because of this great rift, it is usual to divide Israel/Palestine into four main north–south zones: the coastal plains, the central hill country, the rift valley, and Transjordan.

The underlying rock of the whole area is granite, while on the surface the principal rocks are limestone, chalk and basalt. The limestone resists erosion and is useful for building, but eventually weathers into a reddish coloured soil; it predominates in the hill country. The chalk is not useful for building and is easily worn away to form valleys through which roads can pass; chalk predominates in the wilderness of Judah and formed the passes through the Carmel hills and the valley (or 'moat') which separates the hills of Judah from the Shephelah lowlands in southern Israel. The basalt, a hard volcanic rock, is found to the north in the Galilee region and northern Transjordan.

The Coastal Plains The cliffs of Ras an-Naqura (the Ladder of Tyre) form a convenient northern boundary. To the south lies the narrow plain of Acco, reaching to the point where the Carmel promontory juts out into the Mediterranean, reducing the plain to a tiny coastal strip before it broadens again into the plain of Dor. South of the Crocodile river (Wadi Zerqa) is the much wider, and once densely forested, plain of Sharon. Sharon is separated from the plain of Philistia by the valley of Aijalon, along which lay the road to the port of Joppa; it was here that the Philistines settled. A feature of the coastal plains, particularly in the south, is the sand dunes, which extend a considerable distance inland.

The Central Hill Country   Galilee in the north is traditionally divided into Upper Galilee, whose highest point reaches almost 4000 feet (1300 m), and the gentler slopes of Lower Galilee. To the south, the line of hills is broken by the plain of Esdraelon (or Megiddo), an approximately triangular area linking the coastal plain of Acco to the valley of Jezreel and the Jordan valley. The 'base' of the triangle is formed by the Carmel hills as they run inland from the promontory to link up with the hill country of Ephraim.

Ephraim, a region of rolling limestone hills and valleys, was the heartland of the northern kingdom of Israel, containing its successive capitals – Shechem, Tirzah and Samaria. To the south lay the hill country of Judah, separated from the plain of Philistia by the low hills of the Shephelah, whose name means 'lowland' (presumably from the perspective of the higher central hill country). The more rugged hill country of Judah, in which lie such important cities as Jerusalem and Hebron, falls away to the west into the wilderness of Judah. South of Beersheba, the hills continue into the Negeb, a region of steppeland which extends from the coast across to the Arabah and to the south-west merges into the Sinai peninsula.

The Rift Valley   In the area of Dan, the traditional northern limit of Palestine, are the sources of the Jordan, fed by the waters of snow-capped Hermon. The streams flow into the Huleh basin, where there was a lake in biblical times (later known as Lake Semechonitis). From Huleh, over 200 feet (65m) above sea level, the Jordan descends rapidly (its name is probably derived from a root meaning 'go down') to the Lake of Galilee, almost 700 feet (230m) below sea level.

The river continues to drop towards the Dead Sea through a valley known as the Ghor, where it has cut a trench, the Zor, and meanders through dense tamarisk jungle. The distance from the Lake of Galilee to the Dead Sea is about 65 miles (105km), but the Jordan actually flows almost 200 miles (320km) in covering the distance. The surface of the Dead Sea is nearly 1300 feet (430m) below sea level, and its deepest point is 1300 feet lower still. The most notable feature of the Dead Sea is the excessive saltiness of its water, caused almost entirely by evaporation. South of the Dead Sea, the rift valley continues some 100 miles (160 km) to the Gulf of Aqaba (Eilat). This desert region is known as the Arabah, though the term is sometimes used to cover the Jordan valley and Dead Sea as well.

Transjordan   The extent to which Transjordan can be considered part of Palestine is a matter of debate. Here it will suffice to note the main regions.

In the north lay the fertile area of Bashan, then, to the south of the Yarmuk valley, the once thickly forested Gilead. Further south-east was the territory of the Ammonites, an area whose boundaries are difficult to define. East of the Dead Sea was the land of Moab, renowned for its sheep pastures (2 Kgs 3.4). Further south still, separated from Moab by the valley of the Zered, and to the east of the Arabah lay the rugged territory of Edom.

The Main Roads

The importance of the country's roads has already been noted. The lie of the land naturally governs the best routes through Palestine. The most important route was the 'Way of the Sea' (Isa 9.1). Coming from Egypt, it passed through Gaza and the plain of Philistia, running close to the coast, before moving further inland to follow the edge of the hills. It cut through the Carmel hills via the Megiddo pass and across the plain of Esdraelon, continuing towards the northern end of the Lake of Galilee. Having passed close to Hazor, the road crossed the Jordan south of Lake Huleh and skirted the foothills of Mount Hermon as it headed for Damascus. An alternative to the northern section of this route crossed the Jordan south of the Lake of Galilee and reached Megiddo via the valley of Jezreel.

The other major trunk road of the region was the 'King's Highway' (Num 20.17; 21.22). This led from the Gulf of Aqaba through the hills of Edom, Moab and Ammon, then, via Ramoth-gilead, north towards Damascus.

Another important road ran through the central hill country, linking such significant cities as Beersheba, Hebron, Jerusalem, Bethel and Shechem; to the south it linked with the Way of Shur, which led to Egypt. Near Shechem, the road branched to enter the plain of Esdraelon via Ibleam or to head towards the rift valley via Bethshan. There were also a number of east–west roads, linking the main north–south routes and the coast.

Climate

Palestine is sandwiched between the sea and the desert, and its position affects its climate. It is usual to divide the year into two main seasons, the hot, dry summer, and the rainy 'winter'. Summer lasts from June to September; the heat is relieved by the breezes from the west, and the complete lack of rain is relieved by dew on the coastal plains and west-facing hills. The early or 'former' rains fall in October and November, making it possible to prepare the soil for the planting of crops. Rains continue throughout the winter months. In March, April and perhaps as late as May come the 'latter' rains, which are vital as the grain swells and ripens. Rainfall tends to decrease from north to south and from east to west. Between the main seasons are brief transitional periods, during which there can be severe rainstorms in the desert regions, and winds known as sirocco or khamsin blow from the desert, causing a rapid rise in temperature, a drop in humidity, and an irritating fine dust filling the air.

The Archaeological Setting

The material remains of an earlier culture, including written records, are many and varied. Before illustrating this variety, we need to consider the question, what information is it reasonable to expect archaeology to provide? The question needs to be asked because exaggerated claims have sometimes been made on the basis of archaeology, whether of the 'archaeology has proved the Bible' or 'archaeology has disproved the Bible' type. It is perhaps because archaeology is thought to be more 'scientific' than some of the other disciplines involved in the study of the Bible that words such as 'proof' are used, but it is important to remember that interpretation is involved in the understanding of an archaeological discovery. It may not always be the case that an ancient site has been correctly identified, or that a piece of writing has been correctly read and translated, or that the purpose of a building or artefact has been correctly understood. Archaeology's major contribution to biblical study is contextual. It has brought the Bible out of isolation, enabling it to be seen as part of a wider environment.

The Hebrews emerged into a world of civilizations already ancient, and, as, will be seen in the outline of the history of Israel and Judah, their fortunes at most stages depended on the relative strengths and weaknesses of their neighbours, major and minor.(The biblical writings were produced in the wider literary context of the ancient Near East, so that the varied types of literature can be compared with their parallels from neighbouring cultures.) The religion of the Hebrew people developed in the midst of many and varied religious beliefs and practices, and came into conflict with some. Of course, archaeological excavations carried out within Palestine itself will provide a more direct witness to the Hebrew people than those in neighbouring lands, in that they reveal some of the places in which they lived and objects they used; yet in Palestine relatively little written material has been found relevant to our period. All in all, archaeology has shed immense light on the world of the ancient Near East from which the Hebrew Bible emerged.

The relevance of particular archaeological discoveries to aspects of biblical study will be noted at various points in this volume. In a brief introduction it is only possible to illustrate something of the variety of types of material available.

The Tell

Many ancient sites take the form of what is known as a *tell* – an artificial mound, built up as a result of successive towns being constructed on the same spot; after a town had fallen into ruin or been destroyed, new buildings would be erected above the remains of the old. These successive occupation levels, or strata, can reach to a considerable depth (e.g. at Ugarit up to 65 feet or 20m), showing the great antiquity of a site. Where a tell has been built up in this way, it should follow that, the deeper in the mound an object or building lies, the earlier will be its date.

Needless to say, not all tells are built up in this neat, layer-cake way, or the strata may have been disrupted, for example by later builders digging down to bedrock to establish foundations for their structures. The task of the archaeologist is to excavate carefully so as to identify the various levels of occupation, and establish a relative chronology. Occasionally something will be found in a stratum which enables a fairly precise date to be given, e.g. a coin which can be dated or the cartouche of an Egyptian pharaoh. Sometimes such methods as radio-carbon dating will be used. More often, a period of occupation may be estimated by comparison of shape and style of buildings or domestic items, especially pottery, with discoveries from other sites, enabling certain features to be labelled as characteristic of a particular period.

It is often not possible to be sure of the identification of an ancient site. Sometimes the ancient name has been preserved in the modern name of a mound or in the name of a nearby modern town or village. Sometimes a discovery made on a site will provide the clue to identification; the tell of Ras Shamra was identified as the ancient Ugarit thanks to the discovery of a tablet naming someone as 'king of Ugarit'. Hard evidence is, however, often scant, so the identification of many ancient sites remains conjectural and problematic. Few identifications can be regarded as conclusive.

Buildings

Discoveries made on a site can be divided into three broad categories: buildings and artefacts; human and animal remains; and written material. In the first category, excavation may reveal the types of fortification constructed to defend a city – its walls and gateways. Major buildings on a site, often in the most prominent positions, may be palaces, administrative headquarters or temples. Their function may be unclear, or a discovery may help the identification. Statuettes or the presence of animal bones near an altar may suggest a cult centre, while jars with official stamps on the handles may have been used for collecting taxes in kind and therefore suggest an administrative building.

Dwelling-houses, and objects found within them, can show something of the lifestyle of the people. Houses were often composed of several rooms built around a courtyard. It is of course necessary to remember that frequently all that remains of a building will be the foundations of the ground floor. In a dwelling-house the ground floor might be used for animals and storage space, the human occupants living above. Discoveries may include other evidence of the way of life of the inhabitants, such as installations for the production of wine or olive oil.

Frequently the function of a building cannot be decided with certainty. At Megiddo, large structures on the site were identified as 'Solomon's Stables' since 1 Kings 9.15–19 seemed to imply that Megiddo was one of King Solomon's chariotry centres. Subsequent excavations revealed that the structures belonged to a later stratum (perhaps from the time of Ahab) above the level contemporary with Solomon. Then their identity as stables was questioned, and comparison with similar structures at Hazor and Beersheba has led to the suggestion that they were storehouses.

Water Supply

This was of vital importance, and sites would be chosen for their proximity to a spring or river. As the techniques of plastering cisterns and constructing aqueducts developed, settlement became possible over wider areas. A good water supply outside the city's fortifications was vulnerable in time of siege, and remarkable measures were taken. Great tunnels were hewn through rock as at Megiddo and Hazor. At Jerusalem an earlier system of shafts and tunnels constructed to provide access to Gihon spring water provided a threat to the city's defences. So, in the time of Hezekiah, a new reservoir was prepared in the south-west corner of the city (the pool of Siloam) and a tunnel quarried through the rock to bring the water from the Gihon, a distance of 583 yards (533m) because of the curves in the tunnel. An inscription found in 1880 indicates that the tunnel was hewn by two gangs of quarrymen starting at either end and working towards each other. It has been suggested that they were perhaps following the line of an underground stream (cf. 2 Kgs 20.20; 2 Chron 32.2–4, 30). The inscription (*ANET* 321) does not mention Hezekiah or give any indication of date.

Artefacts and Bones

Artefacts often shed light on the life of the people. These include tools and weapons, jewellery, ornaments and statuettes, and domestic pottery, of varied shapes, sizes and quality. The style, shape and decoration of such artefacts provide important clues to finding the date of the stratum or level. Human remains provide information about burial customs, bodily characteristics, diseases and causes of death. Animal bones provide evidence of diet and sacrifices, as well as of the fauna of the region.

Scripts

Two major systems of writing had been developed at either end of the Fertile Crescent before the end of the fourth millennium BCE. The Sumerians in southern Mesopotamia had begun to use simple depictions of objects, drawn on clay tablets with a reed stylus. Gradually the pictures were simplified to a limited number of wedge-shaped strokes pressed into the clay. These are known as *cuneiform* (Latin *cuneus*, wedge). In time, the signs were used not only to stand for the names of the objects portrayed, but for the sounds of the names. Akkadians adopted this script to write their Semitic language which by the second millennium was widely used throughout the ancient Near East. The Akkadian language was deciphered thanks to the discovery of a trilingual (Akkadian, Elamite and Old Persian) inscription carved into the rock of a cliff face at Behistun. The Old Persian provided the key to the decipherment of the Akkadian.

In Egypt, a script based on pictures was developed (*hieroglyphic*). Signs which originally represented a simple object were grouped to express more complex ideas and gradually came to represent sounds. The hieroglyphic script was deciphered thanks to the discovery of the Rosetta Stone, which bore a decree written in Greek, in hieroglyphic and in the demotic script, a cursive development from hieroglyphs.

A major advance in the development of writing-systems can be credited to the Canaanites. The cuneiform and hieroglyphic scripts required large numbers of signs representing *words* and *syllables*; they developed a system based on the simplest consonantal *sounds*. Early this century, inscriptions were found at Serabit el-Khadim in the Sinai peninsula, the work of Semites employed by the Egyptians in mining turquoise and copper in the middle of the second millennium BCE. A few other examples of this script have been found in Palestine. Pictures represented the sound of the first consonant of the name of the object depicted. Further north, the scribes of Ugarit used cuneiform characters, reduced to about thirty relatively simple groups of wedges or single strokes. Thus developed the *alphabetic* form of writing which was later adapted for the writing of Hebrew, Aramaic and Phoenician. The earliest example of the Old (or Palaeo-) Hebrew script is the so-called Gezer Calendar, which lists farming-activities in relationship to the months, and which may date from about the tenth century BCE. The 'square' characters of the Hebrew Bible were adopted from the Aramaic script, which was widely used in the Persian Empire and which gradually supplanted the Old Hebrew script.

Written Documents

Written documents are of a considerable variety. They may take the form of inscriptions carved on the walls of temples and other buildings; or on a *stele* (standing stone) set up to record the deeds of a king (e.g. the Stele of Merneptah from the late thirteenth century BCE, containing the earliest reference to the people of Israel; or the Black Obelisk of Shalmeneser with its reference to, and perhaps picture of, King Jehu); or a law code such as the Code of Hammurabi. Much is on clay tablets, which provided a convenient medium for the cuneiform script. The finished product was baked so that the text could be stored in an archive (such as those found at Mari, Nuzi, Ebla and Ugarit). A piece of broken pot (*ostracon*) would serve as a suitable surface for recording such mundane information as deliveries of produce (e.g. the eighth-century ostraca from Samaria) or for the writing of letters (e.g. the Lachish letters, which shed valuable light not only on the period of the fall of Judah to the Babylonians but also on how Hebrew was written at the time). The use of *papyrus*, prepared from strips of the pith of an aquatic reed, is associated particularly with Egypt, where it was used from early in the third millennium. Papyrus was gradually supplanted by the more durable *parchment*, made from the skins of sheep and goats; particularly noteworthy are the Dead Sea Scrolls from Qumran, which preserve the library of a Jewish sectarian group who lived near the Dead Sea from the second century BCE to the first century CE and which include the earliest known manuscripts of large sections of the Hebrew Bible.

Something of the variety of contents of written material discovered by archaelogists has already been indicated. Considerable attention has been paid to the texts which contain the myths and legends of the Mesopotamians, Egyptians and Canaanites, and which give such valuable insight into the religious beliefs of those from whom and among whom the Hebrews emerged and lived, beliefs with which protagonists of their god Yahweh sometimes had to contend. Important insights into religious beliefs and practices can also be gained from prayers, rituals and lists of sacrifices. Other texts may have a less direct religious significance. Law codes enable the legal material in the Hebrew Bible to be set in a wider context. There has been much discussion about whether the form in which the idea of covenant is presented in the Hebrew Bible was affected by ancient Near Eastern treaty forms, or whether there are parallels to the phenomenon of prophecy in Israel in references to messengers of the gods in such texts as those from Mari. King lists, annals and other historical texts can be of value for establishing chronology, and for setting the Bible in a wider political context. Administrative and legal texts provide insights into the way of life of the peoples of the ancient Near East. Lexical texts provide word lists which shed light on languages or items of vocabulary. Indeed, one of the most important contributions of the written material to biblical study lies in their elucidation of Semitic languages and, in particular, of biblical Hebrew.

The Historical Setting

The attempt to produce a history of Israel, even in outline, is fraught with difficulties. It involves an analysis of the sources available for the task, literary and non-literary, biblical and non-biblical. To what extent do the biblical books which seem to provide historical information actually do so? There are many problems of interpretation both with biblical records and with contemporary ancient Near Eastern material. Is the ancient record of, for example, the exploits of an Assyrian king any more or less likely to be historically accurate and free from propaganda than the biblical accounts of King David? Theology, or propaganda may have influenced both. Biblical narratives provide first-hand evidence of the *writer*, not of the period the narratives purport to describe. History written with a didactic purpose often merges imperceptibly with fiction. The biblical writers used sources, but unfortunately we are almost completely in the dark about them: were they faithfully preserved, or were they modified by the writers?

The Patriarchs

Where should the outline begin? Of course, the Bible begins with creation, then proceeds to recall persons who and events which few would regard as having any historical basis. The more immediate background to the story of Israelites in Palestine lies in the so-called Patriarchal Period, and it is here that some would argue that the history of Israel begins, in the stories about Abraham, Isaac and Jacob. The 'Israelites' own understanding of their past begins with the first couple – Adam and Eve – then groups – including the patriarchs Abraham, Isaac, Jacob – who moved from Mesopotamia, around the Fertile Crescent, and into Palestine. Whether we can place such a folk movement into a clear historical context is more problematic. Recently much has been made of apparent parallels between certain patriarchal customs and practices reflected in the Nuzi texts (dating from the fifteenth century BCE, from a predominantly Hurrian population): if the patriarchal stories could accurately reflect and record customs and practices now known to have been current in the middle of the second millennium BCE, could they not have preserved reliable information about historical figures Abraham, Isaac and Jacob? Such approaches concentrate on the similarities and overlook important differences; they have also often overlooked the possibility that parallels existed at other times. This is *not* to say that the Nuzi texts should not be used in the attempt to provide a historical context for the patriarchs, only to say that they should be used with caution. There may be traditional (or folkloric) elements in the patriarchal stories, but there may also be not a little later interpretation and theological reflection.

Moses

Can the outline begin with Moses? The Bible's own account portrays ancestors of the Israelites moving into Egypt to escape the effects of famine, their subsequent enslavement and their escape from bondage under Moses' leadership. There is some evidence that Semitic people were in Egypt during the New Kingdom and that they were employed on building projects by pharaohs such as Rameses II (1290–1224 BCE), in whose honour the city of Raamses was named (Exod 1.11). There is no extra-biblical evidence for Moses (though it is noteworthy that his name was Egyptian) or, probably, for the exodus; but in view of the importance of the exodus tradition to later generations (especially in the development of a 'new exodus' theme at the time of the Babylonian exile) few would doubt that the story has some historical basis. The date of the exodus has been much debated, but the thirteenth century is the most favoured. The location of the crossing of the Sea of Reeds, ('Red Sea' in English versions) and the route taken by the escaping slaves cannot be recovered with any certainty, as is often revealed by the number of question-marks beside the place-names on maps purporting to show the route!

The Promised Land

It was once customary to speak of the exodus as followed by the 'conquest', although it was noted that Joshua and Judges may contain hints that the settlement was a gradual process, perhaps even absorbing elements of the local population. A subsequent theory, that the Israelite occupation of Palestine took place by a process of infiltration as nomadic people began to settle down, was challenged largely on the basis of archaeological evidence that a number of important Canaanite cities in Palestine suffered destructions in the late thirteenth century BCE. But were these destructions the work of Joshua and the Israelites? And, if archaeological evidence is to be used, what is to be made of such stories as the famous 'battle of Jericho', since archaeology presents an enigmatic picture as to whether there was a major city on the site at the time.

If Jericho is an enigma, Ai is a problem! Here the archaeologists seem confident that the city was not occupied for perhaps as much as a thousand years before the time of the Israelite settlement. Further, cities not mentioned in the biblical narrative were destroyed and resettled in the same period. Does the Bible present the correct picture? Does archaeology? Have both been misunderstood or misinterpreted? Can the apparently conflicting evidence be reconciled? Has the site been correctly identified? What actually happened is still a mystery. We have to piece the evidence together carefully, and attempt hypothetical reconstructions. There seems to be general agreement that by the beginning of the Iron Age (c1200 BCE), about the same time as the Philistines were beginning to occupy the southern coastal plain, the Israelites were settling in Canaan; but was it a conquest or an infiltration, or, as is being strongly argued today, a social revolution focusing around a small group of escaped slaves?

The extent to which there was any factor unifying the Israelite groups at this period, or any unified form of government, has been hotly debated. It is to this time that the biblical tradition assigns the activity of the so-called 'judges'. Whether any of these charismatic deliverer figures held any widespread authority must be doubted. Indeed, how many of the stories reflect real historical figures and events must be questioned. The biblical traditions reflect a time of limited collaboration between Israelite groups in the face of common enemies, and, in the Samson stories, the growth of tension between the Israelites and the Philistines.

Saul and David

The Philistines had designs on territory occupied by the Israelites, and had mastered the use of the chariot and iron. They posed a threat to the Israelites, and got the better of early encounters. It was in this context that Israel's first king, Saul, was chosen. Despite a promising start to his reign, Saul was unable to remove the Philistine menace; he is presented as unstable, obsessed with the new popular hero, David. David was forced to take refuge in the hills of Judah, where he lived the life of an outlaw before becoming a vassal of the Philistine king of Gath. Saul's end came at the ill-fated battle of Gilboa, where the Israelites were defeated by the Philistines on the plain of Esdraelon.

David was declared king over Judah at Hebron. Soon the remaining claims of the house of Saul were removed, and the people of northern Israel accepted David's kingship, enabling him to consolidate his position. He held the two kingdoms together by the force of his personality and his policies. There were two main aspects of this consolidation: the ending of the Philistine threat, and the taking of Jerusalem as a capital city for his kingdom. Consolidation was followed by expansion, as David conquered territory in Edom, Moab and Ammon, and extended his power further north by the defeat of Aramean forces, and the setting-up of garrisons in the area of Damascus. Alliances with the kings of Hamath and Tyre ensured friendly neighbours to the north. David's activity saw Israel at the zenith of its power, yet the biblical account suggests that his later years were marred by dissension within his family and outside as to who was to succeed to the throne. In the end, as a result of palace intrigue, the pro-Solomon party proved successful.

King Solomon and his Successors

Solomon's reign is noted for a number of achievements. He established and maintained alliances with neighbouring peoples, often sealing these by marriage. He instituted a building-programme whose most notable feature was the construction of the Temple in Jerusalem, but which also involved the fortification of a number of cities in key strategic positions. He exploited the land's position to engage in trade ventures and he established an administrative system of twelve districts, though whether Judah was excluded or itself subdivided into twelve districts is unclear. In order to provide for the upkeep of his elaborate court and for his various projects, he imposed heavy taxes and eventually required the Israelites to spend part of the year working in labour gangs. This was to lead to the division of the kingdom.

When Solomon died, the people of Judah accepted his son Rehoboam as king and he went to Shechem to receive the acclaim of northern Israel. But he was confronted with demands that the heavy burdens imposed by his father should be reduced. Rehoboam refused, so the northern tribes declared a rival king, Jeroboam, who had previously been involved in an attempt to separate the northern tribes and been forced to flee to Egypt. Unity between Judah and the northern tribes, always tenuous, now broke down.

Shortly after this schism, the area suffered an invasion by Pharaoh Shishak of Egypt which caused great devastation throughout Judah, and in Israel (the northern kingdom) as far north as Esdraelon (part of a stele of Shishak has been discovered at Megiddo). Tension and hostility between Israel and Judah continued for some half a century.

The House of Omri

From this point, ancient Near Eastern records begin to fill out the wider political details, and the biblical record can be compared with accounts written by the opposing powers. The names of monarchs of Israel or Judah creep into non-biblical records.

After the death of Jeroboam, Israel entered upon a period of instability, culminating in virtual civil war from which Omri, an army commander, emerged to claim the throne, establish a dynasty, and restore stability to Israel. It was he who founded Samaria as his capital city. It is noteworthy that the Assyrians continued to call Israel the 'house (or land) of Omri' long after the dynasty ended. Ahab, Omri's son, married Jezebel, a Phoenician princess, and his reign saw an increase in foreign religious influences. The external threat to Israel was Syria, and it was in battle against the Syrians that Ahab died.

The dynasty of Omri was brought to an end when Jehu, the commander of the troops of Jehoram (the last king of the dynasty), seized power. He killed Jehoram, who was recuperating after being wounded in battle. Ahaziah, the king of Judah, who was visiting Jehoram, was also put to death. Jehu carried out a purge of Baal-worshippers, but lost territory east of the Jorden to Syria. The subsequent resurgence of the fortunes of Israel reached its zenith in the reign of Jeroboam II in the middle of the eighth century BCE. He seems to have restored the northern boundary of the land to what it had been in the time of Solomon, but the prosperity may not have been shared by all the populace, if we may judge from the oracles preserved in the book of Amos.

The Destruction of Israel and Samaria

The final decline of Israel was very rapid. As Assyrian power spread under Tiglath-pileser III, there was dissension and civil war as one king after another sought to establish himself. Eventually Pekah seized power, and joined with the king of Damascus in resisting the spread of Assyrian influence. When Judah refused to join the coalition, the northern confederates sought to remove Ahaz (who had just come to the throne). Ahaz appealed for help to Tiglath-pileser, who moved down the east Mediterranean coast and took over parts of Israelite territory. What probably saved Israel for a few more years was the murder of Pekah by Hoshea, who surrendered. However, not long after the death of Tiglath-pileser, Hoshea saw an opportunity to rebel against the new Assyrian ruler, Shalmaneser V, so withheld tribute and appealed to Egypt for help. Shalmaneser (or perhaps his successor, Sargon II, who claims the achievement) captured Samaria in 722 BCE and deported much of the populace, bringing in new settlers from other parts of the empire.

The Destruction of Judah and Jerusalem

The kingdom of Judah was to last almost another century and a half before suffering a similar fate. The reign of Hezekiah saw an attempt to shake off the power of Assyria, improve the fortifications of Jerusalem, and institute religious reforms apparently with the intention of removing Assyrian elements, and centralizing the cult in one place, Jerusalem. The Assyrians, under Sennacherib, once again turned their attention to the west; one by one the fortresses of Judah were destroyed, but Jerusalem escaped as Hezekiah was forced to sue for peace and accept a heavy tribute. It is possible that Hezekiah rebelled again later in his reign. He was succeeded by Manasseh, who appears to have remained a loyal Assyrian vassal during his lengthy reign.

By the middle of the seventh century, cracks were beginning to appear in the Assyrian Empire, as the power of the Medes and the Babylonians was increasing. Manasseh was succeeded briefly by Amon, who was assassinated, perhaps by anti-Assyrian elements, and his eight-year-old son Josiah was placed on the throne. His reign is perhaps most noted for the religious reform which sought to remove alien elements and centralize worship on the

Jerusalem Temple. Judah became to all intents and purposes independent. When, in 609 BCE, Pharaoh Necho marched north in an attempt to bolster the remnants of Assyria and ward off the threat of the Medes and Babylonians, Josiah sought to intercept him at the pass of Megiddo. Whether this was a bid for complete independence or whether Josiah had already sided with the Babylonians is not certain, but the bid was fatal. Josiah was killed and replaced on the throne by his son Jehoahaz. Necho consolidated his position west of the Euphrates. Jehoahaz was taken to Egypt and his brother Jehoiakim put on the throne as an Egyptian vassal.

The Babylonian advance westward was not long delayed. In 605 the Egyptian armies were defeated at Carchemish on the Euphrates, and the way was open for the Babylonians, led by Nebuchadnezzar. At some point Jehoiakim transferred his allegiance to Babylon, but was not prepared to remain subservient, and, when both Egypt and Babylon suffered heavily in a battle, Jehoiakim rebelled. Before the blow fell, he died (perhaps assassinated in the hope of avoiding the worst consequences of his folly) and his eighteen-year-old son Jehoiachin became king. On 16 March 597, Jerusalem capitulated; the king and other prominent citizens were deported to Babylon, and Zedekiah was put on the throne.

Despite all that had happened, Zedekiah's reign was a time of unrest and sedition, culminating in open rebellion. The Babylonians advanced, laid siege to Jerusalem and gradually destroyed outlying fortresses. In 587 or 586 Jerusalem fell. Zedekiah was blinded and taken to Babylon, with another group of exiles. Gedaliah was made governor, but he was soon assassinated by one Ishmael, with Ammonite backing, and Gedaliah's supporters fled to Egypt.

The Exile and Return

The Jewish exiles in Babylon, although far from their own land, owned their own houses and gardens in which to grow produce, and to meet together. Those left in Judah had to survive in a ravaged land. The fortunes of the Jews changed when Cyrus, king of Anshan in Persia, took control of all Media and Persia, annexing Lydia, and, after extending his power to the east, incorporated Babylon in his huge empire. By 538 BCE his control reached to the frontier of Egypt, thus including Judah as well as Babylon, the land of exile. Persian policy seems to have been to allow exiled groups to return to their homelands and pursue their own religions. Cyrus issued a decree authorizing the return of the Jews to Judah in his first year as king of Babylon (538). Under the leadership of Sheshbazzar, and subsequently Zerubbabel, groups returned and work began on rebuilding the Temple.

The restoration was a very slow process, for almost a century later the walls of Jerusalem had still not been rebuilt. In 445 or 444 Nehemiah, a Jew in the service of the Persian king Artaxerxes I, was given permission to travel to Jerusalem, and despite considerable opposition he was successful in securing the city's defences and in taking measures to give stability to the community. The relationship of the career of Ezra to that of Nehemiah has been much debated. Traditionally he has been thought to have come to Judah before Nehemiah, or it has been argued that he arrived shortly after Nehemiah. Possibly he came to Judah in the seventh year of Artaxerxes II (398), with the task of enforcing the law which governed religious matters in Judah.

A 'Dark Age'

Almost nothing is known of events in Judah during the latter years of the Persian Empire and beyond. It seems to have been a time of worsening relations with the Samaritans and of the diminishing use of the Hebrew language, as Aramaic became more dominant. Alexander the Great (336–323 BCE) brought to an end the power of Persia and stimulated the spread of Greek culture (Hellenization) throughout the Near East. In a series of rapid moves he removed the Persian forces from Asia Minor, gained control of the lands of the eastern Mediterranean (including Palestine), was welcomed into Egypt, and turned his attention eastward, via Babylon, Susa and Persepolis, eventually campaigning beyond the Indus, in India.

Seleucids and Ptolemies

After Alexander's death at the age of thirty-three, his huge empire fell apart as rival generals vied for control in different areas. For the next hundred years Palestine came under the control of the Ptolemies of Egypt, though there is no evidence that they meddled in affairs in Judah. The Jewish population of Egypt increased. They adopted Greek as their language: hence the need for a Greek translation of the scriptures (the *Septuagint*).

The situation in Palestine changed when Antiochus III the Great (223–187 BCE) came to the throne in that part of Alexander's former empire which had been seized by the Seleucids, and reasserted Seleucid power over Asia Minor, Syria, Mesopotamia and lands to the east. The Egyptians were driven from Asia, and Palestine came under Seleucid control. The Jewish historian Josephus records that the Jews welcomed the change; but, when Antiochus sought to challenge the power of Rome, he was defeated.

The impact of Hellenism on Palestine continued and a dramatic turn of events took place. Antiochus IV Epiphanes (175–163) undertook a policy of enforcing Greek culture, which, so far as the Jews were concerned, amounted to a proscription of their religion. Observance of the Sabbath, circumcision and Jewish festivals were forbidden. Altars to Greek gods were set up and sacrifices offered. Jews were forced to eat the flesh of animals they regarded as unclean. In December 168 or 167 an altar of Zeus was erected in the Jerusalem Temple, and pig's flesh offered. This was the 'abomination of desolation' referred to in Daniel (9.27; 11.31; 12.11).

The Maccabees

While some Jews seem to have welcomed the spread of Hellenism, others were fiercely hostile and sought to resist. Rebellion broke out when a priest named Mattathias was instructed to offer a sacrifice to Zeus; he refused and fled to the hills with his five sons, calling those loyal to the Jewish law to rally to them. They carried on guerrilla warfare against the Seleucids and their sympathizers. When Mattathias died shortly afterwards, the leadership of the rebellion passed to his son Judas, known as 'Maccabaeus' ('the hammer'): under his leadership victories were achieved over the Seleucid forces. Jerusalem was entered, and the pagan altar was removed from the temple. In December 165 or 164 BCE the Temple was rededicated.

Since it is widely believed that the latest book in the Hebrew Bible (the book of Daniel) was produced at the time of the persecution under Antiochus IV, just prior to the rededication of the Temple, this marks a suitable finishing point for this historical survey.

The outline began with questions, and it is fitting to finish with questions.

It may appear to the reader that historical certainty increases as the outline progresses, but how true is this?
To what extent are there more reliable sources for the later period than for the earlier?
Have the biblical sources sometimes been taken too much at face value in this survey?
This historical outline has not once mentioned God. The biblical writers would not have written such an account, so should the modern writer?

Some details can be checked against contemporary sources, but in general the biblical historians are theologians, recounting 'historical' events in order to preach a sermon about the goodness (or wrath) of Yahweh, and about the faithfulness (or sin) of the Israelites. Our starting-point must therefore be the *literary* works. We do not know how accurate they are, but we do know they were written, and for a specific purpose. The study of the Hebrew Bible is first and foremost a study of its *writers* – their interests, values and dogmas. Our prime concern is how they composed their works, with what literary skills, and for what purpose.

In this our overriding problem lies in the anonymity of these writers: we do not know *precisely* who they were or when they were writing. The evidence therefore is problematic: there are few firm 'answers', but many questions. There are many rival 'solutions', which can be confusing to the beginner. Hypotheses are a working-tool of biblical historians, who seek a meaningful framework for the very incomplete data at their disposal. Hypotheses are constructed to be tested, to fathom their strengths and weaknesses, and to be modified or rejected. Students regard hypotheses as 'fact' at their peril!

FURTHER READING

Aharoni, Y. 1979: *The Land of the Bible: a Historical Geography.*
Aharoni, Y. 1982: *The Archaeology of the Land of Israel.*
Gottwald, N. K. 1985: *The Hebrew Bible: A Socio-Literary Introduction*, ch. 2.
Miller, J. M. and Hayes, J. H. 1986: *A History of Ancient Israel and Judah*, chs 1–2.

2

The Authority and Use of the Hebrew Bible

THE HISTORY OF THE TEXT

Peter Robson

The Tenakh

The Hebrew Bible is divided into three major sections.

Torah, 'Law'
Genesis–Deuteronomy, sometimes called by the Greek term
Pentateuch (Five Books)

Nebi'im, 'Prophets'
The Former Prophets (the historical works Joshua–Kings)
The Latter Prophets (Isaiah, Jeremiah, Ezekiel, and the Book of the
Twelve or 'Minor Prophets')

Kethubim, 'Writings'
Psalms, Job, Proverbs, Ruth, Song of Songs, Ecclesiastes,
Lamentations, Esther, Daniel, Ezra, Nehemiah, Chronicles.

The word *Tenakh* combines the initial letters of these sections. Later translations did not keep to the order of the Hebrew Bible and included additional books. English versions follow both of these practices, although the Protestant translations keep the additional books in a separate section, called the *Apocrypha*.

That the Hebrew Bible was originally written in Hebrew (except the few sections in Aramaic) is rarely contested. However, the earliest complete Hebrew Tenakh manuscript dates only from the tenth century CE. There are earlier texts of portions of the Hebrew Bible – the most significant being the 'Dead Sea Scrolls', fragments of which were discovered in 1947. A community at Qumran near the Dead Sea had copied books of the Hebrew

Bible for their library from about 100 BCE, a thousand years before the first complete Hebrew text. The earliest translations, into Greek, Syriac, Aramaic and Latin, all bear 'Hebraisms' – features of Hebrew style which strongly suggest a Hebrew original. The Greek translation of Aquila is written in a style so heavily influenced by Hebrew that it has been said not to be Greek at all!

The Hebrew Language

Hebrew is one of a group of Middle Eastern languages called *Semitic* (from *Shem*, son of Noah). Scripts differ in appearance, but the languages in the Semitic 'family' have words and grammar in common. They derive many of their words from verbal 'roots' of three consonants. Most Semitic languages write the text from right to left (the converse of English). Hebrew has only two 'tenses' ('perfect', of *finished* action; and 'imperfect', of *unfinished* action), but verbs have a number of forms to convey a variety of meanings – usually described as simple, passive, reflexive, intensive and causative. Table 2.1 lists forms derived from the root *sh-m-r* (keep).

Scrolls were used at least from the seventh or sixth century BCE. Jeremiah (*c*.600 BCE) describes his scroll as having columns and as written in ink, probably lamp-black (Jer 36). Ezekiel (2.9–10) and Isaiah (34.4) also mention scrolls. Papyrus from Egypt was readily available, but more fragile. The Letter of Aristeas (a fictitious narrative written in the first century BCE) describes the Torah as being written on animal skins. Ezra's Torah may have been written on leather ('parchment'), as was the custom in the Persian administration. Persian parchments of this age have survived. Biblical manuscripts from Qumran are generally parchment scrolls, and samples of ink have survived. The modern book form, or *codex* (plural *codices*), did not become general until the second century CE.

These oldest manuscripts were preserved as traditional sacred texts and commentaries were written on them. To give material a more precise date

Table 2.1   Forms of the Hebrew verb root *sh-m-r* (keep)

Simple	he kept	*shamar*
Passive	he was kept	*nishmar*
Reflexive	he kept himself	*nishmar*
Intensive	he kept for a long time	*shimmar*
passive	he was kept for a long time	*shummar*
reflexive	he kept himself for a long time	*hithshammer*
Causative	he caused [them] to keep	*hishmir*
passive	he caused [them] to be kept	*hoshmar*

requires careful study leading to hypotheses. There are often fierce arguments about whether hypotheses are convincing, and rival hypotheses can be radically different, so it is never wise to take these for granted. One widely used hypothesis is that books with Aramaic text (Ezra 4.6–23; 5.1–6.18; 7.12–26; Dan 2.4–7.28) or showing Aramaic influence are late in date – although Aramaic was also an ancient lanaguage. Sometimes the meanings of individual words are in doubt. A number are found once only (called therefore *hapax legomena*, Greek for 'once read'), so we have to rely on the context, the translations and possible etymologies. One word of uncertain meaning is '*arob* in the third plague in Egypt (Exod 8.21): Jewish tradition gives it the meaning 'wild beasts' but English versions prefer 'swarms of flies'. Often it is clear that early translators were also guessing, so we should not accept their view at face value either.

Sometimes a meaning has to be deduced using another Semitic language (often called 'comparative philology'). There are great dangers in this, as languages are not static. It is easy to jump to conclusions, as Barr (1968) warns. Arabic, often used in the search for parallels, is much younger than Hebrew. Some renderings of the New English Bible stem from the use of this comparative method: for example, the reading 'she broke wind' (Judg 1.14) replaces 'she alighted from her ass' (RSV).

It is widely believed by scholars that the earliest passage to be composed was Judges 5, often called the 'Song of Deborah', about an ancient battle possibly in the eleventh or twelfth century BCE. The latest may have been Daniel, in the second century BCE, much of which is written in Aramaic. During this thousand-year period, Hebrew underwent some changes. Ideas and words were borrowed from other cultures – the Canaanites, Babylonians, Persians and Greeks. The script, too, altered considerably, before reaching its final 'square-script' form (sometimes called 'Aramaic' or 'Assyrian'). In Old Hebrew, *b* and *r*, *h* and *ḥ* (a gutteral), and *m* and *n* could be easily confused. Some textual corruptions can thus be traced back to this time. The Samaritan Torah (see below) and a few Qumran scriptures are written in Old Hebrew, showing that the changeover was gradual. The introduction of the square script is traditionally attributed to Ezra (*c*.400 BCE) and the earliest extant secular example is roughly contemporary with this. By 200 BCE surviving manuscripts are usually in square script. Now *b* and *k*, *d* and *r*, *y* and *w* could be easily confused.

The Dead Sea Scrolls

The library of the Qumran community, hidden during the Roman campaign against Jerusalem and Masada (*c*.67–73 CE) contained scriptures, commentaries and handbooks. They were written during the previous two centuries, on writing-desks and with inkwells discovered in the ruins of Qumran. There were two Isaiah scrolls, a Habakkuk commentary and fragments of many other biblical books. The text of one Isaiah scroll differs substantially from the Masoretic text, but the second is much closer. The first seems to be a popular text, the latter from the text 'family' which the Masoretes later treasured. A Hebrew fragment of Samuel is much closer to the Septuagint than the Masoretic text, which is substantially different. Some Qumran texts are reminiscent of the Samaritan text, and others differ from these three text traditions.

The Masoretes

During the first nine centuries CE, the *consonantal* text of the Hebrew Bible was handed down meticulously by Jewish scholars, first the 'scribes' and later the *Masoretes* or 'transmitters'. The Masoretes were dealing with an ancient sacred text, written without vowels, in a language they no longer spoke. Corruptions had crept in, making some words and passages totally incomprehensible. They invented a system of dots and dashes (*pointing*) to indicate how the word should be read. They added extensive marginal notes (*masora*): these noted any doubts they had, suggested alternative readings, and differentiated between what was actually *written* (*kethib*) and what ought to be *read* (*qere'*). A prime example is the 'perpetual *qere*' *Adonai* (my Lord) for the divine name YHWH. The text was also divided into paragraphs, 452 *sedarim* (weekly lessons for a three-year cycle) and 54 (or 53) *parashoth* (weekly lessons for an annual cycle). (The present chapter divisions stem from the thirteenth century CE.)

Masoretic Manuscripts

A large number of manuscripts have survived, but only a few are from the early period (tenth-eleventh centuries CE). Of these the Leningrad and Aleppo codices from the tenth century are the most important. Since its third edition (1937), *Biblia Hebraica*, the standard Hebrew text, has used the Leningrad Codex, written and pointed in 1008 by Samuel ben Jacob. Shelomo ben Buya'a wrote the very fine Aleppo Codex, and Aaron ben Asher added the pointing and masora notes (*c*.900–50). Damaged and partly destroyed in 1947, a critical text of it is now being published. The Codex Cairensis (895 by Moses ben Asher) contains only the Prophets, but is the earliest extant Masoretic manuscript.

Printed Texts

There are two different strategies in preparing a printed text. One is to follow a particular manuscript faithfully, and add notes to comment on different readings in other early manuscripts. Such a text is *Biblia Hebraica Stuttgartensia* (1977), which notes Qumran variants in footnotes. Another method is to select the 'best' readings from all manuscripts and produce an 'eclectic text' – but who decides which is best? This kind of text is a hypothetical solution based on individual judgements of the editors.

The Samaritan Pentateuch

The text of the Torah preserved by the separated Samaritan community (perhaps by the fourth century BCE) is an early variant, written in Old Hebrew script. It differs from the Masoretic text in around 6000 particulars. Many are *orthographic* – that is, variant ways of writing the same words. In about 1900 instances, the variants agree with the Greek Septuagint where the Masoretic Hebrew differs, and in others the reading corresponds to variants in the Dead Sea Scrolls. Clearly these reflect a form of the Hebrew text in the centuries immediately prior to Christianity. The large number of minor differences suggests that this was not the text form preserved by the Masoretes. The most important extant manuscript dates from the eleventh century CE.

The Hebrew Bible in Greek

According to the legend found in the Letter of Aristeas (*c*.100 BCE), Ptolemy II Philadelphus of Egypt (285–247 BCE) commissioned seventy-two scholars to translate the Torah, which they completed in seventy-two days. The usual name for this translation, the *Septuagint* (*Septuaginta*), means 'seventy' (in Roman numerals, *LXX*, the usual abbreviation for the version) and refers now to the whole Tenakh as translated into Greek by Jews in Alexandra. Alexandria was founded in 332 BCE and a Jewish community soon established itself. In time, Greek became the common language, creating a demand for a Greek translation. There is little consistency in the various books, which suggests they were translated in a piecemeal fashion, and accuracy fluctuates widely. In some cases (e.g. Jeremiah, Samuel), the Hebrew text used by the translators differed significantly from the Masoretic text.

The complete version became a standard text for early Christians, and there is some later evidence of interference by Christian scribes – such as in Psalm 96.10 'the Lord reigns *from the tree*'. In Isaiah 7.14 the rendering of the Hebrew *'almah* (young woman) as *parthenos* (virgin) may have influenced Matthew's interpretation of that text (Matthew 1.23). The manuscripts which form the basis of modern Septuagint editions are Vaticanus, Sinaiticus and Alexandrinus, from the fourth and fifth centuries CE, where they formed the beginning of the Christian Bible in Greek. Many earlier fragments have been discovered, which may lead eventually to a new critical edition of the Greek text.

Aquila produced a new and slavishly Hebraic rendering of the Hebrew Bible (*c*.130 CE) which was favoured by Jewish communities, and later that century Theodotion, a Jewish proselyte, brought out a version in good Greek, revising an earlier Greek version in the light of the Masoretic text. Symmachus brought some literary style to the operation (*c*.170), and Origen (185–254) worked on his monumental *Hexapla* in six columns: the Hebrew text; Hebrew text in Greek characters; Aquila; Symmachus; Septuagint (emended); Theodotion. This was a fundamentally important work of scholarship which had lasting influence.

Translation is a very difficult enterprise, because words and grammatical structures have very different ranges of associations in different languages. The Hebrew *dbr* for instance is translated in twelve different ways (excluding the variant *deber*, 'plague', which the translator did not understand). The fact that there are multiple meanings is important – but a translator has to choose one. So-called 'literal translations' do not make easy reading, and may fail to be meaningful. Translations *interpret* a text: translators look to what they *believe* the text to mean, especially when words and concepts are difficult. Versions are on occasion very free indeed. The Hebrew Bible cannot therefore be properly studied through translation.

The Targums

For Jewish synagogue congregations, there was a need to translate the Hebrew Tenakh into the vernacular Aramaic. An interpreter (*meturgeman*) gave spontaneous interpretations which sometimes reached written form (such as the Targum of Job, and the Genesis Apocryphon, found in Qumran). Material eventually became codified: the Jerusalem Targums (including that of Pseudo-Jonathan); the Palestinian Targum (originally discovered in Cairo, but existing in various forms, notably in the Vatican Neofiti manuscript); and the versions produced in Babylon, attributed to Onkelos (Torah) and Jonathan ben 'Uzziel (Prophets). These date from the sixth and seventh centuries CE. The text was interpreted, expanded, altered and explained, with the result that these provide very valuable evidence about interpretation but very little hard data on textual matters.

The Syriac Bible

Christians in Mesopotamia also translated the Tenakh from Hebrew into the vernacular. Some readings are reminiscent of the Septuagint, others of the Targums, suggesting a complex development. Some books provide useful evidence relating to the Hebrew text. The standard Syriac Bible is called the *Peshitta*, meaning 'simple', and probably dates from the second century CE.

The Latin Vulgate

When Latin supplanted Greek as the language of scholarship during the third century CE, a Latin Bible became inevitable. The *Old Latin* version was translated from the Septuagint: only fragments of it are now available. The first *Vulgate* version of the Hebrew Bible was completed by Jerome (*c.*342–420) in 405, although current manuscripts are from much later and may have been modified with use. His style blended colloquialism with monastic intellectual vigour. He used Greek translations widely, but rarely strayed far from the Hebrew text. The Vulgate gained in popularity only slowly.

English Versions

Resistance to translating the Bible into English was gradually broken down, with William Tyndale playing a decisive role. Early translations include the Matthew Bible (1537), the Great Bible (1539), the Geneva Bible or 'Breeches Bible' (1560), the Bishop's Bible (1568) and the Roman Catholic Rheims–Douay Version (1610). King James I authorized a major translation (completed in 1611 and known as the Authorized Version) which remains in use today. Various revisions have been completed, of which the Revised Standard Version (1948) is still in common use. The Common Bible is a form of this version. Recent versions of note are the excellent New Jerusalem Bible (1966), the New English Bible (1970) and the New International Bible (1978).

The Canon

The idea of *canon*, a list of authoritative books, developed in the Christian period. People in the 'Old Testament' period had no established canon and used a wider range of 'scripture' than preserved in English Bibles. The Hebrew Bible is termed 'Scripture' by the New Testament, Philo, Josephus and the Mishnah, and the Torah was of course pre-eminent. Around the end of the first century CE, Josephus mentions twenty-two books (*Against Apion*, I, 8), and 4 Ezra (2 Esd 14.44–6) gives twenty-four – a variation perhaps pointing to different ways of counting the thirty-nine books (for example, counting the twelve books of the Minor Prophets as one). Legend attributes some decisions to a 'Council' of Jamnia (Yabneh) late in the first century CE – probably a college for Bible study (*beth hammidrash*) and religious court (*beth din*) – but this is not born out by Jewish sources. The Mishnah (Yadaim, 3.5) notes discussions in the period 80–117 CE on the place of the Song of Songs and Ecclesiastes in Scripture. The Talmud notes that there were also questions raised at various times against Ezekiel, Proverbs, Ecclesiasticus (The Wisdom of Jesus ben Sirach), Ruth and Esther.

The real decisions on scriptural status had emerged gradually over the years. The Torah was already accorded high status in Ezra and Nehemiah (unless the writer included it as an anachronism). Jesus ben Sirach, in about 190 BCE, mentions the 'twelve prophets' after Isaiah, Jeremiah and Ezekiel (Ecclus 48.20–49.10), seemingly implying that their prophecies were understood as forming a book complete in itself. Daniel, written after this date, would therefore find no place in the Prophets and is accordingly found in the Writings. Ecclesiasticus talks of the Torah, the Prophets and *remaining books* – referring to the beginnings of this final section. Qumran texts speak of Torah and the Prophets (Damascus Document, 7.14–18; Manual of Discipline, 8.15–16). The Septuagint shows that a wider range of books was treasured in Alexandria, and the Qumran scrolls also reflect this earlier, less rigid situation. Many other Jewish writings have survived from this period, some identified in the Qumran fragments. There are several modern collections of *Apocrypha* ('hidden [writings]') and *pseudepigrapha* ('falsely [i.e. falsely attributed] writings'). The early Christian Church adopted this wider canon, including Jewish works whose ideas influenced Christian thought. These additional books are commonly referred to today as *deutero-canonical* ('deutero-' meaning 'second').

Today, Protestant churches accept only the Hebrew Tenakh as authoritative 'Old Testament'. During the Reformation, Luther followed Jerome in the view that only the Tenakh was 'inspired'. The Roman Catholic Church from 1546 accepted 'deutero-canonical' books (found today in the New Jerusalem Bible) translated from Greek: Tobit, Judith, Wisdom, Ecclesiasticus, Baruch, 1–2 Maccabees, and additions to Jeremiah, Esther and Daniel (the Song of the Three Young Men, or Benedicite; Susanna; and Bel and the Dragon). Orthodox churches include in addition 1–2 Esdras (= 3–4 Esdras), the Prayer of Manasseh, Psalm 151, 3 Maccabees; and some further accept 4 Maccabees, the Odes of Solomon and the Psalms of Solomon. The Ethiopian church adds Jubilees and 1 Enoch.

FURTHER READING

Barr, J. 1983: *Holy Scripture: Canon, Authority, Criticism.*
Childs, B. S. 1979: *Introduction to the Old Testament as Scripture*, chs 2–4.

Eissfeldt, O. 1976: *The Old Testament: an Introduction,* rev. edn, pt 5
Mellor, E. B. 1972: *The Making of the Old Testament.*
Würthwein, E. 1979: *The Text of the Old Testament.*

A JEWISH PERSPECTIVE

Sybil Sheridan and Dan Cohn-Sherbok

The threefold division of the Bible expresses important distinctions in origin, authority and use. The *Torah* is seen as 'direct revelation' – the word of God dictated to Moses on Mount Sinai. The *Nebi'im* (Prophets) are viewed as 'inspiration' – that is, they were written by prophets after they had received some form of revelation. The *Kethubim* (Writings) are best described as 'communication' – written after prophecy was said to have ceased, they represent human initiatives to seek out and understand God.

The Torah therefore has the highest authority, as the word of God: for Jews, Bible study means largely the study of Torah. The Nebi'im and Kethubim are frequently employed as proof texts, but examination of these books as works in themselves is less frequent.

Revelation

The single most profound event in Judaism was the revelation of Mount Sinai, though Jewish groups differ in their understanding of what happened there. Orthodox Jews regard the whole Torah as the word of God dictated to Moses. Moreover, God entrusted Moses with the means of *interpreting* it. This was not written down, but passed on orally to chosen representatives in each generation, and gradually revealed as the times dictated. Thus the later works the Mishnah (*c.*100 CE) and the Talmud (*c.*500 CE) are considered *oral law*, revealed at Mount Sinai.

Reform, Liberal and Conservative Jews do not follow this view, but are of the opinion that, while Moses did receive a revelation at Sinai, it is unclear how much of the Torah was God's original word, and how much was added later. Some laws seem by today's standards inhumane, and possibly reflect the attitudes of a primitive society rather than the wishes of a loving God. Liberal Jews often apply modern biblical criticism in an attempt to separate

God's revelation from those elements which deal with a particular social context. They understand the Mishnah and Talmud (and later codes) as largely products of their own time.

Interpretation of Torah

Torah is a Hebrew word meaning 'teaching': it is full of directives on how to live one's life and how to worship God. To do this properly requires close examination of these directives to ensure that they are correctly interpreted and understood. There are apparent contradictions; the precise meaning of some prescriptions is unclear; and there are concerns about how to observe them in contemporary life. As time went by and society changed, many directives seemed out of date. Scholars and scribes devoted their lives to the reappraisal of Torah, reinterpreting the meaning of the laws to keep them relevant. The process of reinterpretation is called *midrash* (from the Hebrew 'to seek out') and the new regulations derived from it are *halakah* (in Hebrew 'the way to go'). They helped Judaism to survive difficult times, and both continue in Judaism to this day.

This was an oral process. Famous scholars taught disciples who committed their master's words to memory. They in their turn, as leaders, added their own comments to these teachings, and so on into the following generations. There were differences of opinion and discrepancies, and, although oral societies boast excellent memories, there was a limit on how much could be recalled. Therefore, in spite of opposition, it was decided to write the oral law down. This was accomplished at the end of the first century CE by Rabbi Judah Hannasi ('the Prince') and, though by no means all of the legal material available to him was included, it was thought of as *the* oral law *par excellence*, the *Mishnah*.

The process of analysis and interpretation went on, and now the Mishnah also came under scrutiny. *Baraitoth*, sayings of the rabbis that were not included in the Mishnah, were compared with Mishnaic law, discussed and applied. In time, these discussions and decisions were written down, to form the *Talmud*. There were two Talmuds, the Palestinian (*c.*300–400 CE; and the Babylonian (c. 500). The Babylonian Talmud is regarded as authoritative. Talmudic passages begin with a statement from the Mishnah in Hebrew, followed by the later rabbis' discussion in Aramaic, known as *Gemara*. Because of the work of the Rabbis, this period is called 'Rabbinic'. Unlike the Mishnah, the Gemara is interspersed with homilies, jokes and prayers. Jewish rabbinic law is further explored in chapter 6.

Subsequent Jewish legal literature has produced summaries of the Talmud and responses by famous rabbis who, using the same process as the original rabbis, bring the laws of the Torah, via the Mishnah and Talmud, to bear on current concerns.

Homilectic Interpretation and Commentary

Halakah treats the Torah thematically, examining various laws on a set subject and deriving new directives. Alongside this, a different strategy was used, interpreting Torah texts sentence by sentence. This too is *midrash*, but does not result in *halakah*. Some material is legal, but most is *homilectical* (that is, resembling a sermon or homily). Such *midrash* enriched the religious life and has always had great popular appeal. From the second century BCE, and perhaps earlier, charismatic preachers were much in demand. They employed parables, allegories and a great deal of fantasy and this material, *aggadah*, was often reused.

The verse-by-verse form of interpretation gave rise to Bible commentaries in the Middle Ages. In these, midrash was used along with the rediscovered rules of grammar and the personal insights of the author. The most famous commentator is Rabbi Solomon ben Yitshak (known, by the initial letters, as Rashi), who lived in France from 1040 to 1105. His commentary is still used today. In Jewish Bible scholarship, it is generally the most ancient, and not the most modern, that is considered authoritative.

The Liturgical Use of the Bible

The focal point of the synagogue service on Sabbaths and festivals (and Mondays and Thursdays in synagogues which have daily services) is the reading of the Torah. The Torah is handwritten on a parchment scroll for this purpose. It is covered and ornamented, and lodged in the 'Holy Ark' (*aron qodesh*), which is ultimately derived from the Ark of the Covenant (Exod 37.1–4).

On festivals, a part of the Torah relevant to the festival is read. On Shabbat (Sabbath), the weekly readings ensure that the whole Torah is covered each year. Babylonian Jews, in the early days, divided the Torah into fifty-five portions (*sidroth*) to form an annual cycle. There was an alternative triennial cycle with 155 *sidroth* in Palestine. There is a special festival, *Simchat Torah*, 'Rejoicing in the Torah', which marks the point where the last chapters of Deuteronomy are read, and Genesis is begun again – symbolizing that the Torah is eternal, with neither beginning nor end. At each service where the Torah is read, members are called up to read the benedictions before and after the reading. Other congregants will be asked to take the scroll from the Ark, process it round the synagogue, remove the coverings and lift it high for all to see. It is considered an honour to participate, and the ceremony is performed with great panache.

On Sabbaths and festivals, the Torah reading is followed by a portion from the Prophets (or *haphtarah*). Legend has it that this was instituted under the rule of Antiochus IV Epiphanes (175–163 BCE), when the Torah readings were forbidden. Prophetic passages that had some connection with the weekly portion were read instead to keep the idea of Torah readings, and their content, close to people's minds. Certain of the Writings are used as *haphtaroth* – notably the Five Megilloth at festivals (see below, ch. 14) and Jonah, which is read in the afternoon of *Yom Kippur*, the Day of Atonement. Other passages (and in particular the Psalms) are widely used in prayers.

The Torah has been the foundation and mainstay of Judaism through three millennia. It has been the main source of intellectual and literary inspiration of Jewish law and lore. Not only is it used in ritual, and studied, but the laws that developed from it are applied to every aspect of life. The Prophets and the Writings serve as commentary to the Torah. In the words of the Psalmist, 'Thy word is a lamp to my feet and a light to my path' (119.105) and 'thy law is my delight' (119.77).

Rabbinic Theology

The rabbis expressed their theological views through stories, legends, parables and maxims based on Scripture (see Montefiore and Loewe, 1974). God's unity was paramount. Repeatedly the rabbis affirmed that God has many different names, but he is always the same. Thus Rabbi Abba ben Nemel:

God said to Moses, 'Thou desirest to know my name. I am called according to my deeds. When I judge my creatures, I am called Elohim; when I wage war against the wicked, I am called Sabbaoth; when I suspend judgement for a man's sins, I am called El Shaddai; but when I have compassion upon my world, I am called Yahweh.

The rabbis also stressed that God alone is the source of the universe, and directs it according to a preordained plan as a captain directs a ship. Idolatry is condemned vigorously: a midrash on Numbers proclaims, 'He who renounces idolatry is as if he professed the whole law.' For the rabbis, God is a transcendent creator, yet he is also *immanent*. The Talmud explains,

God is far and yet He is near. . . . For a man enters a synagogue and stands behind a pillar, and prays in a whisper, and God hears his prayer, and so it is with all His creatures. Can there be a nearer God than this? He is as near to His creatures as the ear to the mouth.

Although 'all is foreseen, freedom of choice is given; and the world is judged with goodness, and in accordance with the works' (Rabbi Aqiba). God knows all things, yet humans have free will and will be judged on the basis of their actions. This judgement is tempered with mercy, as a midrash on Leviticus records:

In the hour when the Israelites take up their ram's horns, and blow them before God, He gets up from the throne of judgement and sits down upon the throne of mercy and he is filled with compassion for them, and He turns the attribute of Judgement into the attribute of Mercy.

In some rabbinic sources, the Torah is described as pre-existent, the instrument with which the word was created. Thus a midrash on Genesis proclaims, 'God created the word by the Torah: the Torah was his handmaid and His tool by the aid of which He set bounds to the deep, assigned the functions to sun and moon, and formed all nature.' As the word of God, every letter is sacrosanct; and its study is the Jew's most sacred task. Beneath the literal meaning, the rabbis asserted, it is possible to discover layers of deeper meaning in which the divine mysteries are revealed.

The Torah also played a central role in the rabbinic depiction of the afterlife. There is no explicit doctrine of eternal salvation in the Hebrew Bible. According to rabbinic sources, the world to come is divided into several stages. First will come a period of Messianic redemption on earth, fulfilling every human aspiration. Peace will reign throughout nature. Jerusalem will be rebuilt. At its close, the dead will be resurrected bodily, and rejoined with their souls. Then the final judgement will come. Righteous Jews will enter Paradise (the Garden of Eden), together with Gentiles who have lived in accord with the laws which Noah took upon himself.

Early rabbinic authorities discussed a wide variety of religious issues, including martyrdom, prayer, charity, atonement, forgiveness, repentance and peace. They reflected on human life and God's nature and activities. These were not binding but were formulated to educate, inspire and edify. The study of Torah was a labour of love which had no end, a task whose goal was to serve the will of God.

Rabbinic Ethics

The Torah serves as the blueprint for moral action. It is through the admonitions of the rabbis in Mishnaic and Talmudic sources that the Jewish people are encouraged to put its teaching into effect in their everyday lives. The rabbis declared *justice* to be of supreme importance. Rabbi Simeon ben Gamaliel (second century CE) remarked, 'Do not sneer at justice, for it is one of the three feet of the world, for the sages taught that the world stands on three things: justice, truth and peace.' According to Rabbi Elazar (second century CE) the principle of justice underlay the whole Torah, including its narratives: 'Sodom was not overthrown till the men of Sodom neglected justice.' Charity was viewed as an essential virtue: 'He who gives alms in secret is greater than Moses', declared the Talmud. Rabbi Elazer, also in the Talmud, declared on the basis of Proverbs 23.3 that almsgiving was greater than sacrifice: 'But loving deeds are greater than almsgiving, as it says [Hos 10.12], 'Sow in almsgiving, reap in love.' He went on, 'Almsgiving becomes increasingly perfect according to the amount of love that is shown in it.'

Rabbinic ethics requires that each person be treated equally, with a concern for human dignity. Arbitrary distinctions between people should not disqualify them from the right to justice, since everyone is created in the image of God. In this there is no fundamental difference between the Jew and the non-Jew, since God's ethical demands apply to all. In a midrash on the Psalms we read, 'This is the gate of the Lord into which the righteous shall enter: not priest, Levites, or Israelites, but the righteous, though they be non-Jews.'

The Jewish faith is not solely concerned with actions and their consequences; it also demands right intention – motives, feelings, dispositions and attitudes are of supreme moral significance. What kind of person you *are* is as important as what you *do*. It is also concerned with right speech: evil words can destroy relationships and anger can be soothed by gentle words. The rabbis urged also that we include animals in the moral scheme of things, that people are morally obliged not to inflict pain on animals. It was said of Rabbi Judah Hannasi that thirteen years of toothache were caused by his thoughtlessness to animals: as soon as he learnt kindness, it disappeared.

Thus Jewish ethics have a humane orientation. Jews were encouraged to strive for the highest conception of life, and establish the rule of truth, righteousness and holiness among humankind. The coming of God's rule and God's kingdom requires a human struggle for the reign of justice and righteousness on earth.

FURTHER READING

Unterman, A. 1981: *Jews: their Religious Beliefs and Practices.*
Cohn-Sherbok, D. 1988: *The Jewish Heritage.*
Montefiore, C. G., and Loewe, H. 1974: *A Rabbinic Anthology.*
Selzer, R. M. 1980: *Jewish People, Jewish Thought: the Jewish Experience in History.*

A CHRISTIAN PERSPECTIVE

Mervyn Tower

The Hebrew Bible in Christian Worship

Luke, in one of the earliest accounts of a synagogue service in any literature, depicts Jesus worshipping in the Nazareth synagogue, 'as his custom was', on the Sabbath. He was handed the Isaiah scroll, read a portion, returned it, sat, and preached (Luke 4.16–21). This may have been a haphtarah reading following the Torah passage. The sermon was found frequently among early Christians. Paul used synagogue gatherings to preach Jesus as Messiah (e.g. Acts 13.5). It is likely that early Jewish converts to Christianity continued to worship in the synagogue, or, if there was opposition, to adopt a similar type of service in a similar building. The Last Supper (and subsequent 'breaking of bread' – Acts 2.42, 46) may have been related to a form of Jewish worship. Luke 24.13–31 certainly mentions Moses and the Prophets, followed by the breaking of bread (v. 30).

By *c*.155 CE, Justin Martyr, a native of Nablus (ancient Shechem), could say,

On the day named after the Sun, all who live in city or countryside assemble, and the memoirs of the Apostles or the writings of the Prophets are read for as long as time allows. When the lector has finished, the president addresses us, admonishing us and exhorting us to imitate the splendid things we have heard . . . .

The Prophets are presumably the Hebrew prophets – and by this time worship had shifted from Saturday to Sunday. When that change was formally made we do not know. Hebrew scriptures were regularly used in the liturgy, with a particularly central place being given to the Psalms. Hippolytus (*c*.170–236) speaks of psalms being used at evening prayer; Clement of Alexandria (died *c*.215) and Tertullian (*c*.160–225) note that they were also used at other times in the day. It seems likely that the Psalms, and other sections of the Hebrew Bible, were used from the time of Jesus; and they continue to be read and treasured as authoritative texts.

In July 144 a priest named Marcion was condemned for heresy for denying the inspiration and relevance of the Hebrew Bible. He also rejected New Testament books he believed to be 'tainted' with ideas about the Hebrew God, and unwittingly provided the impetus for defining the New Testament canon. Marcion died in 160; but on a popular level dismissive ideas about the value of the Hebrew Bible have remained, and some theologians have argued that these books are *inferior* to the New Testament material. Such an approach misrepresents the authority which early Christians vested in the Hebrew Bible, which was 'Scripture' (Mark 12.24; Luke 24.27; Acts 8.32; Romans 1.2; Corinthians 15.3–4).

Whatever scholars may think of the nature of the evidence about Jesus, there can be no real doubt about his Jewishness. Paul, the convert Pharisee (Philippians 3.5–6), who had such a dominating effect upon the growth of the early Christian communities, is like Jesus indebted to the Hebrew Bible. He not only uses a wealth of quotations, but also used rabbinic methods of argument. In Romans 10.18–20 he uses three texts to prove his point – one each from the Torah, Prophets and Writings. Of the gospels, Matthew has the most quotations (41) but they are not inconspicuous in the other three (Mark 21; Luke 21; John 14). Altogether the New Testament has around 350 direct quotations from the Hebrew Bible, 300 of which are closer to the Septuagint version than to the Hebrew. Nearly half (167) are from the Torah, and 112 from the Psalms, pointing to the popularity and importance of these texts. Only Ezra, Nehemiah, Song of Songs, Ecclesiastes and Esther are not cited.

The Unity of the Bible

Christians began to view the two halves of their Bible as a unity. The relationship was, it was suggested, one of preparation and completion, or prophecy and fulfilment. Quotations are introduced by phrases such as 'it is written', 'as Scripture says', or 'that it might be fulfilled'. Similar phrases are found in the Hebrew Bible itself (1 Kgs 2.27; 2 Chron 35.12) – and also in Qumran texts, the Jewish philosopher Philo (first century CE) and rabbinic texts. This is a clear witness to the view of the early Church that the Hebrew scriptures provided them with a valuable primary source to prove and demonstrate the Messiahship of Jesus. The view that there was an independent collection of 'proof texts' (suggested by J. Rendel Harris) is interesting but not generally held in its extreme form. Borrowing from the Hebrew Bible was also indirect, as where Deuteronomy 18.19 is paraphrased in John 12.49, Deuteronomy 32.5 in Philippians 2.15 and Exodus 19.6 in Revelation 1.6. Luke 1.46–55 may be a midrash on 1 Samuel 2.1–10; and there is an allusion to Numbers 20.1–11 in 1 Corinthians 10.4. Some passages use the language of *type* and *antitype*: 'image' (Greek *tupos*) and 'reality' (Greek *antitupos*). Thus the flood (Gen 6–9) is seen as the 'type' of baptism (see 1 Peter 3.21); Jesus is the 'antitype' of the Holy of Holies (Hebrews 9.24); Adam is the 'type' of Jesus (Romans 5.14). Such an evolutionary view of the relationship between the Hebrew Bible and the New Testament could raise the status of the latter at the expense of the former. Goldingay, speaking from a conservative Christian position, prefers the language of ~~mutuality~~ (1981, 34–5) – that each makes a major contribution, with 'parallel status', but that reading the two in conjunction can be mutually enriching.

The influence of the Hebrew Bible continued after the composition of the New Testament, in prayers, liturgies, sermons, writings and theology. The Church Fathers, making heavy use of allegorical exegesis, were determined to show that the Hebrew Bible was as much the heritage of the Church as of the synagogue. St Augustine of Hippo (354–430) expressed what was probably the common view: 'that which lies hidden in the Old [Testament] is revealed in the New'. The Hebrew Bible thus is viewed as an essential ingredient of Christianity. Allegorical interpretations have been replaced by the much wider critical approach which is developed later in this book. The process of interpretation is called *hermeneutics*. There is no one single hermeneutical method in Christian circles: in fact, the variety can be sometimes bewildering.

God

The developed concept of the Trinity (Father, Son, Holy Spirit) dates from long after the New Testament; but the belief in Jesus's divinity is clear even in early New Testament texts (the title 'Lord' may also suggest divinity), and some texts picture the Spirit as a separate entity (John 14.17; 15.26; 16.13). The New Testament continues to teach monotheism (e.g. Mark 12.29): the one God is everlasting and eternal, his love is boundless, his mercy and forgiveness limitless, his faithfulness unswerving. Doctrines from the Hebrew Bible are continued in the New Testament, as succinctly summarized in the Benedictus (Luke 1.68–79). An emphasis on God as 'father' dominates, sometimes using the intimate Aramaic *Abba*, 'father' – a metaphor found to a lesser extent in the Tenakh (Isa 63.16; 64.8) with a particular emphasis on God as father of the king (2 Sam 7.14). In general, the New Testament continues the fundamental presupposition that God is the one who reveals himself in his words and actions – through creation (Romans 1.20) and through history (Acts 7.2–50). In a sense, the Church was viewed as the heir of Israel as the recipients of God's revelation (Galatians 3.29).

Messiah

If God is viewed as 'father', then the Messiah was above all his 'son'. 'Messiah' means 'anointed' and originally referred to kings such as David, of whom the divine oracle said, 'I will be his father, and he shall be my son' (2 Sam 7.14). This explicitly signifies the paradox of discipline and love: 'When he commits iniquity, I will chasten him with the rod of men, with the stripes of the sons of men; but I will not take my steadfast love from him . . .'.

After the monarchy failed, the Messiah was sought in unlikely places – even the Persian king Cyrus was called 'his anointed' (*meshiho*– Isa 45.1) – and eventually a future king was fervently expected as a coming saviour. In Jesus's day, the Pharisees taught that the Messiah would be of Davidic descent, would display signs and wonders, would be signalled by the return of Elijah, and would fulfil the Messianic mission in his lifetime. There was at least a popular belief of the Messiah's political leadership, judging from John 18.36, when Jesus denied such a role for himself. The New Testament presents Jesus as fulfilling Messianic criteria. His Davidic descent is stressed (Romans 1.3; Luke 1.32; Matthew 1.20) – although Mark 12.35–37 intriguingly presents Jesus as denying this. Messiahship is revealed through a public display of 'signs' (Greek *semeia*), although Jesus denies the relevance of signs in Mark 8.11–13. Matthew 11.14 equates John the Baptist with a returned Elijah; but John 1.21 denies it. The Messianic mission is not fulfilled in Jesus's lifetime; rather the Messianic age is inaugurated and is continued by the Church, which retains a belief in the lasting presence of the Messiah.

It is an interesting question whether or not Jesus thought of himself as Messiah, Son of God, or Son of Man – although clearly the early Church believed this of him. The gospels show that he viewed his own role as triumphing through suffering, as the 'suffering servant' of Isaiah had done before him. New Testament writers used the Hebrew Bible as a quarry for so-called Messianic passages: in one sense they went beyond their brief; but in another they drew out interesting themes to illustrate the nature of Messiahship. Psalm 22 is an excellent example: the graphic picture of suffering ('I am poured out like water, and all my bones are out of joint' – v. 14) becomes the perfect picture for the crucified Jesus. Some Greek manuscripts in consequence interpreted v. 16 as 'they have pierced my hands and feet' (so RSV, Hebrew corrupt?). Jesus himself expressed his despair by using this psalm, using as the opening line on the cross *Eloi, Eloi, lama sabachthani*: 'My God, My God, why hast thou forsaken me?' Texts about the resurrection of the Messiah are less frequent. Psalm 16.8–11 is given such a treatment in Acts 2.25–32. The Church Fathers interpret other texts as indicating Jesus's resurrection (Hos 6.2; Ezek 37.1–14 and Jon 1.17). A more reasoned account of this doctrine is given in detail by Paul in 1 Corinthians 15.

Law

There is both continuity and discontinuity here. The Sermon on the Mount declares that Jesus came to fulfil the Torah and Prophets, not to abolish them. Christians should continue to live their lives in the spirit of the commandments of the scriptures (Matthew 5.17–48) – although this demonstrated that the spirit went far beyond the letter of the law. Jesus's teaching, as depicted in the gospels, challenged a literalistic view of Torah in relation to the washing of hands and food laws (Mark 7.1–23), Sabbath observance (Mark 3.1–6), fasting (Mark 2.18–19); but in each case he invited his hearers to take to heart the main thrust of the regulation. The early Church struggled with the question of literalism for many years – Peter for example was severely criticized for his conservatism (Galatians 2.12–14; cf. Acts 10), and the Council of Jerusalem (Acts 15) reached a compromise solution. Paul was firm in his theological argument: the original purpose of these regulations was to divide Jew from Gentile; Jesus died to reconcile the two (Colossians 3.11; Ephesians 2.11–22) and thus dissolved the whole purpose of the regulations. He saw the Torah as a 'tutor' to reveal sin (Galatians 3.19) but without the power to bring salvation. In general, moral aspects of the scriptures were retained to form the basis of Christian morality: Christians who saw freedom, as preached by Paul, as an excuse for licence and immorality were quickly condemned.

Much of the later debate among Christian theologians lacks an appreciation of the rich role of the Torah. Sometimes, because of thinly veiled anti-semitism, the Torah was caricatured as something which binds, in contrast to the Gospel which releases. Such an attitude can be traced in part to Paul (Romans 3.20; 7.6; Galatians 3.24). This reduction of Torah to legalism is an unpardonable distortion of Judaism which has blinkered many scholars and writers.

Creation

The teaching of God as creator of heaven and earth was incorporated into Christianity. There is, in New Testament writings, a tension between the *already* and the *not yet*. Jesus is seen as the principle of the new creation *already inaugurated*, which he achieved through his resurrection (2 Corinthians 5.17). The individual is incorporated into this new creation through baptism (Romans 6.4; Colossians 3.3; 1 Peter 1.23). Nevertheless, the purpose of creation is *not yet* fulfilled. Such a fulfilment involves *re-creation* (Romans 8.19–22; 1 Corinthians 7.31; 2 Peter 3.13; Revelation 21.5; cf. Isa 66.22) and is linked with Jesus's final eschatological victory (1 Cor 15.22–8; Ephesians 1.10). Until this, the Gospel must be preached, to *all creation*, to all created things, not to human beings alone (Mark 16.15).

Christian theology stressed the principle of creation from *nothing* (*ex nihilo*) to preserve the doctrine of God's unique sovereignty as creator. Since Darwin's work, the Christian debate has often sadly been restricted to whether scientific hypotheses can be reconciled with biblical accounts of creation – which assumes a literalist view of the Bible, and that the creation narrative was intended to be scientifically accurate.

Prophecy

The early Christians had great respect for Hebrew prophecy: of the 144 uses of the Greek word *prophetes* all but twenty-one refer to the Hebrew prophetic books. The belief in the continued existence of prophecy, found in the New Testament and Qumran, contrasts with the later rabbinic view that prophecy ceased with Malachi (see for example Tosephta Sotah, 13.2, and Seder Olam Rabbah, 30). Both John the Baptist and Jesus continue the functions of earlier prophets, speaking out God's will. John dressed and ate like a prophet, and demanded repentance even of rulers such as Herod. He was likened to Elijah who was to return. It is Luke above all who presents Jesus as a prophet. John three times presents Jesus as *the* prophet of Deuteronomy 18.15 (John 1.21; 6.14–15; 7.40), pointing to him as the antitype of all others. Certainly Jesus was conscious of his divine commission, performed symbolic actions, and uttered sayings which pointed to the future consequences of present decisions. He is viewed as the giver of the Spirit – which was itself viewed as a source of continuing prophecy (1 Corinthians 12–14). By the middle of the second century CE, the view developed (dispensationalism) that prophecy had ceased with the death of the apostles – a view intended to cut later 'heretics' down to size.

In general, the Church Fathers interpret the Hebrew prophetic writings *typologically* and reduce the notion of prophecy to foretelling the future, and in particular foretelling the mission of Jesus. Thomas Aquinas (*Summa Theologica*, II, 2a, question 171) quoted the more enlightened Isidore of Seville (*c.*560–636), explaining prophecy as 'speaking on behalf of' rather than 'foretelling the future'; nevertheless this crude evaluation generally prevails in popular circles today.

Ethics

The moral values demanded of the Christian are those spelt out by the Hebrew prophets: charity, humility, truth, justice, peace, unity, fidelity, forgiveness. Moral norms, or rules of conduct, are condensed within the Decalogue (Ten Commandments), which is authoritative for the Christian as for the Jew. Jesus is concerned to stress the importance of *values* over *norms* – as regulations can become ends in themselves. Love for God (Deut 6.5) and for neighbour (Lev 19.18) give rise to the doctrine of *agape*, 'love' (cf. Luke 10.27–8). The *conscience* has an important role in early Christian doctrine, and owes much to Greek philosophy: the word is only found in the Septuagint of the apocryphal Wisdom (17.11). Nevertheless, it picks up the Hebrew notion of personal responsibility (e.g. Ezek 18). Values, norms and conscience are still important areas of debate in Christianity. In a rapidly changing world marked by genetic and nuclear developments, the biblical proclamation of the priority of values should not be neglected.

FURTHER READING

Barton, J. 1988: *People of the Book? The Authority of the Bible in Christianity.*
Ferguson, D. S. 1987: *Biblical Hermeneutics: an Introduction.*
Goldingay, J. 1981: *Approaches to Old Testament Interpretation.*

A MUSLIM PERSPECTIVE

Stephen Bigger

Although revelation in Islam focuses on Muhammad (570–632 CE) as the last, and the 'seal', of the prophets, completing the long process of revelation, the earlier prophets are respected no less:

Say: We believe in Allah [God] and that which is revealed to us; we believe in what was revealed to Abraham, Ishmael, Isaac, Jacob, and the tribes; to Moses and Jesus and the other prophets. We make no distinction between any of them, and to Allah we have surrendered ourselves. (Qur'an 2.136).

Allah, (*al-Ilah*, '*the* God') revealed 'the Book' (scriptures) to herald good news, to guide and to warn (2.213), to lead people from darkness to light, 'to the path of the Mighty, the Glorious One, the path of Allah, to whom belongs all that the heavens and the earth contain' (14.12). The prophets were champions of justice: 'We have sent our messengers with explanations, and sent the Book and the Balance [of justice] down with them, so that mankind may conduct themselves with all fairness' (57.25). 'The Book' was 'sent down to bring the truth' (2.213); this heavenly scripture was revealed in the prophet's natural language (14.4). The Qur'an stresses that every nation has received a messenger to tell them, 'Serve Allah [God] and avoid false gods' (16.36). All messengers are commissioned by God but not all are described in the Qur'an (4.164–5; 40.78). Prophets were not deified: 'The apostles we sent before you were no more than mortals whom We inspired with revelations and with writings' (16.43). Sura 45 reads,

We gave the Scriptures to the Israelites and bestowed on them wisdom and prophethood. We provided them with good things and exalted them above the nations. We gave them plain commandments: yet it was not till knowledge had been vouchsafed them that they disagreed among themselves from evil motives. (45.16–17)

Particular mention is made of the Torah (*Tawrat*) and Psalms (*Zabur*): 'We wrote in the Psalms [Ps 37.29] after an earlier reminder [given to Moses]: "The righteous among My servants shall inherit the earth" ' (21.105).

Prophets convey God's word and will to the world. They are 'bearers of good tidings and of warning, messengers thanks to whose coming mankind could have no possible case against God' (4.163–5). Yet the *nature* of God will always remain ultimately incomprehensible. The tragedy of world history has been people's reluctance to listen: in particular, the reluctance of contemporaries to take a prophet seriously has led to a disregard for the message. Muslims therefore remain sceptical about the extent to which the message revealed to earlier prophets was preserved intact. The words of some have not been preserved at all, others in heavily edited versions which have tended to corrupt the meaning of the text. In contrast, the words revealed to Muhammad between 610 and 632 CE were, Muslims believe, preserved so carefully in the Qur'an that this must be regarded as the final, authoritative word of God. Thus, although the earlier prophets are respected, the writings attributed to them do not constitute Scripture. Information given in the Qur'an takes precedence always over earlier writings, and in effect replaces them. The Qur'an 'is a confirmation of that which was revealed before it, and an explanation of the Scripture' (10.37). Thus there are many passages where a story is clarified, or a regulation explained and on occasions (as with the ban on camel meat–4.160) abrogated.

There are major points of contact between the Hebrew Bible and Islam. The Muslim testimony (*shahada*) 'There is no God but God . . .' echoes the Shema from Deuteronomy: 'Hear, O Israel, the LORD our God, the LORD is one' (6.4, RSV margin). The Hebrew *'ehad* (one) is reflected in Sura 112, although *wahid* is more commonly used in the Arabic: 'Say: Allah is One, the Eternal God. He begot none, nor was He begotten. None is equal to Him.' The aggressive monotheism of prophets such as Elijah and Second Isaiah sets the tone for the Muslim rejection not only of idolatry but of all representational images of God – in line with the commandments (Exod 20.3–5; Deut 5.7–9). God has many attributes, of which the most often repeated are 'the merciful, the compassionate', but Muslims resist physical anthropomorphism and stress God's transcendence. Most importantly, God is our creator, sustainer and teacher who has revealed his will to the world – a will that demands submission (*Islam*) and an ethical response.

Prophets Adam, Enoch (Idris), Noah

The story of Islam begins with Prophet Adam. The prophetic line includes many biblical figures, not all of whom are identified as prophets in the Bible. Adam and Eve were expelled from Paradise to earth, with the fallen angel Saitan (or Iblis, the devil). Adam learnt to pray, and was forgiven (2.37). Traditions refer to him as establishing the first 'house of God', later restored and preserved as the Ka'bah. There is little detail of Enoch, but many stories about Noah – including one in which his son decides not to board the Ark and is drowned: Noah's grief is balanced by the judgement 'what he did was unrighteous'. Noah warned the people to no avail, 'Worship none but God. I am afraid on your account of a day of grievous retribution' (11.25–49). Only the righteous survived.

Abraham, Lot, Ishmael, Isaac

The contribution of Prophet Abraham cannot be minimized. Islam is no less than the pure religion of Abraham (2.132): 'Abraham was neither a Jew nor a Christian, but a *hanif*, a man of pure worship, a *muslim*, not one of the idolators' (3.67). This particularly stresses his *faithfulness* and *obedience*. The message delivered by Abraham is called Qur'an (43.26–31): it is stressed that this came *before the Torah and the Gospel* (3.65–8). Abraham rejected the idols of his father Azar (21.51–73; 26.69–104; 37.83). He perceived the folly of worshipping sun, moon and stars, and broke in pieces the images of his community, except one, the largest. He claimed that the surviving image had cause the havoc. To the reply that it could not have done so, Abraham condemned them for worshipping powerless idols. Monotheistic faith demanded a clean break with idolatry and the 'old' fertility rituals, so this is a recurring theme in the work of the prophets, including Muhammad. Abraham's view was not popular, and there was one attempt to kill him, by burning (21.51–73). Delivered by God, Abraham and Lot departed for 'the land on which, for all humanity, We made a blessing rest'. Later, Lot and his family were found to be the only believers from their city who submitted (*muslimun*) to God (51.24–37). Lot's role was more dynamic and positive in the condemnation of the city; his wife, who was not faithful, remained behind (Sura 29).

Abraham's relationship with his first-born, Ishmael, is given a pre-eminence not found in the Hebrew Bible. Ishmael is, in the Qur'an, the son whom Abraham was instructed to sacrifice: 'together they submitted to God's will' before God intervened (37.83–113). Abraham and Ishmael together built the Ka'bah and established it as a centre of true Muslim worship (2.124–9). Was Abraham's land therefore not Palestine? The Ka'bah is particularly remembered in pilgrimage month, when hajis (pilgrims) travel around the sacred sites, performing established rituals. Muhammad is said to have rededicated the Ka'bah to the true worship of Allah, and laid down guidelines for pilgrimage. Ibn Ishaq, an early Muslim writer, recorded that the sons of Ishmael had taken stones from Mecca, and circumambulated around them as Ishmael did around the Ka'bah: thus began the corrupt worship of stones; Muhammad had to establish again the true spirituality of Abraham. Although many rituals were retained (such as circumambulation around the Ka'bah), their heart was purged of spiritual idolatry. Hagar, Ishmael's mother, is particularly remembered in the *Say* – 'running' in search of water – and in the Zamzam spring, the spring associated with the gift of water for her survival. Abraham's faithfulness was continued in his family, Joseph particularly being described in detail (Sura 12). That community has passed away, enjoying its just reward. The Qur'an, however, encourages Muslims to see themselves as the spiritual heirs of Abraham.

Moses

Moses plays a dominant role in the Qur'an, being mentioned 196 times. He is the only prophet with whom God conversed directly (4.164; cf. Exod 33.11; Deut 34.10). There are echoes of many biblical stories, often with new insights. After killing an Egyptian, Moses says, 'Forgive me, Lord, for I have sinned against my soul' (28.16). This has puzzled Muslim commentators who hold prophets to be incapable of sin. Moses and Aaron together served as prophets. Egyptian magicians are presented, in the Qur'an, as conjurors, easily overcome by God's power. The story of Sinai and the golden calf – including Aaron's part in the proceedings, for which Moses pulls him by the hair as he protests his innocence – is retold in Sura 7, 'The Heights'. Moses was granted 'The Book', the tablets from God in person. 'The Cow', one of the longest suras, tells how the Israelites tried deviously to avoid the sacrifice of the heifer (Num 19).

Other Prophets

David is particularly respected as the author of Psalms (*Zabur*). Solomon 'We tested, placing on his throne a replica body' (38.30–40) – and he was penitent. He had knowledge, and all creation at his disposal, including winds and demons. He communicated with animals and birds: he converted the Queen of Sheba to Islam (27.15–44) after a lapwing had brought him news that she worshipped the sun. Elijah and Elisha were faithful messengers. Ayyub (Job) remained submissive, even after great suffering; and other Hebrew prophets are named. Jonah, 'man of the fish', is frequently mentioned (10; 21.87; 37; 68.48).

FURTHER READING

Cragg, K. 1988: *Readings in the Qur'an.*
Irving, T. B., Ahmad, K. and Ahsan, M. M. 1979: *The Qur'an: Basic Teachings.*

A HUMANIST PERSPECTIVE

Stephen Bigger

Is it possible to appreciate the Hebrew Bible without believing in God? Humanists find theistic assumptions an initial barrier. The first task is to 'translate' the idea of God into concepts which the humanist can accept. For example, ideals such as justice, fairness, compassion and relationship are found as attributes of God; and a transcendent God can be seen as a metaphor of mystery. Not restricted by a framework of religious dogma, humanists can react against metaphors and openly debate their value. The bottom line is the issue of reality: in which sense can religious language be said to be *true*? This debate begins with the issue of whether ideals such as justice can be said to be true. 'God is just' translates into 'justice is a true perception'. The metaphor of 'personhood' of God has given the idea of God a personal, even human, dimension, but it tends to obscure the possibility of treating God as abstract – God is truth, as Sikhs might say; and then the search for truth is the same as the search for God. The idea of mystery relates to the partial nature of our understanding: we observe but cannot fully understand why things are as they are. Attempts to uncover and explain reality make it still more incomprehensible. Transcendence and mystery are constant reminders of human limitations. We can therefore regard God-language as an understandable convention which need not deflect us from reading the texts as interesting human responses to experience. Certainly the writers reflected on thought-provoking questions; and their responses are often far removed from cosy piety – real people in real situations.

Understanding Life

Life is rarely simple, and often moralistic perspectives fail to satisfy. There is not a little moralizing in biblical books – the view that faithfulness is rewarded. Yet that perspective is constantly challenged, even as writers are struggling to express it.

Ecclesiastes wrestles with questions of meaning and purpose in the face of death. It recognizes that there will be few answers – 'As you do not know how the spirit comes to the bones in the womb of a woman with child, so you do not know the work of God who makes everything' (11.5); and not a little uncertainty – 'For in much wisdom is much vexation, and he who increases knowledge increases sorrow' (1.18). True wisdom lies in enjoying life, and work, and company, and quietness – *striving* only produces a greed for more.

Job has a different problem: he needs to understand why his family has been wiped out, his business ruined and his health wrecked. He takes no comfort in advice, debates fiercely, even with God, and finally admits defeat and can accept his lot without rancour: 'I have uttered what I did not understand' (42.3). Much else in the Hebrew Bible is about human existence and meaning, and about ideals which may or may not be achieved.

Understanding Relationships

Society wants harmony but has to cope with tension. Tension often stems from group identity – a certain repression to maintain solidarity, and a consequent aggression with other groups. The social group is centre stage in the Hebrew Bible in its many aspects. Esther explores courage in the face of racial persecution, as a young Jewish girl foils Haman's attempt at genocide – the bitterness, and the joy of deliverance, are celebrated at the Purim festival. The Song of Songs and Ruth focus on romantic love from different directions: the former through love songs, the latter through a story of devious dealings as Ruth won her man. Their festivals – Passover and Shavuoth – focus on rebirth and harvest. Prophets had wide-ranging social concerns, as they struggled towards a fairer society, defending the defenceless in society against greed and power politics. The ethics of business, and of government, both have their roots here with the demand that justice should be official policy and the challenge for society to live up to its ideals. The king, the 'anointed one' (*mashiah*, Messiah) should usher in universal peace and harmony *in this world* – an ideal worth striving for, although no king lived up to this and peace became, as always, a future hope. Sexual relationships were a burning concern and there are responses that are both chauvinistically overbearing (Judah's double standards in Genesis 38!) and deviously feminist (Ruth and the Song of Songs).

Meaning and Value

The crisis between religion and science has focused on literal interpretations both of biblical creation stories and of scientific models. An accompanying technological crisis is forcing us to pay less attention to 'What can we discover?' and more to 'How should we use what we have discovered?' Thus we are turning to questions of meaning and value. Humanists have found the view that Genesis 1–3 provides a blueprint of how the world was made sadly lacking in hard evidence. The notion that a 3000-year-old document could provide a scientific blueprint seems somewhat bizarre. Insights about the human condition, however, are a different matter: wisdom about human values early reached a high level, as the development of major world faiths attest. Genesis 1–3 stresses that the universe has a moral dimension; that it is essentially good, and can be run without greed and aggression; that humans have a position of grave responsibility in caring for the earth and the creatures within it; that we need to stand back from routine tasks, to take stock, and deepen our relationships; that we need to reassert the partnership (Hebrew *'ezer*) between men and women, generally disrupted by self-centred greed. This produces an agenda which deserves to be taken equally seriously today.

The passage raises also the question of God. In Genesis 3 God is anxious and jealous at humankind's newfound knowledge. Adam had 'become like one of us, knowing good and evil; and now lest he put forth his hand and take also of the tree of life, and eat, and life for ever . . . '. God falls silent at the appallingness of this thought and banishes Adam from the garden (Gen 3.22) into a world of suffering and toil. There is an apparent naïveté in this view, but we can have no doubt that Adam was cast into the world we actually inhabit. Once we view God as a conjunction of our most powerful symbols which give meaning to our existence, the expulsion from the garden represents bad faith – not being true to ourselves because selfish greed has dulled our fundamental human values. Our real self (= God) is threatened by new knowledge which is out of tune with our personal values (the disobedience motif). We seek knowledge for the sake of it, for self-gratification, without thought as to how it will be used. We fight against our inner selves, bringing upon ourselves strain, delusion, and the seeds of self-destruction.

This may be reading too much into the text, but we can be too easily satisfied with a surface reading and be patronizing in our assumption that ancient Hebrews were naïve and simplistic. The concept of God can come to life when it is viewed it as a supreme symbol of value. Qualities attributed to God mark justice, mercy, peace, righteousness, loyalty and faithfulness as values to be treasured. The call for faithfulness stresses sincerity; and the rejection of idolatry emphasizes a supreme distaste for 'bad faith', esteeming material objects over human values. Things of human design should not to have a central focus in our lives, as Second Isaiah affirmed acerbically (Isa 44.9–20). Measured by this powerful social critique, the community was found wanting, drifting away from its ideals and adopting lesser, and grosser, ambitions. This kind of idolatry involves a rejection of our true selves.

3

Symbol and Metaphor in the Hebrew Bible

Stephen Bigger

Language expresses what we think, and helps us to clarify our thoughts, but it is inexact and not infrequently ambiguous. We use expression and body language to give an extra dimension. However, when dealing with emotions, with questions about who we really are, about purpose and meaning, about responsibilities, and about deep feelings and insights, ordinary language fails to do justice to what we feel. Religious language attempts to make sense of areas beyond our understanding. Major concepts, such as love, hope, justice, value, are all contained in our concept of God. For a theist, language cannot encapsulate and contain God, who is much greater than we can conceive; for an atheist, the language reflects personal and social ideals. In either case the concepts are human concepts and we need to be cautious about claiming 'truth' for them – and to be open to insights from others. Our culture gives us a traditional framework to help us interpret our world, a framework which needs extending and sometimes challenging to prevent us being hidebound with preconceived notions.

The Hebrews expressed meaning not only through language, but also through objects, gestures, rituals, places, and stories. Symbolism can be an active means of expression, evoking emotions and new insights – although it can also have traditionally understood meanings. A symbol can change over time and take on new and interesting meanings unexpectedly. To be dogmatic closes the mind. 'Is it true?' asks for a literalistic and dogmatic response, when it depends on what is meant by 'true'. 'What does it mean?' and 'Can I enter into this understanding for myself?' provide challenging lines of thought and are more helpful.

Objects as Symbols

Many religions provide visual means to help people focus on the 'reality' that underpins their worship. There is sometimes a significant aspect of the symbol which provides a clear analogy – the light of a candle, for instance.

Or the significance of the object may depend on knowing the story they appear in – the symbols at a Passover meal, for example. We should beware of generalizing, since objects may have had a complex history.

Images, Icons

The Hebrew faith is portrayed as *aniconic* (imageless), in line with the second commandment of the Decalogue, forbidding graven images. No certain image of Yahweh has been unearthed, providing a marked contrast with the iconographies of neighbouring states – Egypt, the Mesopotamian civilizations, and Canaan. Where idols are worshipped in the Hebrew Bible, the practice is condemned. God is depicted without visible form – a voice which uttered God's 'word' (Deut 4.12; cf. 1 Kgs 19.9–13). The Torah speaks of God's *name* and *glory*. There were, however, tensions. The ceremonial bulls of the northern tribes, introduced by Jeroboam, were acceptable in their day although condemned by the later Judaean writers of Kings; and prophetic denunciations of idolatry reveal the existence of socially accepted rituals which did not always meet the prophets' high ideals. 'Idolatrous' worship at high places, with pillars and sacred groves, was common practice. One image banished from the Temple by King Hezekiah was Nahushtan, the bronze serpent created (a wilderness narrative claimed) by Moses himself as a response to plague (Num 21.8f; 2 Kgs 18.4). Later, in taking dramatic action against idolatry, King Josiah (*c*.626 BCE; 2 Kgs 23) had the clear support of prophets such as Jeremiah; but there is strong evidence that 'idolatry' was widespread. Narratives feature images. Rachel is depicted stealing her father's idols (*teraphim*), causing a major incident (Gen 31.34–5). After Jacob had made an altar to God at Bethel, he insisted that the company put away their foreign gods and he buried them under an oak (Gen 35.2–4) – evidence perhaps of an editor's ideology. Princess Michal deceived her father Saul by putting teraphim in David's bed to simulate the sleeping David, who was thus able to escape (1 Sam 19.13–17). Keel (1978, 194) assumes that these were cult masks. Gideon made an ephod of gold, the easiest explanation of which is that it was an image (although a golden garment is possible; see below). Micah's mother made an image of silver to go alongside the ephod and teraphim (Judg 8.26f; 17.4) which the tribe of Dan, in a period of anarchy, stole and subsequently installed in their own shrine. The texts do not condemn these images (except perhaps Hos 3.4). Some may have been Yahwistic; but many, such as the shrine of Gideon's father, were not (Judg 6.25).

The ban on representations of God was part of a determined attack on idolatry. The exilic writer Second Isaiah, stressing the absolute greatness of God, depicted him as incomparable: 'for I am God, and there is no other; I am God, and there is none like me' (Isa 46.9). The image is man-made, created by human skill, without further significance (Isa 44.9–20). There seems to be a clear relationship between this and the first two commandments, demanding the worship of God alone, without representations. To create a representation – a picture or an image – is to confine God to human categories, to create a god from a human idea. These gods are human creations, representing human emotions and needs.

The Ephod

The ephod was a garment worn by the priests, although in some contexts a gold ephod has been viewed as a golden image (Judg 8.26; 17.5; 18.14–31). The linen ephod, such as King David wore for his sacral dance (2 Sam 6.14–20), may have been a simple loincloth. It was viewed as a matter of great importance not to expose the genitals near the altar (Exod 20.26; 28.42–3) – although David's wife Michal still accuses him of exhibitionism! The high priest's ephod is clearly a whole garment, described as finely made and embroidered (Exod 28.15–30). A breastpiece matched the ephod in material and workmanship. Fixed to it were twelve different gems, each representing a tribe of Israel. These sacral garments clearly reached their final form after a long period of development.

Urim and Thummim

The Urim and Thummim were in the 'breastpiece of judgement' on the ephod of the high priest, next to his heart (Lev 8.8). They were used in justice by leaders, who used them to seek God's will (Num 27.21) and they appear again after the exile (Ezra 2.63; Neh 7.65). Two stories in Samuel are interesting – one showing how 'Urim' was one possible response and 'Thummim' another. King Saul 'inquired of God' through them whether he would defeat the Philistines, but received no response. Consulting them again, they placed the guilt for the silence on his son Jonathan (1 Sam 14.37–42). Later, the fugitive David consulted 'the ephod' (which presumably contained the Urim and Thummim) and received two 'Yes' responses (1 Sam 23.6–12). Were they lots? Or flat stones? Were they found early in Hebrew history or an anachronism based on exilic practice? Urim may mean 'cursed' and Thummim 'perfect'; but finding possible etymologies for archaic and obscure terms is problematic and we should not make too much of this, as meanings change over time (see Barr, 1961).

In synagogues today, the scroll of the Torah is wrapped in a finely embroidered cover to recall the ephod, with a breastpiece (or breastplate) attached to or hanging upon the front. This reminds worshippers of how God's wisdom is conveyed today. On the top are *rimmonim*, or 'pomegranates' (cf 1 Kgs 7.18–20, 42; 2 Kgs 25.17), with bells: the high priest's garments in the Tabernacle were decorated with bells and pomegranates

(Ex 28.33–4; 39.24–6). These are topped with the *kether*, or Torah crown. The Tablets of the Law and lions of Judah often appear on the decoration.

The Menorah

In the Tabernacle an elaborate seven-lamped *menorah candelabrum*, made of pure gold with almond motifs, was to be lit from morning to evening (Exod 25.31–40). King Solomon put ten lampstands in the First Temple (1 Kgs 7.49). Light symbolized God's presence, and so today the seven-branched menorah (or the nine-branched *hanukkiah* for the Hanukkah festival) can be seen in synagogues and Jewish homes. Synagogues also have an eternal light (*ner tamid*) to symbolize God's presence, and Sabbath candles are traditional. In two passages light and lamps represent God's guidance and instruction, but these have become central: 'Thy word is a lamp to my feet and a light to my path' (Ps 119.105); 'For the commandment is a lamp and Torah a light' (Prov 6.23). The menorah with its branches is often linked with the tree of knowledge in Eden, signifying understanding; placed in the Temple in front of the Ark it symbolized understanding of the Torah. As the flame of the burning bush, it becomes a symbol of God's revelation to the world.

The Ark of the Covenant

According to Exodus 25.10–22 and 37.1ff, the Ark of Covenant was a rectangular box of acacia wood, with winged beasts (*cherubim*) on the top. It contained relics ('the testimony', *ha'eduth* – Ex 25.16; the NEB's 'Tokens of the Covenant' is a paraphrase). These were the Tablets of the Law, manna, and the rod, used by Moses and Aaron, which budded. The ark was placed in the inner sanctuary, where it symbolized God's presence with his people. The lid, the 'mercy seat', served as God's throne. The whole could be carried on poles to become a mobile shrine.

This description is generally regarded as late, influenced perhaps by Temple design; but the Ark itself may be much earlier. It is associated in the narrative with Moses (Num 10.33–6; Deut 10.1–3); and symbolized God's help in the Ephraimite sanctuary at Shiloh, in the story of young Samuel – although in this case it was captured in battle by the Philistines (1 Sam 4). It was endowed in the narratives with magical properties, killing a man who touched it, and causing plague and disaster (1 Sam 5.1–7.2; 2 Sam 6.6f) and was finally placed in Jerusalem, first in a tent and eventually in Solomon's Temple. It became a focal point for covenant faithfulness: yet Jeremiah looked to a time without the Ark when the whole of Jerusalem would be God's throne. He saw the symbol as limiting; a greater vision is available to those who have eyes to see (Jer 3.16–17). The 'Holy Ark' (*aron qodesh*) has pride of place today in a synagogue, but contains another symbol of the divine presence – the scrolls of the Torah. The Ten Commandments, representing the Tablets of the Law, are generally nearby.

Mezuzah and Tephillin

The *Shema* (Deut 6.4–9: a prayer beginning 'Hear O Israel, the LORD our God, the LORD is One' and stressing the love worshippers owe to God) in sisted that children should be taught the words of the prayer, and that ever yone should be constantly reminded of them: 'You shall bind [these words] as a sign upon your hand, and they shall be as frontlets between your eyes.' Over the ages, Jews have obeyed this using *tephillin*, or 'phylacteries': small boxes bound with thongs onto the hand and forehead. These contain sacred writings – including the Shema and Ten Commandments – and represent mindfulness, devotion and obedience to the Torah.

The Shema continues, 'And you shall write them on the doorposts of your house and on your gates'. The boxes containing these words, the *mezuzah*, has a similar symbolism: to remind people of God every time they enter and leave rooms or buildings. Today, the mezuzah has the Hebrew word *Shaddai*, 'Almighty', written on it.

Tallith and Tsitsith

The Torah also commands (Num 15.37–40) that tassels (*tsitsith*) should be placed at the corner of the garments, with a blue cord, to help Hebrews 'remember all the commandments of the Lord, to do them, not to follow after your own heart and your own eyes . . . . So you shall remember all my commandments, and be holy to your God.' These tassels are today placed at the corner of a *tallith*, or prayer shawl. They have traditionally been made with 613 knots, the number of injunctions (*miswoth*) in the Torah.

The Shophar

The *shophar*, or 'ram's horn' (actually the horn of any ritually pure animal except a bull, because of the idolatry with the golden calf – Exod 32), was commonly used on ceremonial occasions in the Hebrew Bible. It has become particularly associated with penitence and atonement at Rosh Hashanah (New Year) and Yom Kippur (the Day of Atonement) and calls to mind the 'Binding of Isaac' (Gen 22), where a ram replaced Abraham's son as the sacrificial victim.

Hebrew Art

The law forbade the veneration of images in place of God (Exod 20.4–6; Deut 5.8–10). However, decorative art was found in Temple decorations and was also found in later generations in synagogues. The early synagogue (second century CE) at Capernaum contained carvings of plants, fruits and animals – reminding worshippers of God's creation – in addition to examples of the Ark, menorah and shophar. Later mosaic synagogue floors (*c.* fourth century CE) were rich in symbolic representations. The description of the Tabernacle notes that people brought artistic free-will offerings in abundance (Exod 36.2–7). Some art was meaningful – that is, had symbolic significance: the cherubim, the Ark and the menorah, for example. Some told a story, as at the synagogue at Dura Europus (built 224–5 CE). In Judaism, art should serve God and not human appetites. Ceremonial objects in the home and synagogue were embellished as eloquent pointers to the worshippers' devotion. The Hebrew phrase *hiddur mitswah* ('glorification of the command') refers to this (Kaniel, 1979, 2–11).

Many more ceremonial objects have been used in Judaism through the centuries, using symbolism reminiscent of biblical imagery: *qiddush* ('sanctification') cups; *hallah* loaves recalling the biblical manna; *havdalah* candles; a spice 'tower' (cf. Song 5.13), and Passover *seder* symbols: *haroseth* (cement), salt water (tears), bitter herbs (suffering), lamb bone and roasted egg (sacrifice) and green salad (new hope). Other interesting motifs have emerged in various contexts, including Western art – the tree of life, the spies in Canaan, the creation.

Actions as Symbols

Some prophets acted out their message to make it more dramatic: Jeremiah wore a yoke to symbolize defeat, buried a loincloth and broke a jar (spoiling and destruction), and bought a field (hope); Ezekiel lay on a tile for a year; Hosea married a prostitute. Prophets occasionally gave their children symbolic names: for example, Hosea's Jezreel, Lo-'ammi ('Not my people') and Lo-ruhamah ('Not pitied '– 1.4–11); Isaiah's Maher-shalal-hash-baz ('The spoil speeds, the prey hastes' – 8.1–4) and Shearjashub ('A remnant will return' – 7.3). He spoke of the coming of Immanuel ('God with us'), a royal prince (7.14). These actions were out of the ordinary, designed to make people notice and hear the prophet's message. There were other more widespread symbolic actions in common use, rituals which were codified in Torah legislation.

Sacrifices

There are sacrifices in biblical narratives, although we should take care not to draw simplistic historical deductions from them. In Genesis 4, the rival sacrifices offered by Cain and Abel declare animal sacrifices to be acceptable, and plant offerings not. Abraham's covenant with God is marked with a solemn sacrifice of a heifer, she-goat, ram, turtledove and pigeon, in which he cuts the animals in two and passes fire between the pieces (Gen 15). A similar covenant sacrifice is described in Jeremiah (34.18f), which stresses that those who break the covenant's terms will be like the sacrificial victim – cut in two. It is possible that the common phrase 'to cut a covenant' comes from this ceremony. Sacrificial worship began in prehistory, long before the Hebrews. Broadly similar sacrifices took place in Mari to the north, dating into the second millennium BCE, and over a wide area. Abraham's faithfulness to God is an important motif: he agrees to sacrifice his son notwithstanding the child's value to him. The story (Gen 22) points to the seriousness of sacrifice, in which the worshipper should be prepared to surrender something of true worth and not be content with ritual for its own sake. To be devoted to God is a declaration of total submission, holding nothing back. Abraham, 'friend of God', was prepared in this story to give up any hope of the promises made to him. In replacing the human sacrifice with a ram, the story is commenting on sacrifice as a ritual: the ram *represents* what is dearest to us; obviously a replacement is sometimes appropriate, but it reminds the worshipper that nothing among our personal possessions and relationships is so special that it stands outside and beyond devotion to God. In Genesis 31.54 a sacrifice marks a covenant between Jacob and Laban (again symbolizing faithfulness), accompanied by a feast. In Genesis 35 Jacob sets up a pillar, over which he pours a drink offering and oil, hinting at a wider variety of offerings (vv. 1–14).

The exodus narratives give a prominent place to the killing of the Passover lamb (Exod 12), whose blood was painted on the doorposts and lintel of the Hebrew houses. The meat had to be eaten by morning, and any remainder burnt. Exodus also introduces the theme of idolatrous sacrifices, later savagely condemned by Deuteronomy and the prophets. After sacrifices are made to the golden calf (Exod 32), those who survive Moses' retribution face plague. The 'Ritual Decalogue' (Exod 34) commands that idolatrous altars be pulled down, lest the Hebrews make a covenant with the people of the land. The Torah includes precise details of altars, different types of sacrifices, and the whole priesthood organization. Later stories, about Balaam, Gideon, Jephthah, Elijah and others, include sacrifices – offered to Baal, Asherah, Astarte and Chemosh as well as Yahweh (Num 23.1–30; Judg 2.13; 3.7; 6.25–7; 10.6; 11.1–40; 1 Kgs 18.19–39; 2 Kgs 3.27; 23.4).

It is now impossible to write a detailed history of the development of sacrifice in ancient Israel. The Torah as finally edited tells us a great deal, but it is hard to separate within it elements which stem from different periods. For example, was the priest entitled to the shoulder, two cheeks and stomach (Deut 18.3), the breast and right thigh (Lev 7.34) – or would he thrust in his fork (or 'fleshhook') and take whatever came out (1 Sam 2.13–14)?

The Significance of Sacrifice   Sacrifice should be an outward expression of a spiritual state of mind. The action gave a visual shape to the inner feelings of penitence and gratitude to God. Ritual can become formalized and performed out of habit or fashion, but this should not blind us to the deeper significance that it should ideally have. There is evidence in the prophets that some people divorced sacrifice from penitence: the prophets often declared that God hated insincere sacrifices and this often takes the shape of oracles which cast doubt on the value of sacrifices at all: 'For I desire steadfast love and not sacrifice, the knowledge of God, rather than burnt offerings' (Hos 6.6; cf. Jer 7.21–3; Mic 6.8; Amos 4.4f).

Samuel is reported to have uttered similar statements, perhaps reflecting the view of the narrator:

> Has the LORD as great delight in burnt offerings and sacrifices,
>   as in obeying the voice of the LORD?
> Behold, to obey is better than sacrifice,
>   and to hearken than the fat of rams.
> For rebellion is as the sin of divination
>   and stubbornness as iniquity and idolatry. (1 Sam 15.22–3)

Confession was crucial before any sacrifice was offered (Lev 5.5–6; Num 5.6–7) and at Yom Kippur, the Day of Atonement, the high priest confessed national guilt (Lev 16.21). In early Judaism also, it continued to be recognized that Yom Kippur, without national penitence, 'will effect no atonement' (Mishnah Yoma, 8.9). It follows that deliberate, defiant high–handed actions cannot be expiated by sacrifice, since the offender is unrepentant. Such a person 'has despised the word of the LORD' and shall be 'utterly cut off' from his people (Num 15.30–1). So in a sense the sacrifice was a dramatic symbol of repentance, getting its power both from the personal sacrifice it required of one of the flock, and the giving of a replacement life. By placing one's hands on the victim's head, the penitent was symbolically represented by the victim (Lev 1.4; 3.2, 8, 13). The offering had its limitations: it could not put aside crimes such as adultery and murder; for these the offender had to accept the appropriate punishment. Without a sincere ethical base, sacrifice was seen as an abomination (Prov 21.27) and a 'mockery' (Ecclus 34.18): how much better is 'the prayer of the upright', which is God's delight (Prov 15.8). Thus sacrifice should 'foster penitence, thanksgiving, adoration, devotion, and humble surrender and consecration to God' (Rowley, 1967, 142) – an attitude seen best in the 'suffering servant' (Isa 53), whose sincerity, submission, and humble surrender to God depict the true guilt offering (*asham*): by bearing the sin of many, he shall make many be accounted righteous (vv. 10–11).

The 'Peace' Offering (*Shelamim*)   Animals were slaughtered in the local sanctuary in a sacral atmosphere, with the priest sharing the occasion and the food. The taking of life for food was not trivialized. This assumed that each community would have easy access to a sanctuary where this could be done: the sanctuary would become an important spiritual focus in the area. The sacralizing of slaughter ceased when there was a single sanctuary at Jerusalem. There was some spiritual loss, as sacral language is replaced by the language of appetite and craving in Deuteronomy's new law:

When Yahweh your God enlarges your territory, as he has promised you, and you say, 'I will eat flesh', because you crave flesh, you may eat as much flesh as you desire. If the place where Yahweh your God will choose to put his name there is too far from you, then you may kill any of your herd or flock . . . and you may eat within you towns as much as you desire. (12.20–1)

Only the blood, which the priests had once poured out in the sacrifice, should not be consumed. It came to represent the life of the animal, becoming the new focus of 'sacralness', and its avoidance continued. The sacrifices at the appointed sanctuary were to continue, and the flesh could still be eaten (12.27). These offerings involve sharing a meal (and all that implies) in God's presence. The blood and the internal organs are presented at the altar and are particularly significant in their symbolism. The blood represented life; the fat, which belonged to God, fuelled the sacrificial fire and smoke, perhaps symbolizing prayer and devotion (Lev 3.1, 17). Free-will offerings and thank offerings are part of this general class of sacrifices.

The Whole Offering   This can be called *'olah*, (burnt) *kalil* (whole) or *isheh* (fire). A total sacrifice, it gave 'a pleasing odour to the LORD' (Lev 1.9). A public whole offering of a yearling lamb was to be made twice a day. It was offered with a flour-oil dough and some wine, to form a symbolic meal (Exod 29.38–42; Num 28.1–8)

The Sin and Guilt Offerings   These reflect a concern for purification. The sin offering (*hatta'th*) demanded of a new mother and after menstruation (Lev 12.6–8; 15.29–30) clearly serves a *ritual* function, to cover unavoidable impurity. The guilt offering (*asham*) was needed in cases where uncleanness was avoidable. First fruits were offered, both of crops and livestock, and included a family's own children, although these were redeemed. These offerings recognized that life came from God and symbolically it returned to God. Tithes, the offering of a tenth of produce, are demanded in Deuteronomy (Deut 14.22–9; cf. Num 18.21–32) and they appear in some narratives (Gen 14.20; Gen 28.22). The *minhah* (cereal offering) consisted of corn or flour, mixed with oil.

Josiah's reforms and his centralization of sacrificial ritual in Jerusalem did not have time to establish themselves before the exile. Sacrifice may have continued in other sanctuaries, and was reinstated in the restored Temple. It lasted until the destruction of the Jerusalem Temple by the Romans in 70 CE. Sacrifices have not featured in Judaism since that time. Today the concepts of self-sacrifice and giving freely of our time and money are familiar, but they are thorough-going spiritualizations: the idea of shedding blood to achieve forgiveness and atonement is no longer part of our culture; and the secularization of killing for food has diminished our view of animal life.

Purification Rituals

Life is full of mysterious happenings and these caused the Hebrews great concern. Purification ceremonies were their only weapons to keep the danger at bay and to stop it spreading. Numbers, set in the wilderness period, could only recommend exclusion: 'The LORD said to Moses, "Command the people of Israel that they put out of the camp every leper, and everyone having a discharge, and everyone that is unclean through contact with the dead . . . that they may not defile their camp, in the midst of which I dwell" (5.1–3).

A collection of purification rules is preserved in Leviticus 11–26. In the Hebrew world-view, things were either clean or unclean. Uncleanness was contagious, and so contact with it demanded purification. Although the aim of a pure and holy Israel is made explicit, no *moral* stigma attached to impurity. Impurity happened, and could not be prevented; and, when it did, it had to be isolated. Carcases of unclean meat bring uncleanness; so do bodily discharges, whether related to childbirth or sex, and skin diseases or fungal growths. These anxieties may be traditional, but some rules claim to preserve Israel from idolatry. Special rituals were prescribed to achieve national purity, to take place on the Day of Atonement – (Lev 16). The present edition of these laws is normally dated around the time of the exile (sixth–fifth centuries BCE).

Sacrifices were most frequently prescribed – after childbirth, leprosy, sexual discharges, or contact with the dead (in the case of someone who has taken a Nazirite vow – Num 6). Impurity was washed away in ritual ablutions, particularly important for priests preparing for their duties (Exod 29.4; 30.17–21; Lev 8.6). The high priest, on the Day of Atonement, washed before *and after* that most sacred of ceremonies (Lev 16.4, 24). Sacred duties made a person unclean – the sacred released mysterious dangers which had to be neutralized. Defiled objects were similarly washed (see particularly the washing of the sacrificial vessel in Numbers 6.21). There was a particular ceremony involving mixing the purifying water (*me niddah*, 'water of impurity') with the ashes of a sacrificed red heifer 'for the removal of sin' (Num 19). Those who prepared the water had to be particularly clean, and *had to wash themselves afterwards*. People rendered unclean by contact with the dead were purified when the ash from this sacrifice was mixed with running water, and sprinkled on the uncleanness. The water was reddened with red dye mixed in the ashes. Outside Leviticus and Numbers, death is not said to cause uncleanness; and, even in these books, two other passages discussing washing after contact with the dead make no mention of the procedure, or of the 'water of impurity' but detail other arrangements (Lev 22.4–6; Num 6.9–12). Is it ancient? Or did it develop in Babylon during the exile? It is reminiscent of another ceremony, in which a woman suspected of adultery drank water mixed with dust and the ink of a curse – 'water of bitterness' – the effects of which pronounced her guilty or innocent (Num 5.11–31).

For 'leprosy' (not the disease so named today but perhaps psoriasis) the cured sufferer was sprinkled seven times with the blood of a bird sacrificed over running water. A second bird was dipped in the blood and set free. The cured sufferer then shaved and washed his whole body, and offered appropriate sacrifices in a detailed ceremony (Lev 14.1–32). Again red dye is used, mixed with the blood. The cure Elisha offered to Naaman the Syrian was much simpler: 'wash in the Jordan seven times, and your flesh shall be restored, and you shall be clean' (2 Kgs 5.10)

The idea of purification is characteristic of Leviticus and Numbers. It is curious that their detail does not have a close relationship with other material in the Hebrew Bible. It may tie in more closely with the great concern for purity in the post-exilic community, which identified its sufferings as a punishment for sharing in the pollutions, abominations and uncleanness of the local population (e.g. Ezra 9.11; Neh 8.26) and were determined to separate themselves from them both in behaviour and by refusing intermarriage. We are told that these new settlers used the lawbook of Moses as their guide: but we are left to guess about the origin of this work.

The prophetic movement was concerned less with ritual than with right attitudes and behaviour. After rejecting insincere offerings, incense, Sabbaths and festivals, Isaiah appealed to the metaphor of washing:

> Wash yourselves; make yourselves clean;
> remove the evil of your doings
>   from before my eyes;
> cease to do evil,
>   learn to do good;
> seek justice,
>   correct oppression;
> defend the fatherless,
>   plead for the widow.(1.16–17; cf. 4.4)

This metaphor is not found elsewhere, but the idea of turning a ritual into a metaphor of some ethical point is found elsewhere in the prophets. Jeremiah treated circumcision and the covenant in a similar way (4.4; 6.10; 9.25–6; 31.31).

Food Rituals

Eating became for Jews a deeply symbolic action. They were constantly reminded of their obedience to God and the Torah by paying careful and continued attention to what they ate, and with what. Only certain meats and fish were allowed, as listed in Leviticus 11; and even these could not be eaten together with dairy produce. The rules were drawn from the Torah and therefore symbolize in everyday life the whole 613 injunctions. There has been speculation about the origin of these restrictions – e.g. in hygienic considerations in hot climates; in the avoidance of scavenging animals; or in the categorization of anomalous animals – but these are of little practical concern. The restrictions are observed not because they can be understood, but because they are *Torah*.

It may be that some rules developed traditionally. Gen 32.32 (do not eat 'the sinew of the hip which is upon the hollow of the thigh', because God touched Jacob on this spot when they wrestled) refers to a practice apparently common 'to this day'. The law against boiling a kid in its mother's milk (Exod 34.26; Deut 14.21) seems to be ancient, repeated several times in early lawcodes, although its precise purpose can only be guessed at. The rules about clean and unclean animals/meats (Lev 11; Deut 14.3–20), about not eating 'what dies of itself or is torn by wildbeasts' (Lev 17.5; Deut 14.21) and not consuming blood (Lev 17.10–14; Deut 12.16, 23–5; 15.23) appear to derive from Deuteronomy, dating back at least to the period just preceding the exile. They may have been reformulated as an exilic survival package, designed to maintain a Jewish separateness.

Circumcision

The surgical removal of the foreskin from the penis appears to be an ancient custom, judging by the use of flint knives in Exodus 4.25 and Joshua 5.2–3. The first passage is enigmatic in the extreme: Zipporah circumcises her son and touches 'his' (Moses'?) feet, making him a 'bridegroom of blood'. In contrast are comments designed to justify circumcision as a covenant symbol (Gen 17; 21.4; Exod 12.43, 49; Lev 12.3), generally considered to be the final editor's work. The prophets listed other neighbouring nations as circumcised in body but not spirit, so the custom was not unique. The 'spirit' here symbolizes covenant loyalty. Possibly circumcision became even more significant in exile as a sign of unify and identity, as other nations, also exiled and shattered by war, let the custom drop. By the second century BCE we hear of specialist circumcisers (1 Macc 1.61) and the Seleucid king Antiochus IV Epiphanes forbidding circumcision (1 Macc 1.15, 60–1; 2

Macc 6.10) Some hid their circumcision, and others were roused to nationalistic fury. Thus circumcision is undoubtedly early, and was retained as a mark of identity at a time when pressures for assimilation in the Babylonian Empire were strong. It is later referred to as *berith milah* (covenant of circumcision).

Processions

It is hard to claim firm evidence for processions, but they are common in worship, and could well have taken place. Isaiah 40 perhaps suggests a procession from Babylon to Jerusalem, on a specially prepared desert highway, when God's splendour would be revealed. Aubrey Johnson (1967) produced a masterly account of a cultic procession in which psalms might have played a dominant role. Suggestions from others that this was a New Year or a covenant procession are interesting but not incontrovertible.

Special Times: Celebrating Festivals

Celebrations pregnant with meaning break up the year in Judaism today, and most of these times can trace their origin to the Hebrew Bible. The earliest were the three pilgrim festivals – *Pesach* (Passover), *Shavuoth* (the feast of Weeks, Pentecost) and *Sukkoth* (Tabernacles). Their existence is noted in the early laws of the 'Book of the Covenant' (Exod 21–3; cf. 24.7 and see below, ch. 6), but with agricultural names and a clear agricultural purpose:

Three times in the year you shall keep a feast to me. You shall keep the feast of unleavened bread; as I commanded you, you shall eat unleavened bread for seven days at the appointed time in the month of Abib, for in it you came out of Egypt. None shall appear before me empty-handed. You shall keep the feast of harvest, of the first fruits of your labour, of what you sow in the field. You shall keep the feast of ingathering at the end of the year, when you gather in from the field the fruit of your labour. Three times in the year shall all your males appear before the LORD God. (Exod 23.14–17)

The decalogue (ten commandments) of ritual laws (Exod 34) echoes this, but replaces 'harvest' with 'weeks' (Shavoth, seven weeks after Passover), but still linked to the first fruits of the wheat harvest. The lists of Deuteronomy 16, Leviticus 23 and Numbers 28–9 give fuller details. In time the festivals, although still incorporating agricultural themes, came to celebrate historical events: the exodus (Passover), law-giving on Sinai (Shavuoth) and the wilderness wanderings (Sukkoth).

Pesach (Passover) is the day preceding the feast of Unleavened Bread. Its celebration was first recorded under King Josiah, although the Chronicler,

writing later, places it in Hezekiah's reign. Pesach is said in Exodus to re-
collect the story of the ten plagues with the 'angel of death' 'passing over'
(*pasah*) Hebrew homes. After slaughtering a lamb and eating a Passover
meal, the Hebrews escaped from Egypt. The festival is a reminder for
successive generations of salvation and hope of a future in Jerusalem, after
the bitterness of slavery. The hope is tinged with sadness: this is not a time
for exulting over the Egyptian dead. Passover is a particularly important
example of *anamnesis*, a time of remembrance and re-enactment in which
worshippers see themselves symbolically as living through significant past
events. The exodus from Egypt provided a story of salvation and escape that
was later to serve the Hebrews during their Babylonian exile. In Babylon
they hoped for a new exodus, their return to Palestine.

There are other festivals. The *High Holy Days* in Tishri (September/
October) end in *Yom Kippur*, the Day of Atonement, a period of fasting and
penitence. This is closely followed by *Sukkoth* (Tabernacles), eight days of
harvest celebration symbolized today by waving 'four species' (palm [*lulab*],
citron [*etrog*], myrtle and willow) representing the Promised Land; and by
building a *sukkah*, or booth, remembering the wilderness days. The 'four
species' have further layers of symbolism, as reminders of personal devotion
– palm leaves being the backbone, myrtle the eyes, willow the mouth and
etrog the heart. *Purim* dramatizes the Esther story as representative of the
defeat of all evil; and *Hanukkah* celebrates the dedication of the Temple
under the Maccabees and the consequent freedom of worship.

Places as Symbols

The Land

The land of Israel (*erets yisroel*) had a special place in Hebrew thought. The
narratives focus on the oaks, wells and hills which have become linked with
legendary events – such as Gibeath-haaraloth, 'the hill of the foreskins'
(Josh 5.3). The land was clearly full of sacred places – such as Sinai/Horeb,
Seir, Pisgah, Penuel and Moriah, associated with divine appearances
(theophanies). An early custom was to build an altar: sanctuaries may have
been established on sacred sites; and a sanctuary may have developed stories
of theophanies to justify its existence.

The story of Joshua's holy war is based on the theological notion that the
land is sacred, God's gift to Israel occupied with divine help by right of conquest. The metaphor of *inheritance* is used: 'Be strong and of good courage;
for you shall cause this people to inherit the land which I swore to their
fathers to give them' (Josh 1.6). This inheritance was conditional on their
observance of Moses' book of the law (vv. 7–8; cf. Deut 12.8–14). (In

ancient Israel, inheritance or heritage implied responsibilities to past and future family members. Naboth (1 Kgs 21) regarded his property as inalienable, and his determination on this point led to his death. Theft of land cannot be countenanced (Deut 19.14)). Conflict between this account of complete victory contrasts sharply with details in Judges 1, and elsewhere. The editor, in giving Joshua this structure, wished to apply the metaphor of rights through inheritance, and to stress the *condition* that the inheritors should observe and obey the Torah.

The prophets felt strongly that what God had given should not be polluted, by immorality, injustice and idolatry. Jeremiah speaks of Israel polluting the land with harlotry (3.2), of defiling the pleasant land given by God (2.6–7). Jeremiah was writing at the point of dissolution and ruin, the destruction of Jerusalem and the land in 587/6 BCE. The same sentiments are found in Leviticus 18.24–8 – with a vicious phrase: the land vomiting out the guilty Hebrews – and in Numbers 35.33, dealing with pollution and bloodshed. The myth of Cain and Abel makes the point shockingly: Abel's blood cries out from the ground to God; and Cain was cursed from the ground 'which has opened its mouth to receive your brother's blood from your hand' (Gen 4.11) to become a perpetual nomad. The defilement of the land is not a major theme of Deuteronomy, but it is clear that the body of an executed criminal hanged on a tree would defile the land if left; and sexual defilement can 'bring guilt upon the land' (Deut 21.22–3; 24.4). Earlier, Hosea speaks of people, or the body politic (i.e. *the people*) being defiled (6.10; 9.4). The idea of the defilement of the land took on new meaning with the loss of the land in Jeremiah's day, after the Babylonian invasion.

Zion – the Temple

The place which the LORD *your God will choose, to make his name dwell there*: Deuteronomy 12–26 stresses that inheritance brings responsibilities, both ritual and ethical. The identity of this central sanctuary is not indicated, but it came to be identified with Jerusalem (see 2 Kgs 22–3, esp. 23.27). This represents a move from local to a national sanctuary, with sacrifices, offerings and tithes being due only there – a move not officially carried out until the reign of King Josiah (639–609 BCE).

There were many sanctuaries serving local areas. Religion was part of daily life. Regular visits were possible, and festivals could become focal points for the community – at least three times each year, at the great harvest feasts of Unleavened Bread, Harvest and Ingathering (Exod 23.14–17). Some sanctuaries, such as Shiloh (1 Sam 1–4), were well known; others, such as Dan and Bethel (1 Kgs 12.25–30), were infamous. Jerusalem was particularly important as the seat of monarchy. Solomon built a temple (tenth century BCE) on Mount Zion: the remaining (Western) wall is today a focus of worship and pilgrimage. Hebrew exilic literature prayed for a return to Zion: By waters of Babylon, there we sat down and wept, when we remembered Zion' (Ps 137.1). Zion thus symbolized God's presence in the land. The 'comfort' given by Second Isaiah was that Jerusalem's iniquity was pardoned and God would return to Zion:

> Get you up to a high mountain,
>   O Zion, herald of good tidings;
> lift up your voice with strength,
>   O, Jerusalem, herald of good tidings,
> lift it up, fear not;
>   say to the cities of Judah,
>   "Behold your God!" (Isa 40.9)

Jeroboam built rival sanctuaries, at Dan and Bethel, after the northern tribes had seceded from the southern: the idea was that northern tribesfolk should not be required to worship at Jerusalem. The probability, however, is that the author (writing during the exile, since that is the last event referred to) was assuming a situation that did not then apply: in Jeroboam's time, Josiah's reform and Jerusalem's dominance lay well into the future and it is clear that local sanctuaries continued to exist.

Words as Symbols

Words reflect and communicate deep feelings, insights and values: we are edified or diminished by them. Words can misinform and cause confusion, conflict and injustice – or can create harmony and relationship. Words thus inform, clarify situations, change events, vindicate or condemn. They provide a focus and a framework for our thoughts, helping to interpret our experience. Yet they are restricting: the word never quite does injustice to the meaning we are striving for.

Blessings and Curses

Curses rupture relationships, whilst blessings heal rifts. This is an indication that words have power, and should not be used lightly. The story of Rebecca and her son Jacob is telling. Isaac, old and blind, was about to pass his blessing on to Esau, and Rebecca decided to pass Jacob off as his brother. Jacob was worried in case the deception should be recognized, and he be cursed – a worse fate than simply not being blessed! Rebecca persuaded him by saying, 'Upon me be your curse, my son' (Gen 27.13). Jacob duly received his father's formal and irreversible blessing, but no blessing remained for Esau. The blessing clearly served as a will, and is found also in Genesis 49 (of Jacob) and Deuteronomy 33 (of Moses). In general, blessing is a recurrent theme, which begins with creation and marks the high points in the narrative. Possibly the most famous blessing is Numbers 6.24–6:

> The LORD bless you and keep you:
> The LORD make his face to shine upon you, and be gracious to you:
> The LORD lift up his countenance upon you and give you peace.

The curse can be found in the Hebrew Bible as a legal formula – 'Cursed be he who . . . ' (Deut 27.15–26). There are no penalties, but an assumption that the word itself is sufficient. The curse represents a ruptured relationship with God and the community, just as a blessing proclaims a state of relationship. The curse is, in a sense, more severe than even the death penalty: the executed criminal becomes accursed by God when hanged on a tree (Deut 21.22–3). Curses are not to be taken lightly, as the story of Balaam shows. Here a foreign seer is brought in to curse the Hebrews, but is intercepted by God. He can not utter the curse: 'How can I curse whom God has not cursed?' (Num 23.8). The passage of the woman suspected of adultery (Num 5) details how a curse could be legally administered: the written curse was washed into the 'water of bitterness' for the accused to drink. If guilty, there would be a physical effect as God's blessing was withdrawn. Curses were used for offences committed in secret – without witnesses or evidence – receiving their power from the total belief of the accused.

Interpreting Meaning

No statement has a straightforward 'meaning': the task of determining meaning is an exercise in problem-solving. Words do not always have the same meaning, even when used by the same writer. They have a range of meanings which interact with each other, creating ambiguity and deliberate puns. For example, the Hebrew word *ruah* means both 'breath' and 'wind'. It became used as a metaphor for both the human spirit and for God. The context is vital when determining which was intended. According to the RSV, 'the Spirit of God was moving over the face of the waters' (Gen 1.2); but the same words are translated by the NEB ' a mighty wind [*ruah*] that swept over the surface of the waters'. The author probably intended something of each. Ezekiel 37.1–14 uses *ruah* in a variety of ways when the dry bones come back to life:

> the Spirit [*ruah*] of God provided the vision;
> God would cause breath [*ruah*] to enter the bones;
> Ezekiel is told to prophesy, 'Come from the four winds
> [*ruhoth*, plural], O breath [*ruah*], and breathe upon these slain, that
> they might live';
> 'and I will put my Spirit [*ruah*] within you, and you shall live'.

We could interpret 'spirit' as abstract (as in 'spirit of jealousy' – Num 5.12), or concrete in a symbolic way ('breath' = 'life force' or 'words') or concrete in a personal way ('Spirit' as an entity). The last, a personal 'Spirit', may be an over-literal interpretation of a metaphor.

It magnifies our problems that the language of the Hebrew Bible is archaic: some words occur very few times, and some only once. The meaning of words depend on usage: some applications of the word may be well-established and others new and creative. Ideally we need a range of interacting meanings. We have problems in understanding particular usages of words when the word is found in too few contexts. An idea or concept may be expressed using different words and terminology, and one word may service several alternative concepts. What Caird calls 'the word-concept fallacy' (1980, 43) confuses words with concepts. We should be cautious when using dictionary definitions: they deal particularly with what a word means *in the public domain*; and give an etymology which *may* be correct and (less likely) *may* be relevant. Within this framework, each word is used privately by writers, with their own range of understandings and meanings.

Religious Language

Descriptive language creates fewer problems than language that is abstract or emotive. The focus of religious language is beyond the descriptive. I. Ramsey (1957) identified as an important characteristic *depth discernment*, which is life-dominating, totally engaging, involving a commitment in the whole process of living. Imagery has to be used – metaphors, analogies, similes – producing memorable associations and eliciting deep emotional responses. Metaphorical language cannot make statements which are objectively 'true', but it probes our concepts and the frameworks we have adopted. Unexpected associations make us sit up and take notice: a throat like an open sepulchre (Ps 5.9); God as a 'deceitful' brook (Jer 15.18). This is a playful and imaginative use of language, to make a serious point, but not to be taken *literally*: we may 'dig into Sheol [the underworld]' and 'climb up to heaven' to escape God, but cannot (Amos 9.2) – such adventures are not literally contemplated!

Figures of Speech

The Hebrew word *mashal*, often translated 'parable', covers a wide range of non-literal sayings. Ancient Greek rhetoric catalogued different forms or figures of speech, but the Hebrew usage was spontaneous, even playful, rather than analytical and contrived. Writers transcend literalism to create interest and vividness. *Hyperbole* overstates: 'you shall thresh the mountains and crush them, and you shall make the hills like chaff' (Isa 41.15) uses a harvest metaphor to describe total destruction. *Litotes* understates: 'But I am a worm and no man' (Ps 22.6) emphasizes feelings of degradation and humiliation. *Irony* says one thing and means the opposite: 'How the king of Israel [David] honoured himself today, uncovering himself today before the eyes of his servants' maids', says his wife Michal tartly (2 Sam 6.20). *Synecdoche* uses part to describe the whole (or *vice-versa*): wheels (*galgal*) are wheeled vehicles (Ezek 23.24; 26.10); and God's protection is proffered through his (single?) eye – 'Behold, the eye of the LORD is on those who fear him' (Ps 33.18; cf. 34.15, 'the eye*s* of the LORD'). *Metonymy* creates correspondences by finding some form of contact, not through comparison. It transfers meaning to associated objects or attributes: 'sceptre' means *authority* (Gen 49.10); 'sword' means *war* (Lev 26.6). God (metonymically) is love, truth or beauty: Islam rejects these as confusions but retains the attributes – God as loving, truthful, merciful, compassionate, and so on: the Hebrew Bible agrees with this usage. *Euphemism* uses metonymy for politeness: 'knew', 'lie with' and 'uncover the nakedness of' each represent the sexual act through an associated action.

Metaphors

These are covert comparisons, describing an object 'in terms suggestive of another' (Soskice, 1985, 50f) using a range of associations normally used of other things. It links through likeness. God *is* king – hence, royal, regal, just, omnipotent, the sole ruler; yet in a sense he is *not*: 'king' is a human image, and God could not be limited to petty kingship. Muslims prefer to affirm that God 'rules', detaching God from the human image. A metaphor can provide us with a framework to help our understanding, but for a balanced view we need to be aware of its limitations.

Other interesting metaphors of God are as craftsman, father, host, shepherd and judge. Inanimate or non-human metaphors are also used of God – as sun and shield (Ps 84.11), thunder (Ps 29.3), the sound of the sea (Ezek 43.2), a rock, fortress, shield, horn of salvation, stronghold (Ps 18.2), a fountain/spring of living/running water (Jer 2.13), a devouring fire (Deut 4.24), a lion, leopard, bear (Amos 3.8; Hos 5.14; 13.7–8). Some seem designed to shock: God is like a moth or dry rot (Hos 5.12); like a bird-catcher (Hos 7.12); or a dry 'deceitful' river bed (Jer 15.18).

Similes and Analogies

Some comparisons focus on a common aspect of the two things being compared. The shaft of Goliath's spear was 'like a weaver's beam' (1 Sam 17.7). The word 'like' (alternatively, 'as') shows this to be a *simile*. Similes can sound like, look like, feel like, smell like, move like – or simply be like. Proverbs makes thorough use of comparisons. Poverty (Prov 6.6–11) will overcome the lazy like an armed bandit. In contrast, the ant makes careful preparations for the future, without leaders or bureaucrats: 'consider her ways, and be wise'! God provides security: 'The name of the LORD is a strong tower; the righteous man runs into it and is safe' (Prov 18.10).

Analogies compare situations. Can a leopard change its spots? No, and neither can an evil man do good (Jer 13.23). To condemn King David's action of stealing a man's wife, the prophet Nathan used a fictitious analogy (the parable of the ewe lamb – 2 Sam 12.1–7). Rabbinic Judaism regarded Job as a parable of suffering. Jonah also, on the universalistic 'light to the nations' theme, is scarcely written as history: even the name Jonah 'dove' may be symbolic. Analogy gives rise to *typology*. The exodus from Egypt mirrored the return from Babylon, which could be described as a second exodus; the reign of the Messianic king would mirror the reign of King David, the 'son' of God (2 Sam 7.14), in faithfulness and righteousness. This method of interpretation was taken much further by Philo of Alexandria (25 BCE – 40 CE) and New Testament writers (Goldingay, 1981, 97–115).

Allegories

Stories became allegories when the major characters featured are ciphers for something different. Isaiah 5.1–7 begins with a vine metaphor: having planted and cared for a vineyard, the vinedresser found that it produced only wild grapes. Israel also did not come up to God's expectations. The prophet sets this in a *pastiche* of a love song (the vine can be an image for fertility) which comments on the relationship between God and Israel. It outlines the consequences, in that the vineyard was then uprooted and destroyed. All this is to be read on two levels: the story and the political reference to injustice and oppression, with its inevitable consequences – invasion and desolation. The Songs of Songs was read as an allegory of God's love. The imagery is vivid and erotic, much as (from a different point of view) is Ezekiel's account (23.1–49; cf. 16.1–63) of the lewdness (= apostasy and idolatry) of Oholah and Oholibah (= Israel and Judah).

Models

People continually construct and refine their personal framework for understanding the world by enabling metaphors to interact and enmesh. As a metaphor extends its associations and links with other analogies, it becomes a *model*, providing an intellectual – and liturgical – framework for our understanding. God's sovereignty is one such model: it determined the status and behaviour of the worshipper; it suggested political action, at least for believers like the prophets; and it provided infinitely extendible 'networks of associations' (Soskice, 1985, 49) which enabled worshippers to explore the nature of deity through new avenues. In so doing, it raised the status of kingship itself: the king could be called 'God' (Ps 45.6), 'Almighty God' (Isa 9.6) and God's son (2 Sam 7.14; Ps 2.7). A future king, as 'the anointed one' (Hebrew *mashiah*, Messiah), was awaited long after the death of the last king of Judah, either as an earthly or as a symbolic king (John 18.36). God's sovereignty, and the related image of God as judge, provide a dominant model in the Hebrew Bible and beyond, extending into the New Testament notion of God's kingdom or kingly rule.

Authority Models   Not all avenues are equally fruitful – believers need to be critically aware of the limitations of their metaphors and models. As 'ruler', God could be seen as a malevolent and capricious tyrant – a tempting idea after a disaster. He is viewed in the Hebrew Bible as a warrior leading his troops – *Yahweh Sebaoth*, the 'LORD of Hosts'. The idea of holy war, and *herem* (with plunder devoted to God and prisoners therefore killed) stem from this model. Another authority model is that of *master-slave*. Second Isaiah makes particular use of it with 'Jacob my servant [= slave], Israel whom I have chosen' (Isa 44.1), and a servant whose mission was to bring Israel back to God (49.5):

> Behold my servant, whom I uphold,
>   my chosen, in whom my soul delights;
> I have put my spirit upon him,
>   he will bring forth justice to the nations . . . (42.1)

The aspect of the slave-master relationship that is stressed is that of service and mission – there is a task to be performed.

Relationship Models   People are conservative about their traditional models and about accepting new ones. Those used to an *authority model* (king–subject; husband–wife; master–servant; father–child) may resist a *relationship model* (lover, friend). The Song of Songs is rooted in the *lover* image, and met with resistance. The *lover/bride* metaphor was used by the prophets and was not confined to the Song. Devotion and love are obvious themes, although the prophets more often emphasize negative aspects of feminine sexuality – that is, the faith*less*ness of Israel. Female sexuality which went beyond patriarchal authority was clearly threatening!

If the relationship model is expressed as story, an immediate problem emerges: did God sexually father mankind, as happens in some mythologies? In Gen 6.1–4 the sons of God, who appear elsewhere as members of the divine court, father children by the daughters of humankind – presumably giving rise to a heroic giant race, although the present text obscures this causal link. More generally, however, God in creation is viewed as master craftsman rather than as father in a sexual sense. The heavens and the earth are the work of his hands or fingers (Ps 8.3; 19.1; 102.25). He laid the earth's foundations, and raised the heavens like a tent, or like a solid vault (Gen 1.6–8; Ps 24.2; 89.11; 102.25; 104.2, 5). In Genesis 1, God alone creates men and women and commissions them to multiply and fill the earth. God is pictured as both father and creator at the same time (Deut 32.6; Isa 64.8; Mal 2.10). Psalm 139.13 takes this firmly into the realm of human experience, as the mystery behind childbirth: 'For thou didst form my inward parts, thou didst knit me together in my mother's womb.' He is particularly father to the Davidic king (2 Sam 7.14; Ps 89.27) and to the needy (Ps 68.6). The comparison is also made as a *simile*: 'As a father pities [has compassion on, NEB] his children, so the LORD pities those who fear him' (Ps 103.13).

Jeremiah 3 represents Israel and Judah as disloyal children and unfaithful wives. Ezekiel 16 combines the two: Jerusalem was adopted as an infant, and subsequently bethrothed and married. Her infidelities were doubly disloyal, symbolically referring to idolatry and political machinations. The prophet mentions Jerusalem's mother (a Hittite), father (an Amorite), elder sister (Samaria), other northern sisters, and younger sister (Sodom). Ezekiel 23 is equally graphic. It is easy to identify this as a literary fiction; but similar relationships are found throughout Genesis in a historicized form, and their *literary* character can be forgotten.

Kinship Images Through non-physical parenthood, humanity (male *and female*) was created in the image and likeness of God. As they produced children themselves, these were in their parents' 'image' and 'likeness' (Gen 5.1–3). The terms *tselem* and *demuth* suggest *physical* resemblance. Mankind similarly is bloodkin to God (Gen 1.26f). Luke's genealogy of Jesus recognizes this kinship (3.38) by going back to 'Seth, the son of Adam, the son of God'.

Kinship metaphors also explore the relationship between man and wife: they are *bone* and *flesh*. She was created from man's side, using his bone and flesh, so man and woman should regard themselves as 'one flesh'. Both words are important: as *flesh*, they share the same biological need to 'cling' to each other (Gen 2.24); and, as *one*, they are *united*. The image is historicized with an explanation of how they came to share the same flesh, culminating in the key poem in 2.23: the women comes *from man*; the 'one flesh' metaphor ends the incompleteness and loneliness of man and pronounces kinship and therefore kinship obligations. The structure, as Alter notes (1981, 31), reveals woman surrounding, emcompassing and completing the first man: *zoth* (this [female]) is the first, middle and last word in Hebrew. In case the reader should interpret the essentially sexual 'one-flesh' metaphor literally, the narrative continues pointedly, 'and *the two of them* were naked, *the man and his wife* [or *woman*] and they were not ashamed' (2.25).

Anthropomorphic Language God is often given human attributes: he walked through the garden, so that Adam and Eve hid from shame (Gen 3.8); and he visited Abraham in his tents (Gen 18.1–2). On the other hand, God is spirit and not flesh (Isa 31.3): and theophanies focus on God's incomparable glory and power. Exodus 33.20–3 provides an interesting mix of glory and anthropomorphism:

'But,' [God] said, 'you cannot see my face; for man shall not see me and live.' And the LORD said, 'Behold, there is a place by me where you shall stand upon the rock; and while my glory passes by I will put you in a cleft of the rock, and I will cover you with my hand until I have passed by; then I will take away my hand, and you shall see my back; but my face shall not be seen'.

The Psalmist (17.15) can speak of seeing God's face and form: 'As for me, I shall behold thy face in righteousness; when I wake, I shall be satisfied with beholding thy form.'

God is described also by human actions, qualities and emotions – communicating, guiding, appointing, loving, pitying. He is just, merciful and bountiful. References can be found to God's face, eyes, ears, voice, nostrils, arms, hands, palms, fingers, feet, back, heart, bosom (for comfort) and bowels (for compassion) (see Caird, 1980, 172–82), which point to activities – seeing, listening, creating and protecting. Metaphors are drawn from elsewhere also: the 'wings of God' (e.g. Pss 17.8; 36.7; 57.1; 61.4; 63.7; 91.4) offer shelter. Not all 'emotions' are benevolent. The wrath or *anger* of God, taking the form, perhaps, of a plague, fire or earthquake, is well-known. He *regretted* making mankind (Gen 6.6) and *jealously* guarded his privileges (Exod 20.5). The creation 'myth' ends with God's *anxiety* at the threat humans could now pose:

Then the LORD God said, 'Behold the man has become like one of us, knowing good and evil; and now, lest he put forth his hand and take also of the tree of life, and eat, and live for ever' – therefore the LORD God sent him forth from the garden of Eden, to till the ground from which he was taken. (Gen 3.22–3)

God's anxiety emerges again at the building of Babel:

And the Lord came down to see the city and the tower, which the sons of men had built. And the LORD said, 'Behold, they are one people, and they have all one language; and this is only the beginning of what they will do; and nothing that they propose to do will now be impossible for them. Come, let us go down, and there confuse their language . . . .' (Gen 11.5–7)

The 'us' is interesting in both passages (also in Gen 1.26) – a relic of the heavenly court, perhaps. In other passages divine decisions are discussed with the host of heaven / holy ones / sons of God (Job 1.6–12; 1 Kgs 22.19–22) – that is, the stars (Judg 5.20; Job 38.7). In Gen 1.16 God *created* the sun, moon *and stars*, perhaps countering earlier mythologies.

Personification   The personalizing of God is part of a wider metaphorical strategy of *ascribing personality* to things and concepts: 'Wine is a mocker, strong drink a brawler' (Prov 20.1); 'when the waters saw thee, they were afraid' (Ps 77.16); 'all the trees of the wood sing for joy' (Ps 96.12). The personalizing of *wisdom* is particularly interesting – as (possibly: the meaning of the Hebrew word is debated) a master workman, alongside God in creation (Prov 8.30). It was personalized as feminine: 'Wisdom has built her house, she has set up her seven pillars [in order to instruct mankind]' (Prov 9.1–18). *Wisdom* was able to interact with *woman*, extending the network of associations with illuminating parallels (see further Camp, 1985).

Fables personify plants or animals, creating circumstances analogous to a human situation to draw out an appropriate message. In Jotham's fable of the trees acclaiming the bramble as king (Judg 9.7–21), if the people acted rightly they would enjoy shade; if not, they should remember that fire starting in the bramble would consume them all. The irony was that Abimelech, 'the bramble', the pretender king, would bring no shade – only destruction.

Interacting Models   The Hebrew Bible uses a variety of essentially separate models which interact with other models. This is a process of extending possibilities and insights. It matters little if 'rival' models conflict and contradict – indeed, *paradox* (holding two opposites to be true at the same time) is a well-known form of religious expression. The pressure to provide a *systematic* theology or philosophy is a separate one, concerned with producing coherent doctrine rather than expressing insights. Nevertheless, the interaction of models provides a way of guiding the explosion of associations in acceptable ways, just as an authority model tempered with a relationship model rules out injustice and pitiless domination. There is a good example of this in Isaiah 40:10f, with God as strong ruler being tempered with the simile of a gentle shepherd:

> Behold, the Lord GOD comes with might,
>   and his arm rules for him;
> behold his reward is with him,
>   and his recompense before him.
> He will feed his flock like a shepherd,

he will gather the lambs in his arms,
he will carry them in his bosom,
and gently lead those that are with young.

Limitations of Models   Models are symbolic and not real – that is to say, they are contrived ways of explaining and describing our world and our experiences for our personal convenience. The world as we understand it is a world constructed by our intellect and imagination, to help us to interpret and to make sense of life. We can, as P. Berger (1969) observes, forget that we have invented it and assume that it is real (that is, we 'objectify' it). Dogma tries to fix these constructions into incontrovertible frameworks for believers: this is, in D. Nineham's phrase (1976, 25) 'doctrines felt as facts', and it greatly inhibits exploration and change. A model, if accepted uncritically and dogmatically, can cause people to feel *excluded*: feminist theologians feel excluded by patriachal models, which, they feel, raise the status of men at the expense of women (see McFague, 1982). Models can become outmoded and other models become more attractive. Forgetting that our models are tentative and hypothetical can lead to what McFague calls idolatry – where the image or hypothetical model is regarded as reality: for example, thinking that God really is our father instead of regarding the metaphor as nothing more than a tool to assist our understanding.

Metaphors into Stories – Myths

A verbal image can be developed in story form. 'The LORD is my shepherd' (Ps 23) is developed as though the speaker (the King, since he is anointed? – v. 5) were a sheep being protected and led to the still waters. Anthropo-morphic images – God the father, judge, king, craftsman, spouse or 'person', with love, anger and sorrow – are readily capable of developing as story. The results are called *myth*. Expressed in reverse, metaphor lies at the heart of myth and can be the key to its interpretation.

The most difficult thing to put into words is *transcendence* – that consciousness, in R. Otto's phrase (1917), of the 'wholly other' which gives rise to the language of awe, wonder and mystery. Second Isaiah had several attempts: God holds the seas in the hollow of his hands; he sets heaven's limits with his span; places the earth on a balance; the nations are like a drop in a bucket; all flesh is grass, which withers 'when the breath of the LORD blows upon it'. He sits on the earth's vault, looking down on its grasshopper-sized inhabitants (see Isa 40). God's greatness suggests human insignificance. Yet a relationship model interacts with this 'power' model: 'Can a woman forget her sucking child . . . ? Even these may forget, yet I will not forget you' (49.15). The two models come together in the concept of redemption – the authority figure (father, master) purchasing freedom

from slavery, and creating a new relationship with the freed: 'Fear not, for I
have redeemed you; I have called you by name, you are mine' (43.1)
   Second Isaiah uses the picture of God, the *maker* or *creator*, as a *potter*:

> Woe to him who strives with his Maker,
>   an earthen vessel with the potter.
> Does the clay say to him who fashions it, 'What are you making?'
>   or 'Your work has no handles'? . . .
> Will you question me about my children,
>   or command me concerning the work of my hands? (45.9–11)

Jeremiah acted out the notion of God as a potter with absolute power over
his material (Jer 18.1–11). The account culminates in the words 'Behold,
like the clay in the potter's hand, so are you in my hand, O house of
Israel'(v. 6). The potter is a common image for the creator God (see also
Isa 64.7). The story of God creating man from the dust and breathing life
into his nostrils (Gen 2.7) owes not a little to this metaphor. The creator can
also be viewed as a *builder* – building foundations (Pss 24.2; 89.11; 102.25;
104.5), hammering out the earth (136.6) and spreading out the heavens
like a tent (104.2). As a *weaver*, he wove mankind (139.15).
   It could be argued that depictions of God the creator are really about 'me
the creature', that myths are about deeply felt current personal concerns.
Otto (1917) described in his classic study how the feeling of 'creatureliness'
is an important facet of religious experience. For Caird myth is a symbolic
form of expression – evocative, appealing to the imagination and the sense
of wonder or mystery. It appeals to the past to shed light on the present and
the future: 'Like the user of other form of metaphor, the user of myth says to
his audience, "Here is a lens which has helped me to understand the world
you and I live in; look through it yourselves and see what I have seen"
(1980, 224).

Traditional Creation Myths   The creation narrative (Gen 1–3) gives
little hint of ancient creation myths, although some are preserved elsewhere.
A Mesopotamian myth tells how Marduk smote and cut up the dragon
Tiamat, and from her body created the world. In Genesis 1, Tiamat has become *tehom*, the deep, and God *created* the great sea monsters. There were
two Hebrew monsters, Rahab and Leviathan. Psalm 74.13–17 speaks of
creation in terms of defeating these dragons: 'Thou didst divide the sea by
thy might; thou didst break the heads of the dragons on the waters. Thou
didst crush the heads of Leviathan . . . .' Isaiah speaks of a future battle,
when God will defeat Leviathan, the fleeing and twisting serpent, and the
dragon in the sea (Rahab?). Second Isaiah, writing during the Babylonian
exile, exults, 'Was it not thou that didst cut Rahab in pieces, that didst
pierce the dragon?' (Isa 51.9). Yet he is talking about Egypt, during the

exodus: Isaiah calls Egypt 'Rahab who sits still' (30.7). Job describes Leviathan in detail (41.1–34) as a subordinate creature, and interprets Rahab as storms at sea: 'By his power he [God] stilled the sea; by his understanding he smote Rahab. By his wind the heavens were made fair; his hand pierced the fleeing serpent.'

As poetry, the myths provide images to demonstrate God's greatness, as he overpowers the most powerful creatures that the world can offer. Political implications are drawn, comparing the great powers to these dragons, which were developed further in later 'apocalyptic' literature (e.g. Daniel). These too would be overcome by God's greatness.

Elsewhere, God is 'rider on the clouds' (Ps 68.4; Isa 19.1), riding through the heavens to your help (Deut 33.26; Ps 68.33) – above and beyond our world and our experience. 2 Samuel 22 depicts God with smoke coming from his nostrils, fire from his mouth, riding on a cherub (a dragon, representing the storm winds) and on the wind, sending out lightning as his arrows (cf. also Ps 18.11). The traditional pictures expressed the power and grandeur of nature, expressing this in terms of the utter greatness of God, totally beyond human understanding.

God: Overarching Symbol

The concept of God draws together diverse symbols and provides a framework for thought and doctrine. The compilers of the Hebrew Bible generally made monotheistic assumptions – 'Yahweh is our God, Yahweh is One' (RSV 'The LORD our God is one LORD' – Deut 6.4). Of the exilic writers' development of this theme, the strict and scornful monotheism of Second Isaiah is the most striking. However, Yahweh was also viewed as king of a heavenly court of divine beings, sometimes called 'the sons of God/the gods' (the Hebrew is ambiguous; see Job 1.6–12; Ps 29.1; 82.1; 95.3; 97.7):

> For who in the skies can be compared to the LORD?
>   Who among the heavenly beings is like the LORD,
>   a God feared in the council of the holy ones,
>   great and terrible, above all that are round about him? (Ps 89.6–7)

The preference of one God *alongside* others has been called 'monolatry'. Scholars often assume that over time doctrines became more refined and that 'ethical monotheism' represented the final stage of development. We should be cautious about this hypothetical notion of evolutionary development. Real life and public debate are never so simple; and the philosophy which gave rise to evolutionary assumptions in the nineteenth century has been long discredited (although their 'assured results' still linger on).

Another dangerous assumption is that monotheism and 'polytheistic idolatry' are mutually exclusive – a view developed by the prophets. Polytheistic systems can be regarded as *symbol systems* – each deity regarded as a symbolic representation (or manifestation) of the one God: Hinduism is a contemporary example. Our entire understanding of ancient Near Eastern religion, filtered as it is through biblical eyes, may be very wide of the mark. Ancient Egyptian religion, for instance, is best understood not as 'primitive' superstition but as complex symbolism (Hornung, 1983). This could mean that monotheism was common in the ancient world (although God was visualized in diverse forms): the Hebrews would, if so, then differ chiefly for their *rejection of images*.

Yahweh

The general word *Elohim*, 'God', is often used throughout the Hebrew Bible – curious in form as it is a plural used as a singular. The divine name *par excellence* is written with four consonants (YHWH) which are vocalized with the vowels of *Adonai* ('my Lord'). English versions often replace it with 'the LORD'. Of obscure origins, the Torah narrator associates the name with Moses' Midianite connections (Exod 6.2–3), whilst still including stories in which the patriarchs clearly knew and used the name Yahweh (e.g. Gen 14.22; 15.2, 7). This caused scholars to suggest that the work of an earlier narrator, the 'Yahwist', had been incorporated. The meaning of the name Yahweh, is also obscure, most scholars following Exodus 3.14–15 in deriving it from the root *hyh* 'to be' ('I am who I am'), but some preferring the root *hwh*, deriving meanings such as 'blow', 'speak' and 'sustain' (Gottwald, 1985, 212). The shortened form *Yah* is used in some psalms. *Yahweh Sebaoth*, 'the LORD of Hosts', is a common epithet found in the prophets. A fuller form, in the David and Goliath story, is 'the LORD of Hosts, the God of the armies of Israel' (1 Sam 17.45). This is a military and nationalistic concept of God in whose name Amalek was decimated (1 Sam 15.1–3) and whose help was sought to destroy enemies (Ps 44.4–5). Yahweh Sebaoth was particularly associated with the Ark of the Covenant – 'the ark of God, which is called by the name of the LORD of hosts who sits enthroned on the cherubim' (2 Sam 6.2) – and with the Shiloh sanctuary. Psalm 24 is particularly revealing:

> Who is the King of Glory?
>   The LORD, strong and mighty,
>   the LORD mighty in battle! . . .
> Who is this King of Glory?
>   The LORD of hosts, he is the King of Glory (vv. 8–10)

In a sense also the 'hosts' are heavenly hosts – the planets and stars symbolizing the heavenly power – as we see from the very early poem the 'Song of Deborah': 'From heaven fought the stars, from their courses they fought against Sisera' (Judg 5.20).

Many other divine names are found in the Hebrew Bible, often in the poetry of the Psalms. *Shaddai*, 'Almighty', is of uncertain derivation and its translation conjectural. Outside the Psalms, it is featured in Torah narratives as the name for God that Abraham recognized (Gen 17.1; Exod 6.14–15). *El Elyon*, 'God Most High' (which more frequently appears as simply *Elyon*, 'the High One'), is found only in Genesis 14 (see below, ch. 4) and one psalm (Ps 78.35).

Readers will bring their own ideas of God to their reading: their task is to understand why they cherish the pictures and models they use, and to examine the personal experiences they bring to the imagery. They should try to view these models as if through the eyes of others, and be prepared to experiment with alternative models (such as God the mother). This will reveal some of the ways religious language is used, and uncover part of the process of how we construct our concept of God from our experience and from other concepts. Our beliefs about God tell us a great deal about ourselves individually and as a society.

Religious language is *problematic*, in that it seeks to express the inexpressible, to give meaning to experience, to make sense of life. The questions it raises – about the purpose of life, about ultimate meaning, about good and evil, life and death – have no easy answers. It may be that the texts of the Hebrew Bible prove to be helpful for one's personal search for meaning, but we should beware of being dogmatic about our opinions. Whatever our view of the authority of Scripture, our interpretation of it is subjective: others may have clearer insights. It may be that we cannot respond to a text because our experience is lacking in some crucial area. As soon as we cease to regard religious texts as 'problematic' – responses to problems which raise questions rather than providing solutions – we slide into self-centred dogmatism.

There is an important first question to be asked: how do we know? In later chapters, we shall face this question with regard to historical data – to see how far it is possible to reconstruct historical events. Yet in reading accounts of 'Yahweh's saving acts' we have also to face the question of how to interpret these as truth claims. What exactly do we mean by 'true'? In what sense is the Hebrew Bible a 'true' story? Is Yahweh truly God, or nothing but a human idea? What is God an overarching symbol *of*? A reality beyond our comprehension? Or a reality *within us*?

Part II

The Torah

4

Genesis: History or Story?

THE TORAH: SOME PRELIMINARY REMARKS

Stephen Bigger

The Torah consists of the first five books of the Hebrew Bible – sometimes named 'Pentateuch', from the Greek for 'five volumes'. Latinized Greek titles are used in English Bibles: *Genesis* ('beginning'), *Exodus* ('going out'), *Leviticus* ('Levitical law'), *Numbers* (Latin *Numeri*, 'numbering'), *Deuteronomy* ('second law'). Hebrew titles use the first words of the book: *Bereshith* ('In the beginning'), *We'elleh semoth* ('These are the names'), *Wayiqra'* ('And he called'), *Bemidbar* ('In the wilderness') and *Elleh haddebarim*, ('These are the words').

The traditional view of Orthodox Judaism is that the Torah was revealed by God to Moses on Mount Sinai in its totality – thus it is in a special sense revealed Scripture. Belief in Mosaic authorship was dominant in Christianity until this century. Pentateuchal critics view the Torah as the creation of writers and editors, a compilation of various sources from different times merged by editors (or 'redactors'). A supposed fifth century BCE date for the final completion of the Torah was generally accepted after J. Wellhausen's work in 1883. His widely accepted hypothesis assumed a gradual process of composition, with an early Yahwistic source (J, from the German *Jahve*) which used the name Yahweh, an Elohist (E) which used the divine name Elohim, a Redactor who combined the two, a Deuteronomic source (D) and a Priestly Writer (P) responsible for the final editing. More recent work by *source critics* make finer distinctions, often proposing different editions or recensions of each source. In other words, four sources often fragment into many.

There has been constant debate also on the *genre* of the material – a folktale? a song? an official report? history? fiction? If it is assumed that the genre is history, the conclusions drawn will be radically different from those

prompted by a view of it as fiction. Aetiologies explain the origins of institutions and names – are these explanations authentic, or imaginative? The
literary critic is interested in the design, plot, characterization and other
literary features (although literary criticism had in earlier years the more
restricted meaning of 'source critic'). The *form critic* is interested in the form
(and the development of each form) of each unit of tradition. The *tradition
critic* seeks to understand the process which was brought the tradition,
through various stages, into the form in which we now find it: each level introduces a different audience who affected the text. Behind this complexity,
one thing is clear. The narratives were put together for a purpose (whatever
the underlying process). The 'author' had particular interests to communicate, so our first area of study is the final form of the text. An understanding
of how it might have been composed may deepen our understanding. As
historians we are primarily interested in what this final form tells us *of the
age in which the writer lived*. We have to make complex judgements about
the accuracy of the data and the bias of the writer before we can begin to
reconstruct the period the text purports to describe.

The Torah begins with story – narratives depicting, as their themes, how
God intervened in earth affairs and how people responded. It lays
foundations by creating a framework explaining the origins of familiar
peoples, institutions and customs. Readers could see how they fitted into the
scheme of things – why they married, spoke different languages, recognized
kinship, and worshipped. It provided a comfortable world which they could
easily comprehend, making clear who their friends were, and who their
enemies. It revealed *what was expected of them*, in terms of behaviour and
ritual; and *what they could expect*. The Torah thus defined their existence,
offering them a framework for life, a paradigm which helped them to see
their existence as purposeful.

The contents of the Torah may be summarized as in table 4.1.

Theme

If the Torah or Pentateuch was intended by its final author/editor to be
complete in itself, there would have been a central purpose. D. J. A. Clines
(1982, 29) has proposed,

> *The theme of the Pentateuch is the partial fulfilment* – *which implies the partial non-
> fulfilment* – *of the promise to or blessing of the patriarchs. The promise of blessing is both
> the divine initiative in a world where human initiatives always lead to disaster, and a
> re-affirmation of the primal divine intentions for man.*

Although the Torah came together comparatively early, the assumption that
the first five books belong together (as opposed to the first four or six) is not

Table 4.1   The contents of the Torah

Book, chapters	Content
Genesis 1–11	Primeval myths and stories
Genesis 12–50	Stories of Abraham, Isaac, Ishmael, Jacob, the twelve patriarchs, especially Joseph
Exodus 1–19	The Exodus story from Moses' birth to Mount Sinai
Exodus 20–4	The Decalogue (Ten Commandments) and other laws
Exodus 25–40	The Tent of Meeting in the wilderness
Leviticus	Rituals and laws
Numbers	Mainly narratives of the wilderness period
Deuteronomy 1–11	A speech by Moses recounting the Exodus story and recent events
Deuteronomy 12–26	A second formulation of religious and social laws
Deuteronomy 27–34	Miscellaneous material leading to the death of Moses

the only option. M. Noth preferred to regard Deuteronomy as the first work of the 'Deuteronomic History' (leaving a Tetrateuch). Joshua ends with a summary (24.1–13), a call to reject idolatry and to establish the covenant (24.14–25; cf. Exod 34), the completion of the book of the law of God (24.26), a note that Israel served God (24.31) and the return of Joseph's bones promised in Gen 50.24–5 and Exod 13.19 (24.32). Thus Joshua could be seen as the completion of the blessing, the sixth volume of a Hexateuch. There may also have been earlier editors, with their own points of view: reconstructing their achievements will necessarily be more hypothetical.

The Torah opens with Genesis, a largely narrative work covering the period from creation to the patriarchs. The stories in this book raise interesting questions about 'what actually happened'. Are the stories fact or fiction? How best can we interpret them? Can we trace their sources?

Genre

It is important to determine the form or genre of the material. Is it carefully researched archival history? Or fiction? G. W. Coats (1983, 5–10) summarizes the principal *narrative* genres found in Genesis as follows.

Saga: traditional, episodic narrative about the resolution of tension, focusing on the beginning, a family or a hero. Individual units may represent other genres.

Tale: a short narrative, probably oral in origin, with the minimum number of characters, a single scene and a simple limited plot.

Novella: a complex subtle story using a series of sub-plots, with a number of characters. Probably a *literary* creation by an author.

Legend: a story focusing on some characteristic or virtue of the hero. It provides an edifying exemplar, and does not resolve particular tensions as saga does.

History: a record of events, without artistry in presentation, for archives or officials (e.g. the king).

Biography: a historical record about a particular person.

Report: a brief record of a single event, perhaps for the court.

Anecdote: a report about a person.

Fable: a fantasy using non-human character, with a pointed moral.

Aetiology: a narrative designed to lead up to an explanation.

Myth: a narrative which explores the real world in terms of divine categories.

Robert Alter also speaks of *historicized prose fiction* (1981, 24f) and the *type scene* – a typical, conventionally structured story (1981, 47–62). It may be difficult to be definitive in our conclusions; but we should at least tackle the question of whether the narrative is an oral tradition, a literary creation, or a piece of factual reporting. Literary perspectives are further developed by Bar Efrat (1988), Berlin (1983), Coats (1985), Kort (1988), Miscall (1983) and Sternberg (1978, 1985).

GENESIS: THE STORY

Stephen Bigger

Preliminary Reading   Genesis.

The Primeval Age

The story begins with creation, and the progress of humanity from Adam to

Abraham. These two are carefully linked by genealogy. The longest narrative describes the great flood, and the survival of Noah's family.

Abram/Abraham, Isaac and Jacob

The Promise

The Abram/Abraham narratives open with Yahweh (God) making a demand and a promise:

Go from your country and your kindred and your father's house to the land that I will show you. And I will make you a great nation, and I will bless you, and make your name great, so that you will be a blessing. I will bless those that bless you, and him who curses you I will curse; and by you all the families of the earth will bless themselves (12.1–3)

Yahweh (the divine name used in most promise declarations) promises Abram the land of Canaan for his descendants. However, Abram's fear of Egypt leads his wife Sarai into adultery (12.10–19): his fear is illusory, for in reality the Egyptians are afraid of Yahweh. There is irony in Lot's choice of territory: it looks good, but the reader is told that the result will be disaster – Sodom and Gomorrah will be destroyed for wickedness (13.10–13). In contrast, the promise to Abram is reaffirmed (vv. 14–18). Abram's faithfulness to God, and therefore strength, sharply contrasts with Lot's weakness (14.1–24).

Abram and Sarai have no children: the promise of numerous offspring is met by a lack of trust as Abram plans that his slave should be his heir (15.1–6).The repeated promise is sealed by a solemn covenant sacrifice (vv. 7–21). This particular style of sacrifice is not found in the sacrificial rituals prescribed in Leviticus. The promise now encompasses huge boundaries – from the river of Egypt to the Euphrates, the land of ten separate peoples (Gen 15.18–21). To compensate for Sarai's barrenness, her slave-woman Hagar bears Ishmael, who, despite Sarai's harshness, is spared. An angel of Yahweh reaffirms the promise, to 'multiply your descendants'. The promise is now developed in the language of the circumcision covenant (17.1–27), using the divine names Elohim and El Shaddai. This passage changes Abram's name to Abraham ('father of many') and Sarai's to Sarah ('she shall be a mother of nations' – 17.16). In other passages too, El Shaddai is linked with promise (28.3; Exod 6.2–3).

The next narrative brings a problem and a limitation: the promise requires that Sarah, old and barren, should have a son; and Lot's line will be excluded from the promise. After the destruction of Sodom and Gomorrah, only Lot and two daughters are left: they incestuously produce the ancestors of the Moabites and Ammonites, neighbouring but hostile tribes. Ammonites and Moabites were excluded from the assembly of Israel 'even to the tenth generation' (Deut 23.3–6). Sarah's barrenness, a human weakness, is solved by Yahweh: a key phrase is 'Is anything too hard for Yahweh?' (Gen 18.14). Another human weakness is introduced by Abraham: he fears for his life, and selfishly represents Sarah as his sister instead of his wife – for a second time. This threatens the paternity of the promised child, as Abimelech king of Gerar takes Sarah as his wife and brings 'a great sin' into the kingdom. The narrative responds in two ways: by declaring that Yahweh has closed the wombs of Abimelech's women (20.17f) and by noting that Abimelech has not 'approached' or 'touched' Sarah (vv. 4–6). Abraham's weakness almost subverts the promise. Isaac's birth is presented as *Yahweh's act* in fulfilling his promise. Isaac almost perishes at Abraham's hand (22.1–19) in an episode which the narrative presents as a test of the patriarch's faith. God again intervenes, confirming his promises.

The birth of sons to Isaac and Rebecca follows the common barren-wife motif. The pregnant Rebecca goes 'to inquire of Yahweh': the oracle speaks of two divided nations or peoples in her womb, the younger being more dominant than the elder. The promise formulas are repeated to Isaac (26.1–5) and finally transferred to Jacob at Bethel (28.10–17). Thereafter the narrator changes Jacob's name to Israel (with promise language – 35.9–13) and focuses on Joseph's sons, Ephraim and Manasseh (48.16–20.)

Aetiology and Eponyms

Often, stories explain the origin of place-names or customs. Some may be related to incidents, others to dreams. A cairn marks the place where Jacob and Laban have reached agreement – it becomes 'the heap of witness', 'Jegarsahadutha' in Aramaic, 'Galeed' in Hebrew (Gen 31.47). Angels met Jacob at Mahanaim, 'two armies' (32.2), and he fights with God at Peniel, 'face of God' (32.22–32). There Jacob is named Israel, 'for you have striven with God and with men, and have prevailed'. Jacob's injury explains a food prohibition: 'Therefore to this day the Israelites do not eat the sinew of the hip which is upon the hollow of the thigh, because he [God] touched the hollow of Jacob's thigh on the sinew of the hip' (32.32). Bethel, 'house of God', is so named after a dream of heaven opening (28.19), authenticating the Bethel sanctuary. Another sanctuary has the interesting name El-Elohe-Israel, 'El is the God [or gods] of Israel' (33.20).

These explanations have an unchartable background in oral tradition. An interesting group of aetiologies involves the sons of Jacob (Gen 29.31–30.24; 35.16–20):

Reuben	'See a son'
Simeon	'God has heard'

Levi	'My husband will be joined to me'
Judah	'I will praise God'
Dan	'God has judged me'
Naphtali	'I have wrestled with my sister'
Gad	'Good fortune'
Asher	'Happy am I'
Issachar	'God has given me my hire'
Zebulun	'My husband will honour me'
Joseph	'May God add to me another son'
Benoni	'Son of my sorrow'
[= Benjamin	'Son of the right hand']

These names are *eponyms* – names of tribes as names of their 'ancestor'. The introduction of the name Israel links Jacob, renamed Israel on two separate occasions (Gen 32.28; 35.10), into the same scheme. Into social chaos such as is revealed in Judges, a family was created, linked through kinship to Jacob/Israel. The patriarchal stories thus acquired a vital function, uniting the people. About the *historical* patriarchs, we have no direct evidence.

Joseph

The Joseph narrative (Gen 37-50) is noticeably different from the episodic material which precedes it: at its heart is a well-crafted short story. The inclusion – some would say, intrusion – of chapter 38, a separate story of Judah, seems to interrupt the flow of the story. Yet there is irony in the narrator's text. Judah was responsible for Joseph's being sold as a slave into Egypt (37.26–8) and thus indirectly for the pre-eminence of Joseph's son Ephraim, the 'ancestor' of the strongest northern tribe (48.1–20). He was also responsible for the (illegitimate) birth of Perez and Zerah (38.29–30), whose descendant David brought Judah together with the northern tribes, including Ephraim (2 Sam 5.1–5). Ephraim's descendant Jeroboam took the northern tribes, 'the house of Joseph' (1 Kgs 11.28), from David's successor. Thus Judah in Genesis 38 is personally responsible for later problems. It is interesting too that David's line is depicted as illegitimate, and Ephraim's as legitimate!

Jacob blessed Joseph's sons: they would thereafter perpetuate his name (Israel). The 'blessing of Jacob' (Gen 49) reveals a tension between Judah the *ruler* (v.10) enjoying luxury and prosperity (vv. 11–12), and Joseph the recipient of God's blessing and thereby Jacob's blessing (vv. 24–6). Unfortunately, the phrase indicating the end of Judah's supremacy is difficult: the sceptre/ruler's staff shall not depart from Judah 'until Shiloh comes' (Masoretic text). The tribes of Judah and Joseph dominated the scene until allocations for other tribes were made at Shiloh (Josh 18) and tribes were encouraged to become independent. There may be here an interesting relationship between the narrative and tribal politics.

The story of Joseph stands out as a coherent unit. Joseph is sold into Egypt (Gen 37), is imprisoned (for attempted rape) following false accusation (39), interprets dreams (40) and particularly Pharaoh's dream (41). He becomes governor and negotiates with his brothers (without their knowledge) until Judah is desperate (42–4). He reveals the truth (45) and thereafter Jacob and his entire family move to Egypt, where they are granted land in Goshen. Joseph's prudence greatly strengthens Pharaoh's hand (46–7). Jacob adopts Ephraim and Manasseh (48), and after a farewell speech foretelling the future of his sons (49) he dies and is buried in Canaan. Joseph too dies in good old age (50).

There is no external evidence in support of this story, although Egyptian texts do speak of foreigners in Egypt because of famine (*ANET* 259). The attempted seduction of Joseph by Potiphar's wife has a close parallel in an Egyptian story of two brothers (*c.*1200 BCE, *ANET* 23–5). There are a number of parallels in detail in chapters 39–41 – the wise man as saviour; the disgraced official; the money in the grainsack (Hayes and Miller, 1977, 191) – which show that the writer was well versed in Egyptian story motifs. In general Egyptians are portrayed as friendly, and the author speaks well of the Egyptian priesthood (e.g. 47.22–6). Joseph married an Egyptian priest's daughter (41.45) – a point that might have perplexed the prophets. The comment that Egyptians may not eat with foreigners (43.32) is clearly an observation for those who might not know it. There is clear evidence of trade between Palestine and Egypt. Some therefore attribute the Joseph narrative to the time of King Solomon, a time of friendly relations with Egypt, including a royal marriage to Pharaoh's daughter (1 Kgs 3.1).

GENESIS: THE EVIDENCE

Alastair G. Hunter

Assessing the Evidence

Pentateuchal narratives combine a number of genres. Although it is true that the writers (or editors) of the final version crafted their work well, they have not obscured its composite nature. Historians need to ask why there appear to be two creation stories, and why the flood account records both that the animals entered the ark in pairs ('two of every sort . . . male and female' – 6.19) and also 'seven pairs of all clean animals, the male and his mate' (7.2). There are many incongruities of this kind in the historical books. A historian would certainly find the chronology implausible. In Genesis 1–11, ages in the 900s are not uncommon, and there is a deliberate scheme reducing ages to more reasonable proportions. Nevertheless, Sarah was over ninety years old when she bore Isaac (17.17); and the 'young' romantic Jacob working fourteen years for his wives was at least seventy years old. Moreover, the biblical record is largely unsubstantiated by extra-biblical sources. There can be no final answers to many dilemmas. At any given time there may be a consensus of opinion in favour of one view or other, but this is liable to change as more evidence becomes available – better textual readings and different perspectives, or emerging extra-biblical data and archaeological findings. Scholars make assumptions in reaching their conclusions – that the patriarchal stories represent real people (so Bright and Albright) or that they do not; that the geography is, or is not, accurate; that the text is relatively pure, or corrupt. Thus what one scholar might see as sound another will consider to be flawed.

A note of caution should be sounded at this point. In areas where hard information is in short supply, it is very tempting to indulge in reconstructions to fill the gaps in our knowledge, or to argue a plausible case from silence (e.g. 'there is nothing to prove that Abraham did not live in Canaan in the second millennium BCE – therefore the traditions are historical'). Perhaps the most insidious temptation is to set up a string of possible statements, each of which has a low plausibility, and draw from them a 'strong' conclusion. This can appear convincing, particularly if the low probability of the constituent parts is not openly admitted, since it looks as though the view is based on a number of sound arguments. In fact the reverse is true – the combination of a string of hypotheses each of low probability leads to a conclusion very much weaker than the individual hypotheses, since *each* of these weak arguments needs to be true if the case is to stand. As an example, read Genesis 12.10–20 and consider the following propositions.

1 It is possible that camels were domesticated in the early second millennium BCE.
2 Abram seems to have been a wealthy and influential nomadic leader, typical of the Amorite invasion which appears to have occurred around 2000 BCE.
3 The wife–sister combination is witnessed in legal documents elsewhere in the ancient Near East, and may well have been known to Abram.
4 The fact that the Egyptian texts are silent on the subject of Abram is

not surprising; after all, the incident must have been embarrassing for Pharaoh.

5   During the Twelfth Dynasty, Egypt ruled over Canaan with the help of Semitic mercenaries, and there was much traffic between the two regions.

6   Therefore, given the weight of such evidence, surely only a hardened sceptic would deny the historicity of Genesis 12.10–20.

It must be left to the reader to unpack the fallacies in this 'argument'. It is, of course, quite untenable – but it is not much exaggerated from the kind of 'proof' which is often found in studies of the history of Israel.

History and Archaeology

History in the Hebrew Bible is not the kind of critical, analytical discipline which would be expected of a modern scholar. What is common is the urge to make sense of the present in terms of the past; where a radical difference appears is in the method of recovering the past. For, while modern historians much check and cross-check all sources and thereby form a view of 'how it actually was', in ancient times knowledge of the past was assumed (or invented), and was certainly not placed under academic scrutiny. In a sense, society *creates* its history: 'History is the intellectual form in which a civilization renders account to itself of its past' (Huizinga, 1963, 9). From this, van Seters suggests a number of principles applicable to the writing of history in ancient Israel (1983, 4–5).

1   'History' is a specific, deliberately constructed form in its own right, not to be dismissed as an accidental accumulation of traditional material.

2   It is not primarily an accurate report of past events. More important is its role of considering the reasons for recalling the past and the significance given to past events – in other words, how does the past explain the present? In antiquity such explanations were primarily moral.

3   It is national or corporate in character. Accounts of individual patriarchs or kings are directed to an understanding of the present condition of 'all Israel'.

Even in the conditional terms we have described, it remains the case that large areas of the Hebrew Bible do not even pretend to be history. Within the Torah itself, when we exclude the legal and cultic material, the narrative portions are restricted to Genesis and part of Exodus and Numbers. While these narratives are in many ways unlike our concept of history, it seems reasonable to argue that they satisfy the definitions offered by Huizinga and van Seters. The texts do reveal an interest in the past and a desire to use the past to inform the present – that is, the time of writing. It is without doubt the personal search for identity, and moral and religious factors which connect the past with the present.

Despite popular belief, and the optimism of an earlier age, archaeology can only very rarely offer direct verification of specific events or people. For example, the discovery and excavation of a tell which is identified as the site of the ancient city of Ur does not 'prove' the accuracy of the tradition of Genesis 11.31 according to which Abram's father emigrated with his family from Ur to Haran. At the very most, it simply tells us that there was indeed a city, which may have been known as Ur, existing at that time. Since the date of the migration from Ur is impossible to determine from the Bible itself, this information is of marginal value. It is necessary to stress that in many cases the evidence gleaned from archaeological investigations, however valuable it may be for the reconstruction of the life and times of the inhabitants, cannot 'prove' the biblical text. Whilst archaeological *data* are to be welcomed, *interpretations* of these data need to be treated with caution.

The most tempting form of external evidence has been written records. A significant body of parallels for the stories in Genesis 1–11 has been recovered, with a resulting deepening of our knowledge of the milieu in which they were written. Yet these comparative texts can be tempting in the wrong sense, in that they can induce over-optimistic historical conclusions. There may be a close literary interrelationship, or both may have been drawn from the same source of ideas. Patriarchal names are found in comparative literature, but they similarly resist precise dating. There are no references to the patriarchs themselves. Customs (such as the adoption of a slave, the legal defining of a wife as a sister, and others from archives found at Nuzi, Mari and in the Hittite territories) have been used to elucidate incidents in the lives of the patriarchs. On closer examination, similarities tend to evaporate as the 'parallels' prove to refer to different situations or to have been misunderstood in the first flush of excitement. A detailed consideration of these matters is found in van Seters (1975). A more recent case which proves that nothing has really changed involves the finds at Ebla in northern Syria. These were dated around 2000 BCE, and it was very quickly reported that both the names 'Yahweh' and 'Abraham' had been identified amongst the texts from the palace archives. This prompted a (rather optimistic) claim that the patriarchal narratives had been 'proved' though it was not long before these identifications and interpretations were questioned (see Bermant and Weitzman, 1979).

The *personal* nature of the patriarchal narratives and the stories of Israel's wanderings in the wilderness mean that these narratives are in principle not open to archaeological verification. Moreover, their anecdotal and largely legendary nature rules them out as carefully researched history in modern terms. Nevertheless, they offer an interpretation of the origins and rise of Israel, reflecting the perceptions of the generation that produced them.

Genesis 14 is a good example. It is written in the form of a campaign chronicle, referring both to named kings and cities in the ancient Near East, and to the particular family at the centre of the patriarchal narratives. Here if anywhere we might expect archaeology and history to lend support; but the matter turns out very differently. The eastern alliance is mysterious indeed: Shinar is Babylon; Arioch might be a known vassal of the kingdom of Mari, or a king of Nuzi; Elam is a known country to the east of Babylon; Tidal can be interpreted as a Hittite name, since it is known to have been used for five kings of that realm. But the other names resist interpretation, and there is no known period when such an alliance can be plausibly inferred. Further, at the time when Abraham is supposed to have flourished (*c.*2000–1500 BCE), the dominant force in Canaan was Egypt, the one great power not mentioned in the chapter! To this historical implausibility must be added the fact that all archaeological investigation of the region has failed to reveal any signs of cities or towns matching those supposed by this chapter. The presence of Sodom and Gomorrah suggests very strongly that we have here the same legendary traditions as in Genesis 19. It is thus unlikely that archaeological or historical support will be forthcoming. The likelihood is that Genesis 14 cannot provide verifiable information for a modern historical study of the mid second millennium BCE.

The early biblical narratives cannot be assumed to have preserved evidence of the period on which they focus. They are historical documents, but of the periods of the writers; and, since the writers and their times are anonymous, and matters of surmise, we cannot expect easy answers. Yet if we ask, 'What are these stories trying to say?' we can enter to some extent into the writers' experiences, and see them wrestling with age-old, yet still current, human problems and insights.

Oral-Tradition Hypotheses

An important aspect of the analysis of the Genesis texts is the question of possible oral developments. Claims for the role of oral tradition have basically two forms. First, there is the general thesis that small units of tradition were told and retold by word of mouth, changing to suit the different circumstances of speaker and listeners, until in the course of time they were absorbed into a longer written text. This leads naturally to a *form-critical* analysis, a study of oral forms. Secondly, it has been claimed that large stretches of material were preserved more or less accurately for a long period of time until they were committed to writing in the crisis circumstances of the exile, when the destruction of Jerusalem and the loss of the homeland threatened the loss of the religious and historical traditions of the people. This thesis goes back to the Swedish scholar H. S. Nyberg (1935), and was elaborated by H. Birkeland (1938), who drew comparisons with such feats of memory in the Muslim world as the word-perfect memorization of the Qur'an. It became a characteristic feature of the Scandinavian school after the Second World War, represented by I. Engnell, A. S. Kapelrud and E. Nielsen.

The debate is a long one. The assumptions behind this form of the oral-tradition hypothesis are, first, that in a pre- or marginally literate society human memory is much more efficient than in our own highly literate world; secondly, that the preservation of long passages of material is normal; and, thirdly, that the process is essentially conservative – that is, that changes to the tradition are consciously avoided. The first of these assumptions may well be justified; but the other two are very questionable. True, many Muslims memorize the *written* text of the Qur'an, but this is entirely different from committing to memory an *oral* epic. Studies in oral tradition in social anthropology indicate that the storyteller has a pronounced *creative* role to play, and other types of material (genealogies are perhaps the most significant) are subject both to selection and to the limitations of human memory. M. Finley (1964–5, 296f) makes this point very clearly:

Wherever tradition can be studied among living people, the evidence is not only that it does not exist apart from a connection with a practice or belief, but also that other kinds of memory, irrelevant memories, so to speak, are short-lived, going back to the third generation, to the grandfather's generation, and, with the rarest of exceptions, no further. This is true even of genealogies, unless they are recorded in writing; it may be taken as a rule that orally transmitted genealogies, unless some very powerful interest intervenes (such as charismatic kingship), are usually fictitious beyond the fourth generation, and often even beyond the third. There is a nice Greek illustration: the Homeric heroes recite their genealogies frequently and in detail, and without exception a few steps take them from human ancestors to gods or goddesses.

Though Finley's remarks are concerned with Greek traditions, they are valid in the Hebrew context also. The sweeping assumptions which lie behind the oral-tradition approach can hardly be justified, and the more modest reality – that certain stories may have been told and retold until they were finally recorded as part of a written narrative – is of limited value in explaining the history of the traditions.

Form Criticism

There is an alternative – and older – approach to the search for oral traditions underlying the written form of the Pentateuch. H. Gunkel's pioneering work, elaborated by his successors, led to an emphasis on the study of *forms* of Hebrew literature. They attempted to recover the short oral units of material which first emerged, and to reconstruct the development process, through oral stages to the final written form. It must be said (see Whybray, 1987, 138–85) that there is increasing scepticism about the likelihood of recovering oral traditions from *literary* evidence; but form criticism none the less has a place in historical–critical analysis of the Hebrew Bible, and we shall describe it briefly.

1   The first stage is to identify (small) units which may appropriately be described as complete in themselves. To do this it may be useful to look for natural 'beginnings and endings'.

2   The units thus isolated are then examined to see if they display characteristic patterns or formulas, standard phrases which are known to be typical of a particular genre. (In English 'Once upon a time' leads readily to the genre definition 'fairy tale'.)

3   A descriptive category of the form or genre may be attempted. Myth, legend, blessing, hymn of thanksgiving, prophetic oracle are typical examples.

4   Some comparison with other known instances might lead to an assessment of the degree of 'purity' of the form. Has it been adjusted to suit the literary context? Are there awkward or unusual features which might indicate how it had functioned at an earlier stage? (For example, named characters with no real part to play in the narrative as it now stands might have been central to an earlier version.)

5   Finally, some attempt is made to define the original life setting (*Sitz im Leben*) of the unit, and to compare it with its setting and context in the final form of the text.

Hypothetical Pentateuchal Sources

It was noted long ago that there are major difficulties in perceiving the writing of the Pentateuch as a single creative act. Striking changes of style, differences of vocabulary, inconsistencies and double accounts all suggest some more complex process. Perhaps the most obvious case is that of Genesis 1–5, with two radically different approaches to creation, with the style of chapter 1 returning in chapter 5. These basic observations produced two significant consequences: the development of *theories* about the formation of the Torah as we now know it, and the evolving of *methods* of critical analysis of the text.

Broadly speaking, two theories have held the field: the *documentary hypothesis* associated above all with the name of J. Wellhausen, and the *history of traditions* approach dominated by M. Noth. Wellhausen's documentary hypothesis, which has dominated a century of scholarship, identifies several basic documents (traditionally known as J, E, D and P) each enjoying a separate existence before being worked into the main text of the Torah by a series of editors or *redactors*. The whole process is assumed to have begun at an early stage, perhaps the tenth or ninth century BCE, and was largely completed by the end of the fifth century BCE. The tradition-history approach, on the other hand, sees the early development as largely an oral matter, with independent traditions preserved and handed down in the community by different groups and in different places. Only relatively late on, perhaps the seventh or sixth century BCE, did the work of recording and combining these traditions begin, so that what we now have is a post-exilic text with early traditions embedded in later bridging themes and narratives. Both of these general theories have been severely criticized in recent years, most recently by R. N. Whybray (1987). This kind of analysis gave rise to historical-critical methods whose usefulness is not limited by the success or failure of the work of Noth and Wellhausen.

Source Criticism

To give more precise shape to the 'variations in the text' a number of practical criteria have been devised. It must be stressed that these are indicators rather than proofs, and that conclusions based on them are necessarily tentative, open to reassessment in the light of other forms of evidence.

1   *Double or even triple accounts of the same material.* There are three cases of a patriarch presenting his wife as his sister (Gen 12.10–20; 20.1–18; 26.1–11), and two apparently conflicting accounts of Hagar and Ishmael in chapters 16 and 21.

2   *Contradictions.* For example, the flood story notes both that pairs of all animals, and that seven pairs of clean animals, entered the ark. In Exodus 24, it is both stated that Moses alone would approach God (v.2) and that all the leaders saw God (vv. 9–11).

3   *The repetition of certain characteristic words or phrases in some places but not others.* In Genesis a number of phrases recur several times: 'and there was evening and there was morning', 'and God saw that it was very good', etc. These are strikingly absent from the alternative story of creation which begins in 2.4.

4   *The identification of characteristic vocabulary*, such as the use of different names for God (Yahweh by the Yahwist [J], Elohim by the Elohist [E]). A clear pattern emerges of passages which use characteristic vocabulary (e.g. Gen 1.26–30; 5.1–2; 9.1–3).

5   *Digressions and abrupt changes of style.* The story of Joseph (Gen
    37–50) includes an independent account of the misdeeds of Judah,
    one of Joseph's brothers. In Genesis 5.29, in the midst of a very
    formal genealogy, in a chapter which begins with a clear reference to
    1.26–30, we find the abrupt introduction of material closely related
    to chapters 2 and 3.

It must be stressed that the findings resulting from the application of these
techniques do not in themselves prove the existence of separate documents
or even of distinct sources. Nevertheless they do constitute primary evidence
of the specific complexity of the biblical text, on the basis of which theories
of the history of the development of the text may be constructed.

Redaction Criticism

The rationale of historical criticism as we have so far described it includes
the assumption that the form of the Torah as we now have it is the result of a
long process of development. The units identified by form criticism, and the
distinctive materials indicated by source criticism, must have been combined at some time. Redaction criticism looks for signs of editorial work in
the text. This requires rather subtle skills, clearly depends on a close analysis
of the Hebrew text, and is peculiarly resistent to codification by means of
rules and procedures. What we seek are signs of linking passages designed to
connect distinct pieces, explanatory glosses where an older source contains
some obscurities, and material which effectively reconciles contradictory
accounts. Overall we assess the redactor's concerns and interests. The phrase
'that is, Hebron' in Genesis 23.2 looks like a gloss intended to explain a now
unknown place-name to a later reader. Genesis 26, the third account of a
patriarch passing his wife off as his sister, speaks of 'the other famine', since
the first of these accounts also relates to a time of a famine.

A Case in Point: Genesis 14

In this section we shall apply the methods just described to a passage which
we have already used as an example. To begin with, we will note the
probable division into logical units (*form criticism*). The chapter begins with
the story of the invasion from the east (v. 1: 'In the days of Amraphel . . .')
and that account ends naturally in v. 11 ('The enemy took all the goods of
Sodom and Gomorrah, and all their provisions, and went their way'). There
follows what appears to be a footnote or addendum – the use of much the
same words to bring Lot into the story. We therefore take v. 12 to be a unit
deserving attention in its own right. Following that, we have the account of

Abram's dramatic rescue of Lot, reaching its natural conclusion in v. 16. The last section describes Abram's dealings with leading figures from the first unit, with whom he has so far no direct connection. Here we find two units, one 'nested' inside the other; for the narrative concerning the meeting with the king of Sodom (vv. 17, 21–4) is interrupted by the seemingly quite separate story of Abram and Melchizedek (vv. 18–20). Thus, summarizing:

1   The invasion from the east, vv. 1–11;
2   Lot's unwilling involvement, v. 12;
3   Abram to the rescue, vv. 13–16;
4   Abram's encounter with the king of Sodom, vv. 17, 21–4; including
5   Abram's encounter with Melchizedek, vv. 18–20.

Turning now to *source criticism*, we may identify possible evidence as follows.

Double accounts: the capture of Lot repeats the description of the capture of the people of Sodom and Gomorrah and their goods; the meeting with Melchizedek looks like an alternative to the meeting with the king of Sodom.

Contradictions: those who actually fight on the side of Abram (v. 14f) are the 318 men of his household, yet Aner, Eshcol and Mamre are referred to in vv. 13, 24 as his allies; the implication of vv. 13–16 is that Abram acts entirely on his own behalf, whereas both 17, 21–4 and 18–20 imply some kind of allegiance to others.

Characteristic language: explanatory notes of the form 'that is . . .'; frequent use of the word for king; use of lists (vv. 1, 2, 5–7, 8, 9); taking and returning of persons and goods (vv. 11, 12, 14, 16, 21); 'subduing' enemies (vv. 5, 7, 15, 17); 'Lord God Most High' (vv. 18, 19, 20,22); 'maker of heaven and earth' (vv. 19, 22).

Digressions and changes of style: the formality of the campaign account is broken by the story of the bitumen pits (v. 10) and the introduction of Lot in v. 12; a major interruption occurs in v. 18 with the introduction of Melchizedek together with an abrupt change from purely secular to highly religious language.

Some tentative conclusions may be drawn at this stage, on the basis of these observations.

1   The Melchizedek episode bears all the signs of a passage inserted into a previously existing narrative. It breaks into a connected account, with no apparent links beyond the form of reference to God in Abram's oath (v. 22; cf.v. 19), and introduces a cultic religious theme quite absent from the story otherwise.

2   The formality of the first eleven verses (use of lists, explanatory notes, interest in dates and battles) indicates that, however it has now been worked into the story of Abram and his family, this material originates in a quite different context.

• 3   V. 12 looks suspiciously like a bridging verse designed to convert an impersonal campaign account into a family saga.

4   The role of Mamre, Aner and Eshcol in the story is a very strange one, for they play no active part in the events, but are the only individuals who are rewarded in the end. We might surmise either that they represent an alternative tradition which has been overwhelmed by the final form of the narrative, or that their presence is redactionally related to references elsewhere in Genesis to Abram's dwelling at Mamre (cf. 13.18; 18.1).

We are in a position now to return to the task of *form criticism*. Characteristic patterns or formulas have been noted above ('Characteristic language'). They suggest strongly a number of conclusions.

(1)   Vv. 1–11 are essentially in the form of a campaign chronicle, a familiar historical mode in the ancient Near East. However, this had been broken in two obvious ways: the present narrative is third-person, where such a chronicle would more likely be first; and the brief passage of vivid circumstantial detail in v. 10 (again untypical of the formality of the chronicle) is an integral element in the story before us, showing that the present account is more likely to be an original narrative modelled on an ancient form than a genuinely ancient chronicle adapted for later use. This conclusion is further supported by the lack of historical or archaeological support for the passage. We might then not unreasonably classify the form as historical fiction, with a deliberate element of archaizing in the use of familiar names with explanatory notes ('that is . . .').

(2)   If this analysis is correct, then v. 12 must be reassessed as a necessary part of the original narrative: it was evidently within the author's intention to create a story in which Abram figured aa a victorious military man, and the traditional association of Lot with Sodom and Gomorrah provided an excellent hook on which to hang this theme. Thus vv. 10 and 12, though apparently out of

accord with the form which provides the *model* for the chapter, are in fact the key to our understanding of the form now before us: a short tale concerning 'the further adventures of Abram the patriarch'.

(3)   The form of vv. 17, 21–4 could be described as heroic legend: the hero Abram outfaces the king of Sodom and demonstrates, almost casually, his vast superiority to that unfortunate monarch. The passage depends on the oath, and it would be unusual to omit the divine reference. Moreover, the introduction of 'the Lord God Most High, maker of heaven and earth' as Abram's only superior emphasizes still more the distance between the hero and the king. Thus it appears likely that the reference to the deity is original to the primary text of the chapter.

(4)   In terms of form, everything indicates that vv. 18–20 are a later interpolation. The only other place where Melchizedek appears is in Psalm 110.4, with reference to King David. The theme of kingship recurs throughout the chapter. Abram, never labelled 'king', is compared with those who are. It seems likely that the interpolation is made, using Psalm 110, to develop this kingship theme one stage further, elevating Abram (and through him the priest-king leaders of Israel at a later date) to a form of kingship peculiar to Israel and closer to that of the divine monarch himself. Thus the Melchizedek episode, using symbols of bread and wine, and constructing a blessing round the events of the chapter and the language of v. 22, is a cultic legend and blessing subsequent to the chapter as a whole, but developing its central theme in a theologically satisfying manner.

How has chapter 14 been merged with the remainder of the story of Abram (*redaction criticism*)? We note first that the reference to Lot and Sodom assumes the reader's knowledge of the more substantial traditions about Lot. Since these are central to the whole thrust of the narrative in chapter 14, we cannot assume that a separate story was later absorbed into the Abram traditions using Lot as a redactional device. Rather, it would appear that Genesis 14 was deliberately constructed to be included with what already existed. Its position *after* the separation of Lot and Abram, but *before* the disastrous events of chapter 19, is chronologically appropriate. We can go further, and suggest that the placing of this chapter just before chapter 15 might be justified by a reference at the beginning of that chapter: 'But Abram said, "O Lord GOD, what wilt thou give me, for I continue childless, and the heir of my house is Eliezer of Damascus?"' (15.2). Though there is some dispute about the precise form of the Hebrew text here, the connection made between Abram and Damascus is curiously echoed in the reference to Damascus in 14.15, and perhaps helped to suggest the most natural place to insert the additional material.

Secondly, we note that the matter of Mamre, Aner and Eschol is unresolved. A brief treatment cannot hope to dispose of this strange affair; it might be sufficient to suggest that, in view of the reference to Abram's dwelling at the oaks of Mamre (13.18), a subsequent writer has 'improved' the story by making this further connection between chapter 14 and the rest of the traditions. Finally, the Melchizedek incident was included in the only possible place, given that by the end of the chapter Abram has no booty left to tithe!

This analysis helps us to understand how the Torah text reached its fixed form. This task is not just an academic exercise. If properly (and modestly) done, it can aid us in our primary task of understanding the ancient text.

Story

Our first introduction to the Hebrew Bible is through stories – the Garden of Eden, Noah, Abraham's family and Joseph being among the best known. The storyteller's primary concern is to communicate in an entertaining and memorable way. The question of the historical accuracy of the stories is a separate one, which has been discussed earlier in this chapter. Interesting though historical questions are, they do not exhaust the possibilities for interpretation of the text as it now stands.

When we take this position, it is less relevant to ask 'When did this happen?' or 'Where did it take place?' The questions with which we need to concern ourselves are 'Why is this story told at this point?' and 'What is the significance of this form of language, of that turn of phrase?' We might decide that the meaning of a text is intimately related to the person who wrote it, so that the author's feelings, context and specific intentions are all vital ingredients in the text's meaning. This is at first sight an attractive hypothesis. Undoubtedly authors intend certain meanings, stemming from their personal experience and psychology. However, it is not at all clear that the author of a text which has lasting value determines its meaning in more than a preliminary sense. We gain things from Shakespeare that he can hardly have intended. In addition, the notion that we can adequately understand the motivations and experiences that lead an author to write in a particular way is quite unrealistic. Most of the time we cannot even understand our own motivations. To make the interpretation of a text depend on such an insecure basis is effectively to make it meaningless. Finally, for a great many important texts from antiquity we have no secure knowledge of authorship, or at most a mere name to which we can attach no further information. Are we to take it therefore that such texts are closed to us?

What has emerged in literary criticism since 1945 has been a much increased awareness of the importance of the text itself. It has been recognized that, however interesting may be the identity of authors or the process of composition, in the end we are confronted with the text itself and the need to understand it. This has clear implications for the Bible, whose authorship is effectively anonymous, and whose significance is widely held to be inherent to the book itself.

Rhetorical Criticism

Although distance in time, place and language makes the task more difficult, we can approach the biblical text as we would any piece of modern creative writing. This kind of literary criticism has very fluid guidelines: it is not a science with clear rules and predictable outcomes. Those who have written on the subject are clear on this point: what they offer are the strategies by means of which individual readers may become skilled in the art of subtle or 'close' reading.

Two general stages may be recognized. The first is deciding the extent of a unit of text. This is less obvious than it might appear on the surface. The books of the Bible are by no means always well-defined units. The book and chapter divisions with which we are familiar are not original to the text, and indeed vary depending on the tradition to which a translation belongs. Some books require to be subdivided to make narrative sense; others look as if they are the separated parts of a once-continuous narrative. There are persuasive reasons, for example, for taking the Joseph story in Genesis 37–50 as a unit for the purposes of rhetorical criticism; Genesis 5 seems to resume the story of creation in the form and language of chapters 1–2.3, with 2.4–4.26 having the appearance of a narrative from a different hand. On a larger scale, what is the extent of the complete work? The five books of Torah? Genesis–Joshua, or even Genesis–2 Kings?

The second and more challenging stage is a detailed analysis of the unit from the point of view of such features as plot and general structure, motif, keywords, stylistic devices and figures of speech. Literary or rhetorical criticism has the task of investigating how 'story' in general and Hebrew story in particular creates its effects. Events or incidents are reported in such a way as to convey a sense of reality (*mimesis*). It must immediately be clear that this is done by means of literary devices which need not represent reality literally. Thus, when we read, 'and God said, "Let the earth bring forth living creatures according to their kinds: cattle and creeping things and beasts of the earth according to their kinds." And it was so' (Gen 1.24), the mimetic effect of what is written makes the story more vivid, but does not require us to accept at face value the suggestion of an instantaneous creation of the world's fauna. Mimetic effect is only a means to an end – the means by which our interest is attracted so that we may then register the various and subtle devices used to convey meaning. We shall misunderstand the biblical writers if we remain oblivious to their literary artistry, their metaphors, irony and wordplay.

There are a number of special characteristics of Hebrew narrative that need to be considered if we are to overcome the gap that separates us from these ancient texts.

Fictionalized History

The genre we are dealing with is neither pure fiction nor pure history. R. Alter (1981, 24) speaks of 'historicized prose fiction', a description which seems particularly well-suited to the narrative portions of the Pentateuch. Even later books such as Kings, which are closer to the events that they describe, tell a theological story.

We could perhaps speak of 'fictionalized history'. This is not to discredit the writers. Both descriptions seek above all to encapsulate the recognition that what we have in the narrative sections of the Bible is prose which has been constructed with great skill and subtlety, demanding of the reader a similar subtlety of interpretation in response. The Torah contains powerful stories. They are in another sense historical sources, giving us information about the writers' time.

Episodic Character

Unlike the extended epics of other societies, biblical stories are characteristically short, almost laconic in their lack of detail and their elaboration, and frequently disconnected from their immediate context. Longer works, such as the patriarchal traditions in Genesis 12–50, give the appearance of a number of short episodes strung together. The episodes have been put together deliberately by a writer or writers, for a particular purpose; but, unlike a modern novel (or history book), they do not obtain their final effect from a sustained development of plot and character. Indeed, *character* itself is not fixed, but is allowed to change as the narrative develops – to the extent that it might well be said that the events of the narrative create the character which emerges gradually.

Genesis has a framework within which individual episodes are included and the various characterizations explored. Questions can be raised about this framework: did the final writer invent it, or use one already traditional? Even if a traditional framework was used, why did it develop in the way that it did? Some scholars assume (J Bright, 1981) that to some degree events were accurately remembered; others (Noth, 1960; Thompson, 1987) that the narrative framework was *created* to fulfil a particular theological or sociological function. Take, for example, the twelve sons of Jacob, who in Genesis 32–50 give rise to the twelve tribes of Israel. Is there, underlying this, a *recollection* of an actual family, actual ancestors who gave their names (as *eponyms*) to later tribes? Or did the later tribes assume that such people must have existed? Could the narrative of their family relationships, and the genealogies which stem from these stories, have been deliberate political fiction to underline national unity, at the instigation perhaps of a monarch for whom unity was vital? If so, our basic paradigm (that is, our set of assumptions) has shifted – from the assumption that the stories reflect the period they purport to describe, to one in which they reflect the period of their creators. The stories may thus uncover struggles for status between tribes (the 'slave-girl' tribes?); or there may have been folktales about particular tribes working together (as Levi and Simeon did in defeating Shechem in Genesis 34). Thus we may be asking literary questions about several periods at once – earlier traditions, and a final writer who built these earlier episodes into his work, perhaps in the process modifying what the tradition actually said. Often the truth is hard to untangle.

In Genesis 18, Moab and Ben-ammi, eponymous ancestors of the Moabites and the Ammonites (so often in conflict with Israel) are conceived after incestuous relationships between a drunken Lot and his two daughters. The incident is full of humour – but who first perpetuated such scurrilous libel, and what did they mean by admitting *kinship* with their enemies?

Dialogue

This is a remarkably dominant feature of Hebrew prose, with much of the action and comment that we may expect from third-person narrative being presented through the words of characters in the story. Language is in the main formal, lacking in idiosyncratic detail to distinguish characters. Instead, individuals are defined by means of contrasts, and by what they say and do not say. The normal convention is to limit scenes to two characters or groups of characters, so that their differences are presented very clearly. A neat example of this may be found in the conversation between Abraham and God in Genesis 18.23–33 about the fate of Sodom and Gomorrah. The language is formulaic in the extreme, full of repetitions, yet conveys to us strikingly the contrast between Abraham arguing voluably and excitedly for the reprieve of Sodom, about to be destroyed by God for sin, with God responding as briefly as possible, quite clearly humouring Abraham although knowing full well the outcome of the argument.

Repetition

This leads to what must be one of the most puzzling and yet most pervasive aspects of biblical prose: the extensive use of repetitions. It was common in the past to regard repetitions as evidence either of a primitive style of com-position (directly indebted to cultic or oral models) or of the composite nature of the text – each different occurrence of the words in question had to be from a different source. We cannot dismiss this possibility completely, but the phenomenon is so ubiquitous that it is hard to believe that it is not deliberate. In the Joseph story, for example, though Pharaoh's dreams are described in full twice in Genesis 41, and referred to a third time, the repeti-tions are not unimportant. For, when Joseph, fresh from prison and facing the test of his ability to interpret a dream, stands before Pharaoh, we are reminded (while the king recounts his vision) of the different fates of the butler and the baker in chapter 41, and of Joseph's own chequered career (including his own ill-fated dreams about his brothers). Much hangs on this incident, and it is a sign of the writer's artistry, not his pedantry or his dependence on earlier sources, that he chooses this moment to keep us waiting in suspense, and does so precisely by focusing our attention on a central motif of the story: the role of dreams.

Repetitions can take several forms (see Alter, 1981, 95–7):

Keyword. A particular word or group of words is explored in various forms throughout a text. A striking example is the use of 'earth' (*erets*), 'ground' (*adamah*) and 'dust' (*'aphar*) in Genesis 1–3, with the pun on the name Adam ('man', created 'out of the ground') and the fate of humans to return to the dust from which they came (2.7). In fact, a close reading of the text might even suggest that it is the rela-tionship between humankind and the earth which is one of the central concerns of the creation stories – a conclusion which has obvious significance for contemporary society faced with an ecological crisis.

Motif. A particular image, action or object which recurs in the course of a narrative: for example, the significant role of personal garments or possessions in the Joseph story.

Theme. An idea which forms part of the purpose of the narrative, giving it shape and meaning, and is repeated in various ways through the story. With the patriarchal narratives a very clear example is the repetition, in different forms, of the promise to Abraham, Isaac and Jacob of land, descendants and blessing. We can extend this theme back into the primeval history in Genesis 1–11 by recognizing the same promises to humankind in chapter 1 and to Noah in chapter 9.

Repeated Action. A phenomenon which belongs to originally to the folktale genre. In the classic folktale pattern a sequence is usually repeated three times, with sometimes a fourth and climactic occur-rence. This precise scheme is not obviously present in Genesis–except, perhaps, in the three stories of a patriarch passing off his wife as his sister (Gen 12, 20 and 26). Whatever the original intention of the earliest version of the story, the cumulative effect is in the direction of an increasing moral and ultimately innocent presentation of the patriarch.

Phraseology. Very often in biblical stories we find, within a rather shorter sequence, several occurrences of the same or very similar phrases, perhaps spoken by different characters, or recorded by the narrator, in which small changes of nuance carry a considerable weight of narrative development. There is a fine example of this process in Genesis 2–3, in which the drama of Adam and Eve, the serpent and the tree, and the instructions of God is presented with repeated reference to the tree, its properties and God's wishes on the subject.

Type Scenes. Alter was struck by the recurrence of a number of scenes and plots, and regarded them as a literary convention. For example, Isaac, Jacob and Moses all meet their future wife at a well and then rush off to her parents to seek their consent to a betrothal. Alter further identified in the Hebrew Bible examples such as the annunciation of a hero's birth to a barren mother (e.g. the birth of Isaac), the epiphany in the field (Abraham, Jacob, Moses), danger in the desert associated with discovery of a well or other source of sustenance (Gen 26), and the testament of the dying hero (Gen 49; Deut 33). In biblical narratives, such stereotyped scenes are given a twist or an unusual feature which, by breaking the standard form, attracts the reader's attention. Perhaps the analogy with *parody*, where the conventional form is given a startling meaning, may be helpful.

Interpreting the Story. Genesis 14: the Battle of the Kings

In this section we shall apply to Genesis 14 the strategies set out above. It is clear that the chapter forms a unit. It has no integral connections with the chapters before or following, and has long been recognized as a kind of 'erratic' block of material which intrudes somewhat awkwardly into the main body of the Abraham story. The chapter itself consists of a number of episodes quite briefly described, yet the overall effect is powerful. For, even though questions have been raised about the unity of the chapter, in its final form it communicates effectively a portrait of Abraham as a warrior chief, on more than equal terms with the great kings of his age, and favoured by a very special relationship with God: in short, a picture of Abraham the priest-king.

The final picture owes much of the use of *contrast*: the ineffectual valley kings, some of whose followers fall into bitumen pits (v. 10), are juxtaposed with Abram and his picked band of 318 men routing the invaders (v. 15); the hapless Lot (v. 12) is rescued by a triumphant Abram (v. 16); the mighty emperors from the east with their long catalogue of successes (vv. 1, 5–12) are humbled by Abram's tiny guerrilla force (vv. 14–15); the king of Sodom's indecent eagerness to get down to practical matters (v. 21) contrasts with Abram's high-minded devotion to God (vv. 22–4); and, finally, only Abram of all the combatants has any experience of God or uses his name.

Dialogue is, untypically, not a major feature of this narrative. Nevertheless it does display some typical features. Thus, though there is no idiomatic speech, the different characters are sharply distinguished: Melchizedek speaks in formal poetic/cultic phrases; the king of Sodom is terse to the point of rudeness (in the Hebrew, the imperative forms of the verbs are remarkably short) and we are given the strong impression that his only interest is to settle the practical matters and get rid of Abram as soon as possible; and Abram expresses himself in mature, thoughtful, considered tones – he is obviously master of the situation in his dealings with both Melchizedek and the king of Sodom. The use of dialogue to convey information about character and events can also be seen in what Abram says: the reference to the vow tells us something about which we were previously in the dark; and the concluding part of v. 23 – 'lest you should say, "I have made Abram rich"' – adds to what we have already discerned as the materialistic character of the king of Sodom, and stresses Abram's independence as an agent free from all *human* constraints.

We turn now to the study of *repetition* in Genesis 14. Motifs which may be recognized are the association of a valley with kings (vv. 2–3, 8, 10, 17); lists of names (vv. 1, 2, 5–7, 8, 9, 13, 24); an interest in dates and numbers (vv. 1, 4, 5, 9, 14, 20); and the movement of booty (vv. 11, 12, 16, 21). The chapter is more than usually replete with repetition, revealing a highly formalized narrative style.

The important *themes* are (1) the meeting in highly charged circumstances of various protagonists – the two sets of kings (vv. 3, 8f), the refugee with Abram (v. 13), Abram with the king of Sodom (vv. 17, 21ff), and Abram with Melchizedek (v. 18); and (2) the routing of enemies (vv. 5f, 7, 10f, 15, 17). It is through these two themes that the central message of the narrative is conveyed.

There are a number of repeated phrases: (1) the formula 'that is . . . ' (vv. 2, 3, 7, 8, 17); (2) 'God Most High' (vv. 18, 19, 20, 22); and (3) 'maker of heaven and earth' (vv. 19, 22); and (4) words to the effect 'the enemy took the goods and went their way' (vv. 11, 12; cf. 16). The chapter also contains a very high proportion of *keywords* which contribute to the meaning of the story. Most obvious is the frequency of the word for 'king' (*melek*) – twenty-six occurrences. There can be no doubt that kingship is a central concern – yet the one who emerges as most king-like in character is in fact the only leading actor who is *not* described as king in the text. There is cunning artistry at work here: the sheer volume of repetition of the title (and the actions with which it is associated) diminishes our respect for the people who bear it (Melchizedek is a special case) and leaves us fully persuaded of Abram's unexpressed but clear claim to be the only one worthy to be king.

Other keywords support this central thesis. The verb 'serve' (*'abad*) is used twice; once (v. 4) to describe the relationship of the valley kings to Chedorlaomer and his allies prior to their revolt, and later (v. 15) with reference to Abram's followers with whom he defeated the latter: here again, Abram is supreme over *both* sets of kings (having defeated the alliance which earlier subdued Sodom)! 'To smite' (*nakah*) is used twice of Chedorlaomer's defeat of the nations (vv. 5, 7), and twice of Abram's defeat of him in turn (vv. 15, 17). We might also note play on the words for 'take' and 'give'. Whereas Chedorlaomer and his allies are shown to take what is not theirs (vv. 11, 12), Abram refuses to take anything except that which is to be returned to others (vv. 23, 24). And, whereas God gives Abram's enemies into his hand, and Abram gives (not the same word in Hebrew) tithes to Melchizedek (v. 20), the king of Sodom issues orders: 'Give me', 'take' (v. 21).

One other, more complex keyword pattern merits attention. The chapter contains seven verbs of motion, with a total of eighteen occurrences spread evenly through the narrative. They create, in broad terms, a clear contrast between the two sections (vv. 1–12 and vv. 13–24), a contrast which is fully supported by an analysis of the particular relationships at work. In the first section all of these verbs deal with the victorious campaign of the eastern alliance (vv. 5, 7, 8, 10, 11, 12); in the second section they are associated with Abram's ascendancy (vv. 13, 14, 15, 16, 17, 18, 24).

One of these verbs, *yatsa'*, is specifically connected with the three major encounters in the narrative: 'the king of Sodom . . . *went out*, and they joined battle' (v. 8); 'the king of Sodom *went out* to meet [Abram]' (v. 17); on his meeting with Abram 'Melchizedek . . . *brought out* [a causative form of the same verb] bread and wine'. It thus acts as a positive bridge between the two parts – we have already noted the theme of encounters as a major one in the chapter. The other verbs all set up significant contrasts (with the exception of the first example, the verb in each part of the contrast is the same). The king of Sodom and his allies flee and fall (v. 10) in the face of Chedorlaomer; Abram goes in pursuit (vv. 14, 15). Chedorlaomer comes to Canaan (vv. 5, 7); a fugitive comes to Abram (v. 13). Chedorlaomer turns back in the direction of his rebellious vassals (v. 7); Abram brings back the booty (v. 16) and returns from defeating the alliance (v. 17). Finally, Chedorlaomer goes off with Abram's nephew and the people of the valley (vv. 11, 12), whereas Abram's men go with him (v. 24). What all this reveals is how the writer breaks up the monolithic power of the eastern kings, who are the main subject of the first section, through the three subjects of the second section – the fugitive, Abram, and his men. Yet at the same time Abram is given the central role. Thus the isolated, intrusive, illegitimate power of the eastern kings gives way to the integrated, socially responsible and legitimate power of Abram (validated by none other than God himself).

A brief mention of *type scenes* will lead to our concluding remarks on this fascinating episode. There are two scenes which might appropriately be described thus: the account of the invasion (vv. 1–12) and the encounter with Melchizedek. The first has some of the characteristics of a military chronicle of the kind known from great rulers of the ancient world; but it has been sufficiently altered to alert the reader to its special function. Thus, it is in the third rather than the expected first person, and, whereas there would normally be little concern for individual victims, we find Lot introduced in such a way as to switch the emphasis from royal chronicle to patriarchal saga. The other type scene belongs to the realm of the cult, the blessing of the king by a temple priest. It is presented as the performance of a mysterious sacramental rite by a priest-king with no known antecedents, and the subject is Abram the patriarch, rather than the king. Once again the reader is alerted to the fact that something unusual is afoot.

In conclusion, though this analysis has of necessity been brief, it demonstrates the kind of information that a rhetorical-critical reading can produce. What seems on the surface to be an inappropriate intrusion into the patriarchal saga is revealed as a carefully wrought presentation of the founding father of Israel as king and priest, favoured alike by God and humankind, vastly superior to the most impressive of secular forces, yet humble in his service of God. It is *this* man who will, in the very next chapter, be given that special covenant which is for ever to define the relationship of God to the people of Israel.

Myth in Genesis 1–11

It is impossible to read through the first eleven chapters of Genesis without becoming aware that they are very different in character from the rest of the book. The claim of historicity is particularly difficult to sustain – the themes treated are often described as *primeval*, belonging to that mysterious 'time before recorded time' when wonders happened in the world. Yet, as is evident from the heated and extensive controversy to which they have contributed, these chapters handle matters of importance. In our efforts to understand biblical narrative as story we have stressed the importance of the form of the narrative and the techniques used to present it. The study of Genesis 1–11 must take note of another factor: the demands made on the form of narrative by the nature of what is to be communicated. The issues involved are deeply serious, and outside the scope of normal historical discourse. How was the world created? Why are humans as they are? Where did evil and death come from? What are the origins of the immense diversity in human race and language? Does sin result in punishment? What is the relationship between the gods and humankind?

These questions are not unique to the Hebrew Bible. Anthropological studies of human societies in widely differing times and places have revealed the universal nature of these fundamental issues. They have also revealed a human tendency to give expression in the form of stories to questions of ultimate meaning, about deity, about creation, and about humanity. The term used to describe such stories is 'myth'.

Unfortunately the word 'myth' is popularly used to mean something false or misconceived, which devalues the stories thus denoted. There is no doubt that this contributes to a certain amount of ambiguity and confusion, but there is not really a satisfactory alternative term. We are not, in the Hebrew Bible, dealing with 'raw' myth. Genesis 1–11 as a completed text was deliberately shaped by the author as an elaborate and structurally complex introduction to the books which follow. Therefore its use of myth is always secondary to its anthropological and theological purpose: an account of how the present condition of humankind came about and an elucidation of the first stages of the great plan of God's salvation for fallen humanity (often referred to in technical terms as 'salvation history'. This is worked out in three cycles, each focusing on one major mythic theme: the *creation*, the *flood*, and the *Tower of Babel*.

The Creation Myth

Critical studies of Genesis 1–3 suggest that two separate literary traditions lie behind the creation stories: the 'Priestly' narrative in 1.1–2.4a and the 'Yahwistic' account in 2.4b–3.24. Differences in the order of events, serious incompatibilities as to the relationships between men, women and the animal world, and radically different styles, vocabulary and structure show that the narrator of the complex whole was primarily concerned not with history or scientific fact but with inner truths. Therefore, when we observe that well-known ancient Near Eastern mythic themes have been woven into this fabric, we are alerted to two equal and opposite errors: on the one hand, the error of dismissing of these texts as ancient, pre-scientific myth of merely antiquarian interest; and, on the other, the folly of attempting to claim objective, historical realism for accounts that were never conceived in such terms. The 'creationist debate' which has spawned lawsuits in the United States is not just obscurantist: it is *and always was* quite irrelevant to the Bible. The concept of creation by a God or gods is virtually universal to the human race and is certainly not confined only to the Bible.

Among the themes that Genesis shares with other Near Eastern myths we can see the following. The primeval watery waste from which the world is created has parallels in Egypt (Beyerlin, 1978, 3) and in the Akkadian *Enuma Elish* (O'Brien and Major, 1982, 16). The Hebrew word for 'the deep', *tehom*, is etymologically related to the dragon Tiamat in *Enuma Elish*, whose slain body is split to form the heavens and the earth. The separation of the waters in Genesis 1.6 echoes the Mesopotamian myth. The story in *Atrahasis* (O'Brien and Major, 1982, 82ff) of the creation of human beings from a mixture of clay and the blood of a god may stand behind the account in Genesis 2.7 of the creation of man from the ground with the life-giving breath of God. The extended myth of the Garden of Eden, with its hint at the possibility of eternal life, and the underlying stratum dealing with the loss of sexual innocence and the unfortunate effects of being civilized (that is, 'knowing good and evil'), has significant parallels in the *Epic of Gilgamesh* (Sandars, 1972).

These themes belong to the natural metaphoric and explanatory stock-in-trade of the world of the writer's time and are used partly with the direct intention of substituting the God of Israel and his story for the claims of other gods and other myths. It is therefore of prime importance for the understanding of Genesis 1–11 that we are alert to the larger purpose of the author in basing the account on traditional material.

The Great Flood

Stories of a great flood are widespread in human myths and legends: the Babylonian flood story featuring Utnapishtim which is contained in the *Epic of Gilgamesh*, the Greek flood tradition associated with Deucalion, and legends from many other parts of the world all testify to the popularity of this myth (Keller, 1980, 43–58; Beyerlin, 1978, 89–97). Although it is possible that these flood stories reflect a world catastrophe, such as the end of an Ice Age (Keller, 1980, 43), there are really no grounds for arguing from archaeological evidence of *local* flooding to the historicity of *universal* flood legends. The most we can usefully say is that the experience of floods is within human experience and comprehension and that this contributed to stories of a universal flood.

Originally a separate myth but now presented as part of the reason for the flood is the strange episode in Genesis 6.1–4 when the sons of God (or of the gods) couple with human women. The beginning of the passage, which clearly introduces the whole flood narrative, closely resembles the corresponding text in the Atrahasis epic: 'The land became great, the people multiplied . . .' (*ANET* 104). Stories of the birth of heroes as a result of the intercourse of gods w: h human women are commonplace in the Greek tradition. At another level the myth is one of rebellious gods reduced in status. Psalm 82.6 speaks of God's judgement on the 'gods'. This suggests that the story is also designed to reduce in status the council of the gods (sons of God) which surrounds Yahweh in popular theology (Job 1.6; 2.1; 38.7; 1 Kgs 22.19–23) and which derives from the Canaanite pantheon headed by El. These elements are no longer primary: the passage has a rather different function in the final form of the text, reducing the span of human life to a mere 120 years (Gen 6.3).

The Tower of Babel

The myth of the Tower of Babel shows people deciding to build a tower to heaven to make a name for themselves. At this stage humankind has one common, simple language. Building the tower is a test of solidarity and co-operation, to prevent social break-up and therefore dispersion. God sees this co-operative enterprise as a threat: 'nothing that they propose to do will now be impossible for them' (Gen 11.6). The confusion of their language is his effective response.

It has often been remarked that the Tower of Babel recalls the ziggurats of Mesopotamia, which in turn were a cultic representation of the sacred mountain. The story may now be indicating that the ziggurat is not a legitimate shrine. Close parallels to the story are lacking in the ancient Near East, though its themes can be traced, often linked with flood stories (Westermann, 1984, 537–8). Once again we must stress that these echoes and parallels are no more than a background to the main thrust of the mythic narrative of Genesis 1–11. It is to that central structure that we now turn.

The Structure of Genesis 1–11

The myths of Genesis 1–11 have been woven into a sophisticated narrative in which key theological questions are raised. The chapters develop the myth of salvation history (*Heilsgeschichte*: the story of a God who has great plans for the creation and who reveals these plans gradually but irresistibly through the events of human experience). It is in Genesis 1–11 that the need for salvation history is established (the myth of the fall) and its mechanism defined: the choice, by God, of a faithful remnant and the sealing of that choice by means of a covenant (the myth of the flood). This provides a basis for the patriarchal narratives which follow. In interpreting these stories from an apparently historical world, we must take with us the essentially ahistorical nature of the theological truths which the primeval narrative has established. The stories, whether primeval or patriarchal, describe *our* condition, not that of some hypothetical original ancestor. In the myth of the fall (Gen 3) it is *we* who experience failure to reach the ideal. It is *our* hope which is given expression in the assurance of a faithful survivor of the flood: despite all appearances to the contrary, we may be optimistic about the ultimate bridging of that gap between the actual and the desirable, the real and the ideal.

We noted above that the final form of Genesis is viewed as the work of the Priestly Writer: his style can be seen in the formula 'these are the generations [*toledoth*] of '. When the formula is used it normally introduces information about the *descendants* of the individual named. In Genesis 37.2 it can be translated, 'this is the history of the family of Jacob', and introduces the story of Joseph and his brothers. In Genesis 1–11, there are seven instances of *toledoth*. Three of these (in 10.1, 32; 11.10) refer to the same generation: thus we have five stages in our narrative. The first use of the formula is in 2.4: 'These are the generations of the heavens and the earth when they were created.' In view of the consistent use elsewhere, it seems appropriate to regard this also as *introducing* what follows, rather than (as is commonly claimed) summing up what precedes. The other natural breaks are to be found in 5.1 ('the generations of Adam'), 6.9 ('the generations of Noah'), 10.1 ('the generations of the sons of Noah') and 11.27 ('the generations of Terah'). This provides a structure for the story of humanity's gradual debasement, involving the breakdown of relationships between individuals and between humanity and the earth. This debasement is seen as a consequence of failed attempts to usurp the place of God. At the same time a thread of hope develops towards its final blossoming – the promise of God's saving activity in 'history'. Winding through this is a refrain concerning the relationship between humanity and the earth, from which the first of the species was drawn and to which we must all return. The first creation story, in 1.1–2.3, and the call of Abram, in 11.27–12.4, frame and bracket this pattern and so prevent it from being merely an endless and unbreakable cycle.

The detail of this structure is set out below.

Original Creation (1.1–2.3)

Perfect harmony; everything is for the best in the best of all possible worlds ('God saw everything that he had made and behold, it was very good' – 1.31), yet we know that this is a delusion. Reality awaits just around the corner.

Creation Corrupted (2.4–11.26)

See table 4.2.

Table 4.2   Creation Corrupted (2.4–11.26)

Chapter, verse	The sin	The loss	Hope	The land
2.4–4.26	WILL: disobedience to be like God, knowing good and evil	Break in relationship between God and humankind	The name Yahweh is known (4.26)	'Cursed is the ground' (3.17)
5.1–6.4	FLESH: intercourse between gods and women	Break between men and women; shortening of life	A man (Enoch) walks with Yahweh	Reversal of the curse (5.29)
6.5–9.29	MIND: God replaced by unrestricted human imagination	Break between humankind and animals (fear introduced – 9.2)	The Noahic covenant is established (9.8–17)	Curse no more (8.21), blessing (8.22)
10.1–11.26	SPIRIT: humankind aspires to take over God's realm	Complete breakdown of all human communications	Fulfilment of the word to Noah – 'be fruitful'	Confusion over all the earth

Creation Restored (11.27–12.3)

The various failures described in 2.4–11.26, with its four stages, have gradually distanced humanity as a whole from God; but a contrary theme has seen a chosen vehicle for salvation gradually distinguished:

all humanity (Adam) → Noah's family → Shem's family → Abram

With the introduction of Abram we leave the primeval narrative and enter the 'history of Israel', in which a new people is created through a man of faith (15.6), a nation which will be great, will possess its own land, and will be a source of blessing for all the earth (12.1–3).

Myth? or history? or neither? The analysis which we have carried out for Genesis 1–11 demonstrates that these questions cannot be simply answered.

Certainly the narrative contains myths, and is mythic in scope; but it is closely linked with the 'historicized fiction' (or fictionalized history) which follows. Ultimately the meaning and meaningfulness of the text lie in the theology the author develops of the relationship between God and humankind.

FURTHER READING

Alter, R. 1981: *The Art of Biblical Narrative.*
Berlin, A. 1983: *Poetics and Interpretation of Biblical Narrative.*
Kirkpatrick, P. G. 1988: *The Old Testament and Folklore Study.*
Ramsey, G. W. 1981: *The Quest for the Historical Israel: Reconstructing Israel's Early History.*
Seters, J. van 1975: *Abraham in History and Tradition.*
Thompson, T. L. 1974: *The Historicity of the Patriarchal Narratives: the Quest for the Historical Abraham.*
Westermann, C. 1984: *Genesis 1–11.*
Whybray, R. N. 1983: *The Making of the Pentateuch.*

5

Moses

Stephen Bigger

Preliminary Reading   Exodus; Numbers; Deuteronomy.

The story of the exodus from Egypt, with its central character Moses, has been remembered, repeated and celebrated for almost three millennia. The story's themes have inspired profound reflection, particularly during during the Jewish festivals of Pesach (Passover), Shavuoth (Weeks) and Sukkoth (Tabernacles). In art and literature, Moses – prophet, deliverer, lawgiver, judge – speaks to generation after generation. The Hebrew Bible itself identifies Moses as prophet, man of God and servant of God (e.g. Hos 12.13; Num 12.7; Deut 18.18; 33.1; 34.10; Josh 14.6). The exodus themes create a vision of freedom from servitude (real or metaphorical), and explore the responsibilities this implies.

The story of Moses explains, verifies and reaffirms fundamental Jewish beliefs, in God, the covenant, the law and the land. Through Moses, God confirms his promise that the Israelites are 'a kingdom of priests and a holy nation' (Exod 19.6). The narrative provides Judaism with a *raison d'être* and a basis for future hope. On the slopes of Jebel Musa (the traditional site of Mount Sinai) St Catherine's Orthodox Christian monastery had a long history of worship and meditation. Muslims too honour Moses as Prophet Musa and regard the words revealed to him *then* as authentic revelation, but unfortunately, not accurately recorded. Alternative sites for Sinai have been suggested in volcanic regions of western Arabia, the focal point of Islamic revelation.

External Evidence

No direct evidence exists for the events in the Moses story, although our knowledge of affairs in Egypt is quite extensive. Herrmann (1973; 1975, 58f) shows that there were Semitic groups in Egypt from early times, some

in extensive settlements. He cites as an analogy a letter from a frontier
official reporting the arrival of some 'Shasu' tribesfolk from Edom who
sought permission to enter. The biblical Edom was south of Palestine. He
notes Helck's view that the Shasu were the southern equivalent of the *'prw*
(= *hapiru, habiru, ?*Hebrew) from Palestine and the north. The story relates
that the Hebrews worked on the 'store cities' Pithom and Raamses, the
latter suggesting Pharaoh Rameses of the Nineteenth Dynasty. A hypothesis
can be built (Herrmann 1975, 59) linking the Hebrew servitude with the
building of pr-Itm (Pithom) and a delta residence for Rameses' dynasty near
Tanis. The usual deduction is that the events took place at the end of the
thirteenth century BCE, with Rameses II (*c.*1304–1237 BCE) as the
oppressing pharaoh, and his successor Merniptah as the exodus pharaoh.
The name Israel appears on the Merniptah stele (*c.*1220 BCE; *ANET* 378),
which praises Pharaoh's victories for propaganda purposes. Israel (this is the
first historical reference) 'is laid waste, his seed is not'. The biblical account
places Israel in Egypt for 430 years (Exod 12.40f), although only four
generations elapsed (Gen 15.16). 1 Kgs 6.1 dates the exodus 480 years
before Solomon's temple, suggesting a date in the fifteenth century BCE.
This would place Joseph in the nineteenth century BCE – a time when
foreigners (Hyksos) took over the Egyptian throne.

Thus there is no compelling evidence that Moses existed or that the events
recorded in Exodus occurred. The only point of which we can be sure is that
the present literary version of the Moses story was written for reasons which
can be guessed and with concerns which can be seen in the texts. A great
deal requires explanation, so hypotheses are gradually refined to explain the
most and present the fewest problems. For J. Bright (1981, 122), the story
is so 'impressive' and the exodus theme 'so ancient and entrenched' that
there can be 'no explanation save that Israel actually escaped from Egypt to
the accompaniment of events so stupendous that they were impressed
forever on her memory'. Yet we can also view the material as the stuff
legends are made of: we could argue that 'anything said is largely guesswork'
and therefore 'decline any attempt to reconstruct the earliest history of the
Israelites' (Miller and Hayes, 1986, 78f). In an effort to explain the tensions
and incongruities in the present text, we could view the Moses narratives as
folk tradition (Hayes and Miller, 1977) or as a development of literary
sources through creative editors (Coats, 1988). The reader should be willing
to learn from each of these approaches – to appreciate what the final narrator
was trying to do; to understand what part earlier sources played and hence to
understand how the text reached its present form; and to understand that at
some stage the folk tradition may have been a significant factor. Although
we should be very cautious when attempting to reconstruct what actually
happened, we need to have an open mind about the possibility of success.

The Name Moses

A Hebrew etymology is given in Exod 2.10, noting that Moses (Hebrew *Mosheh*) was 'drawn forth' (*mashah*) from the water. The name Moses appears in many Egyptian names (Thutmoses, Ramoses, which mean 'Thoth is born','Ra is born'). Rameses means 'Ra bore him'. In Moses' case, the theophoric element (the name of the deity) has been omitted (Herrmann, 1973, 43–5).

Hypothetical Sources

Scholars have found it difficult to separate the strands of the J and E sources in Exodus. W. Rudolph denied the existence of E altogether; G. Fohrer proposed a nomadic source ('N'). G. W. Coats (1988) attributes a heroic view of Moses to the Yahwistic (J) redactor, often obscured by later redactors who downgraded Moses in order to emphasize Yahweh's saving power. The Priestly source (P) is often described as being intermeshed with earlier sources, sometimes flowing consistently like an independent source, sometimes seeming to have an editorial function. Some argue for a Deuteronomic redaction, and others deny it. Important studies (Noth, Zimmerli) suggest that P did not know the Sinai traditions; but others feel that such a conclusion is not necessary (Childs, 1979, 172-3). There is dispute too about the sources of the legal material (particularly Exodus 20–4 and 34 and Leviticus). As can be seen, the situation is very complex; the sources of Exodus have not been definitively explained.

Among the form critics, J. Pedersen's view of Exodus 1–15 as a cultic legend surrounding the Passover festival was influential. G. von Rad identified a number of liturgical formulas as belonging to two circles of early ceremonies, one based at Gilgal and the other (the Sinai tradition) at Shechem. On this view the narrative developed in the sanctuaries to accompany various festivities or ceremonies. This proved to be a useful model, although the subsequent debate also exposed its limitations.

The Message of Exodus

The exodus story depicts how the God of Israel, through Moses, fulfils his threefold promise to bring the Israelites out of bondage in Egypt, to take them to be his own people, and finally to bring them to the promised land which he will give them as a possession (Exod 6.6-8). Important themes are developed – the triumph of good over evil, and of freedom over bondage. In particular the narrative tells of a people special to God but unworthy, set apart to fulfil a particular destiny which brings with it solemn obligations (which are frequently ignored). (Literary analyses can be found in Childs, 1974; Coats, 1988; Gunn, 1982; Isbell, 1982; Nohrnberg, 1981; and Vater, 1982.)

The Birth and Upbringing of Moses (1.1–2.22)

The narrative opens with the birth of the deliverer, setting the scene for the story and opening up major themes. The situation into which the future deliverer is to be born is one of despair, with liberation a most unlikely prospect. The Hebrews are enslaved in appalling conditions, burdened with Pharaoh's projects. The keyword, often repeated, is '*ebed* (root '*bd*), 'slave'. Numerically, the Hebrews thrive; but any optimism this prompts is dashed by the administration's neurotic fear that the slaves will make war against them. Ironically, it is *because of* this fear that later on the slaves *do* make war – successfully, since their God fights for them (Exod 14.14, 25). The severity of the situation is marked by words such as 'ruthlessly' (twice; RSV 'with rigour'), 'bitter' and 'hard' (1.13–14). Another blow falls with Pharaoh's command to the two midwives, Shiphrah and Puah, to kill male Hebrews at birth. Slight hope is introduced as the courageous midwives subvert Pharaoh's intention and the Hebrews 'grew very strong': that hope is immediately dashed when Pharaoh commands 'all his people' to cast Hebrew newborn sons into the river, though the daughters are allowed to live. The evil persecution is institutionalized, exacted by the whole population of the oppressors. Two key themes are introduced here. The midwives *fear* their God, who rewards them with families. Their 'fear' of God – an important motif – contrasts with fear of Pharaoh, a temporal yet very dangerous 'god'. This is the beginning of the conflict between Yahweh and Pharaoh: God acts through those who fear him; Pharaoh acts through his people (cf. 14.10, 31).

When the birth of Moses is announced, the normally happy birth announcement now becomes a source of tension at the calamity which is about to fall. The birth of a son is not the blessing it usually is; hope instead comes through the *daughters*. The daughter of Levi ironically turns the tables on Pharaoh by obeying his order: when Moses can be hidden no longer, she casts her son into the river *in a basket*, so ensuring his survival. Her daughter Miriam keeps watch and negotiates for Moses' mother to become his nurse for a fee – and thus totally responsible for his early upbringing. Pharaoh's daughter adopts him, giving the future deliverer an Egyptian name, and bringing him up in the Egyptian court; but even the name is Hebraized and subverted. Yet the normally happy adoption formula 'and he became her son' marks another note of despair.

A key focus is water. Moses is said to be so named because he was drawn out (*mashah*) of the water. It is a common legendary motif that the life of a future leader is preserved in association with water. Sargon king of Akkad was saved from the river Tigris; Romulus and Remus were saved from the Tiber. The conflict between the Hebrew God and the Pharaoh takes place at the edge of (*'al sephath*) water throughout the story. The challenge to Pharaoh's authority represented by the plagues occurs 'at the edge of the river'. The central act of salvation, at the Sea of Reeds, takes place 'at the edge of the sea'. Water, with its dual capacity to bring life and to destroy, is in the hand of the God of Israel. God created order out of a watery chaos (Gen 1.1–5). The forces of chaos, represented here by Pharaoh, challenge God's authority at the edge of that water – and lose.

As Moses grows up, hope re-emerges – he has not changed sides. He opposes Egyptian oppression, and he *acts*. He recognizes the Hebrews as 'his people' (2.11). The fight which ends in the death of the brutal taskmaster is the first blow for freedom. The word 'smite' is next used of the ten 'smitings' (RSV 'plagues'), also a prelude to freedom; but the story dashes hope even before it can surface. The liberated Hebrew talks; two Hebrews reject Moses' intervention – 'Who made you a prince and a judge over us?' (2.14) – and he is afraid, his anti-Egyptian act now in the open. There is to be no quick resolution. The 'hero' flees into the desert, opting for a simple life shepherding in Midian. True, he remains a hero of sorts, *delivering* (a key term) seven *daughters* from oppression at the *hand* of some local shepherds. The 'hand' is used as a symbol of power – either the power to oppress, or the power to save. As the story develops, it is the hand of God which oppresses ('behold, the hand of Yahweh will fall with a very severe plague' – 9.3) or saves ('by strength of hand Yahweh brought you out from this place' – 13.3). The power of Moses' hand is not to be overestimated. He marries one of the 'daughters': he had been saved by 'daughters', and now he redefines his life in terms of 'daughters' – as a sojourner (*ger*) or resident stranger content to live away from his kin. His *son* Gershom symbolizes the abandonment of hope: the name is said to mean, 'I have been a sojourner in a foreign land' (2.22). In this story the birth of sons, usually a happy event, signals despair; the 'deliverer' has chosen to deliver someone else, somewhere else. The word 'deliver' is next used in 14.30, when God delivers the Hebrews from the hand of the Egyptians. The human deliverer was unworthy, and the people undeserving.

The king of Egypt dies; but the servitude has been fully institutionalized, and the Hebrews continue to groan under oppression under a new pharaoh. The word 'bondage' recurs. Hope returns through the compassion of God: he *hears* the Hebrews' cry, *remembers* his covenant, *sees* the people and *knows* their condition (2.24–5). Pharaoh, by contrast, fails to hear, since his heart has been hardened; he fails to remember past agreements ('Now there arose a new king over Egypt, who did not know Joseph' – 1.8); he fails to see the

Hebrews as people, as first the midwives and later Moses had done (1.16; 2.12); and he does not 'know', he has no understanding. The plagues are inflicted to give him this understanding (cf. 7.17; 8.10) but still he fails to perceive (14.5, 18).

Vocation Tales: Moses' Call at Horeb (3.1–4.31)

In this section, Moses' father-in-law is called 'Jethro, the priest of Midian', although he has already been introduced as Reuel (2.18). This has been taken to be a clear indication that different sources have been used. Moses is shepherd to Jethro's flock, which brings him westward to Horeb, 'the mountain of God'. The tending of flocks is a dominant motif in stories of people fulfilling a special religious role – Abraham, Isaac, Jacob, David and Amos among the ancient Hebrews, Muhammad in Islam. Shepherding involved long periods of solitary reflection which could lead to an acute awareness of the divine presence. It developed vigilance, resourcefulness and self-sufficiency – all vital leadership qualities. Moses' shepherd role prefigures his leadership of the Hebrews in the wilderness: he is not the military leader who leads them out of it. In a sense, the experience of Moses in the wilderness – his escape from Egypt, his life in the wilderness, his meeting with God at Horeb – parallels Israel's experience (see Nohrnberg, 1981, 40–2). Deuteronomy underlines this link by referring to Mount Sinai as 'Horeb' (5.2). Jeremiah uses a marriage motif – as Moses married Zipporah, so Israel married its God: 'I remember the devotion of your youth, your love as a bride, how you followed me in the wilderness, in a land not sown' (2.2).

Moses encounters God at 'the mountain of God'. Mountain sanctuaries were common throughout the ancient Near East, viewed as points closest to God. The ziggurat temples in the Tigris – Euphrates valley (the Tower of Babel in Genesis may have been the Babylon ziggurat) are generally interpreted as symbolic mountains. God's active presence can be more readily seen in a volcano: it is said that at Mount Sinai God 'descended upon it in fire; the smoke of it went up like the smoke of a kiln, and the whole mountain quaked greatly' (Exod 19.18). God's revelation to Moses is both visionary and auditory. He *sees* a bush burning but not consumed. He *hears* a voice inviting him to holy ground. Explanations of this event are usually psychological – although a bush with flame-like flowers is still grown in the Jebel Musa area.

The deity identifies himself as 'the God of your father' – specifically Amram (Exod 6.20), but through him 'of the Hebrews' (see 3.18). He is also the God (Elohim) of Abraham, Isaac and Jacob, linking this story with Genesis. The deliverance that has so far evaded the Hebrews is promised, and with it possession of 'a good and broad land, a land flowing with milk and honey' (3.8). Moses is commissioned to liberate the Hebrews. As a sign, 'you shall serve [root '*bd*] God upon this mountain' (v. 12). As a sign, the revelation at Sinai would come too late to convince either Pharaoh or the Hebrews, although it would lead the Hebrews to new understanding. It creates the link in the story between the two revelations. This passage looks back (to the patriarchs) and looks forward (to Sinai and the Promised Land) and is therefore pivotal.

In response to Moses' persistent objections of his inadequacy, the deity identifies himself in two ways. Moses is first told to say, 'I am [*ehyeh*] has sent me to you' (v.14); and, secondly, 'Yahweh [RSV "The LORD"], the God of your fathers, the God of Abraham, the God of Isaac, and the God of Jacob, has sent me to you: this is my name for ever, and thus I am to be remembered throughout all generations' (v. 15). The first appellation is mysterious but suggests that the name Yahweh was linked with the root *hyh*,'to be'. The second fits in well with the narrator's development of the story. The name Yahweh had been used by the patriarchs (e.g. Gen 15.2, 7f) and is now introduced to Moses. The Hebrews would depart for a new land 'flowing with milk and honey', but unfortunately occupied (Exod 3.17). The king of Egypt would be asked to release them to sacrifice to Yahweh in the wilderness. The story could, if it wished, build up the tension, keeping readers wondering if freedom would be achieved; but instead the outcome is made to appear inevitable. God has spoken and it will be done. The forthcoming plot is summarized with Yahweh's words: 'I know that the king of Egypt will not let you go unless compelled by a mighty hand. So I will stretch out my hand and smite Egypt with all the wonders which I will do in it; after that he will let you go' (vv. 19f).

The narrator heavily underscores Moses' ineptitude, with God's anger kindled because of his reluctance. The help of his brother Aaron would be sought. This downrating of Moses contrasts starkly with the powerful man who stands before Pharaoh: 'The man Moses was very great in the land of Egypt, in the sight of Pharaoh's servants and in the sight of the people' (11.3). The story reveals here that this power is an illusion: Moses' power stemmed from God; his wonders were God's wonders. There may well have been separate traditions: the hero Moses; and Yahweh's mighty acts. Yet in the present text they are held together in creative tension, carefully balancing each other and reminding the reader that Moses was great − but not that great.

Moses sets off, with Jethro's permission taking his wife and sons with him. They are not mentioned again in Egypt; but they rejoin him in the wilderness in 18.1-7. They had been, we are there assured by way of explanation, sent back to Jethro. The narrator wants the reader to know the danger that Pharaoh's stubbornness invited and does so through the theme of the 'first-born son': 'And you shall say to Pharaoh, "Thus says Yahweh, Israel is my first-born son, and I say to you, 'Let my son go that he may serve me'; if you refuse to let him go, behold, I will slay your first-born son" ' (4.22–3). This is the point of tension. The conflict between God and Pharaoh begins. The Hebrews will 'serve' (root '*bd*) God, not Pharaoh.

An old and strange tradition notes that, after Yahweh had 'sought to kill him' at a halt, Zipporah circumcised her son and touched 'his' feet with the foreskin, declaring 'you are a bridegroom of blood to me' (4.24–6). Who is the intended victim and whose feet are touched? The RSV assumes it to be Moses and the final editor may have intended this – although Moses is not mentioned by name. If he is meant, the intention might have been to show how the fragile Moses once again owed his life to a woman's intervention.

On Yahweh's initiative, Aaron meets Moses at 'the mountain of God'. Aaron announces Moses' message to Israel, who 'believed' and 'worshipped'.

Confrontation with Pharaoh (5.1–15.21)

Moses negotiates with Pharaoh to allow the Hebrews to leave Egypt. The narrative is composite. The Hebrews leave Egypt in great haste, without time for the bread to rise; and yet they plan carefully, having time to take plunder from the Egyptians (11.1–2; 12.35–9; 13.18f; 14.5). It has been common to see the hand of the sources J and possibly E, as well as P, in the account. Coats (1988, 89–108) identifies separate 'sign schemas' in J and P (ascribing to P the 'hardened heart' formula). If E appears at all, it is in brief glosses. J, he concludes, gave a heroic role to Moses. The Passover plague has a different structure from the rest, and was included as an appendix: the Hebrews made a rushed escape, taking with them plunder from the Egyptians. P focuses primarily on God's intervention, and on the institution of Passover.

Setback; Covenant and Promise (5.1–6.30)   There is an initial setback when Pharaoh retaliates by increasing the Hebrews' workload (5.1–21). This creates hostility to Moses (and to Yahweh) among the overseers and Hebrews, whose spirit is broken. The story asserts that Yahweh's purpose is not assisted by popular support – that the Hebrews did not deserve to be delivered. After this comes a discussion between God and Moses (6.2 – 13), designed to link the Moses narrative with the covenant and promise motifs to Genesis. Three promises are made: to deliver the people from bondage in Egypt; to take them as God's people; and to give them the Promised Land. There are close links in language and ideas with Genesis 17, which is alluded to in Exodus 6.4. The covenant with Abraham has been remembered, and Yahweh promises future deliverance: 'I will take you for

my people, and I will be your God' (v. 7). That this passage duplicates the
vocation tale (3.6–22) has often been noted: Yahweh introduces his name
again, the same promises are made, and Moses once more protests his
incompetence. The declaration that the name Yahweh was not known to the
patriarchs (6.3) contradicts narratives of Genesis in which patriarchs deal
with Yahweh by name.

The Plagues (7.1–11.10) Moses negotiates for the people's release, but
the reader knows that ultimately the power is God's. Signs and wonders are
promised, so that the Egyptians 'shall know that I am Yahweh' (7.5) when
the exodus is achieved. Thus, the plagues function as *signs* rather than punishment: the earlier signs are repeated by the Egyptian magicians. This
theme emphasizes Yahweh's victory over Egyptian magic: the failed
magicians announce, 'This is the finger of God' (8.19) and are finally driven
out (9.11). Each time God hardens Pharaoh's heart – his stubbornness
deliberately caused by God. There is evidence of another point of view, in
which Moses takes the credit for the wonders (9.11; 11.10; Deut
34.10–12). Two observations about the form of the signs are of interest:
that there are three groups or 'sets' of plagues, each introduced in
characteristic ways (plagues 1, 4, 7; 2, 5, 8; 3, 6, 9); and that the signs have
a *chiastic* structure – that is, the first sign linking with the tenth, the second
to the ninth, and so on (Coats, 1988, 91–5) (see table 5.1).

In each case, the tenth plague (eleventh sign), the death of the first-born,
lies outside the structure and acts as an appendix introducing the Passover.
After the ninth plague (darkness), Pharaoh refuses to negotiate and Moses
accepts this as the end of his attempt to achieve his ends by persuasion
(10.28f). Appending the tenth plague ('Yet one plague more . . .'– 11.1)
seems clumsy, with Pharaoh still involved in 11.8. Coats (1988, 100–8)
identifies two separate lists of eight signs, the earlier from J and JE, and the
later from P.

After the final, terrible plague the Egyptians press the Hebrews to leave
Egypt immediately and are even ready to give them their treasured
possessions. Pharaoh gives Moses permission to leave. The crowning victory

Table 5.1

1 Aaron's rod becomes a snake	10 Darkness (9)
2 Nile water turned to blood (1)	9 Locusts (8)
3 Frogs (2)	8 Hail (7)
4 Gnats (3)	7 Boils (6)
5 Flies (4)	6 Disease on cattle (5)

Note: The numbers in parentheses are numbers of *plagues*. The first *sign* is not a plague.

for God is manifest in Pharaoh's final words: 'and bless me also' (12.32).
The narrative makes it clear that God is totally in control. He is responsible
for every reaction of the Egyptians; he hardens Pharaoh's heart so that his
revelation can ultimately be universal. God's message sums up the divine
purpose: 'By now I could have put forth my hand and struck you and your
people with pestilence, and you would have been cut off from the earth; but
for this purpose I have let you live, to show you my power, so that my name
may be declared throughout all the earth' (9.15–16).

The Feasts of Passover and Unleavened Bread (12.1–13.16). The

pilgrim festival which celebrated the exodus from Egypt was *Matsoth*,
'Unleavened Bread' (23.15; 34.18), which required unleavened bread to be
eaten for seven days. A separate law about the Passover *sacrifice* (not feast) is
given in 34.25. They are joined here in Exodus, as they are in Leviticus
23.4–8, Numbers 9.1–14 and 28.16–25, and Deuteronomy 16.1–8: the
precise dates of these passages are not certain, but there is no evidence to
demand them to be early. Thus it would not be surprising if the plague
narrative once set up the feast of Matsoth (Exod 12.14–20, 34) before a
hasty exodus (v.33). The 'despoiling the Egyptians' theme (vv. 35f; cf.
3.21f) implies substantial time and planning. 2 Kgs 23.21–3 reports that
the Passover was not observed after the judges (Joshua 5.10f reports the first
Passover in the land), and that King Josiah (639–609 BCE) introduced it
(c.620 BCE) after a lawbook was discovered in the Temple: 'For no such
passover had been kept since the days of the judges who judged Israel, or
during all the days of the kings of Israel or of the kings of Judah' (2 Kgs
23.22). In Chronicles, however, King Hezekiah (727–698 BCE) began his
reign by repairing and sanctifying the neglected Temple and ordering a
Passover in the *second* month (since the repairs had prevented it at its proper
time). Possibly the link between Passover and Matsoth was not original and
Passover was not regularly observed until late in the monarchy. Post-exilic
texts and post-biblical sources developed the ritual considerably (see Bokser,
1984).

Whatever the historical background to the feasts, the narrative insists that
they commemorate deliverance by the God of history in response to his
covenantal promises. The Passover ascribes final victory to Yahweh: the
death of Egyptian first-born was so devastating that Pharaoh acknowledged
Yahweh's power (12.32). The need to eat unleavened bread draws attention
to the speed of the departure: there was insufficient time for the bread to
rise. The Hebrews, under Moses' leadership, had to respond promptly when
God intervened. The suddenness of escape stands in dramatic contrast with
the long years of bondage. The feasts encapsulate and celebrate the freedom
of God's people; the narrative gives the celebrations their *raison d'être*. The

exodus is made possible by the proper performance of the rituals; and there is a demand that the Passover be celebrated in Palestine (13.3–16).

Yam Suf: the Reed Sea (13.17–15.21) The Hebrews leave equipped for battle; yet the story stresses their faint-heartedness. The quick coastal route is avoided, 'Lest the people repent when they see war, and return to Egypt' (13.17). This emphasizes that the escape should be viewed as God's saving act – and so the 'faint heart' motif reappears in 14.10–14. Even after the momentous signs and portents, Pharaoh again changes his mind and sends his army in pursuit. This sudden and irrational U-turn is directly attributed to God, who uses his enemies to implement his purpose:

For Pharaoh will say of the people of Israel, 'They are entangled in the land; the wilderness has shut them in.' And I will harden Pharaoh's heart, and he will pursue them and I will get glory over Pharaoh and all his host; and the Egyptians shall know that I am the LORD. (14.3–4)

This sign against Egypt brings God's strength home to the Hebrews: 'And Israel saw the great work which the LORD did against the Egyptians, and the people feared the LORD; and they believed in the LORD and in his servant Moses' (v. 31).

The act of dividing the waters to provide safe passage for the fugitives is, furthermore, deeply symbolic. Just as God's first act at the beginning of time was to divide the waters of chaos in order to create the world, so now he divides the Reed Sea to create a people. Passing through the waters is the definitive experience in the formation of God's people. Those who survive the waters are true Israelites.

The deliverance narrative closes with the first celebration of a free people. The poetic exaltation of God, the 'song of the sea', is placed in the mouth of Moses, God's instrument of deliverance. It stresses that the victory is attributable not to man but to the God of history:

> I will sing to the LORD, for he has triumphed gloriously;
> the horse and his rider he has thrown into the sea.
> The LORD is my strength and my song,
> and he has become my salvation;
> this is my God and I will praise him,
> my father's God and I will exalt him.
> The LORD is a man of war;
> the LORD is his name. (15.1–3)

The first two lines recur in v. 21, where they are sung by Miriam. Miriam is described as 'prophetess', and as leader of the women. Given that there are few references to prophetesses, and that there is an anti-Miriam tension

(Num 12), this detail is not likely to have been invented but may well belong to an earlier tradition. If so, the expansion in the mouth of Moses (the 'song of the sea') is likely to represent a later hymn in the same tradition. There are several other 'Reed Sea' hymns: Psalms 77.16–20; 78.13–16; 114.1–8; 136.10–22; Isaiah 51.9–11. Psalm 105, recounting the exodus events, curiously omits the crossing of the Red Sea. It also lists only eight plagues: two of the present ten are joined (flies and gnats), and one is new (destruction of vines, figs and trees), although now linked with the hailstorm. Could this be an earlier tradition?

Both prose and poetic accounts present the crossing of the Yam Suf as a miracle (14.22; 15.8), performed by Yahweh and not Moses (see Coats, 1988, 157–65). Yam Suf, 'the sea of reeds' (RSV 'Red Sea'), may have acquired its name from the marshy lakes on the Egypt–Sinai border: that the Hebrews knew a path through this reed marsh is often suggested. It is less easy to connect events with the eruption of Thera in the fifteenth century BCE (see Luce, 1969, 132f). The first part of God's threefold promise is now fulfilled – to 'bring out', 'deliver', 'redeem' (6.6): the Hebrews have been brought out of Egypt. The focus of attention now shifts: God accepts them as his people and demands their obedience.

In the Wilderness (15.22-17.16)

The key theme here is *complaint*: again the people show faint hearts. The place-names Massah ('proof') and Meribah ('contention') are attributed to this fault-finding, perhaps by way of popular etymologies. In the narrative, this again stresses the unworthiness of the Hebrews to receive salvation. Hostile Israelite elements make a dramatic contrast to what one would expect of people who have been offered salvation.

God's response to their murmurings is to provide for their immediate needs throughout a series of miraculous signs – sweet water from bitter at Marah; quail and manna in the wilderness of Sin; and water from the rock at Rephidim. These interventions demonstrate God's concern for human needs. It is in this context that the notion of the Sabbath is explained, albeit in the face of some opposition (16.22–30). The last external enemy to strike at the Hebrews is the tribe of Amalek. Joshua is victor (17.13) with some magical help from Moses (who in turn needs the help of Aaron and Hur to keep his arms raised). The narrator thus gives ultimate victory to God (vv. 14–15). The attack, immediately prior to the lawgiving at Sinai in which the special relationship between God and Israel is sealed, is symbolic of the final vanquishing of external opposition as God creates a people for his own possession.

Jethro: Moses Delegates Power (18.1–27)

Jethro is the central figure in what follows as the Hebrews enter Moses' old haunts. This is used as an opportunity to praise Yahweh their God for deliverance, and to show Moses' dependence on Jethro: he 'did all that he had said' (18.24). He delegates judicial authority to able, trustworthy, God-fearing men, removing any trace of autocracy whilst maintaining his authority as the one who represents the people before God. Jethro's advice also emphasizes the need for law, providing a preface to the lawgiving at Sinai: 'you shall teach them the statutes and the decisions, and make them know the way in which they must walk and what they must do' (v.20). Jethro's reintroduction into the story underlines Moses' subordination. He does what Jethro tells him, and ceases to be an authoritarian ruler. The narrator introduces a jarring note. Moses wife and sons also come (that they had returned to Jethro is not mentioned earlier) but Moses kisses *Jethro* – and the two disappear into the tent together. The appearance of Moses' family ends his emergency leadership and restores the family normality which preceded the exodus.

Israel at Sinai (19.1–40.38)

Up to this point, God has acted of his own volition to end Israel's servitude: 'The LORD will fight for you, and you have only to be still' (14.14). However, it has also been made clear that maintenance of the special relationship between God and his people will depend on obedience:

If you will diligently hearken to the voice of the LORD your God, and do that which is right in his eyes, and give heed to his commandments and keep all his statutes, I will put none of the diseases upon you which I put upon the Egyptians; for I am the LORD, your healer. (15.26)

Israel's role, if it is to be God's people (the second promise), is to fulfil the law which God will reveal. Only if Israel is obedient will it become 'a kingdom of priests and a holy nation' (19.5f). The law is revealed on the mountain where Yahweh revealed his name. Moses has fulfilled the commission there given, that of deliverer of the chosen people. Now he becomes mediator of the law. It is clear that this new law springs from God's act of deliverance. The *Decalogue* (Ten Commandments) encapsulates the whole of the law. Other laws are also placed in this context to give them the authority of the Sinai revelation. They demand a settled agricultural existence, unlike the nomadic background that the story gives Israel at this point – and so deliberately look forward. The narrator is introducing the third aspect of God's promise, the provision of a land in which to settle: at the end of these laws, Israel is told how to deal with the inhabitants they will replace or live alongside. Accepting and obeying the law is a necessary response to deliverance, and bound up with the future gift of land. The narrative of the first lawgiving concludes with a covenant-making ceremony. Moses reads the law; the people agree to keep it: 'All that the LORD has spoken we will do, and we will be obedient' (24.7). Their crucial decision is then sealed by sacrifice.

The traditional site of Sinai, the mountain of God, is Jebel Musa. There is some evidence that this was a later Nabataean pilgrimage area: but the Exodus account uses volcanic imagery (e.g. 19.18), which would not fit. There can be no certainty, and a case has been argued for a north-west Arabian location (cf. Noth, 1960, 130–2; Herrmann, 1975, 72f).

The narrative's great emphasis here is in Moses the lawgiver, and this is strongly underlined by Deuteronomy, in which Moses interprets the law of God. Coats (1988, 155–78) argues that this theme lies behind Moses' other roles (shepherd, man of God) and dominates; and this is certainly true of the final redaction now available to us. It leaves open the question of whether this always was the case. After the first lawgiving the narrative elaborates further on how the covenant will be perpetuated. Where is God's presence be found? How will God communicate his will? How will his cult be organized? How should Israel worship?

The Tabernacle (25.1–31.18; 35.1–40.38) Details are given of a portable tent on which the worship of Yahweh will focus. Its specifications are given; and the task of construction is given to Bezalel, son of Uri, of the tribe of Judah (for which he is filled with the Spirit of God, with ability and intelligence, with knowledge and all craftsmanship – 31.3). He has Oholiab, son of Ahisamach, a Danite, as his assistant. The materials are brought by the people – far more than needed (36.5–7). At the centre of the Tabernacle is the ark and, at its completion, 'the cloud abode upon it, and the glory [or "fire" – v.38] of Yahweh filled the tabernacle' (40.35). There is some overlap between the 'tent of meeting' (33.7–11) and the ornate Tabernacle which may suggest separate sources.

The Great Apostasy (32.1–35) The narrative also contains a major test of the covenant. Whilst Moses is on Sinai, receiving more instruction about how worship should be conducted, Aaron his brother (the priest) supervises the erection and worship of a golden calf, made from the people's jewellery. True worship is set in stark contrast to the sinfulness of Israel. The relationship so recently forged is broken. God wishes to destroy what he has created, and Moses has to take on the role of intercessor, reminding God of his promises to former generations. The outcome is that those guilty are punished, but the promise remains – a pattern to be followed in later narratives: 'Whoever has sinned against me, him will I blot out of my book.

But now go, lead the people to the place of which I have spoken to you; behold, my angel shall go before you' (32.34).

Moses' final role is to lead the Israelites towards the Promised Land. This is to take a complete generation: when the nation completes its journeyings all who participated in the apostasy are dead. Moses himself dies when the task is complete. His last sight is of the land stretching out before him, beyond the Jordan he will never cross.

Numbers: the Wilderness Wandering

The narrative of Numbers describes the organization of the Hebrews in the wilderness, with details of tribes and clans. The folk tradition is not oblivious to contemporary concerns, and we cannot assume unquestioningly that genealogies are authentic or accurate. Kirkpatrick (1988, 101–10) shows this not to be the case when social anthropologists study genealogical lineage traditions today. Therefore, the biblical details may reflect the narrator's time rather than giving an accurate portrayal of ancient social history: if so, part of the purpose of the narrative may have been to legitimate tribal groups, rituals and institutions. The strongest theme here is *murmuring*. The people complain, and fire breaks out (at Taberah, 'burning' – Num 11.1–3). They complain about their food, and are given quails but die of plague before they can enjoy them (at Kibroth-hattaavah, 'graves of craving' – vv. 4–35). Miriam and Aaron rebel, and Miriam is struck with leprosy (ch. 12). They murmur against the Promised Land, and are condemned to wander for forty years so that none of the murmurers shall enter (chs 13–14). Korah, Dathan and Abiram rebel with substantial following: they are swallowed up into the earth, fire destroys their support, and plague takes another 14,700 casualties (ch. 16). After further complaints, venomous snakes take more lives. The raising of a bronze snake averts further deaths (ch. 21).

Throughout these stories, the narrative develops the character of Moses as the humble servant of God, who speaks to God face to face. This is made to contrast with two things: with the complainants' view of Moses as an autocrat; and with the prophets. Any tyranny in the stories focuses on Yahweh, quick to anger and savage in his punishment – Moses intercedes where possible to *minimize* the calamities. Prophets are recognized in the camp – Eldad and Medad, for example (11.26–9). Not only are they tolerated, but Moses adds, 'Are you jealous for my sake? Would that all the Yahweh's people were prophets, that Yahweh would put his spirit upon them!' (v. 29). Moses is distinguished from these prophets: they perceive through dreams and visions; Moses looks on Yahweh's form, and speaks with him face to face (12.8).

Moses leads Israel in many battles against local tribes, particularly in the

Transjordan. One conflict, against Balak, king of Moab, introduces the splendid character of Balaam (chs 22–4). The story develops a humorous tension as Balaam, paid to curse Israel, proves unable to prophesy anything but good about it. Balak's anger increases to fever pitch, to no avail. Balaam, whose talking ass steals the show with perceptive and devastating logic, has his eyes opened to see what the ass sees. He meets God face to face (23.4) and thenceforward can only prophesy truthfully, ascribing present *and future* victories to Yahweh.

Another conflict is more subtle: attracted to Moabite women, the Israelites begin to worship their gods – especially the Baal of Peor (Num 25). Apostasy through intermarriage is a strong theme of Deuteronomy, forbidden in the laws of Exodus (e.g. 34.16) and after the exile by Ezra and Nehemiah (e.g. Ezra 9). Numbers 25 is a conflation of several accounts: the guilty are executed, and separately 24,000 die in a plague; the villains change from Moabites to Midianites, as the narrative makes this the excuse for war. Phinehas becomes the hero, by killing the Simeonite Zimri and his Midianite woman Cozbi: Phinehas makes political capital out of this incident in Joshua 22.17 – stressing, incidentally, the clear continuity between the Torah and Joshua.

Moses in Deuteronomy

The fundamental concept of this book lies in the words, 'Beyond the Jordan, in the land of Moab, Moses undertook to explain this law' (Deut 1.5), teaching the people what God had declared to him alone. He is the *authorized and authoritative interpreter of God's word for Israel* (Polzin, 1980, 10).

Most of the material is cast as a speech by Moses to the people, outlining events and commenting on teaching. The material recalls much that has already been recounted in Genesis to Numbers; but it is perplexing that there seem to be two separate introductions (Deut 1–4 and 5–11; see Nicholson, 1967, 19f). Chapters 12–26 consist of a body of statutes for their occupation of the land – again with links particularly to Exodus, but rewriting the laws with a very individualistic flavour. Moses' speeches continue in chapters 27–33 with the particular theme of blessings and curses. There is a song in chapter 32, and Moses' final blessings, in poetic form, in chapter 33.

The Death of Moses (Num 27.12–33; Deut 31.1–23; 34.1–12)

Moses does not enter the Promised Land, but has to be content with viewing it from a mountain vantage-point – Abarim (Num 27.12), or Nebo and

Pisgah (Deut. 34.1). The hero of so important a story might be expected to be present at the final triumph; Numbers therefore offers a reason for his absence: 'you rebelled against my word in the wilderness of Zin during the strife of the congregation, to sanctify me at the waters before their eyes' (27.14). A further note identifies this with the incident at Meribah (Num 20, esp. v. 12), where Yahweh 'showed himself holy' (v.13; cf. 27.14: 'to sanctify me at the waters before their eyes'. The point at issue is that Moses struck the rock twice, instead of *telling* it to produce water, thus reducing the wonder. More significantly, the narrator reduces the stature of Moses relative to God, minimizes his heroic role and magnifies God's holiness. Joshua is appointed as Moses' successor, to be a shepherd to the community invested with *some* of Moses' authority (27.20). Moses' very significant role here runs counter to the narrator's minimalist view.

Deuteronomy attributes Moses' premature death to incapacity stemming from old age (31.2). Joshua is commissioned as successor (although God is seen as the real leader – 31.3–8). A bleak future of apostasy is forecast. The concluding chapter of Deuteronomy notes Moses' death at the top of Pisgah, on Mount Nebo – a point from which the land could be viewed. It reaffirms God's promise of land (34.4) and that Moses will not enter the land (but without the reason given in Numbers). It gives a general location for his grave, but stresses that the exact location is a mystery (v. 6). A eulogy stresses Moses' *vigour* – 'his eye was not dim, nor his natural force abated' – in contrast to 31.2. The mourning leads to the announcement of Joshua's leadership ('for Moses had laid his hands upon him' – v. 9), which leads easily into the next part of the narrative, the conquest of the land under Joshua's leadership. The concluding phrases give a high estimate of Moses' contribution:

And there has not arisen a prophet since in Israel like Moses, whom the LORD knew face to face, none like him for all the signs and the wonders which the LORD sent him to do in the land of Egypt, to Pharaoh and to all his servants and to all his land, and for all the mighty power and all the great and terrible deeds which Moses wrought in the sight of all Israel. (vv. 10–12)

There is no downrating of Moses here!

In the Moses narrative, Yahweh moulds human activity to achieve his purposes, winning victory when defeat seemed inevitable; and yet allows free will in his people, who must accept the consequences of their actions. This main thrust is, as we have seen, developed in a variety of subtle ways (and not just in a redactional framework). Other conflicting voices may also be heard. They may stem from separate sources but readers should be open

6

Covenant and Law

Dan Cohn-Sherbok and Stephen Bigger

Preliminary Reading   Exodus 20–4, 34; Leviticus; Deuteronomy.

God's covenant with Israel serves as the basis for the Jewish faith. The Torah is traditionally said to contain 613 commandments (*miswoth*), which Jewish 'rabbinic' scholars – referred to as Tannaim and Amoraim – interpreted from the first century BCE until the sixth century CE. According to Pharisaic Judaism, both the written Torah (the Pentateuch) and the rabbinic interpretation (oral Torah) were given by God to Moses on Mount Sinai. This belief implies that God is the direct source of all laws recorded in the Torah, and is also indirectly responsible for the authority accorded the legal judgements of the rabbis – such a doctrine served as the justification for the rabbinic exposition of scriptural ordinances. Alongside this exegesis of the Jewish law (*halakhah*) scholars also produced interpretations of Scripture in which new meanings of the text were expounded (*aggadah*) in rabbinic commentaries (*midrashim*) and in the Talmud. Within these 'aggadic' texts is found a wealth of theological speculation about such topics as the nature of God, divine justice, the coming of the Messiah, and the hereafter. In addition, the rabbinic authors devote considerable attention to ethical commandments, and recount their mystical reflections about God and his creation. Early rabbinic Judaism thus covered a wide variety of areas all embraced by the holy word revealed on Mount Sinai, and this literature served as the foundation of later Judaism as it developed through the centuries.

Covenant

A major theme of the Torah is that of *covenant* – the solemn and binding agreement between God and his people. The act of establishing a covenant between two or more parties was widely practised in the ancient Near East.

135

The derivation of *berith* (covenant) is uncertain: it has been suggested that it is related to the word for 'father', or to the idea of sharing a meal or cutting. The origin of the term is not vitally important, as it acquired a precise technical sense. (Today, pronounced *bris*, it refers also to circumcision as a mark of the covenant.) Other Hebrew parallel terms are used – *'eduth* (testimonies) and *alah* (oath). An interesting expression is 'to cut a covenant', often associated by source critics with the J (Yahwistic) source but used very widely, perhaps hinting at a ceremony involving the sacrifice of an animal, as in Genesis 15.

In the Hebrew Bible, covenants were of different types. Frequently two individuals made a covenantal agreement, as in Genesis 21.27 between Abimelech and Abraham: 'So Abraham took sheep and oxen and gave them to Abimelech, and the two men made a covenant.' The purpose of the covenant is given in the story of Jacob and Laban (Gen 31.43f). As Laban's daughters and their children leave the orbit of his protection, the covenant becomes a witness between the two which symbolically prevents Jacob from ill-treating his wives or taking new wives. This covenantal witness has divine validation: 'although no man is with us, remember, God is witness between you and me' (v. 50). In other cases, a covenant was made between rulers or states – between David and Israel, to establish David on the throne (2 Sam 3.21); between Israel and Tyre (1 Kgs 5.12) and Israel and Assyria (Hos 12.1). In 2 Kings 11.17 Jehoiada the priest 'made a covenant between the LORD and the king and people, that they should be the LORD's people; and also between the king and the people'. The first covenant was sacred, effecting a special relationship between God and Israel, which wished to rededicate itself after the apostasy of Athaliah; the other was secular, establishing the new king's position. Of course, the Hebrews did not distinguish between sacred and secular, since the whole of life was in God's orbit. Marriage is depicted as a covenant: 'Because the LORD was witness to the covenant between you and the wife of your youth, to whom you have been faithless, though she is your companion and your wife by covenant' (Mal 2.14). Again the covenant brings with it the idea of divine witness: God witnesses the agreement when there are no human witnesses to enforce it. Hosea speaks of God reaching a covenant agreement with the animal world not to harm humankind in an oracle promising future security (2.18). Covenants were often agreements in which a superior party (such as the king) made a pact with an inferior, providing protection with loyalty as a condition. Thus the people of Jabesh-gilead sought the protection of Nahash, the king of Ammon (1 Sam 11.1). The Israelites were forbidden from making such pacts with the Canaanites, including mixed marriages, in case it caused them to serve other gods (Deut 7.1–5).

Frequently covenantal relationships were accompanied by external signs to remind parties of their respective obligations. Jacob and Laban raised a cairn of witness. Isaac and Abimelech ate a meal together (Gen 26.29f) to seal their oath/covenant. Sacrifice was used to confirm covenant responsibilities: 'Gather to me my faithful ones, who made a covenant with me by sacrifice' (Ps 50.5). Abraham's covenant sacrifice (Gen 15) was the basis of common practice, attacked by the prophet Jeremiah for hypocrisy and insincerity: 'And the men who transgressed my covenant and did not keep the terms of the covenant which they made before me, I will make like the calf which they cut in two and passed between its parts . . . ' (Jer 34.18f). The famous sign or token of Israel's covenant with God is circumcision, the cutting-away of the foreskin from the penis. Demanded in law (Lev 12.3), its origin was traced to God's covenant with Abraham (Gen 17).

The covenantal relationship between God and Israel is a central feature in the Hebrew Bible. A number of ancient Near Eastern treaties have been discovered in which a common pattern can be observed. Many were agreements between a king and his subjects, stating the duties and responsibilities of each side. Since the work of Mendenhall (1954) the suggestion has often been made that the Hebrew writings were influenced by this treaty pattern. The case has been overstated, as McCarthy shows (1963, 1972), but it still remains a plausible hypothetical model. In particular, the treaty pattern emphasizes the concept of the kingship of God in relation to his chosen people. McCarthy's definitive study finds convincing arguments for supposing that Deuteronomy and certain Deuteronomic passages (e.g. 2 Sam 7) exhibit this pattern, but finds the case for the Sinai narrative much less compelling.

In the light of such scholarly investigation, it is now evident that the idea of God as king need not have originated during the monarchy but was an ancient doctrine. In the period of the judges the tribes are seen resisting kingship because of the belief that God was the true king: to appoint an earthly king would betray this conviction. When kingship was accepted, the king and the nation together were viewed as vassals of the divine suzerain. The Israelites believed that both land and dynasty had been granted by God and, as was common in the ancient Near East, this relationship was expressed in written form. It is not surprising, therefore, that the tablets of the covenant played such an important role.

A major problem relates to when the concept of covenant became central in Hebrew thought. Circumcision as a sign of the covenant (Gen 17) has generally been attributed to the latest source, P. An influential case for viewing the Sinai narrative as reflecting a covenant-renewal festival liturgy has been made by W. Beyerlin (1965) using source analysis and tradition-historical investigation. He concludes that the setting of the festival was in Kadesh, in the wilderness period.

The Sinai narrative (Exod 19–24) ends with the reading of the 'book of the covenant', a blood sacrifice and a meal; but the literary history of this section is very complex. In particular, the passage which contains the idea of covenant (24.3–8) seems to interrupt the natural flow of 24.1–2 and 9–11 with its climax in a solemn meal before God. Although *berith* is not mentioned in vv. 1–2, 9–11, some scholars interpret the meal as a covenant occasion – but there are other possibilities. The mention of *berith* comes in connection with the sacrificial rite (24.8) in a passage that is reminiscent of the Deuteronomist, i.e. from the time of the exile (see further Nicholson, 1973, 65–77). A case can be argued for viewing the covenant language in Exodus 19, 24.3–8 and 34 as Deuteronomic – if it is not, it certainly *influenced* Deuteronomy. We have already seen how Deuteronomy may have been influenced by ancient Near Eastern treaty forms. Nicholson notes,

fresh consideration must surely be given to the fact that the very distribution of the word $b^e r\hat{\imath}th$ is concentrated to a pronounced degree in the Deuteronomic literature and literature which can be shown to be either dependent upon or at least influenced by it. (1973, 77)

Thus it cannot be assumed that the earlier form of the Sinai narrative was interpreted as a covenant, or that references to covenants in passages earlier than Deuteronomic literature bore the theological weight that it was later to acquire. The socio-political covenant found in everyday relationships could have provided a useful metaphor or model, and the language of international treaties may have had an effect. Many of the examples of everyday covenants are in Deuteronomic literature, or in narratives which could have been influenced by the Deuteronomist. It is possible that the major emphasis on covenant was a late development.

Biblical Law

Within the Torah there are several collections of law. One task we have is to determine the background and characteristics of each collection; but at the same time we should not forget that all have been brought together in the Torah deliberately. In the final text of the Torah, all collections have a part to play and were clearly designed to interact.

The Decalogue (Exod 20.1–20; 34.1–28; Deut 5.1–21)

The phrase 'the ten commandments' (literally, 'the ten words') appears only in Exodus 34.28, but the list which precedes it differs substantially from the mainly ethical collection generally recognized as the Ten Commandments. The laws relate to ritual and ceremony, so this is often called the Ritual

Decalogue, although it does not naturally break into ten laws. Exodus 20 is often called the Ethical Decalogue, but herein lies a problem: the commandments here are spoken and not written on tablets of stone – these come at 31.18, when ritual is being discussed. The language throughout Exodus 34 is reminiscent of Deuteronomy, with its emphasis on avoiding idolatry; and yet Deuteronomy 5.22 appears to link the ethical Decalogue with the stone tablets.

Two versions of the ethical Decalogue are given, in Exodus 20 and Deuteronomy 5: there are numerous differences between them, mostly minor except for the Sabbath law, which Exodus explains in terms of the creation story (Gen 2.2, when God rested), and Deuteronomy in terms of slavery in Egypt – the slaves rest, recalling how the Hebrews escaped from slavery in Egypt. Early dates have been argued for both versions, but evidence is inconclusive. The hand of late redactors has been traced in all three Decalogues.

The contents of the Ritual and Ethical Decalogues may be summarized as in table 6.1.

Table 6.1   The Ritual and Ethical Decalogues

Ritual Decalogue	Ethical Decalogue
No molten gods	No gods before Yahweh
Feast of Unleavened Bread	No graven or molten images
First-born (animals)	Misuse of name Yahweh
First-born sons	Sabbath
Sabbath	Honour parents
Feasts of Weeks and Ingathering	Do not kill
Sacrifices: separate blood and leaven	Do not commit adultery
Passover sacrifice	Do not steal
First fruits	Do not give false evidence
Do not boil a kid in its mother's milk	Do not covet

The Book of the Covenant (Exod 20.22–23.19)

The phrase 'the book of the covenant' is used in Exodus 24.7 of the material which precedes it. The collection is generally dated early, but its background is agricultural rather than nomadic. Of all the legal compilations in the Torah, this one has the closest connections with Mesopotamian law. Nevertheless, the laws are well adapted to the Hebrew situation: the legal tradition has been utilized, but individual laws have not been inappropriately borrowed. The laws in the 'book of the covenant' are mostly civil – to do with offences and disputes that might disrupt communal harmony.

There is a greater concern to uphold individual rights than in ancient Near Eastern codes.

The following list summarizes the contents of the 'book of the covenant'.

Hebrew slaves (21.1–11)

Murder and manslaughter
   (21.12–14)

Striking parent (21.15)

Stealing (kidnapping) a person as
   a slave (21.16)

Cursing a parent (21.17)
Assault (21.18–27)
A goring ox (21.28–32, 35–6)

An open pit (21.33–4)
Theft (22.1–4)
Wrongful grazing (22.5)

Fire damage to crops (22.6)
Breach of trust (22.7–15)

Seduction of a virgin
   (22.16–17)
Sorceress (22.18)

Bestiality (22.19)
Sacrifice to foreign god (22.20)

Oppressing strangers
   (22.21–4)
Lending to the poor
   (22.25–7)

Reviling God and ruler
   (22.28)
Giving surplus crops to poor
   (22.29)
First born son (22.29–30)
Do not eat torn flesh (22.31)
False witness (23.1–3)
Care of enemies' animals
   (23.4–5)
Perverting justice (23.6–8)
Oppressing strangers (23.9)
Fallow Sabbath year
   (23.10–11)
Sabbath day (23.12–13)
Three annual feasts
   (23.14–17)
Sacrifice: separate from leaven;
   do not let fat remain till
   morning (23.18)
First fruits (23.19)
Do not boil a kid in its
   mother's milk (23.19)

The Priestly Code (Exod 25–Num 10)

The laws in this section are interspersed with narrative. Although varied, they mainly cover regulations involving ceremonial and cultic matters – sacrifices, purity, the priesthood, ceremonies. The name 'Priestly' is therefore descriptive, and was used to describe what was thought to be the latest Pentateuchal source. Much of the material clearly circulated among priests and Levites, who are often mentioned. There may have been several major collections incorporated into this section, such as those on the Tabernacle (Exod 25–40), on offerings (Lev 1–10) and on holiness (Lev

11–26; see below). Authorship used to be credited to a hypothetical 'Priestly Writer'; but today scholars are more cautious on the subject. However, a date during or after the exile is still commonly advanced for the present collections.

The Holiness Code (Lev 11–26 or 17–26)

This has been identified as a separate law code, although its full extent is debated. It particularly deals with various kinds of pollution, such as through food (ch. 11) childbirth (12) disease (13–14), sex (15) blood (17) incest (18, 20) injustice (19) and death (21). Purification rituals are given, and priesthood and ceremonial are discussed in detail (16,21–6)

Deuteronomy

The name is Greek, meaning 'the second law'. Moses reiterates, in a speech on the plains of Moab just before his death, the story and laws found in the previous books. The writer drew heavily on the 'book of the covenant', producing in effect a second edition, with modifications and new laws. Although there are some who argue for an early date for Deuteronomy, most regard it as the major work of a group influenced by the prophetic movement.

Dating books in the Hebrew Bible is not without its problems. Nicholson notes about Deuteronomy,

At one time or another almost every period in Israel's history from Moses to the exile has been advocated as the date of its composition, whilst its authorship has at various times been attributed to Moses, Samuel, levitical priests, the Jerusalem priesthood, or prophetic circles. Similarly the origin of the book has been traced to Jerusalem, Shechem, Bethel and elsewhere. (1967, 37)

The fact that Ezra reads the law of Moses publically (Neh 8.1–2) may mean that it was completed by this time (fifth century BCE) or that the writer wants us to believe that it was! Furthermore, this 'law of Moses' cannot be straightforwardly identified with Deuteronomy or with the Torah. Deuteronomy has been linked with the religious reforms of King Josiah (c.620 BCE; 2 Kgs 22–3), since these were based on the teaching of a lawbook found in the Temple during his reign. His reforms correlate closely with the teaching of Deuteronomy. Yet still there are problems. How reliable is the Josiah narrative? Was that lawbook ancient or modern? And was it the *whole* of Deuteronomy? Or was it substantially edited when it was incorporated into the Torah? Probably no more than the laws of chapters 12–26 were found and used by Josiah. Clearly, Deuteronomy uses the narratives and laws of Genesis – Numbers as a source, and must be dated later than this. A date for Josiah's lawbook during the century before its discovery (roughly between 721 and 620 BCE) is that most favoured (see Nicholson, 1967, for the arguments). Many scholars date the final redaction of Deuteronomy during the exile (sixth century BCE), incorporating and interpreting earlier materials. Polzin reminds us to take the contribution of the *narrator* seriously: as Moses interprets God's words, so the narrator interprets Moses' words. Yet he keeps in the background – only fifty-six verses explicitly give the narrator's view; the remainder is placed in the mouth of, and presented from the point of view of, Moses himself (Polzin, 1980, 10).

A strong connection has been noted in language and theology with the redactors of Joshua–Kings, and to a lesser extent Genesis–Numbers. In other words, the Deuteronomists seem to have been involved in providing the final polish to a major portion of the Hebrew Bible.

Apodictic and Casuistic Law

Much has been made of two different types of legal statement:

(1)   casuistic or case law, generally beginning 'If a person . . .' or 'The person who . . .', and stating the penalty;

(2)   apodictic law, usually prohibitions beginning 'You shall not . . .', and not stating the penalty.

Another form occasionally found (e.g. Deut 27) is 'Cursed [*arur*] be the person who . . .' Apodictic law is characteristic of the Torah, but not of ancient Near Eastern law in general. As it is a simple statement of prohibition it raises the question of what happened to offenders. Some apodictic laws exist also in casuistic versions with penalties attached. It is possible that penalties were imposed by elders or judges in the light of their more detailed knowledge of legislation. Among the common penalties imposed in casuistic law in the Torah are 'shall be put to death' (*moth yumath*: cf. Exod 21.12, 15, 16, 17; 22.18); 'shall pay for the loss' – sometimes double (cf. Exod 21.19, 34, 36; 22.4); 'shall cut the person off from among his people' (cf. Lev 20.6).

The death penalty is to be executed by stoning (Lev 24.23; Deut 21.21) or, exceptionally, by burning (Lev 20.14, for a sexual relationship where a man takes a woman and her mother). Deuteronomy gives an interesting account of the procedure, to conclude the case of the rebellious son:

Then all the men of the city shall stone him to death with stones; so you shall purge the evil from your midst; and all Israel shall hear, and fear.

And if a man has committed a crime punishable by death and he is put to death, and you hang him on a tree, his body shall not remain all night upon the tree, but you shall bury him the same day, for a hanged man is accursed by God; you shall not defile your land which the LORD your God gives you for an inheritance. (21.21–3)

The hanging seems to have been not a form of execution but a public exhibition of the body. The law limits the exhibition on the grounds not of propriety but of defilement. Deuteronomy legislates to check abuses: the evidence of two or three witnesses is demanded (19.15–21), with a malicious witness liable to the penalty for the charge he has supported. Deuteronomy is specific in indicating that such penalties were expected: in earlier laws it is an open question whether the formula *moth yumath* means execution or sudden death (i.e. at the hand of God) – in a dangerous society, with wars, wild animals and disease, sudden death could be seen as a result of some offence. Compensation was affixed to several early laws and there was a tendency to give this more widespread application later. The meaning of 'to be cut off from among his people' is uncertain – banishment comes to mind as a possibility.

'*An Eye for an Eye*'

Another form of compensation was provided by the *lex talionis*, 'the law of equivalents', involving 'an eye for an eye' and so forth. The fullest form is given in Exodus 21.23–5, generally regarded as an early law in an early law code. The context is the case of a pregnant woman who is unintentionally knocked during a brawl which causes her to miscarry. If she is not hurt, a fine is imposed – claimed by the husband and adjudicated by the judges. If she is hurt, 'then you shall give life for life, eye for eye, tooth for tooth, hand for hand, foot for foot, burn for burn, wound for wound, stripe for stripe'.

Leviticus 24.19–20 gives the rule for the case of a man who causes disfigurement: 'as he has done it shall be done to him, fracture for fracture, eye for eye, tooth for tooth; as he has disfigured a man, he shall be disfigured'. 'Life for life' is missing, but two preceding laws stipulate the death penalty for murder (v. 17); and 'He who kills a beast shall make it good, life for life' (v. 18). 'Life for life' suggests compensation, perhaps replacing the life with a beast from the offender's own herd, not the execution of the offender, which would be clearly stated as it is elsewhere. In either case, the possibility that the damage was accidental is not an issue: rather, a victim who has been diminished is offered compensation in goods and in honour. The result is a deterrent for all, since this law applied 'for the sojourner and for the native' (v. 22): one law for all.

A third compensation law involves the malicious false witness who attempts to diminish his neighbour through the process of law: 'you shall do to him as he had meant to do to his brother . . . . Your eye shall not pity; it shall be life for life, eye for eye, tooth for tooth, hand for hand, foot for foot'

(Deut 19.19, 21). As Deuteronomy emphasizes the execution of the death penalty, 'life for life' may here imply that; but loss of eyes, teeth or feet were not, as far as we know, prescribed punishments. Some form of compensation would be expected, to the value of an eye, tooth, hand or foot – and possibly a life. In Exodus, the *lex talionis* can be interpreted as retribution; but it can also be read as a compensation formula: either another life (wife) must be offered, to replace the deceased wife, or there should be appropriate financial compensation; eyes, teeth, and so on, cannot be replaced in fact, and burns, wounds and stripes are not replaceable – the compensation would therefore be financial. There may have been flexibility within the legal texts themselves; and, as Exodus 21.22 states, in cases of individual dispute the judges would decide.

Ancient Near Eastern Law

Despite differences in detail, the law codes described above have much in common: all condemn murder, robbery, incest and adultery; each requires respect for parents and strict justice in the courts; they protect the rights of the stranger and the impoverished; provision is made for freeing slaves; certain locations are set aside as refuges for manslaughter; destruction of idols and a ban on divination are stipulated; observance of the Passover and festivals is required; tithes are to be given to Levites and priests; the first-born of animals should be given to God, but the first-born of their own families should be redeemed. This compilation of moral, civil and criminal law draws extensively on ancient Near Eastern precedent. Some ancient Mesopotamian law codes have been discovered by archaeologists: the codes of Lipit-Ishtar, Eshnunna and Hammurabi. There are also middle and late Assyrian and Babylonian codes, contemporary with biblical material. All can be found translated in *Ancient Near Eastern Texts Relating to the Old Testament*, edited by J. Pritchard (*ANET*). The most complete surviving code is that of Hammurabi, king in Old Babylon (1728–1686 BCE), on a stele with a relief picture of the king receiving the lawbook from the sun god Shamash. A long prologue praises the king through a long list of epithets ending with 'I established law and justice in the language of the land, thereby promoting the welfare of the people.' The laws relate to issues such as buying and selling, hiring, property, the family, slavery, assault, medicine, farming. The epilogue further lands the king, but attributes the laws to the gods and invokes the gods to curse offenders. There are parallels with biblical laws, particularly with the 'book of the covenant' (Paul, 1970), and a similar ideology of theocratic law mediated by a leader. Laws on ritual do not dominate, as they do in the final biblical legal collections (e.g. in Leviticus) and for parallels we should need to examine ritual texts which deal more with sin – the breaking of ritual or religious law – than with crime. The Neo-Babylonian laws, closest to the period of exile, are not well-preserved.

It is clear that biblical law was not created in a vacuum. The biblical writers utilized concepts of election and covenant to give authority to the legal system. God was conceived as supreme and worthy of worship; Israel was therefore obliged to serve him faithfully. Justice for all was a cardinal obligation, firmly based on the nation's relationship with God. The study and interpretation of law therefore became a religious preoccupation and dominated the subsequent history of the Hebrew, and later Jewish, people.

Rabbinic Law

The exegesis (drawing-out of meaning) found in rabbinic literature of the Tannaim (first century BCE – second century CE) and Amoraim second – sixth centuries CE) is largely of two types: direct and explicit exegesis which comments on the text to clear up possible confusion; and indirect exegesis which cites the text to support an assertion. The rabbis frequently reinforce their exhortations with a text which expresses their sentiments (see Montefiore and Loewe, 1974). Termed 'homilectical', this use of Scripture is illustrated by Simon ben Shetach (first century BCE), who declares,

When you are judging, and there comes before you two men, of whom one is rich and the other poor, do not say, 'The poor man's words are to be believed, but not the rich man's.' But just as you listen to the words of the poor man, so listen to the words of the rich man, for it is said, 'You shall not respect persons in judgement' [Deut 1.17].

It was also usual in rabbinic circles to cite a text and then draw out its meaning. For example, the verse, 'You shall open wide your hand to your brother' (Deut 15.11) is explained as meaning that one should give according to particular needs: 'To him for whom bread is suitable, give bread; to him who needs dough, give dough; to him for whom money is required, give money; to him for whom it is fitting to put food in his mouth, put it in.'

It was a principle in rabbinic hermeneutics (interpretation and exposition) that a word should be taken in its most strict sense. In the Talmud, Rabbi Meir (second century CE) says, 'Where is the resurrection derived from the Torah? As it is said, "Then will Moses and then will the children of Israel sing this song unto the Lord" [Exod 15.1]; it is not said *sang* but *will sing*.' Hence, he argues, the resurrection is deducible from the Torah. Sometimes typology is used: the Talmud to Isaiah 43.9 understands Edom (cf. Gen 36) as prefiguring Rome. Some passages are treated as allegories: Bar Kappara (second century CE) interprets Jacob's dream as referring to the Temple

(= the ladder), the sacrificial smoke (because the ladder reaches to heaven) and the priests (= the angels).

Hillel the elder (first century BCE) lay down seven rules for scriptural interpretation, later expanded to thirteen by Rabbi Ishmael ben Elisha (second century CE), mainly by subdivision. The first rule, the inference from minor and major, states that restrictions or allowances applying to matters of minor importance are applicable also to matters of major importance and *vice-versa*. In the Mishnah, for example, the Sabbath is in some respects regarded as being of more importance than a common holiday. If, therefore, a certain kind of work is permissible on a Sabbath, we may infer that such work is more permissible on a common holiday; conversely, if a form of work is forbidden for a common holiday, it must be all the more forbidden on the Sabbath. Rule six allows interpreters to solve exegetical problems by reference to other texts. Rabbi Ishmael's thirteenth rule states that two passages which seem to contradict should be reconciled by a third if possible. Thus Exodus 13.6 ('Seven days you shall eat unleavened bread') and Deuteronomy 16.8 ('Six days you shall eat unleavened bread') are resolved by reference to Leviticus 23.14, where no use is to be made of the new corn until a formal offering is made on the morning after the first day of Passover: thus the unleavened bread can be eaten only on the six remaining days. The unleavened bread made from the previous year's corn can be eaten for seven days.

These various methods of exegesis were based on the conviction that the Torah is sacred, that it can be understood, and that, properly understood, it guides the life of the worthy. By devoting their lives to its proper interpretation, the rabbinic authorities were able to infuse the tradition with new meaning and renewed relevance. The literary outpouring of the first few centuries of Pharisaic Judaism bears witness to the fervent conviction that God's eternal word can have a living message for each generation.

From Mishnah to Talmud

Utilizing many of the rules of scriptural interpretation, the rabbis attempted to draw out what they believed to be the implications of the written law. Rabbinic exegesis, known as 'oral Torah', consisted of ancient legal traditions, enactments by men of the great assembly and the Sanhedrin, and laws deriving from the Tannaim in the Palestinian academies. The transmission of this material was at first through verbal recitation. As time passed, the oral Torah reached enormous size and some scholars felt it necessary to systematize the material.

Mishnah   The first attempt to organize this mass of tradition was made by Rabbi Hillel, president of the Sanhedrin in the first century BCE, by arranging it into six divisions. Later, Rabbi Aqiba subdivided the subject matter, grouping laws according to their subject matter or on a system of mnemonics; and Rabbi Meir completed the collection and improved its order. Eventually, using this as a framework, Rabbi Judah Hannasi, 'the prince' (head of the rabbinic academy at Jamnia in the second century CE), attempted to establish a general code of oral law. Where there was a divergence of opinion, he named the authors of individual opinions, and noted the prevailing consensus. This work was initially called the Mishnah of Rabbi Judah (to distinguish it from those of Rabbi Aqiba and Rabbi Meir); but, when it was generally accepted as authoritative, it was designated simply *Mishnah*. It is divided into six main sections.

1 *Seeds* embraces the ritual laws concerning cultivation of the soil and its produce. It is introduced by a treatise on prayer and benedictions.
2 *Festival* treats the laws concerning Sabbath and other festivals.
3 *Women* outlines the regulations concerning marriage and divorce.
4 *Damages* details civic and criminal law.
5 *Sacred Things* treats the sacrificial law and the Temple service.
6 *Purification* deals with the laws concerning clean and unclean.

The rabbinic authorities mentioned in the Mishnah – scribes, *zugoth* (pairs) and Tannaim – belong to three distinct periods. The scribes were learned men who succeeded Ezra, referred to as the men of the Great Assembly, which consisted of 120 members; *zugoth* denotes pairs of learned teachers who served as heads of the Sanhedrin; the Tannaim continued until 200 CE, and used the term 'rabbi' for ordinary scholars, 'rabban' for the president of the Sanhedrin.

Gemara   As the Mishnah became established as the authorative code of oral law, scholars studied it in Tiberias, Sepphoris and Caesarea in Palestine, and in Nehardea, Sura and Pumbaditha in Babylonia. They aimed to explain its meaning, delineate its reasoning, determine its sources, reconcile seeming contradictions, and apply its decisions to new situations. The period of the Amoraim began with the death of Judah Hannasi and extended until the completion of the Babylonian Talmud at the end of the fifth century CE. The collection of these commentaries on the Mishnah is referred to as *Gemara*.

The legal material in the Gemara is referred to as *halakah*. The ethical teaching, theological speculation and historical material are called *aggadah*. There are six main categories.

1 *Exegetical aggadah*, explaining biblical texts.
2 *Dogmatic aggadah*, discussing doctrine.

3 *Ethical aggadah*, illustrating moral duties.
4 *Historical aggadah*: traditions and legends of biblical and rabbinic personalities.
5 *Mystical aggadah*, developed by Kabbalist mystics.
6 *Miscellaneous aggadah*: anecdotes, observations, practical advice, and so on.

The Talmuds Separate Gemaras were developed in Palestine and Babylonia. These finally became known as the Palestinian and Babylonian Talmuds. They differ in language, style and content, with the Palestinian text only a third of the length of the Babylonian. Not only is the Palestinian Talmud more succinct, but it is also more historically accurate, without the frequent flights of fancy of the Babylonian Talmud. The Babylonian Talmud established itself in North Africa and Europe, where it was rigorously studied.

Later Codes

After the Talmuds, a number of other law codes were formulated: those of Rabbi Jehudai Gaon of Sura (eighth century CE) and Rabbi Simon of Kahira (ninth century); Rabbi Isaac Alfasi's *Halakoth* and Moses Maimonides' *Mishneh Torah* (eleventh century); the code of Rabbi Moses of Coucy (twelfth century); Rabbi Jacob's *Tur* (thirteenth century); and Rabbi Joseph Karo's *Shulchan Aruch* (sixteenth century). The last subsequently became accepted as the standard lawcode of the Jewish world.

FURTHER READING

McCarthy, D. J. 1972: *Old Testament Covenant: a Survey of Current Opinions*.
Montefiore, C. G. and Loewe, H. 1974: *A Rabbinic Anthology*.
Musaph-Andriesse, R. C. 1981: *From Torah to Kabbalah: a Basic Introduction to the Writings of Judaism*.
Nicholson, E. W. 1973: *Exodus and Sinai in History and Tradition*.
Nicholson, E. W. 1986: *God and his people: Covenant and Theology in the Old Testament*.
Phillips, A. 1970: *Ancient Israel's Criminal Law*.

Part III

Nebi'im: the Prophets

7

The Former Prophets

Keith W. Whitelam

Preliminary Reading   Joshua; Judges.

The 'Prophets', the second section of the Hebrew Bible, consists of two major collections of books: the 'Former Prophets' (Joshua, Judges, 1–2 Samuel, 1–2 Kings) and the 'Latter Prophets' (Isaiah, Jeremiah, Ezekiel and the twelve 'minor' prophets). The Former Prophets includes narratives of early prophets, such as Samuel, Elijah and Elisha (see further, chapter 9); but it is in essence a narrative account covering the winning and losing of the Promised Land – beginning with Joshua's conquest and ending with the fall of Jerusalem and the exile in Babylon. The Torah and Former Prophets are certainly linked, at least editorially – but there are a range of views on exactly how. The textual tradition treats 1–2 Samuel and 1–2 Kings as single books, divided simply to fit on conventionally sized scrolls. The versions present these books as a unit, named Kingdoms (*Basileiai*). The prophetic sympathies of the writer are clear; much later, the Talmud (Baba Bathra, 15a, *c.*500 CE) suggests that the author of Kings was the prophet Jeremiah. The names Joshua, Judges and Samuel reflect the *subject matter* of these books and not the authors. The books of the Latter Prophets bear the names of individual prophets. These writings may ultimately derive from the prophet's ministry, but it is beyond the evidence to claim that they were written and edited by the prophets themselves. Indeed, Isaiah 45.1 mentions the Persian king Cyrus over 150 years after Isaiah's ministry, among oracles clearly contributed by a later hand. Scholars identify these later oracles as the work of Second ('Deutero-') or even Third ('Trito-') Isaiah.

There has been a tendency in scholarship to view texts as small units, looking primarily for sources and historical verification of details. Yet it is important not to forget that the complete texts were put together for a purpose, by writers who imposed their views on the material and provided a *literary* context. Our crucial first critical focus is on the text as it now stands: only from an adequate understanding of this can we hope to penetrate behind it to identify strands and sources.

Joshua

The book of Joshua deals with the conquest of the Promised Land under God's initiative and Joshua's leadership, and its eventual partition between the tribes. It ends with a homily at Shechem stressing the ideal relationship between Yahweh and Israel. The theme of the promise of land is highlighted in Deuteronomy 30.20, a speech of Moses, just before the transition to Joshua – 'the land which the LORD swore to your fathers . . . to give them'. This 'gift of land' theme is picked up in Joshua 1.3 – 'as I promised to Moses'. The difference in perspective concerning whom the promise was made to may suggest separate authorship – or may be due to the different point of view of the character, Moses basing his claim on ancient history, and Joshua basing his on Moses' authority. In Joshua 23.14–16 the theme divides – to stress that the promises have been fulfilled, and that the people will be destroyed if they transgress the covenant and worship other gods. This leads on, in 24.19, to the concept of the holy and jealous God who *will not* forgive sins. Chapter 23 is a key chapter in Joshua's presentation of God's point of view, relating *future* disaster (recounted in Judges) to the past promises. It takes its inspiration from Deuteronomy 7, with its warnings against idolatry.

Joshua is in Moses' shadow (Childs, 1979, 244–5). The law of Moses is central – the *sepher torah* (Josh 1.8), the *book* which 'shall not depart out of your mouth'. Whoever acts on its injunctions shall be 'prosperous' and 'have good success'. The blessings and curses uttered at Mounts Ebal and Gerizim (Deut 27) are *read* in Joshua 8.34. The Torah is fixed, and clearly authoritative. Links with Deuteronomy predominate, but the appearance of Phinehas (22.30–4) also presumes the narrative of Numbers 25. The book of Joshua typifies covenant faithfulness and its consequences, a 'paradigm of obedient Israel' (Childs, 1979, 249). There are examples of broken faith: at Ai (Josh 7.1), going against Deuteronomy 7.25; and the Gibeonite trick (Josh 9), which should have been prevented by Deuteronomy 20.16–18.

The division of land ideally rounds off the conquest; but into this material have been introduced unsettling traditions with an alternative view, in which settlement is presented as patchy and gradual (Josh 15.63; 16.10; 17.12). Some view the lists as historical retrojection of future ideals, and 'priestly'; others see evidence of actual historical lists. Some apportioned land clearly has still to be conquered. Israel will not be successful if it allows the Canaanites to become a 'snare and a trap' (23.13). Idolatry could cause the tribes to lose territory – as is made so very clear in Judges.

The question of where the editor obtained his information has been widely discussed in a century of study. The presence of Pentateuchal sources is frequently claimed. We have already noted the possibility that the book of Joshua, describing the conquest as a fulfilment of the promise of land, originally formed the end of the P corpus, in which promise and fulfilment loom so high. If so, we have three perspectives at least: that of the final or major editor, who saw the conquest as the beginning of problems caused by disobedience; that of P, seeing the events as a remarkable triumph of divine grace, fulfilling earlier promises; and that of the earlier source or sources, each with its own concerns which may or may not have been obscured by later editors. The stories, steeped in the ethic of divinely sanctioned war and designed to legitimize the Israelite land claim, do not always inspire general sympathy, but there is some fine characterization. Rahab of Jericho is finely painted, a marginalized young woman prepared to subvert the community which keeps her in her place – the righteous enemy. Achan epitomizes greed and self-seeking which threatens the common good – incidentally turning 'holy war' into banditry.

Judges

Judges is about *human endeavour*, tracing the struggle experienced by some tribes in maintaining their territory, and the heroes who helped them to victory – Ehud, Deborah and Barak, Gideon, Jephthah, Samson. The introduction is a relentless mass of detail cataloguing disobedience and failure, setting the picture for the reversal in the nation's fortunes. Each character and plot that follows is a variation on a 'deliverer' stereotype – but the story is one of failure, a picture of disobedient Israel. The stories are well told, full of tension and excitement, and rich in detail. The pattern is made explicit:

Whenever the LORD raised up judges for them, the LORD was with the judge, and he saved them from the hand of their enemies all the days of the judge; for the LORD was moved to pity by their groaning because of those who afflicted and oppressed them. But whenever a judge died, they turned back and behaved worse than their fathers, going after other gods, serving them and bowing down to them; they did not drop any of their practices or their stubborn ways. So the anger of the LORD was kindled against Israel; and he said, 'Because this people have transgressed my covenant which I commanded their fathers, and have not obeyed my voice, I will not henceforth drive out before them any of the nations that Joshua left when he died . . . .' (2.18–21)

The judgeship of Othniel (3.7–12) follows the pattern, and others provide unpredictable variations. The cycle of disobedience, God's anger, repentance and salvation becomes the framework of stories coming from an earlier age. Some leaders are more briefly mentioned (generally called 'minor judges'); the brevity of the accounts of them create an illusion that the judges of whom more is said flourished longer (Kort, 1988, 30). Some stories *break* the pattern (e.g. that of Shamgar in 3.31) and others offend it. Abimelech contrasts with Gideon in every way – he seeks office, kills the innocent, and dies shamefully. These stories speak of a society without a king (18.1; 19.1; 21.25) in which the misplaced and displaced of society long for the identity, peace and security that comes with attachment to *land*. The narrative powerfully describes the fears, hopes and aspirations of the alienated of society – political, religious or social refugees. The promise of land, and the fulfilment or withdrawal of that promise, is a major theme running through the Hebrew Bible (Brueggemann, 1977); and the issue of rights to that land still troubles Middle Eastern politics today.

Most scholars are agreed that chapters 17–21 are appendices, added on to the structure of the main book; yet they complete the picture of the chaos resulting from human endeavour. The stories are of theft, idolatry, rape, murder and genocide, all summed up by two statements: there was no king in Israel; and everyone did what was right in his own eyes (21.25). The result was nothing to be proud of.

Judges may have existed as a separate entity before incorporation in the 'Deuteronomic History'. It is reasonably complete in itself (some question whether the point of division from Joshua is now in the right place) and ends sharply before 1 Samuel begins. B. G. Webb (1987) argues that Judges addressed the issue of non-fulfilment of the promise to the patriarchs. Themes are developed artistically throughout the book, leading to a finale in the concluding chapters. Webb finds rhetorical artistry and inner coherence, even when the Deuteronomic passages are removed. If so, the book was *incorporated* but not *created* by the Deuteronomic editor.

Samuel and Kings

The books of Samuel describe the rise of Samuel the prophet and seer in particular, and the appearance of the prophetic movement. The introduction and development of the monarchy are a theme within this, which continues through Kings, giving us detailed information about politics and society in Israel and Judah. This material contains some of the finest artistic creations of the Hebrew Bible. The cycle of narratives about the rise to prominence of Saul, and his tragic decline (1 Sam 8–31), together with the gripping stories of David (1 Sam 16–1 Kgs 2) have been recognized as major artistic achievements (Gunn, 1978; 1980). The books of Samuel and Kings are more fully discussed in chapters 8 and 9.

The Former Prophets: Deuteronomic History?

There are many questions to be asked of these books, and on many issues there is fierce debate amongst scholars as to their historical significance. Many scholars now acknowledge that the stories in the books of Joshua, Judges, Samuel and Kings need first to be read as literature whose narrative artistry can be appreciated. The stories provide evidence first and formost of the *writers*, and of their concerns and theology. Others feel that the primary questions relate to the historical accuracy of the details in these books. Ideally, both approaches should be employed together. What to one scholar may be a clumsy division between two sources may to another be evidence of literary skill. Our judgements need to be finely balanced – and even after the most careful of studies conclusions will be essentially provisional.

How did the narratives originate? Is there significance in their order and chronology? Is there an overall plan? The study of this corpus of literature was decisively shaped in the 1940s by the German publications of M. Noth in which he advanced the theory that Joshua – Kings had been compiled as a unified narrative by an individual during the sixth century BCE, in the early years of the exile (see Noth, 1981). Noth called this work the 'Deuteronomic History' since he believed that it used Deuteronomy (or at least an early verson of it) as its introduction and reflected its language and theological outlook. He held that the 'Deuteronomic historian' used a number of sources. The most extensive, the 'Succession Narrative' or 'Court History' (2 Sam 9–20; 1 Kgs 1–2) tells of how Solomon won the bloody struggle to succeed David on the throne. The Deuteronomic historian was, however, much more than a mere collector of traditions. He compiled and rearranged his material, skilfully weaving together the traditions with speeches and editorial links. These speeches were placed in the mouths of central characters – Joshua (Josh 1, 23) Samuel (1 Sam 12) and Solomon (1 Kgs 8). The editorial sections (e.g. Josh 12; Judg 2.11–23; 2 Kgs 17.7–41) occur at crucial points in the history of the nation.

According to Noth, the Deuteronomic History attempts to come to terms with the traumatic events of 587/6 BCE, when Judah and Jerusalem were humiliated at the hands of the Babylonians. The Deuteronomic historian has *selected* his material and edited it in such a way that it tells the story of Israel from the perspective of trauma and defeat. His purpose was to explain how Israel had gained possession of the land with divine help, had been frequently warned of its solemn obligations and the dangers of apostasy, particularly through the prophets, and yet, through accelerating moral decline, had exhausted God's patience. The Deuteronomic History therefore describes a just retribution, expressed in terms of Deuteronomic law, visited on the community. For Noth, the ending of the work in 2 Kgs

25.27–30 indicates that the judgement on the community was definitive and final:

And in the thirty-seventh year of the exile of Jehoiachin king of Judah . . . Evil-merodach king of Babylon, in the year that he began to reign, graciously freed Jehoiachin king of Judah from prison; and he spoke kindly to him, and gave him a seat above the seats of the kings who were with him in Babylon. So Jehoiachin put off his prison garments. And every day of his life he dined regularly at the king's table; and for his allowance, a regular allowance was given him by the king, every day a portion, as long as he lived.

Noth believed that the point was that the last heir of David's throne was now dead, emphasizing the hopeless situation of the community in exile, and the abrogation of the promise made to the house of David (2 Sam 7).

The structure of the Deuteronomic History, as construed by Noth, may be summarized as follows.

Deuteronomy. Mosaic discourses (e.g. 1–3, 29–30) surround a central core relating to the giving of the law.

Joshua. The theme of obedience and conquest, concluding with a final speech of Joshua (Josh 23)

Judges. The theme of apostasy and decline after Israel occupies the land.

The cycle of sin, punishment, repentance and salvation. The editorial passage 2.11–21 provides the format for the 'deliverer stories'.

1–2 Samuel. The rise of the monarchy, continuing the theme of the people's rejection of Yahweh their God.

Samuel's programmatic speech in 1 Samuel 12 emphasizes that, unless Israel and its king remain obedient to God, they will be rejected and punished.

The tragedy of Saul and the story of David further illustrate the continuing themes of obedience/disobedience, sin, repentance and deliverance.

1–2 Kings. Solomon's speech at the dedication of the Temple (1 Kgs 8).

The apostasy of the monarchy, especially the northern kings, resulting in the destruction of the northern kingdom, Israel (2 Kgs 17).

The chequered history of the southern kingdom, Judah, reaching a climax in the destruction of Jerusalem. The loss of political and religious autonomy and, for many of the community, exile from the land.
The work finishes with the release of Jehoiachin, the last Davidic king.

Assessing Noth's Theory

Noth's hypothesis of a unified Deuteronomic History achieved widespread support. However, there is currently no agreement on the location of its composition, whether in Palestine, as Noth believed, or in Babylonia; or on whether it was the product a *single* author or is the result of a more complex process of composition. Cross (1973) and Nelson (1981) argue that the work in its original form was completed during the reign of Josiah, before Judah's defeat and exile. This Josianic edition was then edited during the exile in the light of the crushing defeat. Others, particularly in Germany, have proposed several editors, with differing concerns. Despite the sustained debate, there remains strong scholarly support for Noth's innovative recognition of the Former Prophets as an entity, even if the precise details and stages of its composition still elude definitive description. Most importantly, the theory gives this body of material a meaningful, coherent structure, in which a clear theological message unfolds. It seems to explain a great deal while creating relatively few new problems – the test of all hypothetical reconstructions. Material which does not fit in with or contradicts a hypothesis causes it to be reformulated or abandoned. Works continue to appear reformulating the details of the Deuteronomic historian's achievement, but there is no move to abandon Noth's theory altogether.

A reading of the major speeches and analyses of history throughout the work illustrates the force of Noth's view that there is a large degree of unity in the final composition. It soon becomes clear that there are common themes and a distinct theological perspective of the history of Israel designed to drive home the lessons of that history to the community. The repetitive Deuteronomic language and the associated theological interpretation of history, seen particularly in the speeches and editorial links (Josh 1, 12, 23; Judg 2.11–23; 1 Sam 12; 1 Kgs 8.14–61; 2 Kgs 17.7–41), provide a recognizable structure and shape to the Deuteronomic History in its final form.

The way in which the ending of the work is understood has important implications. On Noth's view, after the death of Jehoiachin little hope remained for the community reading this treatise of God's dealings with Israel. However, these concluding verses can be read more positively. G. von Rad (1953) proposed an alternative interpretation by arguing that the release of Jehoiachin and upturn in his fortunes offered a lifeline to the defeated exiles. Hope was not entirely lost. There was still an honoured Davidic king, heir to God's promise. The community had not been completely abandoned. Or could there be an implied criticism of an 'evil' king (2 Kgs 24.9) *enjoying* his exile? All great literature has a dynamic open-ended quality. Both views constrain the text too rigidly. Both negative and positive poles are present together, in a tension which allows the material to be reinterpreted in changing circumstances. H. Wolff (1975) sees conditional hope in the Deuteronomic History. If the community *repent*, Yahweh their god will respond and save them. The book of Joshua stresses obedience, which brought clear success. Judges demonstrates what happens when the community forget their obligations to the law. Only when they repent is a deliverer sent: for the exiled community also, repentance and obedience to the law give them their only hope of return and restoration. The conclusion is therefore open-ended – with the possibility of restoration; and the threat of continued estrangement if the exiles do not respond positively. On this view, Noth's Deuteronomic History has the richness, diversity and adaptability of a well-crafted literary work.

The Historical Value of the Deuteronomic History

Noth believed that the work was based on material already available, including a self-contained and detailed account of the occupation. The author did not fabricate the history of his people but presented it clearly. He transmitted traditional accounts with reverence and accuracy, if selectively. His purpose was to teach the true meaning of the history of Israel. In Noth's view, this great work shares with modern history-writing the concern to make the past relevant to the present.

Noth's assessment of the historical value of this work has come under closer scrutiny in recent years. The process of selection must raise questions about value judgements and bias, as in all history-writing. It is important to ask a number of questions. Why did the compiler select particular episodes and omit others? What was the purpose of his work in the first place, and how has this coloured the presentation of particular episodes? The speeches and structure show that the Deuteronomic History is a theological interpretation of history, a *secondary* source which historians should use only with great caution. Even Noth acknowledged that, despite the author's fidelity to his sources, he nevertheless made 'corrections' to the traditions. The way in which traditions were combined and incorporated into the overall structure placed a distinctive interpretation upon them. Noth was well aware of the problems this posed for the historian and concluded that the Deuteronomic historian had significantly affected the presentation of the story.

The entertaining and skilful compositions challenge the reader to consider the possibilities and pitfalls of a theological reading of history. The presentation of particular reigns has been dictated and constrained by a rigid and dogmatic framework. Where data can be checked against archaeological evidence and inscriptions, it is clear that theology is more important than faithful recording. Omri, king of the northern kingdom, Israel, and founder of the city of Samaria (876–869 BCE), a powerful king according to Assyrian records, is dismissed in a mere eight verses (1 Kgs 16.21–8) with the negative judgement that he 'did what was evil in the sight of LORD, and did more evil than all who were before him'. The material from Judges is often used to reconstruct the period of settlement. Noth, for instance, believed that the list of so-called 'minor judges' (Judg 10.1–5; 12.7–15) was based on official records of an ancient office. However, the *message* of the work is central, and this must raise questions about historicity.

It is clear that the modern historian using the Deuteronomic History should proceed with caution. It is clearly a complex and selective theological interpretation of history. Modern research needs to decide to what extent the writer was influenced by the concerns of the community which he was himself addressing – a community exiled from its homeland, without a temple, without a king, wondering if they had been abandoned by their god.

The Settlement of the Land

Anyone who reads the books of Joshua and Judges closely cannot help but be struck by a number of important differences in the presentation of Israel's acquision of the land. The impression that most people have of the 'conquest' of Canaan is that of a swift, successful and miraculous campaign in which Israel, aided by Yahweh their god, swept all before it. The book of Joshua describes how Joshua masterminded the defeat of the Canaanite cities in a brilliant and swift military campaign. There is such a wealth of detail in the narratives that at first reading it is not possible to appreciate subtle differences in some of the accounts. Judges cannot fail to provoke many questions. The reader is informed of a number of Canaanite cities which have not been captured or destroyed by Israel, calling into question the authenticity of the material. When referring back to Joshua, it soon becomes apparent that the account is not consistent even with itself. A number of passages are in accord with Judges 1 and suggest that Israel did not enjoy the unhindered success its own narrative suggests (Josh 15.13–19, 63; 16.10; 17.12). Can we evaluate these differing accounts from a historical point of view? Or is the theological message more central? Is the tension between the two accounts perhaps deliberate? Most of Joshua illustrates the rewards of obedience. For a community outside their homeland, the story presents the view that Yahweh their god can intervene. Yet they are not to expect divine help as a matter of course: it depends totally on their own worthiness and faithfulness. The story therefore introduces a note of caution. God will not act on Israel's behalf at *any* cost. If the people fail to live up to the covenant obligations as outlined in the Deuteronomic law, and reject God to pursue other gods, then they will suffer the consequences. Judges drives home the endless cycle of apostasy. God is portrayed as compassionate and long-suffering in the face of blatant disobedience. When the people repent, they *will* be delivered.

The disturbing and frightening stories which form an appendix to Judges (chs 17–21) describe the worship of images, rape and murder, confirming the sad religious and moral decline of Israel. The narrator drives this home with a repeated 'in those days there was no king in Israel', emphasizing the lack of leadership in the community. The conclusion of the book adds the words, 'every man did what was right in his own eyes' (21.25). Was early Israel like this, anarchic, without social constraints? Or is this royal propaganda, suggesting that order could only be brought about once Israel had a strong monarchy? The books which follow tell the story of the leadership which emerged – judge – prophets such as Samuel, who governed effectively, and kings who persisted in ruling badly, in the narrator's view. The criticism of kings is explicit, and the presence of true prophets is presented as a thorn in the sides of the dynastic kings. The narrator's exiled readers had no political leadership. The king was banqueting in comfort. Their only hope lay in the prophetic message, of hope conditional on obedience and repentance, in the certain knowledge that their plight could have been avoided. This understanding shaped their present – and must also shape their future.

In the Hebrew Bible, it is not insignificant that the prophetic *writings* immediately follow this powerful analysis of failure.

Historical Models

Three main proposals have been put forward by historians to explain the emergence of Israel in Palestine. These are hypothetical models, attempts to set the material in a framework that gives it more coherence. Such hypotheses should be exposed to critical debate and tested to ensure their appropriateness and to discover their limitations. New archaeological evidence and methodological changes in the study of the text have both contributed to and shaped the debate.

The Infiltration Model In 1925 A. Alt published an important study of the Israelite occupation of Palestine which offered a fresh perspective on the biblical narratives (see Alt, 1966). He utilized important Egyptian documents, including the 'Amarna letters' (a group of letters written by rulers in various Canaanite cities to the Egyptian pharaoh during the fourteenth century BCE), to illustrate the topography and settlement patterns of Palestine at the end of the Late Bronze Age (1500–1200 BCE). These documents give valuable information about Palestine in the fourteenth century BCE Palestine. Alt demonstrated in particular that the lowlands were densely populated and controlled by a network of small city states, whereas the highlands were only thinly populated and outside the control of the urban centres. This comparative study of biblical and extra-biblical material claimed that Israel had settled in areas, such as the central hill country, which had previously been only sparsely populated. Alt came to the conclusion that the Israelites were semi-nomads, dependent upon flocks and herds of domesticated sheep and goats, and that they entered Palestine over a protracted period in search of pasturage. He proposed a gradual and mostly peaceful infiltration from outside by groups who settled first in the southern hills. It was only later, when they tried to move to the lowlands (during the period of Saul and David), that they came into conflict with the Canaanite cities. This view gives priority to those traditions which describe a gradual and complex process of settlement. Alt placed little store in the historical authenticity of Joshua's military campaign.

Alt's views were followed and further developed by his pupil M. Noth (1960) and later by M. Weippert (1971). Noth developed a theory of settlement now known as the *amphictyonic hypothesis*. It is one of the great landmarks of biblical scholarship in the twentieth century. It is discussed later in this chapter.

The strength of the infiltration model lies in the way it deals with the tensions in the biblical narrative. It stresses the complexity of settlement, and how long it took. It takes seriously the biblical narratives and acknowledges the difficulties involved in trying to interpret this material. The major objection is that it relies heavily on an outdated view of nomadism. It has been common in the past to attribute changes in material culture to the influx of new ethnic groups from outside. Recent studies of nomadism, utilized in biblical studies first by G. E. Mendenhall (1962) and later N. K. Gottwald (1979), have completely undermined theories of nomadic and semi-nomadic incursions into Palestine. The traditional understanding is that nomads were violently opposed to settled communities, often erupting into settled areas. In the course of time the nomads adopted agriculture and became settled themselves. However, it has become clear that the interrelationship is much more complex. Villagers kept herds of cattle, sheep and goats to protect themselves against crop seizure or failure. These flocks and herds had to be moved seasonally to find pasture, and highlanders would often need to graze their animals in the lowlands. Settled villagers were therefore also pastoralists. There would undoubtedly be quarrels over grazing and wells, but also co-operation. There is great doubt also over the presence of camel nomads, and whether the camel was domesticated by this time. Camel nomadism is, at any rate, not a useful analogy or model for early Israelite nomadic practices. In addition, the deserts around Palestine have never been able to support a large nomadic population, which undermines the view that Israel *en masse* emerged from the desert in the thirteenth century to take the land either by force or infiltration.

The Conquest of Palestine W. F. Albright and G. E. Wright, American biblical scholars and archaeologists, were convinced that the biblical account of the violent destruction of major Palestinian cities was historically accurate. They pointed to archaeological discoveries of poor rural sites in the uplands which contrasted with the rich lowland sites, and to apparent innovations in the finds at the upland sites: four-roomed houses and a distinctive form of pottery known as collared-rim ware because of the distinctive shape of the neck. All this seemed to provide evidence for an Israelite presence. Archaeologists already knew the biblical framework of violent battle (e.g. Josh 10.40) and the deep-rooted enmity between Israelite and Canaanite. Archaeology appeared to confirm that there had been a widespread destruction of Canaanite cities around the thirteenth – twelfth centuries BCE: Hazor, Megiddo, Ashdod, Tell ed-Duweir, Tell el-Hesi, Tell Deir 'Alla amongst others. These finds offered an impressive demonstration of the biblical destructions of Hazor (Josh 11.10–11), Lachish (10.31–3), Eglon (10.34–5), and Debir (10.38–9). There was evidence also of a new culture on some destroyed sites (e.g. Hazor, Succoth, Bethel and Debir) and in new villages in the hill country. There seemed no doubt whatever that the Israelites had been responsible. The argument was neat and powerful: the biblical text had been confirmed by outside, objective and independent evidence. This view became – and remains – very influential in the United States and in Britain.

However, a closer examination of the evidence and arguments reveals significant weaknesses. We have already explored problems in the historical account of the conquest, and in the concept of nomadism; but the greatest irony is that the case foundered on archaeological evidence, the very linchpin of Albright's case. Jericho (Josh 6) and Ai (Josh 8) play a central role in the account of the conquest, but excavations at each site (Tell es-Sultan and Tell et-Tell) have failed to find any signs of major occupation around the thirteenth century BCE. Attempts to explain away these discrepancies have not been successful. There is also no positive evidence that it was Israelites who were responsible for those destructions that have been convincingly dated to this time, and destructions are found in areas well out of Israelite range. There are other ways of accounting for the evidence – Egyptian campaigns (which are well-documented), the incursions of the Sea Peoples, conflicts between Canaanite cities, domestic fires and earthquakes. Furthermore, the 'distinctive' collared-rim ware and four-roomed houses have now been found elsewhere in Palestine and Transjordan. It is now clear that it is not sound to attach ethnic labels to these remains. It seems more likely that the poor material culture once identified as Israelite was more specifically the result of a general drop in material prosperity over an area rather larger than that involved in biblical conquest narratives.

It has to be admitted that the conquest model is selective in the presentation of both the biblical material and the archaeological data. Knowledge of the biblical framework can easily seduce even archaeologists into believing that they have found what they wanted to find. It is most important that the two fields are examined *independently*, if we are to have any confidence in the 'evidence' which emerges.

Peasant's Revolt Model   The questions and difficulties which we have raised about the conquest and infiltration models were examined further by Mendenhall (1962), who developed the controversial thesis that 'Israel' was formed in large part from native Canaanites who revolted against their rulers. These disaffected peasants were aroused by a small group of fugitives who had escaped from forced labour in Egypt. Canaan had long been dominated by various city states under the nominal control of Egypt. The urban elite, petty kings with their bureaucracy and religious officials, extracted the agricultural surplus from the surrounding countryside in order to feed and pay the urban specialists. The peasants were subjected to continuous taxation in the form of produce and forced labour, and were required for military service. The Amarna letters (fourteenth century BCE) clearly show the political turmoil and social strife around the Canaanite cities as various petty kings vied for power and greater control of strategic areas. Mendenhall argued that the numerically small exodus group acted as an important catalyst for social unrest and grievances. They brought with them potent traditions of escape from bondage in Egypt with the help of their god Yahweh. The peasant communities of Palestine, who had been subjected to continuous exploitation by the urban elite under the aegis of the Egyptian imperial power, were able to identify with such liberation traditions. 'Israel' was formed when large numbers of disaffected peasants rejected the exploitative social set-up of urban Canaan and joined in the covenant with Yahweh.

N. K. Gottwald has elaborated this hypothesis with a detailed study (1979) of the development and social organization of Israel. He sees an early

Israel which included peasants, pastoralists, mercenaries, bandits, itinerant crafts specialists and others. Israel was, he argued, an egalitarian tribal confederation organized to resist the exploitative hierarchy of urban Canaan. Although in Mendenhall's view early Israel chose a theocracy, rejecting forms of earthly power, Gottwald and M. Chaney (1983) argue that an alternative power structure soon developed.

The peasants' revolt model has become extremely influential, particularly in the United States, but there have been criticisms. Some label it 'Marxist': arguments through labels are notoriously emotive and fail to grasp the essential issues. The focus of rational criticism has been directed to the point that this reconstruction runs counter to the biblical traditions, and does not explain the deep-seated enmity between Israelites and Canaanites. The most extensive critique comes from N. Lemche (1985), who questions basic assumptions derived from American evolutionary anthropology. In response, some biblical support has been claimed, with the general disclaimer that texts edited in the monarchy would not consciously preserve and legitimate traditions of co-operation between Canaanites and Israelites. That some such traditions have been preserved is therefore particularly significant. Rahab's aid to the Israelites (Josh 2.1–14; 6.22–5) and the treaty with the Gibeonites (Josh 9, 10) provide examples. Joshua 24 may portray an alliance with Shechemites. It was the royal hierarchy which was the target of opposition, as seen in the list of defeated kings in Joshua 12. Judges 5, an ancient poem, speaks of 'the triumphs of the LORD, the triumphs of his peasantry in Israel' (v. 11) in a battle against Canaanite *kings*. The hostility to Canaanites focused on the ruling aristocracy, the urban centres. The revolt model is further strengthened by extra-biblical data such as the Amarna letters, raising the question of a possible connection between the 'Hebrews' (*'ibri*) and the *apiru* (outlaws) of the letters – or whether at least an analogy can be claimed. Lemche, in response, doubts that many of the biblical texts are early.

Thus, even strongly supported hypotheses provoke controversy. It cannot, however, be doubted that this elaboration of the social organization has added a new perspective to the study of early Israel which has helped to break the sterile impasse over infiltration or conquest. The model has forced scholars to reassess the kinds of presuppositions which inform their study of the text of the Hebrew Bible, and has encouraged the exploration of methodologies from other disciplines. Although we see that the process of Israel's emergence was extremely complex, new and exciting possibilities are now opening up, stimulating the search for more information on the nature and structure of early Israelite society.

Indigenous-Development Model   Recently a number of scholars, while broadly accepting the revolt model, have pushed the debate in new directions. These support the view that Israel emerged in Canaan, but do not regard the *revolt* as being necessary or significant. Some, but not all, draw explicitly on the work of Mendenhall and Gottwald but feel that conflict and unrest was not the decisive factor in Israel's formation.

One of the interesting features is the number of scholars who approach the study from the perspective of the growing archaeological data, studied *independently* of the biblical text. D. C. Hopkins (1985) has studied the agriculture of the period. J. A. Callaway (1985), who was responsible for the important excavations at Ai and Raddana, two rural sites in the Palestine hills, proposes that population movements came from the west (that is, from the lowlands) rather than from the east as the biblical story presupposes. Lemche (1985) accepts that the formation of Israel was largely indigenous to Palestine; R. B. Coote and K. W. Whitelam (1987) link this indigenous development to the collapse of international trade. The emergence of the rural villages in the central hill country was a *result of*, and not *a cause of*, the decline in trade which undermined the lowland urban centres. These reconstructions which stress the indigenous formation of Israel tend to treat the biblical text as secondary to the interpretation of archaeological data. It must however be recognized that archaeological data are ambiguous and notoriously difficult to interpret. It remains to be seen how successful these reconstructions will be and what changes will be made as future excavations in Israel, Jordan, Lebanon and Syria are used to test the hypothesis.

The Nature of Early Israel

Even if the question of how Israel emerged within Palestine can be resolved, an equally fundamental problem remains: *what was Israel?* What kind of society was it, and how was it organized? Do the stories reflect society, or are the details just as much larger-than-life as the central characters? It may appear startling to note that there is no longer any agreement among scholars concerning the nature of early Israelite society. It is not clear what the term Israel referred to in this early period. The earliest reference to Israel outside the Bible is in the Egyptian Merniptah stele, *c.* 1220 BCE. This monumental inscription was set up to commemorate a victory over Libyans, but concludes with details about the pacification of Syria – Palestine. In exaggerated language, it claims that Egyptian troops had wiped out 'the seed of Israel for ever'. No further details are known.

The Amphictyonic Hypothesis From the 1930s until comparatively recently, part of the bedrock of biblical studies was Noth's view (1930) that early Israel was organized as a twelve-tribe religious confederation devoted to the worship of Yahweh at a central sanctuary. Noth's detailed analysis of genealogies and tribal lists focused on the recurrence of the number twelve. Even when the tribe of Levi was omitted, the number twelve was maintained by dividing the Joseph tribe into two, Ephraim and Manasseh. Noth drew cross-cultural analogies with similar 'amphictyonic' leagues attached to religious centres in ancient Greece and Italy – particularly those around the shrines at Delphi and Pylai. He argued that the twelve-tribe system was similar, with the twelve tribes being responsible, on a monthly basis, for the maintenance and upkeep of the shrine. Israel, represented by the leaders of the tribes (e.g. Num 1.5–15) would meet at the sanctuary for religious festivals and the proclamation of sacral law. The Israelite amphictyony had central officers, the so-called 'minor judges' (Judg 10.1–5; 12.7–15) responsible for the administration of law. Noth believed that the account of the covenant-renewal ceremony in Joshua 24 preserved important information on the founding of the amphictyony at the central shrine at Shechem. The shrine became the amphictyonic centre when the Ark was present; Bethel, Gilgal and Shiloh also served as centres on other occasions.

Noth's amphictyonic hypothesis was remarkably influential. The Greek amphictyonies are well-documented, and the model gave a compelling shape and order to the fragmentary biblical traditions. His reconstruction provided a context in which to understand and interpret wide-ranging traditions concerning national unity in which the cult of Yahweh was seen as central and unifying. This understanding of the nature and organization of early Israel dominated the presuppositions of biblical scholars for several decades. Even Albright and other proponents of the conquest model (e.g. Bright, 1981) accepted Noth's analysis.

The collapse of the hypothesis occurred suddenly and dramatically as its central tenets dissolved under sustained scrutiny. It has now become clear that the biblical texts offer little support for the view that particular shrines acted as central sanctuaries for some pan-tribal organization encompassing all Israel. Nor is there any proof for an inter-tribal body of officials. On further investigation, it has been found that Mediterranean amphictyonies were not exclusively organized around twelve tribes or cities. Moreover, here the amphictyony held together *pre-existent* tribes or city states. The religious confederation posited for early Israel was claimed to be responsible for the *formation* of the nation.

The success, and ultimate failure, of Noth's amphictyonic hypothesis demonstrates an important methodological concern. His cross-cultural analogy was used to explain ambiguous and difficult biblical material. The hypothesis appeared to work, in relation to the texts examined. Subsequent studies searched for anomalies to test the hypothesis, and these gradually weakened the case. Eventually the anomalies were more significant than the ability of the hypothesis to explain – it raised more problems than it solved. At that point the hypothesis was considered to be fundamentally flawed, and abandoned. As greater use is made of anthropological, ethnographic and sociological studies, it is important to ensure that theories and data imported from other disciplines, often from societies far removed in time and space from early Israel, *have been sufficiently understood in their own context* before meaningful comparisons can be drawn. The scholar is involved in a dynamic process of research and testing. Testing and modifying models and hypotheses is essential if the study is to develop.

With the demise of the amphictyony, the search has continued for an alternative. There still remains, despite the extended critique of Noth's work, an underlying assumption that early Israel possessed national identity and was a religious and tribal confederation. Will this survive future analysis?

Segmentary-Society Model It has recently become common to describe early Israel as a segmentary society. The model has been drawn from anthropological studies, particularly the work of M. Fortes and E. E. Evans-Pritchard (1940) on African political systems. A. Malamat (1973), R. R. Wilson (1977), N. K. Gottwald (1979) and A. D. H. Mayes (1985) have recently applied the segmentary-society model to early Israel. A segmentary society is one in which there is no centralized political authority but rather a number of clans make up larger tribal groupings who maintain a balance of power, often through competition. The basic unit of the political system is the extended family under the authority of a single head, who may represent it in political and religious situations. *Unilineal* descent and genealogical relationships (i.e. through *either* the male or female line) are of paramount importance. Although the society is not politically centralized, there are examples of more coherent political leadership during periods of crisis, when an individual may temporarily exercise power over several tribes.

The features of segmentary societies outlined above appear to offer a very close analogy to early Israel as presented in Judges and Samuel. Gottwald's extensive analysis (1979) of the extended family, clan and tribe in biblical traditions has greatly strengthened the case for using this model. Judges, in particular, illustrates temporary charismatic leadership and the lack of centralized authority. Israel, like segmentary societies, nevertheless possessed a notion of national unity. We should, however, be cautious in the use of cross-cultural analogies. Mayes (1985), although generally supporting the use of the model, finds no correspondence in African society to the worship of Yahweh as the basis of unity. J. W. Rogerson (1986) and D. Fiensy (1987), drawing on current anthropological discussions, have raised serious questions: they point out that the social and political organization of 'segmentary' African societies differs in important ways from that of early Israel, and that we must therefore beware of generalizing. Evans-Pritchard's claim that the Nuer of the Sudan were achepalous (without continuous leaders) has been questioned by others in his own field. Social anthropologists of his time were not averse to using biblical examples as explanatory models for *their* observations, implicitly or explicitly; so we, in using their analyses, run the danger of constructing a circular argument. Further, it should not be forgotten that the biblical traditions are not in their present form the product of pre-monarchic Israel.

Thus the material in Joshua and Judges has proved to be frustrating for the historian attempting to reconstruct the processes involved in the emergence of early Israel and the nature of its social organization. The regional archaeological surveys and excavations at present being undertaken in the area may shed further light on the complex processes at work, and attempts to reconstruct the history of Palestine from a primarily archaeological perspective may have far-reaching implications. It has brought to the fore the fundamental question of how to read and interpret the Hebrew Bible – if not as history, then as a complex narrative and a rich collection of religious traditions of high literary quality, the end product of a protracted process of interpretation and adaptation.

The following two chapters give a detailed account of Samuel and Kings. Chapter 8 looks at the central focus on Jerusalem; chapter 9 discusses the stories of significant prophets.

FURTHER READING

Coote, R. B., and Whitelam, K. W. 1987: *The Emergence of Early Israel in Historical Perspective.*
Finkelstein, I. 1988: *The Archaeology of the Israelite Settlement.*
Klein, L. R. 1988: *The Triumph of Irony in the Book of Judges.*
Mayes, A. D. H. 1985: *Judges.*
Noth, M. 1981: *The Deuteronomic History.*
Ramsey, G. W. 1981: *The Quest for the Historical Israel: Reconstructing Israel's Early History.*

8

Jerusalem

Philip Davies

Preliminary Reading   2 Samuel; 1 Kings.

Early Jerusalem

Jerusalem owes its existence, first of all, to the Gihon spring, where the earliest evidence of human occupation has been found (about 3000 BC). The hill above it (later called the Ophel) was the site of the earliest Jerusalem, from which the city spread in the biblical period, although it lies outside the present walls. It is surrounded by valleys on three sides; to the north rises the more imposing hill on which the Temple of Solomon and its successors stood – now occupied by the Dome of the Rock and the el-Aqsa mosque. The earliest claimed reference to Jerusalem in ancient documents is among the texts from ancient Ebla (Tell Mardikh in Syria), dating from *c*.2500 BCE, which mention a city called Salim. More certainly, the Egyptian execration texts, curses against enemies written on pottery vessels and dating from the nineteenth–eighteenth centuries BCE, include 'the kings of Rushalimum'. Further direct evidence of settlement, including traces of a city wall, and tombs across the valley on the slopes of the Mount of Olives, confirms that the city is at least a thousand years older than King David. In the fourteenth century BCE 'Urusalim' is mentioned among several Canaanite cities in the diplomatic correspondence recovered from the then Egyptian capital at el-Amarna; we even know the name of its king, Abdi-Heba.

The early Israelites did not found the city of Jerusalem: they acquired it by capture. The written records of the acquisition of the land are none too clear about how or when this happened. According to Joshua 10, Joshua defeated a coalition of kings including Adoni-zedek of Jerusalem and killed them all (see also Josh 12.10), but, although the chapter ends with a note that 'Joshua defeated the whole land', the capture of Jerusalem itself is not specifically recorded. Joshua 15, part of a survey of Israelite tribal

169

allotments, mentions Jerusalem again; in v. 8 the border of Judah skirts round the southern side of 'the Jebusite (that is, Jerusalem)', but the city was not yet part of Israel: 'But the Jebusites, the inhabitants of Jerusalem, the people of Judah could not drive out, so the Jebusites dwell with the people of Judah at Jerusalem to this day' (v. 63). 'To this day' is an interesting remark, because it means that in the writer's time the city had been occupied by Israelites, who had nevertheless not displaced the earlier inhabitants. The statement also assigns to Judah the responsibility for failing to capture the city.

These traditions about Jerusalem reappear in Judges 1. Here Joshua's fight with Adoni-zedek becomes a fight between the tribe of Judah and Adoni-*bezek* (vv. 7–8), while v. 21 reaffirms that Jerusalem itself was not captured, but this time puts the blame onto the tribe of Benjamin: 'But the people of Benjamin did not drive out the Jebusites who dwelt in Jerusalem; so the Jebusites have dwelt with the people of Benjamin in Jerusalem to this day.' Here is a problem. Which tribe *did* occupy Jerusalem alongside the Jebusites? And when did this occupation occur? Certainly not by the time referred to in Judges 19.11, where the travelling Levite approaching the city of 'Jebus' hears his servant suggest entering this 'city of the Jebusites' and replies, 'We will not turn aside into the city of foreigners who do not belong to the people of Israel.' So, the biblical story tells us, even late in the period of the Judges, the city of Jebus was occupied by Canaanites who took their name from it.

The capture of Jebus was, it seems, actually one of the achievements of David's men and is described in 2 Samuel 5. Here the city, again called Jebus, is also named the 'stronghold of Zion', which, we learn, becomes the residence of David and is thereafter called the 'city of David'. Why David wished to take the city is not clear. The story suggests that it was taken as a challenge, because of the saying that even blind and lame people could ward off an attacker. Such a proverb may suggest that the city was in an almost impregnable position and thus ideal as a capital for an ambitious king. The conflicting statements in Joshua and Judges may give us a further clue: it lay in territory assigned both to Judah and to Benjamin, and was therefore on the borders of the kingdoms of Israel (of which Benjamin, King Saul's tribe, was the southernmost tribe) and Judah, David's realm. As a capital city of a united Israel-and-Judah it was well placed; and, indeed, during his reign it seems to have remained David's own city rather than an official part of either kingdom, by right of personal conquest.

We have so far encountered many names for the city; Jerusalem, Jebus, city of David, Zion. 'Salem' and 'Moriah' are two other names, occurring in two very interesting stories involving Abraham. The first is in Genesis 14, already discussed in Chapter 4.

This is a curious story. After the defeat of four still-unidentified kings, Abraham is met by the king of Sodom 'at the valley of Shavneh (that is, the king's valley)'. Here 'Melchizedek king of Salem brought out bread and wine; he was priest of God Most High [El Elyon]'; and he blessed Abraham, receiving in return a tithe of Abraham's goods. Who is this Melchizedek? The sudden appearance (and just as sudden disappearance) prompted later speculation (in a text from the Dead Sea Scrolls) that he was an angelic figure, while his dual kingly and priestly role is referred to in Psalm 110, probably addressed to the Israelite king.

Three clues point to a connection between Melchizedek and Jerusalem. The first and most obvious is 'Salem', which in Psalm 76.2 is also used as an abbreviation for the city. Second is the expression 'El Elyon', an ancient title for God used at Jebus/Jerusalem and later applied to Yahweh, particularly in the Psalms. Third, 'zedek' is also an element in the name of another king of Jerusalem, Adoni-zedek in Joshua 10.1, and, although it can be translated as 'righteousness', it might be the name of the deity of the city. These clues are far from conclusive historically; 'Salem' might be another place altogether – but there is hardly any doubt that Melchizedek was subsequently thought to have come from Jerusalem. The story of the meeting between Abraham and Melchizedek, brief and curious though it is, makes the important connection between the great patriarch and the great holy city. Apart from this, although Jebusites are occasionally mentioned, the city of Jebus/Jerusalem is not mentioned before the book of Joshua. The 'adoption' of Abraham by the city through its king–priest who received tithes and gave a blessing was no doubt of great religious and political value to the city and its rulers. It is not inconceivable that this explains why the story was told.

The account of the near-sacrifice of Isaac fulfils a similar function. The story is set in the 'land of Moriah', a name which occurs elsewhere only in 2 Chronicles 3.1: 'Then Solomon began to build the house of the Lord in Jerusalem on Mount Moriah, where the Lord had appeared to David his father . . . . ' It is strange that this very important identification was not made in the account of 2 Kings but only in a book composed in the period of the Second Temple, in the fifth or fourth century BCE. This may suggest that the identification is a late fiction, whose purpose is quite clear. The sacrificial system of Solomon's Temple, implies the story, was inaugurated on the very spot by Abraham, whose near-sacrifice of his son serves as the prototype of all subsequent sacrifices in the Temple. If this connection was not important in the first Temple period before the exile, it was certainly valued later, after the traumas of exile and partial restoration, when the Temple and its rituals became a central symbol for the Judahites who sought precious links with the ancient past.

Jerusalem and the Ark of the Covenant

Thus Jerusalem became David's capital; but more than a geographical bond was needed to unite the two kingdoms successfully. A symbol of religious unity was required in the newly won city. One of the chief cultic objects was the Ark, which lay several miles outside Jerusalem at Baale-Judah (Kiriath-jearim according to 2 Sam 7), and had been there for twenty years (1 Sam 7.2). Of the origin of this wooden box we cannot be very certain. It is said to have been manufactured in the wilderness under Moses' instructions (Exod 25, Deut 10), brought into Canaan with Joshua (Josh 3) and used in the capture of Jericho (Josh 6). It was taken later to Mount Ebal (near Shechem; Josh 8.33) after which time we hear nothing of it until Judges 20.27, where we are told, in passing, that it happened to be in Bethel. By the beginning of 1 Samuel it is lodged in Shiloh. If these reports are at all close to the facts, the Ark, which had begun life as a moving object, had increasingly been set down at sanctuaries. From Shiloh (1 Sam 4) it had been carried out to the battlefield and captured by the Philistines, who, blaming disasters on its presence, had let it go. David's plan to move it to the 'city of David' (1 Sam 6) was surely intended not only to further its prestige, but also to underline David's defeat of the Philistines, and present him as the God-given saviour of the nation.

Despite a slight hitch, a man's death blamed on the Ark's power, the move was accomplished and the Ark was housed in a tent which David had made for it. This tent introduces us to another religious symbol and another historical problem. From its very beginnings, the Ark is housed, according to Exodus 26, in a tent (or 'tabernacle'). In fact, the tent is often referred to apart from the Ark, and it may well be that the association of tent and Ark is not original. Indeed, the tent entirely disappears from the books of Joshua and Judges: it is clear that the biblical picture is not as simple as it appears at first sight. We are faced, then, with two alternative explanations of the origin of the association of tent and Ark. The biblical explanation is that the two belonged together from the time of Moses. Accordingly, it could be argued, the Ark was always supposed to be housed in some kind of structure, but, when not being transported, it would rest in a sanctuary (Shechem, Bethel, Shiloh, for instance). Thus, when David recovers it, he naturally provides for it a housing, because it has no sanctuary. David's next step would then be to provide a permanent house for it, as indeed he proposes in 2 Samuel 7. The divine reply to this suggestion is 'I have not dwelt in a house since the day I brought the people of Israel from Egypt to this day, but I have been moving about in a tent for my dwelling' (v. 6). Yet this seems to be contradicted by 1 Samuel 3.3: 'Samuel was lying down within the temple of the Lord, where the ark of God was.' This first explanation, then, runs up against a flat contradiction.

The second explanation assumes that the Ark is already housed in the Temple at Jerusalem, as it was, apparently, after the time of Solomon. As an ancient precedent, the tent was justified by an extremely elaborate description in Exodus 26 and 36. This is no flimsy covering, but a highly ornate mobile 'temple', and, in the view of most scholars, is intended by the author of Exodus to be the Temple's prototype, sanctioning the later royal decision to house the Ark in a temple. Did such a decision need justifying? The divine response to David just quoted may suggest just that: there was a strong feeling that the Ark did *not* belong in a permanent house, but belonged in a tent. On the other hand, it was housed in places such as Shiloh, which might have been sufficient precedent for the building of a temple.

While we would obviously like firm historical conclusions about arrangements for the Ark, we have to recognize that the biblical stories were written later than the events they describe, when conditions had changed, and that they were written partly to justify later situations by explaining how they preserved ancient practices. When we meet conflicting claims, we are dealing with two different views of the link between Ark and Temple: one view sees the Temple housing as a divinely disapproved innovation; the other implies that the ark had already been housed in a temple. The compromise between these two conflicting views is to say that the Ark had *not* previously been housed in a building, only in a tent, but that the tent was a forerunner of the Temple and came to be described as if it were a rudimentary temple. It is difficult to discover the truth behind the complex biblical picture, which suggests a society in which institutions are being evaluated and re-evaluated by creative use of the past. Seen in this way, texts can become three-dimensional, revealing more about the conflicts and concerns of the society in which the stories were created and re-created than about the past that they reconstruct. The biblical writers' view of the past is being constantly 'updated' in the light of later reflection. A minor example of this is the concern to express the continuity between Shiloh and Jerusalem, which is effected very neatly by the little remark that, as the Ark came into the city of David, David wore a 'linen ephod'. The first we hear of this garment is in 1 Samuel 2.18, where it is worn by the young Samuel at Shiloh. It is also worn by the priests at Nob whom Saul slew (1 Sam 22.18). After David, the garment entirely disappears from the Bible. But it has served as a sort of marker to indicate continuity between Shiloh and Jerusalem, reinforcing the legitimacy of David's bringing of the old Israelite religious symbol to his new (and previously non-Israelite) city.

Kingship

The biblical writer's concern to express continuity covers up a *lack* of continuity. David was a king of Judah who supplanted Saul on the Israelite throne; and, although the Bible presents him as the *second* king, his reign is very different from Saul's. Whereas Saul had no capital city, no court, no private army, and was really no more than an elected military leader (like Abimelech or Gideon) with a new name ('king'), David developed all of these regal trappings. Solomon was even grander, with many wives, foreign alliances, temples (including Yahweh's next door to his own palace), trading-ventures, a new administrative structure and a system of taxation. Although the Bible seems to see a cut-and-dried distinction between 'monarchy' and 'non-monarchy', its own accounts of Saul, David and Solomon demonstrate that, in historical terms, 'monarchy' emerged gradually.

However, the biblical account is more interested in the theological issues. It explains that there was legitimate opposition to the idea of a king, but that kingship eventually acquired divine approval. Kingship remained a disputed institution, nevertheless. Some texts approve it, others (such as Hosea 10.9, where 'Gibeah' refers to the anointing of the first king) disapprove. If one adds up the verdicts in 2 Kings on the various kings, one appreciates that most of them were bad, not good. Yet, despite the failings of most monarchs, the biblical verdict in the end is approving of the institution, or at least of the Davidic dynasty (e.g. 2 Sam 7; Ps 2). And, just as those individual verdicts on kings entirely ignore all criteria except cultic orthodoxy (as defined by the writers), so the biblical view of kingship remained a theological ideal, largely untainted by the blemishes of the historical experience. The Deuteronomic historian, for all his idealism of kingship, nevertheless acknowledges that neither David nor Solomon was a paragon: David's adultery with Bathsheba and his murder of Uriah (2 Sam 11) and Solomon's weakness for foreign wives (1 Kgs 11) are noted, as are the punishments they incurred. But, for all that, David and Solomon are projected largely as ideal figures. In Chronicles no such criticism is to be found, and in later tradition both kings are credited with scriptural books. For the Deuteronomic historian the question is, is kingship God's choice of political leadership for the chosen people? The answer was undoubtedly 'Yes', although not quite everyone agreed. For the Chronicler, writing after the demise of monarchy, it was necessary to adopt a *symbol* of monarchy, namely the Temple, and to stress the creation of Temple and cult as David's essential achievement.

In the first century BCE, after centuries of rule by foreign kings and Jewish priests, we encounter a projection of the ideal Davidic king into the future as the 'Messiah', the true heir and successor of David who would finally made the ideal into the real. 'Messiah' means 'anointed'; anointing was a ritual of pouring oil upon the head and signified divine election to office. It was performed on high priests and kings (e.g. Exod 30.30–3; 1 Sam 10.1) and hence Messianic figures were either royal or priestly – or both.

King and Temple in Judah and Israel

The united kingdom lasted only through the reigns of David and Solomon: Rehoboam lost most of the territory to Jeroboam, who established an independent kingdom ('Israel' as opposed to 'Judah'). Jerusalem was replaced as administrative capital by Shechem, an ancient sanctuary. Jeroboam built no temple there; instead he constructed two new royal shrines at Dan and Bethel, at the extremities of his kingdom. According to 1 Kings 12.28–30, 'the king took counsel and made two calves of gold. And he said to the people, "You have gone up to Jerusalem long enough. Behold your gods, O Israel, who brought you up out of the land of Egypt."' Jeroboam apparently initiated cultic festivals to coincide with those in Jerusalem, and set up an official priesthood, which, according to the Judahite Deuteronomic historian, were non levitical and therefore invalid. The king also offered himself, like the previous Judean kings, as head of the cult and offered sacrifices. The opposition in Judah to the golden calves is thought to have influenced the story of the golden calf in Exodus 32, which in its present form comes from a later period.

The constitution of the northern kingdom was different from that of the southern. Judah was small, relatively poor and dominated by Jerusalem, where its kings lived and its temple stood. Its political and social stability, with a single dynasty on the throne until the exile, was greater than Israel's. In the north, there were several *coups d'état*, and successive dynasties chose and built their own capital cities. In Israel, not Judah, we encounter continual opposition to the monarchy from a series of named and unnamed prophets who opposed the politics and the religion of the monarchs. We need to bear in mind that the united kingdom was an exceptional interlude in the history of the Israelite people and not the norm. The Judahite biblical writers naturally imply otherwise, and wish to compare Israel unfavourably with Judah. From a religious point of view, no Israelite king was acceptable, while a few Judahite kings were. From the political, economic and social points of view, we should judge Israel and Judah, and their kings, rather differently. While Israel was at times wealthy and powerful, Judah was relatively speaking a backwater.

During much of their history, the two kingdoms were in fact at war. Baasha, who had King Nadab, son of Jeroboam, assassinated (1 Kgs 15.27), started building a (capital?) city at Ramah, close to Jerusalem. After being attacked by Benhadad of Damascus, he retreated and built a capital at Tirzah (Tell el-Far'ah?). Baasha's son Elah was assassinated by Zimri, who after seven days (according to 1 Kgs 16.15) fell at the hands of Omri. Omri and his son Ahab brought stability: Samaria became the capital, and remained so until the end of the kingdom. Even Ahab's usurper Jehu, pictured in submission on Shalmaneser's 'Black Obelisk', is described by the Assyrians as of the 'house of Omri'. Of a central temple in Samaria we are told nothing except that Omri 'erected an altar for Baal in the house of Baal, which he built in Samaria' (1 Kgs 16.32).

The Deuteronomic historian paints a simple picture of the religion of Israel and of Judah. The northern kingdom is presented as religiously apostate in two respects: it maintained worship in the royal sanctuaries at Dan and Bethel (the 'sin which Jeroboam made Israel commit'); and it regularly resorted to worship of the Canaanite god Baal. The two accusations do not amount to the same thing. The cult of the royal sanctuaries is not said to have been non-Yahwistic. Indeed, its sin was that it apparently depicted Yahweh as a calf. As for Baal worship, it is not at all easy to draw the hard-and-fast distinction which the Deuteronomist requires between Yahweh and Baal, for religious syncretism was undoubtedly widespread and Yahweh not only attracted to himself many of the features of Baal but was probably identified with Baal among those whose livelihood depended on agriculture and for whom the cult of Baal was especially important, since Baal was a god of vegetation. The story of Elijah and the priests of Baal sets out to show that Yahweh can perform Baal's main function of bringing rain. How many Israelites cared which name they used for the deity who guaranteed their harvest? A recently discovered inscription at Kuntillet Ajrud mentions 'Yahweh and his Asherah', showing that it is oversimplifying to treat the religion of Israel and the religion of Canaan as clearly separate in the life of pre-exilic Israel. The difficulty of an accurate description of Israelite religion in the eighth century BCE is illustrated by the fact that the book of Amos makes no accusation of worshipping gods other than Yahweh but criticizes the hypocrisy of excessive religiosity combined with social injustice, while the book of Hosea criticizes the nation's desertion of Yahweh in favour of Baal. It is hard to credit that both books are describing the same society; we can only suppose that each is focusing on a different aspect of a varied pattern of religious behaviour.

Hosea apart, the biblical books generally agree in placing responsibility for Israel's (or Judah's) religious behaviour on its monarchs. These are not perceived simply as political leaders but as religious figureheads. In Judah, Temple and monarchy were dominant symbols as never in the kingdom of Israel. The king's role in the Temple cult is attested by the number of 'royal psalms': in these either the King himself speaks (Ps 59) or the psalmist intercedes for him (Ps 20) or proclaims his divine sonship (Ps 2) or invincibility (Ps 21). In Judah the stability of the Davidic dynasty and the divine election of the great city of 'Zion' were the twin pillars of the cult ideology. Yahweh was frequently said to reign from Zion, in language reminiscent of descriptions of the northern mountain Zaphon as the seat of the gods in Ugaritic myth (Ps 48.3). The Davidic king's reign in Zion was held to be guarante' d by a divine promise (2 Sam 7), which scholars often refer to as the 'Davidic covenant'.

The Jerusalem Temple: Construction, Personnel and Cult

A description of the Temple built under Solomon is given in 1 Kings 5–7. It was built by Phoenician workers using Phoenician materials and, we may suppose, according to Phoenician conventions. Certainly the description given corresponds to Canaanite and other ancient Near Eastern temples excavated by archaeologists. Undoubtedly the Temple cult also followed Phoenician customs, though we cannot expect the Bible to say so. According to 1 Kings 9.25, Solomon sacrificed at the altar three times a year: we are given little other information here about the Temple routine. 1 Chronicles, on the other hand, provides detailed lists of personnel and their functions, the allocation of which, along with the design of the Temple itself, it attributes to David rather than Solomon. This contradiction of 1 Kings may perhaps be accounted for by the Chronicler's desire to represent the contemporary, post-exilic Temple as not only the lineal successor of the pre-exilic house of Yahweh but also the promised eternal 'house' of David, at a time when there was no King of Judah. We can have little confidence that the Chronicler's descriptions of the Temple personnel and routines correspond very closely to pre-exilic reality. To reconstruct that reality, we must use evidence preserved in the Psalms and in the legal portions of the Pentateuch, distinguishing as best we can between description and idealization.

The Construction of Solomon's Temple

We know that the Temple of Solomon was Phoenician in design. According to 1 Kings 5–8 it was a rectangle sixty cubits long, twenty wide and thirty high (a cubit is about half a metre). Three storeys of rooms supported the exterior walls. Possibly the structure stood on a terrace. The main entrance was from the east, and from this point of entry the first chamber was a vestibule (the *ulam*) ten cubits long, windowed and containing doors opening onto the nave (*hekal*), which, forty cubits long, was the main room. At its far end, though twin cedar doors, was the shrine (*debir*, or 'most holy place'), a twenty-cubit cube. The interior walls were lined with cedar, the floors with cypress. Furnishings were overlaid or inlaid with bronze and gold. Beside the main door were two huge pillars. A particularly interesting item is the 'sea', a large bowl, presumably holding water, resting on the backs of twelve bronze oxen. Of the internal furnishings we know of ten golden lampstands in the nave, an incense altar before the 'most holy place', a table for the 'bread of the presence' somewhere in the nave and, in the 'most holy place' itself, the Ark, topped by two cherubim. The Chronicles description adds a bronze altar and a 'veil' in front of the shrine. Otherwise it mainly follows that in Kings, with larger dimensions and more gold! Ezekiel's description (Ezek 40–3) is intended as an idealistic description. It may preserve some data from the Solomonic structure, which the prophet could have seen, but it differs in several details from 1 Kings. Successive kings made alterations to the Temple (Joash, Manasseh). The final biblical source is Exodus 25–31, 35–40, describing the wilderness Tabernacle. It is thought that this account, given by the Priestly writers, is modelled on the Temple, since the dimensions of the nave and shrine are exactly half; but the Tabernacle has no vestibule.

There is no remaining archaeological evidence of Solomon's Temple, and comparative evidence from Palestine is meagre. Canaanite or Phoenician temples at Hazor and Beth-shan have the same basic plan of three adjacent chambers. Lampstands, cherubim and pillars are also included in other temple sites in Syria-Palestine. The remains of a temple at Arad, possibly built under Solomon, suggest a similar, thought smaller, layout. The postexilic Temple we shall not describe here. We know little about its layout, except that it was more modest than its predecessor. Herod's ambitious rebuilding is described by Josephus (*Antiquities* XV, 11; *Jewish War*, V, 5) and in the Mishnah (Middoth).

Personnel

For the clergy of the first Temple there are few preserved regulations. Kings frequently offered sacrifices, especially on national festivals, and David is said to have both sacrificed, and made his own sons priests (2 Sam 6.13; 8.18). Of the two priests in charge of the ark in David's day, Abiathar came from the sanctuary of Shiloh, where the ark had once been housed; Zadok is a mystery, though it is widely conjectured that he belonged to the old Jebusite priestly class. It was Zadok who triumphed under Solomon, his dynasty ultimately winning a monopoly of the high-priesthood after the exile, as the sole eligible group. The biblical genealogies which trace his ancestry back to Aaron are performing the proper role of such genealogies and creating the necessary (fictional) lineage to meet the requirements of prejudice, tradition and decorum. By the time of the Chronicler the priestly castes, including the Levites, had been precisely worked out. It is impossible to define any such precise prerogatives at the time of Solomon, and the exclusive claims of the tribe of Levi to the priesthood are impossible to retrace with any confidence. Possibly the Levites acquired a place in Jerusalem in the aftermath – or as part – of the Josianic reform (*c*.621 BCE) which abolished other sanctuaries. The absence of a king after the exile gave the Temple and its personnel the prestige of a royal palace and administration, with the high priest recognized internally and externally as head of the nation. How elaborate and extensive the pre-exilic Temple hierarchy was we can only guess, and such arrangements were subject to royal control. The story of Athaliah's murder (2 Kgs 11) suggests that the Temple priests were very much subject to the royal administration. (Likewise at Bethel, also a royal sanctuary, Amaziah the chief priest reported to the king.) Again, we shall give no description of the post-exilic Temple cult.

Cultic Activities

Once again, the problem is of dating the information in the relevant sources. Assuming, however, that the Pentateuchal material assigned to the Priestly writer is unreliable for the pre-exilic period (although this is far from universally agreed), we have to exclude the twice-daily offering, which was the staple activity of the Temple, and the Day of Atonement, the most important. We are left essentially with occasional rituals for the benefit of the king, such as those prior to warfare (inferred from Psalm 20, for example) and national festivals. The three major celebrations of Passover, Shavuoth (Weeks or Pentecost) and Sukkoth (Booths or Tabernacles) are probably all older than the Temple. Both Hezekiah (2 Chron 30) and Josiah (2 Kgs 23.21) are said to have tried to centralize the Passover at the Temple. The Passover legislation of Deuteronomy 16 reflects such a reform, while Exodus 12 describes a non-centralized feast. According to 1 Kings 9.25, Solomon offered at the Temple three times a year; Deuteronomy 16.16 specifies three times a year for 'males to appear before Yahweh your God' (i.e. at the Temple). After the exile, certainly, and into the New Testament period, the Temple was the site of three annual *pilgrim* festivals, on which many of the Psalms were recited, including probably 23, 24, 121–2, 125–8, possibly 132 in a ceremony involving the Ark, and doubtless many others. Many reconstructions of pre-exilic major festivals have been offered, including a New Year festival akin to the Babylonian *akitu*-festival, which might have involved the celebration of Yahweh's conquest of the watery chaos and renewed kingship; or alternatively a festival celebrating the divine election of Zion and including an Ark procession; or a covenant-reading ceremony at Sukkoth. In truth, however, we know very little of the pre-exilic cult. We can say, however, that in Jerusalem the Temple grew continuously in importance. As a house for the Ark, it symbolized Yahweh's election of the city as a home. In Deuteronomy, Yahweh 'causes his name to dwell' there. And, if this localization of God waned under the more transcendental theology of the Priestly writer, it was no doubt popular belief in post-exilic

times that the presence of Yahweh was really to be found in the Holy of
Holies, which the high priest entered once a year only, amid clouds of
incense (deliberately reminiscent of the pillar of cloud by which Yahweh's
presence was signified in the wilderness).

Destruction and Exile

The destruction of the Temple and exile of king, court and most of the
Temple priesthood affected the various communities differently. Those who
were left behind have been largely ignored by the Old Testament writers, or
dismissed as of impure stock. Some of those who fled to Egypt built their
own temples there. We know of one at a military colony in Elephantine, and
another built by a fugitive high priest, Onias IV, at the beginning of the
second century BCE in Leontopolis. There is no evidence that a temple was
built in Babylon, to which the elite were exiled. This is possibly because the
Babylonian exiles included those to whom the Jerusalem Temple was
especially a symbol of national religion and identity, to whom the idea of
'singing Yahweh's song in a strange land' (Ps 137) would be tantamount to
'forgetting Jerusalem' (v. 5). Even so, most of those exiled in Babylonia, as
elsewhere, did not wish to return when permitted. Those who did, and who
wrote and preserved the biblical literature, had a vested interest in restoring
Jerusalem, its temple and its priesthood, for temples and their associated
services provide a livelihood for many people – livestock-breeders, priests,
traders, shopkeepers. The Second Temple was not only the kernel of a small
religious economic and political community but also the centre of Jewish
devotion throughout the Diaspora, or Dispersion, of the Jewish people,
whose donations and visits helped substantially to sustain the economy of
the 'Promised Land', now reduced to an area of about 400 square miles
(around 1000 sq. km). The piety of Diaspora Jews is eloquently expressed
in the book of Daniel. The exiled hero prays towards the city (6.10), and
receives a visitation in answer to prayer 'at the time of the evening offering'
(9.21). In the vision of chapter 2, the 'stone' that 'became a great mountain
and filled the whole earth probably includes a reference to the 'holy hill' of
Zion from which the final kingdom will arise. The desecration of the
Temple vessels spell the doom of the one foreign king whose death is
described (5.3).

Jerusalem in Three Religious Traditions

The history of Jerusalem after the biblical period falls into five phases.
Jewish occupation continued until 135 CE. Then Jerusalem was for 200
years a Roman city from which Jews were barred. With the adoption of
Christianity as the state religion of the Roman Empire, it became a

Christian city for 300 years. From the middle of the seventh century CE until the early twentieth century the city was Muslim, except for a short interval during the Crusades. After the Great War of 1914–18 the city, while retaining its Islamic character under a British mandate, saw increased Jewish immigration and Western Christian presence. The rights of the Arab inhabitants and the more recent Jewish settlers, mostly fugitives from persecution in Europe, resulted in a partition of Palestine, with the city divided. Since 1967 it has all been under Israeli administration. It remains at present a mixture of Muslim, Jewish and Christian cultures.

Judaism

'Zion' is historically the name of the hill on which the Temple stood (although what is called 'Mount Zion' in modern Jerusalem is a different part of the city altogether). Zion has been a symbol for the city and the nation. 'Zionism' springs historically from a yearning to return to the historical 'land of Israel', a yearning which dates from the forcible expulsion of Jews from the city in 135 CE. It has never been absent from the Jewish consciousness, but was particularly intense during the Middle Ages, when, after centuries of relative 'toleration', the Jews suffered persecution, expulsion and displacement (for example, to Spain and Portugal) by Muslims in the eleventh century and Christians in the fifteenth. Yearning for pilgrimage to, and piecemeal settlement in, the Holy Land have attested to the spiritual exile which many European Jews, in particular, have felt. At the very centre of Jewish pilgrimage is a section of the wall of the platform on which Herod the Great built his massive Temple complex. This wall, long known as the Wailing Wall, because it attracted grief for the loss of land and Temple, is now known as the Western Wall: since the Israeli annexation of the whole of the city, including the walled Old City, grief is less appropriate.

In the twentieth century Zionism has come to stand for the doctrine of Jewish resettlement in 'Palestine' and the creation of a Jewish state. It represents both a religious ideal and a secular one: alongside the symbolism of Jerusalem as the spiritual home of Jews and the focus of their future hope lies the desire to escape the vicissitudes of life among Gentiles and to establish a 'national homeland'. There exists today in Israel a certain tension between political and religious forms of Zionism – the former dedicated to the maintenance of Israel as a political state, the latter seeing Jerusalem in particular as the focus of Jewish religious hopes, where by divine rather than human agency the Messianic age will be brought in. But throughout its history Jerusalem has stood as a symbol of the conflict (sometimes harmony) between politics and religion. Along with this goes the problem of defining 'Jewish': does it denote adherence to a religion or racial identity? Since

David's choice of Jerusalem to fuse the religious and political into a single symbol, the city has remained such a symbol.

Christianity

For Christians Jerusalem is pre-eminently the 'city of Jesus', the scene of his passion and resurrection. The city now contains many Christian pilgrimage sites, with varying degrees of authenticity. The earliest place of devotion was the tomb, which from earliest times Christians have assumed lay adjacent to Golgotha/Calvary. Christian pilgrimage to the Holy Land was frequent during the Byzantine period, when many churches were built at places of religious importance, monasteries were built, and many individual monks took up residence in caves, in the Judaean desert between Jerusalem and Bethlehem on the west and the Dead Sea on the east. Jerusalem was indeed a Christian city for 300 years, and, even today, at or near the vast majority of ancient biblical sites a Byzantine church or monastery can be found.

Christians remained in the city after the Muslim conquest, and Christian control was briefly re-established by the Crusaders. The Crusaders contributed many fine buildings to the city, including churches such as that of St Anne by St Stephen's Gate, taken to be over the home of Jesus' mother. St Anne was venerated as the mother of the Virgin, and the church illustrates the proliferation of sites sought out by Christians but hardly authentic. It is important that, while the Crusaders were Roman Catholics, the Byzantines represented Eastern or Orthodox Christianity, with different holy days, different rites, and differences in theology too. Even within the Orthodox churches, which are divided into national institutions, there are differences, and the Armenians, one of the oldest national churches in existence, differ in several respects from other Orthodox churches, and occupy their own quarter of the Old City.

A third phase of Christian 'occupation' of Jerusalem begins in the nineteenth century, when Protestants from Europe began to take an interest in the history of the Holy Land. Protestant churches now also occupy parts of the city, and, although there are not many holy sites exclusive to the Protestants, there is one famous exception. General Gordon visited the city and identified as Golgotha a rocky hill bearing the shape of a skull. To this day, some Protestant Christian groups venerate this quiet garden as the site of the tomb. There is no archaeological basis for this; on the other hand, the ornate Church of the Holy Sepulchre, venerated by Orthodox and Catholics, is very likely to mark the site.

Islam

Jerusalem is the second holiest city of Islam, and is known to Muslims as al-Quds, 'the holy [city]'. It owes its status to two traditions. The first is common to all three religions: Abraham sacrificed his son on Moriah, a place identified in later biblical tradition with the Temple mount. Abraham is, of course, the father not only of Jews but of 'many nations', of which the Arab nation is one, tracing its descent from Isma'il (Ishmael). The Qur'an teaches that this son was Isma'il and not Isaac. Abraham himself was one of the followers of the true religion (called *Hanif*), and is as much the ancestor of the Muslim as of the Jew. The second tradition about Jerusalem is that of Muhammad's night journey, related in the Qur'an, at the beginning of Sura 17: 'Praise be to him who transported his servant by night, from the sacred mosque to the farther mosque, whose surroundings We have blessed, that we might show him [some] of our signs'. The 'sacred mosque' is the Ka'bah at Mecca; the 'farther mosque' has always been understood as the site of the Jerusalem Temple, and accordingly the first mosque to be built in Jerusalem was named, and is still named, el-Aqsa, 'the farther'. The Qur'an says no more, but early Muslim commentators and biographers of the Prophet relate that Muhammad was taken, either in a vision or bodily, to al-Quds and thence to heaven, to see the 'signs' of Allah. In the centre of the Temple mount in Jerusalem, alongside the el-Aqsa mosque, stands the Mosque of Umar, known also as the kubbat as-Sakhra, 'Dome of the Rock'. The rock which it houses is venerated both as that on which Abraham nearly sacrificed Isma'il and also as the place from which the Prophet ascended to heaven on his night journey. The footprint of the Prophet is believed to be visible on the rock. Other traditions hold that it is literally the nearest place on earth to heaven, that Noah's ark rested there, that the last trumpet will be blown on the Day of Resurrection from there. At the beginning of the Prophet's career, he and his followers observed the practice of the Jews and prayed facing the direction of al-Quds (the orientation at prayer is known as the *qibla*). Soon after, the *qibla* was changed towards Mecca, as it remains.

FURTHER READING

Avigad, N. 1983: *Discovering Jerusalem.*
Jeremias, J. 1969: *Jerusalem in the Time of Jesus.*
Kenyon, K. M. 1974: *Digging up Jerusalem.*
Prag, K. 1988: *Jerusalem.*
Wilkinson, J. 1978: *The Jerusalem Jesus Knew.*

9

Stories of the Prophets

Michael E. W. Thompson and Stephen Bigger

Preliminary Reading   1 Samuel; 1 Kings 17–2 Kings 14 and 22; Jonah;
Daniel.

Although there are occasions in the Hebrew Bible when Abraham and
Moses are described in prophetic terms, this motif is never dominant. The
characteristic stories of early prophecy are found in the books of Samuel and
Kings, which together form a consecutive piece of history-writing that opens
with stories of Samuel (*c*.tenth century BCE). The work closes with an
account of the exiled king Jehoiachin (died 563 BCE), which gives us an indication of the date of final publication of the work (although some scholars
argue for a seventh-century-BCE edition). We have seen that the 'Deuteronomic historian' was guided by the same theological principles as are found
in Deuteronomy. It is in the interpretation of what happened in the past
that we see the theological thought of Deuteronomy coming out particularly
clearly in Joshua, Judges, Samuel and Kings. For example, the book of
Deuteronomy sees that the people of Israel are totally dependent upon what
God has done for them in love and devotion (4.32–35; 7.7–8), and is concerned that these people for their part should remain faithful to God – to
this God alone! They must have nothing to do with other gods – but
Yahweh God of Israel they must never forget (8.2–3). Especially they must
not forget God when things are going well for them (6.10–16; 8.11–17;
10.20–2). Deuteronomy maintains that, if the people of Israel remain
faithful to God, all will go well with them (11.8–9, 22–3); if they are not
faithful, death will overtake them (11.16–17).
   Disaster and death overtook Israel and Judah. In 722 BCE the Israelite
capital, Samaria, fell to the Assyrians, and in 587/6 BCE the capital of
Judah, Jerusalem, fell to the Babylonians. In the light of these catastrophes
the Deuteronomists saw the past as an object lesson for their own generation.
They wished to *interpret* the past; and Deuteronomy was the interpretative
message which 'fired' them. In their gathering, organizing and presenting of

185

their materials, they sought to demonstrate that when people had been faithful things had gone well for their nation, but that after times of religious unfaithfulness catastrophes had befallen them. The story is thus a theological interpretation of history, the story of people's response to Yahweh their God and his faithfulness in return. In Samuel and Kings the writers used earlier sources – the so-called 'Succession Narrative' or 'Court History of David' (2 Sam 9–1 Kgs 2); the 'Book of the Acts of Solomon' (1 Kgs 11.41); and the 'Book of the Chronicles of the Kings of Israel' and the 'Book of the Chronicles of the Kings of Judah' (both frequently mentioned in Kings). (These are not the biblical books of Chronicles, which themselves use Samuel–Kings as a source.) Certainly, then, stories of prophets existed before the Deuteronomic historian completed his work. There are many references to prophets in Samuel–Kings. This says a great deal about the nature of the tradition, and also about the writer's interests. There are further hints: the historian saw the fall of both northern and southern kingdoms as the fulfilment of judgements uttered by prophets (2 Kgs 17.23; 24.2); and he understood the prophets' role as that of calling people to return to God (17.13).

Deuteronomy portrayed Moses in prophetic terms: 'Yahweh your God will raise up for you a prophet like me from among you, from your brethren – him you shall heed . . . ' (18.15). The writer went on to justify the work of later prophets with a divine oracle:

I [God] will raise up for them a prophet like you from among their brethren; and I will put my words in his mouth, and he shall speak to them all that I command him. And whoever will not give heed to my words which he shall speak in my name, I myself will require it of him. (vv. 18–19).

The idea here is that, just as Moses had been appointed to the particular role of mediator between the people and Yahweh, responsible for bringing to the people authoritative divine words, so Yahweh would send a succession of faithful prophets who in a series of situations would declare to them the word and will of Yahweh. It is therefore interesting that, upon the discovery of a lawbook in the Jerusalem Temple, King Josiah is said to have taken immediate advice from Huldah 'the prophetess' (2 Kgs 22.14–20). Deuteronomy is aware of false prophets and the dangers they pose (18.20–2), and says that true and false may be distinguished by whether their prophecies are fulfilled or not. Unfortunately, it could take some time to find out.

Nevertheless, it is clear that the authors of Deuteronomy and the Deuteronomic History held a high view of prophecy. Their historical presentation portrays Israel as continually falling away from Yahweh, who in the first place has so graciously come to these undeserving people. In this presentation, the prophets have no small part, preaching repentance and threatening disaster. They are depicted as trying to slow the decline; but, since the people take little notice, the prophecies of doom have to be fulfilled (Koch, 1982, 23). They can also be seen not as retarding but as advancing Hebrew thought. They are presented as projecting the ideal of traditional faithfulness, but the tradition, and the response of the people, indicate that this 'old' message was in fact *new*. The people were more used to syncretism, allowing them freedom to worship how they wished. The career of many of the prophets was a constant struggle to impose monotheistic exclusivism on a people who did not want it.

The Chronicler further adapted the stories in line with his own interests at a time when national and religious life was being re-established after the exile. He says nothing about Samuel, and omits most of the story of the northern kingdom. He believes that the will of God was revealed through the prophets and that, to live successfully, one has to obey the prophets: 'Hear me, Judah and inhabitants of Jerusalem! believe in the LORD your God, and you will be established; believe his prophets, and you will succeed' (2 Chron 20.20).

Thus we should read our biblical sources with a critical eye. They are not concerned to give us 'bare facts', but like all history-writing are an interpretation which fits in with the author's scheme of things. They have strong views about the role and work of prophets. This means that, when we turn to these works in order to gain information about early prophets, we must exercise critical caution and accept that the materials we are studying are themselves interpretations of what *might* originally have taken place. Yet, if we find the early prophets hard to grasp historically, we shall find the views of the Deuteronomic historian (and indeed the Chronicler) to be of great historical interest. Whether or not we regard what they have to say as representing commonly held views in their own day will depend on how we assess them. Were they expressing current ideas? Or were they protesting about contemporary beliefs and attitudes?

Samuel

An ancient narrator introduces the story of Samuel's call to prophethood with these words: 'And the word of Yahweh was rare in those days; there was no frequent vision' (1 Sam 3.1). His readers were intended to understand that there was little direct communication from God to the people of Israel and that things were at a low level, spiritually speaking. Grave sins were committed by the family of Eli the priest, under whom the boy Samuel was ministering (vv. 12–14). Yet, with the call of Samuel in the sanctuary at Shiloh, the writer was hinting that dramatic changes were coming. God announced to Samuel that he, Yahweh, was about to do things in Israel 'at which the two ears of every one that hears it will tingle' (v. 11). What was about to take place was the punishment of the family of Eli for their sins – the neglect of the things of God. So, the narrator continues,

And Samuel grew, and the LORD was with him and let none of his words fall to the ground. And all Israel from Dan to Beersheba knew that Samuel was established as a prophet of the LORD. And the LORD appeared again at Shiloh, for the LORD revealed himself to Samuel at Shiloh by the word of the LORD. Thus the word of Samuel came to all Israel. (1 Sam 3.19–4.1a)

Thereafter, God's word, spoken through Samuel, came more regularly to Israel. There was an important political dimension. The Philistines, based on the coastal strip, began to press inland. They posed a threat to the Israelites, who found themselves to be in need of leadership. Samuel was concerned with the proper establishment – and development – of Israelite kingship.

Samuel is portrayed in a number of roles – as prophet, seer, judge and sacrificial intercessor. The story opens with Samuel called by God in Shiloh. The background is one of human weakness, and decadence; and out of this comes the means whereby the word of Yahweh is to be declared to Israel. Many scholars have noted that the interpretation of the name 'Samuel' (1.20, 27–8) as 'lent' or 'asked' (Hebrew *Sha'ul*) does not really fit his name – it relates rather to Saul, the first king. Could this story have originally been about Saul? In the account we now have, the writer wishes to portray Samuel as the one who was *asked* by Yahweh, and *lent* by his parents for divine service.

In 1 Samuel 7.3–14 is a rather different picture of Samuel. Here he is a judge, with a local circuit around Mizpah. In vv. 8–14 Samuel intercedes through sacrifice, bringing about a victory against the Philistines. Samuel's intercession – offering prayer on others' behalf – is remembered in Jeremiah 15.1 and Psalm 99.6. In 1 Samuel 7.15–8.3 Samuel is spoken of as a *judge*, as one travelling around the various sanctuaries of Israel interpreting the Torah of God.

Samuel established Saul as the first king. This account is critical of the institution of kingship and Samuel is portrayed as the mouthpiece of this criticism. Nevertheless, it is stressed that the word of God to Samuel is that the people's wish to have a king should be granted (8.7–9, 22). The people are warned of the dangers of kingship and of the demands a king will place upon them (8.10–18). When we read this passage it is hard to resist the conclusion that it is the third king of Israel, Solomon, who is intended, with later negative experiences of kingship being read back into the story. This theological criticism of kingship must colour our view of these passages as 'historical' accounts of the beginnings of kingship.

In a further account of the establishment of the monarchy, kingship is spoken of positively. Here Samuel is portrayed as a 'seer' to whom people can go for guidance. There are, in Hebrew, different words for 'prophet': the most common is *nabi'*, which later served as the wide general term. There are also *hozeh* (visionary), *ro'eh* (seer) and *ish elohim* (man of God). 1 Samuel 9.9 notes the difficulty: 'Formerly in Israel, when a man went to inquire of God, he said, "Come, let us go to the seer"; for he who is now called a prophet was formerly called a seer.' The next verse notes, 'So they went to the city where the *man of God* was.'

The scene changes in 13.8–15 and 15.10–31; now there is opposition between Samuel and Saul, and Samuel is sharply critical of some of Saul's actions – particularly his assumption of ritual responsibilities. In the first passage, Samuel speaks as if Saul will not be allowed to remain king much longer; the second passage speaks of the rejection of Saul. It seems that here Samuel represents a strand of thought in Israel that was not happy with the institution of kingship. Samuel chooses David from Bethlehem to be king in place of the rejected Saul (16.1–13). Even after Samuel's death (ch. 25) his ghost is called up by Saul (ch. 28), stressing Saul's disobedience.

Thus the stories have been overlaid with theological interpretation, even in some cases protest. This may have originated as much in tradition as in the mind of the final editor. A 'tradition-historical' study would seek to unravel the different layers and uncover the process of the tradition's development. Modern scholars would be cautious about details of the historical Samuel, but we can say that the stories reflect the transitional period between the judges and the monarchy when many things were unclear and events were in a state of flux and change. The Samuel legend grew on traditions about bands or groups of possibly charismatic prophets, called *bene nebi'im* (sons of the prophets), and about judges. It was the concept of prophethood which was central to the Deuteronomic historian. He viewed Samuel as a prophetic prototype, seeing things as they really are (*ro'eh*, seer), deciding disputes (judge), in communion with God, as one of the sons of the prophets, and as the spiritual mentor of society. Few kings would match his standards!

Gad

Samuel was not the only prophet who was concerned with politics. King Saul felt threatened by David, causing David to withdraw to Maspha in Moab with 400 supporters. The prophet Gad advised David to seek support in Judah (1 Sam 22.3–5). The narrator does no more than record

David's obedience to his wise counsellor. Later, with David established as king, Gad is mentioned as the 'seer' (*ro'eh*) who criticized a census conducted by David. David's plan was to raise a standing army, a distinct move to a new style of kingship. The historian has already placed in the narrative a marker critical of this. He criticizes many later monarchs for doing evil in God's sight; on this occasion Gad is the mouthpiece of this message, uttering a word of judgement against David (2 Sam 24.11–17; cf. 1 Chron 21.9–17). Gad also commands David to purchase the threshing-floor belonging to Araunah the Jebusite as a site for an altar (2 Sam 24.18f; cf. 1 Chron 21.18f) – the site of Solomon's Temple. The writer views David as an ideal monarch with whom an everlasting covenant is made (2 Sam 7), promising a perpetual dynasty. On doing wrong, David accepts criticism by the prophets – and his punishment. It is difficult to be sure of what role Gad played historically. We are given the impression that he was a counsellor and adviser to David on political and religious matters. It is possible that he blamed the devastating plague (which caused 70,000 casualties) on a census which had broken the mould of Israelite politics. Both the Deuteronomic historian and the Chronicler present him as being the bearer of God's message to David.

Nathan

The prophet Nathan plays a significant part in three events in David's reign. David wishes to build a temple in Jerusalem (2 Sam 7.1–17). At first Nathan approves, but a later divine message rejects the plan, replacing it with the promise of a dynastic house. The historian had a particular concern with the royal house (see 2 Sam 7): Nathan is a mouthpiece for this concern, in a chapter which contains themes such as punishment of faithlessness, so characteristically Deuteronomic. Solomon is given leave to build the Temple – by a *direct* word from God (1 Kgs 6.11–13). After David committed adultery with Bathsheba and arranged for the killing of Uriah her husband (2 Sam 12), Nathan recounts to him a fictitious case in which a rich man takes away the only lamb possessed by a poor man. When David judges that the offender should die, Nathan replies, 'You are the man!' (v. 7). Justice for the poor is a common prophetic theme. Nathan is also involved in the choice of David's successor (1 Kgs 1.5–48). He champions Bathsheba's son Solomon, acting in the role of privy counsellor.

Ahijah

With Ahijah of Shiloh we have a prophet whose recorded actions are all in the political sphere. He appears as supporter, and later as opponent, of

Jeroboam's kingship over Israel, the northern kingdom. Ahijah represents opposition to the injustices of Solomon's reign (1 Kgs 11.26–40). He meets Jeroboam and in a dramatic act of prophetic symbolism proclaims the division of Solomon's kingdom by ripping his new garment into twelve pieces, indicating that Jeroboam would receive ten of them (symbolizing the ten northern tribes). The historian uses Ahijah's prophecy to declare Jeroboam's northern kingdom to be legitimate, against the tyranny of the Solomonic dynasty: 'for it was a turn of affairs brought about by the LORD that he might fulfil his word, which the LORD spake by Ahijah the Shilonite to Jeroboam' (12.15). Ahijah's prophecy (11.31–9) criticizes Solomon for encouraging the worship of foreign deities. Rehoboam is left the rump of the kingdom 'for the sake of David my servant whom I chose, who kept my commandments and my statutes' (v. 34) so that 'David my servant may always have a lamp before me in Jerusalem, the city where I have chosen to put my name' (v. 36). This language reflects Deuteronomy (12.5, etc.) and Second Isaiah (Isa 42.1). Yet the same Ahijah makes a devastating denunciation of Jeroboam, indeed a devastating critique of kingship itself. Jeroboam, once a bright hope, has fallen far short, constructing hill shrines with bull–calf images – understandable in political terms, as they wean his people away from Jerusalem, but clearly not acceptable in religious terms. The message of condemnation and eventual doom echoes throughout the chapters on the northern monarchy – so that the description of its destruction by the Assyrians is an inevitable punishment.

Shemaiah

Shemaiah the man of God successfully orders Rehoboam not to attack the Judahites' northern kinsfolk (1 Kgs 12.21–4). Whatever the historical background to this episode, the narrator is saying that God's hand was in evidence in the political rift. Rehoboam's political ambitions are thwarted by the word of the man of God. The *people* are reminded of their *kinship obligations*; any further disputes are the responsibility of the kings who have brought them about.

The Man of God from Judah

The main purpose of the story in 1 Kings 12.33–13.31 is to condemn Jeroboam's shrine at Bethel: no official alternative to Jerusalem should be allowed. The man of God prophesies that King Josiah will come and sacrifice the northern priests on the altars, a detail which is surely editorial. The story includes two acts of divine power – withering and healing the king's hand, and tearing down the altar. Every decision the man takes is informed by a word from God, including a prophecy not to eat or drink. The story moves to a second scene (some say it was originally a separate story) at which an old prophet from Bethel meets the man of God and persuades him to stay for a meal by claiming that he has received a counter-prophecy. After the meal, a further prophecy condemns the man of Judah; and on the way home he is killed by a lion. There is an important lesson here for the exilic community for whom the story was intended. In condemning northern schismatics, it is easy – and fatal – to rest on one's laurels and neglect *obedience*. It is also dangerous to lay too much emphasis on religious authority: the man of God failed; the prophet was untrustworthy. The story ends more positively. The prophet asks to be buried with the man of God, and declares that his prophecy about Josiah will come true – clearly an editorial note. Perhaps also there is an aetiology here – a story suggested by the grave of two unnamed prophets? Or perhaps apostate Bethel was viewed as the only fit place for the disobedient man of God's grave!

Jehu

Jehu, son of Hanani, foretells the destruction of the dynasty of Baasha, king of Israel, for following the ways of Jeroboam (1 Kgs 16.1–4). He had destroyed the house of Jeroboam – but behaved no better! The same prophet is reported in 2 Chronicles 19.2f as censuring Jehoshaphat of Judah for joining Ahab of Israel – but there are favourable words in this later narrative that are not found in the earlier Kings: 'for you destroyed the Asherahs out of the land, and have set your heart to seek God'.

Micaiah

In a story full of humour, and mocking kings and prophets, a group of prophets prophesy success for the kings of Israel and Judah in their proposed attack upon Syrian-held Ramoth-gilead. Micaiah, already unpopular with the king of Israel for his 'past record in opposition' (Auld, 1986a, 143), first prophesies success – which is so unexpected that the king sharply requires him to speak the truth (1 Kgs 22.16). The second oracle, full of horror, tells of sheep without a shepherd (v. 17) – clearly the offensive would fail. Micaiah appears to contradict himself, and provides an example of prophets in violent disagreement. Micaiah's 'vision' offers a theological commentary:

I saw the LORD sitting on his throne, and all the host of heaven standing beside him on his right hand and on his left; and the LORD said, 'Who will entice Ahab, that he may go up and fall at Ramoth-gilead?' And one said one thing, and another said another. Then a spirit came forward and stood before the LORD, saying, 'I will entice him.' And the LORD said to him, 'By what means?' And he said, 'I will go forth, and will be a lying spirit in the mouth of all his prophets.' And he said, 'You are to entice him, and you shall succeed; go forth and do so.' Now therefore behold, the LORD has put a lying spirit in the mouth of all these your prophets; the LORD has spoken evil concerning you. (vv. 19–23)

This is a powerful message, which challenges notions of prophetic inspiration, as Jeremiah also did. In the end the test of genuineness is whether the prophecy comes true (v. 28) – although, had Ahab listened and not gone to war, Micaiah's word would not have been fulfilled. Ahab is concerned enough to go to battle in disguise, but is killed as an archer shoots an arrow '*at a venture*' which happens to find the chink in the king's armour (v. 34). He dies by chance – a chance now rich with implied theological comment: the prophetic word makes explicit, for this historian, God's intervention in world affairs.

Elijah

The Elijah narrative (1 Kgs 17–2 Kgs 1) is more extensive than most of the accounts already discussed. Neither Elijah nor Elisha is mentioned in the Chronicler's narrative, which is surprising for such a substantial body of material. The setting is the northern kingdom during the reigns of Ahab (875–854 BCE) and Ahaziah (854–853 BCE). Ahab's long reign is seen as one of religious crisis, occasioned by the king's wife Jezebel, daughter of the Phoenician king Ethbaal (1 Kgs 16.29–34); she is portrayed as a zealot for the worship of Baal. Elijah champions Yahweh, as his name, meaning 'Yahweh is my God', implies. Baal worship is anathema to the narrator, who is deeply concerned about religious purity (involving the exclusive worship of Yahweh), as revealed sharply in the Josiah narrative. This deep concern makes it difficult for us to be sure about the accuracy of details. When so many events are portrayed as scandalous and distressing, one wonders how dispassionate his stories are. Ahab gives his children Yahwistic names (e.g. Ahaziah, 'Yahweh has grasped') and supports the Yahwistic prophets (22.5–12); but alongside this he gives Jezebel a free rein in establishing sanctuaries to Baal of Tyre. It may be true that she began to have ambitions for Baal to replace Yahweh, for the narratives report persecution of Yahwistic prophets and demolition of altars (18.3–4). This caused the narrator deep concern and he may have exaggerated the seriousness of the situation. Elijah is portrayed as the faithful prophet who stood up to Jezebel's threat and her encroaching religion.

Elijah the prophet is portrayed as larger than life. Legends of miracle and magic associated with him may have grown over time. He is fed by ravens (17.4 – although 'Bedouin Arabs' is a plausible alternative reading) and by an angel (19.5–8); he controls the weather (17.1), multiplies food (vv. 8–16), raises the dead (vv. 17–24), performs feats of endurance (18.46; 19.8) and levitates (18.12; 2 Kgs 2.1–2, 16). Possibly the narrator selected material to illustrate themes from Deuteronomy – rain and fertility (Deut 7.13; 8.7; 11.11–17); defeat of Baal (12.1–3); the voice at Horeb (5.1–5); the extermination of the unfaithful (13.1–18); social justice, as with Naboth's vineyard (19.14–21); death by stoning (21.21); prophets (18.15–22) and the monarchy (17.14–20). Elijah enters the story abruptly. His curse causes a drought (1 Kgs 17.1) which does not come to an end until idolatry has been removed (18.40–6) in line with Deuteronomy 11.17. Three incidents during the drought have a legendary feel – Elijah fed by ravens at the brook Cherith (17.2–6) and by a widow at Zarephath whose jars replenish themselves (vv. 7–16) and whose son he resuscitates (vv. 17–24).

In the great contest on Mount Carmel between Elijah and the prophets of Baal fire comes down from heaven to consume Elijah's sacrifice, thus securing his triumph over the rival prophets. The story looks consistent on the surface, but there are curious features. The setting is one of a disagreement between Ahab and Elijah (18.1–20, 41–6), yet Ahab is not mentioned at Carmel. In spite of the drought, there seems to be no water shortage, as barrel after barrel is filled (vv. 33–5, 38). The story may once have been separate from its present setting; and was the altar really built from *twelve* stones, or was the narrator exercising literary licence and portraying this as an occasion when *all* the tribes came together? Is Elijah being portrayed as a new Joshua, who raised up twelve stones at Gilgal (Josh 4.1–24), or a new Moses, building an altar with twelve pillars (Exod 24.4)? The choice of Mount Carmel for the contest is not accidental: close to the Phoenician border, it is deliberately chosen to present a real challenge to Jezebel and the prophets of Baal. Yahweh's triumph is made greater in that *one* prophet overcomes *many* – the number 450 is stressed. Another contrast is that between Elijah's quiet, calm prayer and the frenzy of the Baal prophets. *All* the people confess that Yahweh is God. The story cannot finish until Deuteronomy 13 is fulfilled, with the death of the false prophets: thus Elijah butchers them by the brook Kishon. With idolatry eradicated, rain can fall again (Deut 11.17) – the first for three years. At this point Ahab returns to the narrative and clouds appear. The 'hand of Yahweh' helps Elijah to run faster than Ahab's chariot! (1 Kgs 18.46)

It is a different Elijah in the following chapter – fearful and fleeing for his life before Jezebel. For the narrator, Jezebel was the real threat, so the sombre atmosphere and menace of this story are very appropriate. It is set at

'Horeb the mount of God' (19.8): Horeb is the name for Sinai in Deuteronomy (e.g. 5.2) and it is not essential to the story – it may be an editorial addition. The narrative, in 1 Kings 19, breaks into four sections. Vv. 1–3a provide the continuity. In vv. 3b–6 Elijah is provided with angelic food (whether from a human or heavenly 'messenger'), in an echo of the manna in the wilderness. Vv. 7–18, a scene which owes not a little to Exodus 33.17–23, tell of a mighty theophany at Horeb, in which Elijah hears God as a 'still small voice', or, more accurately, mystically, a "voice of fine silence'. He is commissioned to anoint three men: Hazael as king of Syria, Jehu as king of Israel, and Elisha as his own successor. Their task is to wipe out the unfaithful (cf. Deut 13), leaving only a faithful remnant – 7000 unsullied worshippers. Finally, vv. 19–21 move the story on to Elisha, who leaves his old life and everything associated with it. As Joshua ministered to Moses (Exod 24.13), so Elisha serves Elijah.

The taking of Naboth's vineyard (1 Kgs 21) illustrates covetousness, dishonouring parents (by seizing Naboth's inheritance), false witness, murder and stealing. Ironically, the trumped-up charge against Naboth reflects another commandment, cursing God. The main actor in the travesty is Jezebel, but Ahab is implicated with the words, 'Ahab rose to go down to the vineyard of Naboth the Jezreelite to take possession of it' (v. 16). The charge is brought by two bribed witnesses – so Jezebel makes herself liable to the death penalty (Deut 19.19). The sentence delivered by Elijah is savage: she is to be eaten by dogs. Elijah also prophesies disaster to Ahab and his dynasty. Ahab has sold himself to do evil (vv. 20, 25), as if sold into slavery to it; but, because Ahab repents (vv. 27–9), the curse is held over to future generations. The narrator expresses judgement on Ahab in terms of the general direction of his reign. He duly notes fulfilment of Elijah's prophecy (2 Kgs 10.10, 17) once Jehu has killed Ahab's sons and so destroyed the house of Omri.

In the last story of Elijah before his translation to heaven, Elijah summons fire from heaven to kill two troops of soldiers – a theme related to Deuteronomy's view of God as a consuming fire (9.3) and its repeated demand to Israel to burn the evil from its midst. Yahweh's authority has been challenged by the king: 'Is it because there is no God in Israel that you are going to inquire of Baal-zebub, the god of Ekron?' (2 Kgs 1.3). The narrator pauses to mock the Philistine god, changing Baal-zebul ('noble Baal') to Baal-zebub ('Lord of the flies'). The king once again has not lived up to the Deuteronomic ideal (Deut 17.14–20) and will die (2 Kgs 1.4) – as he shortly does (v. 17).

Elijah departs as mysteriously as he came – in a whirlwind after passing his mantle (really and symbolically) to his disciple Elisha. The narrator does not intend the whirlwind to shock readers. Instead of building up tension, he tells the reader the conclusion before the story starts (2.1). We remember the wry comment of Obadiah, Ahab's negotiator: 'as soon as I have gone from you, the Spirit of the LORD will carry you whither I know not' (1 Kgs 18.12). Really, Elijah could have departed in no ordinary way! Elijah is thus marked out as different. Just as he departs alive – in a whirlwind accompanied by a fiery chariot and horses – so he will return. For the prophet Malachi, Elijah is an agent of reconciliation:

Behold, I will send you Elijah the prophet before the great and terrible day of the LORD comes. And he will turn the hearts of the fathers to their children and the hearts of the children to their fathers, lest I come and smite the land with a curse. (4.5–6)

The Deuteronomic narrator thus uses the Elijah stories to emphasize God's triumph over Baal, to condemn Ahab's kingship, and to express a deep concern about social justice. They provide a clear commentary on Deuteronomy's message, set in history and providing a critique of the northern monarchy.

Elisha

Elisha has to 'see' Elijah's departure – to 'comprehend' as well as to 'witness'. The prophets send out a search party, thinking that the Spirit of Yahweh has taken him elsewhere – as usual! – but Elisha knows they will find nothing (2 Kgs 2.16–18). Elijah's mantle has power, at least to part water (2.8); and, by receiving it, Elisha of Abel-meholah inherits a double portion of Elijah's 'spirit' (2.9–12). The stories recorded in 2.12–10.36 give an impression of Elisha trying to outdo Elijah's achievement with miracle after miracle; and yet Elijah continues to 'shine through as the more important and significant figure of the two' (Auld, 1986a, 162). There is great subtlety here. The Elisha tales have a flavour of folk tradition, presenting a disordered jumble of miracles and wonders which the narrator has made no attempt to diminish. Elijah has been placed in the framework of the Deuteronomic message with stories that are powerful but sparing; and his influence is felt even within the Elisha chapters (2 Kgs 9.36; 10.10). Elijah's career comes across as more meaningful than Elisha's aimless feats. As his solo career begins, Elisha apes Elijah by parting the water – with *Elijah's* mantle, and in the name of 'Yahweh, the God of Elijah' (2.14). He is 'ashamed' (v. 17), and, although he can bless (vv. 19–22), he can pointlessly curse boys who tease him (2.23–5). His wonders are without divine *authority*, and without even a consistent divine *reference*; and there are crucial things which God keeps from him (4.27). This is really no Elijah!

Both at this stage and later, Elisha travels with the prophetic 'guilds', the 'sons of the prophets'. Under Elisha, these bands of prophets are presented as a sizable group. The Jericho community of prophets come to accept Elisha as a result of his parting of the Jordan (2.13–18). Many tales centre on the Gilgal shrine and most involve miracles – parting the Jordan, making iron float, neutralizing poison and purifying foul water; even she-bears act on Elisha's behalf, tearing apart forty-two youngsters who have taunted him for being bald (2.23–5). Stories of multiplying oil reserves and reviving the dead seem closely related to stories told about Elijah: the 'borrowing' could have happened in the tradition or could be the work of the narrator; and it may not be easy to determine which prophet has historical priority. A final anecdote tells how a dead man is cast into Elisha's grave and returns to life upon touching Elisha's bones.

Some stories are well-told. Befriended by a wealthy woman in Shunem (4.8–37), Elisha seeks to repay her. Her laconic replies punctuate the story: to proposed advancement, 'I dwell among my own people'; to the promise of a son, 'No, my lord, O man of God; do not lie to your maidservant'; to Elisha's greeting, 'It is well'; on breaking the news of her son's death, 'Did I ask my lord for a son? Did I not say, "Do not deceive me?"'; on departure home, 'As the LORD lives, and as you yourself live, I will not leave you'; and, at the emotional high point, with her son alive, she says nothing at all. Yet her reactions structure the entire story. (An epilogue in 8.1–6 tells of how Elisha advises her to escape famine, and how she returns to reclaim her property.)

The story of the Syrian Naaman, cured of his 'leprosy' (probably the skin disease psoriasis – see Auld, 1986a, 167) by Elisha on the advice of a Israelite slave girl (5.1–27) has a central sub-theme of national pride: Naaman is unimpressed by Elisha, the setting, and the prescription – seven dips in the river Jordan. He is persuaded not by mighty advisers but by a humble slave. There is humour too in his fundamental misunderstanding: 'Behold, I know that there is no God in all the earth but in Israel' (v. 15). As if the universal God were tied to Israel, he takes home with him two loads of Israel's *earth* so that he can sacrifice to Yahweh! The fate of Gehazi, Elisha's servant, is a warning to dishonest servants everywhere – he is struck with Naaman's leprosy for his greed.

Other stories show Elisha's political significance, in conflict with Moab (3.4–27) and Syria. One siege (6.8–23) is foiled when Elisha prays that the Syrians' eyes be opened so they can see the army of fiery horses and chariots surrounding them. Struck blind, they are easily captured – *but are freed*: the vision has ensured they will no longer raid Israel. 'Afterward' (v. 24) they clearly do, however, for we see Ben-hadad of Syria besieging Samaria (6.24–7.20). There is horror in the story of the woman boiling and eating her son, and black humour in the case of the doubting gatekeeper who, as Elisha prophesies, is crushed in the stampede for food. The Syrians flee after hearing another heavenly (or at least mysterious) host. Elisha's intervention leading to a change of monarch is strangely contradictory (8.7–15). The sick Ben-hadad consults him through his son Hazael. Elisha replies that Hazael should tell Ben-haded that he will recover, but says that God has shown him that the king will die. He stares meaningfully at the crown prince, and tells him that he will be the next king. The prince delivers his message of recovery but 'took the coverlet and dipped it in water and spread it over this face, till he died' (8.15). The vision of power has been too great.

Elisha sends one of the 'sons of the prophets' to Ramoth-gilead to anoint Jehu king over Israel (9.1–13). The narrator describes Jehu as a zealous remover of Baal worship and religious reformer (2 Kgs 9, 10). When the prophet is on his deathbed, King Joash, Jehu's grandson, visits him. Elisha commands him to shoot an arrow eastwards, linking this symbolic action with future victory over Syria. He then tells the king to strike the ground with the arrows. He does so three times and stops – at which Elijah announces that he will have limited success. Had he struck the ground more, the victory would have been complete (13.14–19).

There seems to have been a large fund of stories at least about Elisha, and perhaps collections were available to the Deuteronomic narrator. Most of the references to the 'sons of the prophets' in the Hebrew Bible occur here, perhaps pointing to the group responsible for these stories. They clearly believed that God had given great powers to men such as Elisha and used the legends to explain their own existence and origins. Whatever the truth about the Elisha of history, his wonders and miracles enhance his standing and exalt his memory. The Deuteronomic narrator used these traditions carefully, limiting Elisha's contribution in subtle ways to strengthen the prophetic profile of Elijah.

Jonah

There is scant reference to the prophet Jonah, son of Amittai, from Gath-hepher (2 Kgs 14.25). He lived in the reign of Jeroboam II of Israel (786–746 BCE), who in the view of the narrator did evil in God's eyes, made Israel sin and continued the policies of Jeroboam I. Yet he restored Israel's borders, 'according to the word of the LORD' through Jonah. God had seen the Israelites' plight and so 'saved them by the hand of Jeroboam [II] the son of Joash' (v. 27). The prophecy was clearly one of hope and deliverance for Israel. There is, curiously, no reference in Kings to the prophets Amos and Hosea, whose prophetic books are dated in the same king's reign.

Another story of Jonah is preserved in the 'minor prophets'. It is in story form, unlike other prophetic books. Jonah is commissioned to go to Nineveh, capital of Assyria, an 'exceedingly great city, three days journey in breadth' (Jon 3.3), to denounce the inhabitants' wickedness. The plot does not move forward easily, since Jonah is mentally unprepared for this task: like Moses, Isaiah and Jeremiah (but more so), he is initially reluctant. Jonah is the 'hero' of the story but it is hard to sympathize with him. We are invited to be critical of his point of view, since we are informed of God's plan which Jonah is frustrating. Jonah's limited horizons are exposed and rejected: the plot always urges us to look carefully beyond them. The story is given a broadly 'chiastic' structure: that is, the central section is the heart, and thought-provoking; the second and fourth sections interrelate, as do the first and last. The story examines the particular situation through the eyes of each of the main characters. The action is seen from the following points of view.

God, Jonah, God (1.1–4)	Disobedience
Mariners (1.5–16)	Fearing God
God, Jonah, God (1.17–3.2)	Repentance
Ninevites (3.3–9)	Fearing God
God, Jonah, God (3.10–4.11)	Disobedience

Thus the centre focuses on repentance, through Jonah's prayer (a psalm) from the fish's stomach and subsequent actions, and through its effect on Nineveh. Surrounding this are examples of outsiders fearing God – first the mariners (including the captain), and second the Ninevites (including the king); and surrounding these sections is comment on Jonah's lack of understanding – first, in fleeing from God's presence (ironically at great personal cost), and, latterly, in viewing himself as a prophet of inevitable doom rather than new hope and new possibilities through repentance. There is deep irony in the statement. 'I am a Hebrew; and I fear the LORD, the God of heaven, who made the sea and the dry land' (1.9) – for he does not fear God but the outsiders *do*, their penitence sharply contrasting with Jonah's egotistical pride. The centre should be the kernel, describing Jonah's faithful execution of the commission; but Jonah is unconditional ('Nineveh *shall be* overthrown' – 3.4) and as a result his message is overthrown as the Ninevites repent and are spared the punishment.

The whole rejects teaching – *all* teaching, whether prophetic, priestly or wisdom (see Kort, 1988, 39) – that is insular and unconditional. The book is about controversy, with each of the human characters responding to God differently. Prophecy, as practised by Jonah, is exposed as being solely concerned with retribution for sin (unlike, curiously, the message of the Jonah of 2 Kings) and ignorant of the problematic nature of God's approach to sin. Like controversy, the book is in danger of going in a circle, ending as it started with Jonah's truculence. However, divine authority breaks through to end the debate: 'should I not pity Nineveh?' (4.11) demands 'Yes' as an answer. Job 40.1–9 would not be out of place here: 'Shall a fault-finder contend with the Almighty? . . . Will you condemn me that you may be justified? Have you an arm like God . . . ?'

On date and authorship we can say little. Had the story been preserved in Kings, its form would not have occasioned great surprise – notwithstanding the different tone of Jonah's one reported prophecy – as there is something of the flavour of Elijah about the story, and there are other psalms incorporated in the Deuteronomic narrative (e.g. 1 Sam 2.1–10). The main thrust of the book of Jonah, penitence leading to deliverance, is close enough to Deuteronomic theology. There is an interest in universalism which has led some scholars to date the book to the time of Ezra and Nehemiah and to see it as a protest against insular policies; and there are hints of wisdom writings in the resolution. The book was certainly in existence by 200 BCE, as it was known by the authors of Ecclesiasticus (49.10) and Tobit (14.4, 8), written around that time. The biological possibility of survival within a 'big fish' need not detain us (although on this much has been written), any more than suggested estimates of the population of Nineveh: whatever the story is, it is not a newscast.

Huldah

Of the prophets discussed in this chapter, Huldah is the only woman and her contribution can be easily missed; yet her words, more than those of any other prophet, helped shape the Hebrew Bible as we know it today. Her prophecy led to Josiah's reform which shaped the Deuteronomic History, and Deuteronomy, into their present forms. There is no reason to suspect fiction – in that case some much more famous name could have been chosen: Jeremiah was active at the time but is not so much as mentioned in Kings.

Josiah, the boy king now in his mid-twenties, orders restoration of the Temple, and in the course of the work a lawbook is discovered. Josiah rends his clothes and says,

Go, inquire of the LORD for me, and for the people, and for all Judah, concerning the words of this book that has been found; for great is the wrath of the LORD that is kindled against us, because our fathers have not obeyed the words of this book, to do according to all that is written concerning us. (2 Kgs 22.13)

Huldah prophesies disaster because of the nation's idolatry. It is *unconditional*: 'my wrath . . . will not be quenched'. Josiah's sincere penitence and humility mean that he will not see the disaster but will die in peace. The judgement on Judah will not be turned aside by Josiah's strenuous efforts to eradicate idolatry (23.1–25) and is prefigured again by the narrator in 23.26–7: 'I will cast off this city'. Yet there is a tension in the account. Josiah does not die in peace, but is killed in battle – although Huldah was right that he would avoid the coming calamity. The glowing testimonial of v. 25 – that there was no better king before or after him – fits well with Huldah's prophecy, and evidently finds no problem in the manner of his death. It is, however, followed by a judgement, certainly from another hand (Nelson, 1981, 84), declaring that, after the 'provocations' of Manasseh, not only were Josiah's efforts not enough but they were irrelevant: it was as if he had never bothered. By the time of writing, Babylon had achieved its victory: the theologians now needed to justify it.

Daniel

The book of Daniel opens with the fall of Jerusalem in 587/6 BCE and quickly paints a scene in Babylon in which Daniel's piety and wisdom become proverbial. In particular, Daniel understands visions and dreams. He proves this when Nebuchadnezzar, the king of Babylon, has a dream that he cannot remember but still wants interpreted: the magicians of Babylon cannot help, but Daniel (threatened like them with death if the king is not satisfied) has the mystery revealed to him 'in a vision of the night' (2.19). He tells the king his dream (of a huge image breaking in pieces) and interprets it in political terms.

Achieving high honours, Daniel is in a position to help his fellow Jews. His friends Shadrach, Meshach and Abednego receive a severe test after they refuse to bow down to a golden image raised by Nebuchadnezzar. This account is serious but comic. Condemned, the three are thrown into a furnace seven times hotter than normal: they survive thanks to an 'angel' (3.28) and their survival promotes the official recognition of the Jewish God – 'for there is no other god who is able to deliver in this way' (v. 29). The humour lies in the pomp of the occasion. The officials present are listed at length twice (vv. 2, 3) and then mentioned again more briefly (v. 27). The long list of musical instruments accompanying the worship is repeated four times (vv. 5, 7, 10, 15), achieving a theatrical effect with a mocking edge.

Nebuchadnezzar has another dream, prophesying his downfall: a year later he loses his sanity and eats grass like an animal, just as Daniel has predicted. When his reason returns, he 'blesse[s] the Most High' (4.34). In the next chapter, Belshazzar is king: here Daniel interprets mysterious words which an unearthly hand has written on the plaster. Even though the words are a prophecy of doom, Daniel is honoured! Belshazzar is killed the same night. Darius the Mede takes over (6.1). He is tricked into an irrevocable decree which forces him to throw Daniel into a lions' den, but Daniel survives. Again the 'God of Daniel' is victorious and Daniel prospers.

The stories inhabit a supernormal world in which a mysterious disembodied hand writes on a wall, a 'watcher, a holy one' comes from heaven (4.13) and miraculous deliverances occur. The book resembles Esther, but in comparison that tale is slow and sedate; in Daniel each story is rushed through so that the next episode can begin. An assumption throughout is that the Jewish god impressed first the Babylonians and later Darius the Mede by his acts of power and revelations of mystery. This is summed up by a decree of Darius: 'I make a decree, that in all my royal dominion men tremble and fear before the God of Daniel, for he is the living God, enduring forever; his kingdom shall never be destroyed, and his dominion shall be to the end . . . ' (6.26). Daniel's own dreams are described in the final six chapters, and complex interpretations given.

The book of Daniel is written partly in Hebrew and partly in Aramaic, whether deliberately or by chance. Since the visions in the latter part of the book are in the first person, 'I', it was widely assumed from the first that Daniel was a historical figure, exiled in 605 BCE. Yet the dreams and their interpretations show a detailed knowledge of the political situation at the time of the Seleucid king Antiochus IV Epiphanes, who desecrated the Jerusalem Temple in 167 BCE, and to most scholars this demands a date after this time (generally given as 167–163 BCE). The dreams and their interpretations seem therefore to be a response to Antiochus's challenge – deliberately obscured so that only the faithful can understand. Seen in this way, the prophecies point to the destruction of the Seleucids and the establishment of God's kingdom. The background may not be the same for the first six (narrative) chapters, which have no certain Seleucid references. These chapters may have arisen earlier, as Esther had done. P. R. Davies (1985) explores these issues in fuller detail.

FURTHER READING

Auld, A. G. 1986a: *Kings.*
Clements, R. E. 1975: *Prophecy and Tradition.*
Davies, P. R. 1985: *Daniel.*
Eslinger, L. 1985: *Kingship of God in Crisis: a Close Reading of 1 Samuel 1–12.*
Gordon, R. P. 1984: *1 and 2 Samuel.*

10

Prophecy and the Prophets

A. Graeme Auld

Preliminary Reading   Joel; Amos; Hosea; Isaiah 1–9; 40–55.

Some of the best known and most strangely fascinating material in the Bible is from its prophetic books, the 'Latter Prophets': Isaiah's vision of the divine king with the ministering seraphim (Isa 6); his dream of the holy mountain without hurt or destruction where the lion eats straw like the ox (Isa 11); Jeremiah's eloquent scorn of a people abandoning the true god for useless substitutes (Jer 2.9–13); exotic Ezekiel – from the beasts and the wheels and the honey-sweet scroll of his vision (Ezek 1–3) that have fascinated so many mystics since, to the valley of dead bones (Ezek 37), which inspired a well-known negro spiritual; the passionate, disappointed love of Hosea's God (Hos 11); Micah's outspokenness (Mic 2–3); Zechariah's weird visions (Zech 1–6); Malachi's promise of the messenger to prepare Yahweh's way before him (Mal 3); and the haunting portrait of a silently suffering servant in Isaiah 53. No chapter in a volume such as this can substitute for sampling such passages at leisure and at first hand.

Who were the 'Latter Prophets'?

Biblical prophets were deeply involved in affairs of state and their community, and were not much given to long-term prediction – despite the usual meaning of 'prophetic' in English. There is a great difference between the prophet figures of the books of Samuel, Kings, and Chronicles, and those in Isaiah, Jeremiah, Ezekiel and the 'Book of the Twelve' (the 'minor prophets').

In the narrative books we find stories about prophets, who sometimes speak in these tales; but what they say is often not the main point of the narrative in which they appear. However, in the 'Latter Prophets' the spoken words themselves are the main point. There is a further surprise. Few prophets appear both as characters within the stories in the narrative books and as the speakers or writers of words in what are called the prophetic books. Isaiah is an exception; and yet his presence in 2 Kings 18–20 (and 2 Chron 32) is no real help towards a portrait of Isaiah of Jerusalem. The stories of his dealings with King Hezekiah at the time of the Assyrian invasion are found in the book of Isaiah also (Isa 36–9) and are clearly legendary when compared with other material in that book.

All this being so, we should be even more sceptical about using the stories of Elijah to help us understand what sort of role Micah may have played in his society, or taking the words (and actions) of Ezekiel as any sort of pointer to how Nathan may have behaved in front of David and Solomon. The prophets of the narrative books and the prophetic speakers are not completely distinct; but they are very different.

As we look more closely at the prophetic books, we notice that very few of the figures after whom they are named are actually called 'prophet' or said to 'prophesy'; that such language is commoner in the later (post-exilic) than in the earlier (pre-exilic) elements in these books; and that some (especially earlier) figures denounce prophets, and Amos actually appears to disclaim being one himself (7.14–15). The mainstream view is that when we find Isaiah or Micah or Jeremiah criticizing the prophets we are glimpsing a feud within a profession, or a struggle for the soul and conscience of a party. The dialogue between Jeremiah and Hananiah in Jeremiah 28 can be claimed as good evidence for this way of looking at things. However, there is an alternative approach. I take seriously Amos's denial that he was a prophet, and the scorn poured on prophets by such men as he. There is also a rather different version of the encounter between Jeremiah and Hananiah in the Greek Septuagint: here Jeremiah is never called 'the prophet' – and, when Hananiah is introduced as one, we, the readers, are invited to expect the worst.

To sum up: Amos, Isaiah, Jeremiah, Micah and their like would not have been seen dead as prophets! Only when they were dead, and probably long dead, could a tradition that revered them also call them 'prophets'. The title 'prophet' had been revalued and rehabilitated in the intervening period. These figures came to be held in high esteem not for how they understood themselves, nor even for how they really were, but for how they came to be remembered.

The 'Latter Prophets' and their Editors

We have to recognize that the books which we who inherit that tradition call 'prophetic' were not transcripts of original oracular performances filed for posterity. They do contain the remembered words of honoured spokesmen of a bygone age – remembered as a still-vital divine message which could be presented anew for a much later age. Yet other parts were anonymous and became attached to the books where they now appear. Other parts again were pseudonymous: compositions deliberately attributed to an authoritative name from the people's past. The book of Daniel, discussed in the previous chapter, provides a good example of this practice, which became common in the intertestamental period.

We cannot choose between Isaiah of Jerusalem and the book of Isaiah, but must try to hold on to both together. We do actually have the book in our hands for inspection and study. The book speaks in its own right; Isaiah himself, reconstructed imaginatively from the book, is important as the crafter of some of the book's great utterances, and as the fount and hero of the tradition it represents. Even if we see him only from a distance, and glimpse him past many obstacles, we have to keep aiming for a better perspective and a more adequate view.

In brief, the growth and development of the fifteen prophetic books was complicated, as will emerge further in the course of our discussion. Here I offer just one rule of thumb – and it is no better than that: poetry is more likely to take us close to the form of the original message than prose. Unfortunately its very compactness and terseness also mean that assured interpretation often eludes us.

The fifteen Latter Prophets are as follows. All dates are BCE.

The 'Major Prophets'

Isaiah. – Eighth century, based in Jerusalem. The book includes extensive anonymous additions, especially in chapters 40–66.

Jeremiah. – Seventh-sixth century from Anathoth in Benjamin. His prophecies focus on coming disaster, blaming faithlessness. The book includes a large amount of narrative.

Ezekiel. – An exilic prophet. Much of the book consists of visions and prophecies of doom, but there are also prophecies encouraging the remnant in exile.

The 'Minor' Prophets'

Hosea. Eighth-century northerner, who prophesied just before the fall of Samaria.

Joel. Fourth century or earlier, from Judah. Uses swarms of locusts as a vivid picture God's anger, demanding repentance.

Amos. Mid eighth century, from Tekoa, near Jerusalem. Active in the northern kingdom. His major concern was *righteousness.*

Obadiah. Possibly fifth century. Prophecies against Edom leading to universal judgement.

Jonah. Mentioned in 2 Kings 14.25. The book named after him is in story form, relating the repentance of Nineveh. (See discussion in ch. 9.)

Micah. Late eighth century, from Moresheth, in the Shephelah (lowlands). Prophecies of judgement and hope.

Nahum. Possibly seventh century, before the fall of Nineveh in 612. The book proclaims the doom of Nineveh.

Habakkuk. Late seventh century BCE. Addresses the question, how can God be using the inhuman Chaldeans (Babylonians) as his instrument of judgement?

Zephaniah. Seventh century contemporary of King Josiah. The book is mainly about the Day of Yahweh.

Haggai. Sixth century. The book relates to the rebuilding of the Temple, c. 520.

Zechariah. Sixth century. The early chapters relate to the rebuilding of the Temple, c. 520. Also anonymous additions.

Malachi. 'My Messenger'. Post-exilic. The book condemns sin and promises hope only for those who repent.

Religious Purity

The prophetic books are more concerned with public religion than with private observance. In the main they address or complain about the whole community, or the capital city, or the king and leading classes. 'Religious purity is thus a matter of the quality of 'established' religion and its public rituals. We are dealing with sacred actions and cultic personnel associated with the cycle of annual festivals or the daily worship at the national shrine. We are not talking about private behaviour or spiritual attitudes.

   The people of the Bible, no less than the other peoples of the ancient Near East, believed there was an intimate relation between how they treated their

god(s) and how their god(s) treated them: that is, how their flocks and crops
fared, and how they prospered in their relations with their neighbours and
the great powers. This widespread view is reflected in the prophets. The
poetic images of Joel 1–2 make enjoyable reading and are easily understood,
once we take our clue from 1.4 and realize that the powerful nation
described as having lions' teeth, advancing like war horses and climbing into
houses is a devastating plague of locusts. For Joel, public fasting and
lamentation are the answer to the invasion – not forgetting a challenge to
their god's reputation: why should he risk the reputation of failing to
support his people (2.17–19)? The opening verses of Hosea 6 express the
same popular belief:

> Come, let us return to the LORD;
>   for he has torn, that he may heal us;
>   he has stricken, and he will bind us up.
> After two days he will revive us;
>   on the third day he will raise us up,
>   that we may live before him.
> Let us know, let us press on to know the LORD;
>   his going forth is sure as the dawn;
> he will come to us as the showers,
>   as the spring rains that water the earth. (6.1–3)

If we turn back to God, he will come and revive us as showers of rain. In a
similar way Haggai, after the first return of Jerusalem's deportees from their
Babylonian exile, explains the fact that 'the heavens above you have
withheld their dew, and the earth has withheld its produce' as being
'Because of my house that lies in ruins, while you busy yourselves each with
his own house' (1.9b–10). Malachi makes a rather more precise complaint
against the priests of his time (1.6–14): they are cheating their god by offering blemished animals in sacrifice, and still hope for his favour – though
they would not be so naive as to treat their Persian provincial governor so
slightingly. Malachi blames the people as a whole (3.6–12) for similar
double-dealing over their tithes (religious taxes paid in the form of
agricultural produce). Human cultic behaviour and divine favour reflected
in the orderly beneficent working of what we today call the natural world
were held to be intimately interrelated.

A well-known series of prophetic 'purple passages' appears to take
criticism of public religious behaviour even further.
Amos is both comprehensive and brief:

> I hate, I despise your feasts,
>   and I take no delight in your solemn assemblies.

> Even though you offer me your burnt offerings and cereal offerings,
>> I will not accept them,
> and the peace offerings of your fatted beasts
>> I will not look upon.
> Take away from me the noise of your songs;
>> to the melody of your harps I will not listen. (5.21–3)

A little earlier in the book of Amos it seems to be suggested that the very act of attending the ancient sanctuaries of Bethel and Gilgal counts as rebellion against Yahweh (4.4–5). Of course, post-exilic Jews might well have supposed that Amos's problem was with the locations Bethel and Gilgal – simply because Jerusalem was the true place of worship. Two factors suggest that they would have been wrong: first, Amos suggests that seeking the Lord means not attending any holy places but rather taking a public stand against evil in one's own community; and, secondly, his Jerusalem contemporary Isaiah is quite as eloquent in condemning the sacrifices, offerings, festivals and prayers even in that city (1.10–17).

Jeremiah appears to reinforce what we have detected in Amos. The passage that begins

> Stand by the roads, and look,
>> and ask for the ancient paths,
> where the good way is; and walk in it,
>> and find rest for your souls.
> But they said, 'We will not walk in it' (6.16)

continues,

> To what purpose does frankincense come to me from Sheba,
>> or sweet cane from a distant land?
> Your burnt offerings are not acceptable,
>> nor your sacrifices pleasing to me. (v. 20)

The prose sermon in chapter 7 goes even further by suggesting that the rules for sacrifice were not part of Yahweh's teaching of his people in the exodus period: at that time he simply instructed them to obey the moral law (7.21–3). This theme is by no means confined to the specifically 'prophetic' books. It is found in the Psalms, for example in 50.7–15, and more briefly in the classic penitential psalm (51.15–17). It is also part of the splendid climax of the story of God's ultimate rejection of Saul through Samuel (1 Sam 15.22–3).

The key question is this: are we dealing, in this range of texts, simply with rhetorical exaggeration or poetic licence, or do these passages represent an important line of tradition which accorded ultimate significance to moral behaviour before God? Did the prophets speak in such a way only to shock people into realizing that bad living could invalidate their worship, or did they really mean, 'Forget worship and live aright'?

If the latter, then, whether we are literary critics trying to understand ancient texts or historians of religion attempting to reconstruct what happened in the past, the ramifications are considerable. During the Second World War, Dietrich Bonhoeffer wrote moving but elusive sketches of a 'religionless Christianity' in letters from a Nazi prison. Was he recapturing an ancient prophetic insight? Or are modern scholars simply reading the ancient world through twentieth-century spectacles when they depict a prophetic vision of 'religion' without religious practice?

The other general point we have to raise is this: whatever may or may not have been the prophetic message, that message has been passed down to us and preserved for us by a religious, cultic, worshipping tradition – the Judaeo-Christian tradition. That tradition in its many forms has tolerated a prophetic critique of worship while continuing its own familiar religious practices. In doing so, has it successfully drawn the sting of a movement which, if properly fostered, might otherwise have destroyed it?

Since, as we have seen, the words of earlier 'prophetic' figures (like the other writings of the Hebrew Bible) received their final editing long after Judah's exile in Babylon, we can not always be sure whether we are reading their words or the editors' intermingled comments, developing a particular interpretation of the prophetic message. It is easier when we can orient ourselves by material which we know is from this later period. The prose sermon in Jeremiah 7.21–3, mentioned above, is a case in point. It seems to dispute the claims in the Torah (Exod 25 – Num 10) that Israel's offerings and sacrifices was revealed through Moses at the holy mountain in the immediate aftermath of the deliverance from Egypt.

Two other important pieces of post-exilic evidence are Zechariah 7–8 and Isaiah 58 (which, as we shall see later, cannot be attributed to the eighth-century Isaiah of Jerusalem). Both passages are about fasting. In Zechariah God questions whether his people's fasting is really undertaken to please him, when in their eating and drinking they are clearly pleasing themselves (vv. 5–6). The talk moves immediately from Jerusalem's pre-exilic prosperity to the prophets of that time who preached justice in God's name, but to no avail (vv. 7, 9–14).

Isaiah 58 is both easier to read and at the same time much more scathing:

> Yet they seek me daily,
> and delight to know my ways,
> as if they were a nation that did righteousness

and did not forsake the ordinance of their God;
they ask of me righteous judgments,
they delight to draw near to God. (v. 2)

Such a chapter should be read carefully in its entirety. Its moving poetic rhetoric is the highwater mark of this tradition within the Hebrew Bible. Attention has shifted from sacrifices and attendance at sanctuaries (as in the earlier texts we have reviewed) to fasting and Sabbath observance. What are we to deduce from this? Some see it as evidence of a development from merely public cultic religion to a more individual spirituality, alongside collective or corporate forms. Yet the fasting in Isaiah 58 seems to be quite as public or corporate as the sacrifices mentioned in the passages from Jeremiah and Amos cited earlier. The difference should be described in another way: Isaiah 58 is addressed to a people physically removed from their sanctuary and the possibility of sacrificing; for them public religion has become the communal fast and weekly Sabbath observance. These exiles are taught that God's chosen fast is 'to loose the bonds of wickedness, to undo the thongs of the yoke' (v. 16).

It is not easy for many Jews or Christians to accept the possibility that a major strand of biblical tradition does not see sacrifice or any other public rite as absolutely essential to the relationship between God and his people. Although Judaism has been a non-sacrificial religion since the Roman destruction of the Jerusalem Temple in 70 CE, Jewish teaching has taken a minute interest in all the rites once associated with the Temple. Christians for their part, from the New Testament onwards, have portrayed the death of Jesus not just as a sacrifice, but as *the* sacrifice which once and for all fulfilled the requirements of the true religion of the Hebrew scriptures. From such perspectives, it is difficult to reach dispassionate historical conclusions about the prophets' attitudes to sacrifice and public religion.

Political Influence

It is sometimes said that kings and prophets needed each other, that it is hard to think of the one group without the other. It is not surprising that the narrative books of Joshua, Judges, Samuel and Kings are called the 'Former Prophets'. When we turn from these stories to a careful, critical reading of the 'Latter Prophets' we have to keep some important questions in mind.

1 Were all the biblical prophets of the sort we find in Kings?
2 Are all the stories in Kings good evidence for the periods they talk about? How many reflect the situations and interests of later storytellers?

3 Did the fall of Jerusalem and the Davidic monarchy create a wholly new situation for prophecy?
4 Have the materials in the prophetic books also been adjusted and supplemented to highlight the political influence of their heroes?

It is certainly true that kings and their courts are seldom explicitly mentioned in the Latter Prophets. Isaiah's audiences with Ahaz (Isa 7) and with Hezekiah (Isa 38–9) and the expulsion of Amos from Israel to Judah by a royal agent are the sort of exceptions that make us aware of more than one relevant rule: they bring issues of royal and divine authority out of the shadows onto centre stage; and they are recounted in narrative prose, clearly distinct from the normal poetic rhetoric of the prophetic books.

Yet is this metaphor of shadows and centre stage the right one? Do these rare narratives simply make occasionally explicit what we should understand as always implied: that in the pre-exilic 'prophetic' oracles the king and his court are being addressed or talked about much of the time? Even although the 'royals' are rarely mentioned, would it not have been obvious to them as to all other hearers of the original words that it was they and their officials who were meant? Or are these occasional royal scenes an intrusion into the books in which they appear? Do they attempt to impose on the Latter Prophets the views of the books of Samuel and Kings on the relationship of kings and prophets? Inevitably there are good arguments on either side.

On the one side, the fact that the oracles of the pre-exilic prophets were re-edited when the monarchy was defunct suggests that allusions to king and court have been played down by the editors. Moreover, we, who belong to a world that is more individualistic and more egalitarian than that of the Bible, may miss such allusions even when they are there. It is hard enough for us to pick up the political realities and social codes of the Near East today, let alone the Near East of over two and a half millennia ago.

On the other side, we have to make two obvious remarks about the literary character – the style and placing – of the narrative episodes in Amos and Isaiah mentioned above. First, some of them appear to disrupt the wider literary structures within which they appear: Amos 7.10–17 separates the fourth from the third of Amos's visions, and yet these reports of his visions appear to have been structured in close pairs; and Isaiah 6.1–9.7 separates chapter 5 from similar material in chapters 9–10. There are grounds for claiming that these sections are intrusions into earlier prophetic collections.

Secondly, these narratives are not just similar, but in fact are closely related, to passages in Kings (Amos 7 to 1 Kgs 13; Isa 7 to 2 Kgs 16; and Isa 36–9 to 2 Kgs 18–20).

Since the preliminary arguments are finely balanced, we must inspect the relevant passages with particular care. But first, to set the scene, let us consider a passage from Isaiah that perfectly encapsulates ideal monarchy. In memorable language with apt metaphors Isaiah 32.1–5 sketches the following dream: give us a king and court that reign justly, and they will both defend us and provide life support. Those who lack principle will no longer enjoy position and honour. Both the over-hasty and the hesitant will be given a context in which they can develop. These verses depict feudal society at its best. They offer a heady vision; and yet similar passages in the Psalms and from elsewhere in the ancient Near East show that the passage is quite in the spirit – at least, the best spirit – of its times. We can see the other side of the same coin earlier in the book, in Isaiah 3.1–15, where the poet vividly portrays the devastating social results of removing from Jerusalem and Judah their court and aristocracy. A king was obviously worth influencing, if one wanted some policy achieved. Our question must be: was the king the only figure in those times worth influencing – to the extent that we should presume that any and every serious appeal we read was originally intended for his ears?

The book of Amos is short enough to review quickly from the standpoint of our question. The following are some passages that may relate to king and court.

1   3.9–11 calls on distant foreigners to view Israel's capital city on its hill. Who controls its strongholds and defences but the king?
2   3.13–15 is spoken against the 'house' (rather than 'people') of Jacob and closes with a mention of its 'great houses'. Does not this at least hint at the royal house?
3   Similarly, the oracles on wholesale army losses (5.1–3) and official sanctuaries (5.4–6) are addressed to the 'house of Israel'.
4   The court and upper classes are clearly the butt of 6.1–8.

Now, it may well be true that the narrative about Amos's verbal tussle with Amaziah is a later composition added to the report of Amos's visions; and it is a fact that the book of Amos contains only one direct mention of the 'house of Jeroboam', the royal house of the northern Kingdom (this occurs in 7.9, just before the Amaziah episode, and so within the report of one of Amos's visions, which we are nowhere told he made public). Yet, after reading the passages listed above, we should not be too surprised to be told that Amaziah warned the king about Amos, claiming that he was involved in nothing less than conspiracy and sedition (7.10–11).

Isaiah's poetry gives a similar impression. It is easy – once you start looking – to see the princes and their retainers as the object of the criticism voiced in the series of 'woes' in Isaiah 5.8–23. 'Those who lead this people lead them astray' (9.16) is at the very heart of the three-stanza poem in 9.8–21. The warnings against an alliance with Egypt in face of what would appear to be the threat from Assyria (30.1–5; 31.1–3; and probably 28.14–22 as well) are clearly directed against manoeuvres by the court, although the king is never directly mentioned.

A word that many of the prophets use is *'etsah*, which is translated in different ways: 'policy', 'plan', 'counsel'. Like its English counterparts, it does not belong exclusively to the world of politics; but it is an important part of that world. It suggests a wish on the part of those who use it to influence affairs. No one uses it more than Isaiah. It can be no accident also that Isaiah includes two famous poems embodying the royal ideal (9.2–7; 11.1–9), and that this key term has a vital part in both: 'Wonderful Counsellor' (9.6) and 'the spirit of counsel' (11.2).

It would be an interesting and useful exercise to read more of the prophetic books with this same question in mind: how much of the material can be read as concerning the king and court circles, and how much is addressed to the wider population. Some of the evidence can only be properly scrutinized in the original Hebrew. A single example will suffice. The common Hebrew verb *yashab* means both 'sit', when used of an individual, and 'inhabit', when used with a people as its grammatical subject. Its present participate (*yosheb*) can mean both 'one who is seated or enthroned' or 'an inhabitant'. In Isaiah 5.3 and 9.9 (9.8 in the Hebrew), for example, the RSV has taken this singular participle to refer collectively to the 'inhabitants of Jerusalem' and 'inhabitants of Samaria'. This is perfectly possible, and an English reader sees no problem lurking; but the Hebrew can be interpreted to refer to the king, 'the enthroned one of Jerusalem/ Samaria'. Which reading is right?

This sort of ambiguity is not at all uncommon in the Hebrew scriptures. It is one of the reasons why Bible translations differ considerably from each other in what they say as well as in how they say it. However, the words of the classical prophets, like much high poetry in any language, often deliberately suggest different meanings at one and the same time. Translation leads to the impoverishment of such poetry, through the loss of some of its multiple meanings. We have to consider the possibility that Isaiah deliberately intended his audience to hear both 'enthroned ruler' and 'inhabitant' in his single word *yosheb*.

Yet we have to mention another possibility too. Even within the tradition and development of a single language, new circumstances can lead to a new decision about which is the most obvious meaning of a text. Many passages in Shakespeare are strange to modern ears, not because the words themselves are unknown, but rather because we now use these same words in a different way. Returning to where we began: even when there were no longer kings sitting (*yosheb*) on the throne of Israel and of Judah, there were still people inhabiting (*yosheb*) Samaria and Jerusalem who could feel themselves, no less than their predecessors, addressed by God through such poetic words as those of Isaiah 5.3 and 9.9. It is possible that they did not hear what Isaiah had intended; yet his words were still a vehicle for God's communication with them.

While we cannot pretend to any certainty over just how much material was in fact directed towards the nation's rulers, it is even less possible to estimate its effectiveness. We may speculate about attempts at political influence, but hardly about its results. It seems that the Latter Prophets were not voices 'crying in the wilderness' – though we should be cautious in any attempt to distinguish between 'central' and 'peripheral' prophets. They do not seem to have occupied a protected position within established religion, but neither do they appear to have been marginal figures, divorced from the society of their time and its centres of power.

The book of Jeremiah, which contains much more extended narrative than any of the other books we are concerned with here, offers several pictures of the personal cost to Jeremiah of his role: he is put in the stocks (20.1–6), debarred from the Temple (36.4–8) and imprisoned (37.11–21). Clearly, his message was heard and understood by officialdom!

Social Justice

Christians have traditionally understood the prophets as foretelling the coming and significance of Jesus and so have seen that as their main role. However, for many readers in the modern world, concern for social justice was the hallmark of the classical prophets. In our own time, this perception has led many Christians towards renewed interest in the prophetic books, as potent charter for civil liberties and human rights. This fresh emphasis is especially obvious among the 'liberation theologians' of South America.

In this section we shall examine three issues: First, is a concern for social justice a prominent feature of classical prophecy throughout its history – and did all the Latter Prophets espouse this cause? Secondly, did they mean what they said? And, thirdly, were those we have learned to call 'the prophets' the source of this biblical tradition – and did they themselves claim originality?

In reply to our first question, social justice was certainly a live issue throughout the history of classical prophecy, from the eighth-century prophets Amos, Isaiah, Hosea and Micah, who are particularly famous in this respect, down to the later post-exilic prophets. Zechariah BCE urges his contemporaries, 'Be not like your fathers, to whom the former prophets cried out, "Thus says the LORD of hosts, Return from your evil ways and from your evil deeds." But they did not hear or heed me, says the LORD' (1.4). Here 'former prophets' simply means earlier prophets. Yet it does show that Isaiah and the others were now known as 'prophets', whatever they might have called themselves. Zechariah 1.2–6, and the similar passage in 7.7–14, restate the old 'prophetic' standards as still valid – and underscore them with the proof of experience: the old threats had been fulfilled.

It is not easy to sort out the argument behind all the complaints in Malachi 2, but the prophet's final protest is plain enough:

You have wearied the Lord with your words. Yet you say, 'How have we wearied him?' By saying, 'Every one who does evil is good in the sight of the LORD, and he delights in them.' Or by asking, 'Where is the God of justice?' (v. 17)

Both parts of this critique bring to mind Isaiah 5:

> Woe to those who call evil good and good evil,
> who put darkness for light
>   and light for darkness,
> who put bitter for sweet
>   and sweet for bitter! (v. 20)

and

> who say: 'Let him make haste,
> let him speed his work
>   that we may see it;
> let the purpose of the Holy One of Israel draw near,
>   and let it come that we may know it! (v. 19)

It is in fact hardly surprising that we find such concerns in the prophets, for they are not just a prophetic topic but (like the issues of religious purity) recur in the narratives and the Psalms. The evidence does not justify a claim that such moral concern provides the single distinguishing feature of the biblical prophet. There are prophets who remain silent on such issues. Joel calls for fasting in response to a devastating locust plague, nowhere suggesting that moral improvement is required. One of the several points that mark out the contribution of the anonymous 'Second Isaiah' from the rest of the book of Isaiah is the complete absence of ethical analysis or moral exhortation from chapters 40–55.

The reasons for these exceptions differ from case to case. The business of the great exilic poet Second Isaiah is to offer to his uprooted, shattered people promise of deliverance and return. His concern is more with God's intentions towards them than with theirs towards God. Joel, on the other hand, is typical of much biblical and non-biblical religion in holding that a cultic response is what is needed in time of national disaster – like holding a national day of prayer in time of war.

The next problem we must face is that of deciding just what the prophets' criticisms really mean. When Micah asks,

> Is it not for you to know justice? –
>   you who hate the good and love the evil,
> who tear the skin from off my people,
>   and their flesh from off their bones;
> who eat the flesh of my people,
>   and flay their skin from off them,
> and break their bones in pieces,
>   and chop them up like meat in a kettle,
>   like flesh in a cauldron (3.1b–3)

are we to imagine cannibalistic behaviour in the royal dungeons or should we instead suppose gross rhetorical exaggeration? And to whom are these denunciations addressed? If the royal court was in the poet's firing-line, there was good reason for him to speak obliquely. If the cap fitted, then let it be worn!

Another issue that has long vexed commentators is what Hosea and Jeremiah mean when they condemn sexual misbehaviour. Are they speaking literally of personal relationships, or metaphorically of 'improper relationships' with gods other than Yahweh? When Hosea says,

> Rejoice not, O Israel!
>   Exult not like the peoples;
> for you have played the harlot, forsaking your God.
>   You have loved a harlot's hire
> upon all threshing floors (9.1)

he may be implying any one of three things: that Israel's women are misbehaving sexually; that Israel has neglected Yahweh in favour of other divine guardians of the harvest; or that Israel is honouring fertility deities in rites that also involve sexual activities. His comments may be literal or metaphorical or deliberately double-edged. Whichever way we read such words, Hosea can be taken as representing the tradition we find in the Ten Commandments, which first ban other gods and later forbid adultery: these are a distillation of non-cultic religion, neither forbidding nor enjoining any specifically cultic actions.

It could be argued that all parts of the Bible with such a point of view were later than, and infuenced by, the prophets; and this may well be true of the Ten Commandments in the form in which we know them. However, it would be difficult (and beyond the evidence) to extend the argument convincingly to all other parts of the Hebrew Bible. It is much more probable that the 'prophetic' poets themselves drew on the poetry of the Psalms (e.g. Pss 15, 24, 50, 51) and on the equally poetic legacy of the wisdom teachers in Israel. Did they intensify this teaching? Did they isolate the theme of social justice from this inheritance and give it an even more central and privileged and even unique status? Was there perhaps a mutual interaction between prophets and other writers on religious and ethical matters?

What we do find in those prophetic books which highlight the theme are brilliantly memorable statements of several social issues. When Isaiah says,

> Woe to those who are heroes at drinking wine,
>   and valiant men in mixing strong drink,
> who acquit the guilty for a bribe,
>   and deprive the innocent of his right! (5.22–3)

we can readily picture those who measure their 'quality' by their appetites and not by their commitment to justice.

What is said about consequences is often not intended literally, or as the final word. The pre-exilic prophets painted the situation sombrely – not just because they saw it that way, but also for effect, so that their hearers might be shocked into changing their ways. Even Amos includes the idea that God may 'perhaps' be gracious to the remnant of Joseph (5.15). One expects that he hoped for this much more warmly than he allowed himself to say. He was not simply shouting after a condemned people on their way to execution that the death sentence was justified. Rather, in attempting to prepare grounds for clemency, he was making the defendants fully aware of the gravity of their situation.

It is interesting that no special claim to originality or novel revelation is made by those prophets who put issues of social behaviour centre stage. They appeal instead to a common morality which, although endorsed by God, should also win assent beyond as well as among their own people. This is true of Obadiah's complaint against Edom's behaviour at the time of Jerusalem's fall (Obad 10–14), and of Amos's critique of several neighbouring peoples before homing in on Israel (Amos 1.3–2.16). Whether they are talking about situations abroad or, as most often, at home, the prophets' words compel by their own passion and appropriate-

In short, we have to conclude that the prophets shared a wider concern for justice and equity, but stated it particularly memorably. They did not present themselves as innovators; and addressed other peoples in much the same terms as they used in speaking to Israel and Judah.

Prophetic Call

This leads us naturally to consider the prophets' divine impulse or compulsion, often held to characterize the beginning of a prophet's mission. Here too we tend to generalize on the basis of too little evidence, some of which is dubious anyway.

We find 'call' narratives in the three largest prophetic books – in Isaiah 6 (and perhaps 40.1–11), Jeremiah 1 and Ezekiel 1–3 – but hardly at all elsewhere (there is perhaps a hint in Amos 7.10–17). Are we to suppose that Isaiah, Jeremiah and Ezekiel are the norm, and that the shorter books reflect more fragmentary records of other prophetic figures? If so, we must recognize that tradition did not find these details essential to the record. Should we then turn our comparison on its head, and examine what is exceptional about the longer books with their distinctive call stories?

Even here we have to start by drawing distinctions. Only Jeremiah and Ezekiel have straightforward 'call' stories – and at the obvious place, the very beginning of the record. The vision of Isaiah which many people read as his inaugural call (Isa 6) is not presented at the beginning of the book and may well have a different function altogether. Further, the books of Jeremiah and Ezekiel have a special and repeated interest in the status of these men as prophets and in their difference from other prophets. Jeremiah 1 talks of Jeremiah's appointment as 'prophet to the nations' (v. 5); while important conflict narratives such as Jeremiah 26 and 28 help to define what is different about this divine appointee. In similar vein, Ezekiel's divine summons includes the words, 'The people also are impudent and stubborn . . . And whether they hear or refuse to hear (for they are a rebellious house) they will know that there has been a prophet among them' (2.4–5). These words are repeated at the end of chapter 33 with its presentation of Ezekiel as his people's true watchman by divine appointment.

I have suggested that it is the books of Jeremiah and Ezekiel, and especially their opening chapters, that we have to thank for our traditional view that the great biblical prophets were men who had experienced and reported a special call from God; and that their evidence is a minority witness. To see the other side of the case we must look in a little more detail at Amos and Isaiah.

There are two relevant passages in Amos. In the course of his dialogue with Amaziah, priest of Bethel (7.10–17), Amos rather oddly responds to being called 'seer' (v. 12) by stating, 'I am no prophet, nor a prophet's son; but I am a herdsman, and a dresser of sycamore trees, and the LORD took me from following the flock, and the LORD said to me, "Go, prophesy to my people Israel"' (vv. 14–15). Amos is still a farmer and disclaims being a 'prophet', despite his obedience to the divine summons; and yet he says that he has been sent to 'prophesy': he 'prophesies' without being a 'prophet'. A similar point is made poetically in Amos 3.8:

> The lion has roared;
> who will not fear?
> The Lord GOD has spoken,
> who can but prophesy?

Just as you do not require to belong to a special class of human beings in order to experience fear in face of a roaring lion, so too anyone at all may prophesy who has heard the Lord speak. (This point is rather deftly undercut before it is ever made, by the preceding verse 7. That verse is in prose and is probably a later intrusion into the poetic context.) Again the verb 'prophesy' is acceptable; but anyone could do it. It may be compared to people admitting to 'playing the piano' whilst denying being 'pianists' – not so much out of modesty over the quality of their playing as because they neither have nor wish professional status.

The 'action' in Isaiah 6 is conducted without using the technical terms 'prophet' and 'prophesy' at all. In fact these words are extremely rare in Isaiah. We find occasional criticism of prophets in Isaiah's poetry (3.2; 28.7); Isaiah is himself styled 'prophet' in the narratives (Isa 36–9) shared with 2 Kings (18–20); but in Isaiah 40–66 we find no trace of this language. Isaiah's vison of the divine king in his court leads to his 'sending' (v. 8) – and on a very odd mission.

Fortunately this powerful and important but very difficult chapter is not quite unique in the Bible. It shares several features with the more extended and often amusing story of Micaiah, son of Imlah, told in 1 Kings 22. That story should be read in its entirety, but with special attention to vv. 19–23. These sketch the scene in the divine court more briefly than Isaiah 6; but we find the same essential features in both stories – and the two reports of visions and missions are much closer to each other than either is to any other biblical passage.

It is when Micaiah is challenged over the authenticity of his prophecy that he counters with a report that he has enjoyed privileged access to God's very inner court and is party to a divine enterprise of deception. We may suppose similar dynamics in the situation that gave rise to Isaiah 6. Vv. 9–13 (apart from the very last words) paint as bleak a picture as any in the Bible of a darkness poured over his own people by God himself – and through Isaiah. Isaiah's own suggestion that this can only be for a limited period (v. 11a) is brushed aside and the threat intensified. Inevitable criticism of this improbable and distasteful mission is neutralized in advance by the report of Isaiah's presence in God's privy council and his commission there.

One last comparison between Micaiah in 1 Kings 22 and Isaiah 6 and our short argument is complete. The king of Israel was unwilling to summon Micaiah because he already knew him well as an established prophet whose prophecies he found disturbing. This story depicts Micaiah as a prophet among prophets. Clearly, Micaiah's vision of God was not his inaugural call, but was directed to a specific challenge within his career. Isaiah's vision can be similarly understood. Nothing in the book of Isaiah suggests otherwise, and the placing of the vision narrative in chapter 6, well into the record of Isaiah's words, simply underscores our conclusion.

Appeals to intimate knowledge of God were occasionally made in the books associated with the earlier biblical prophets, but normally only as a response to exceptional pressure. Isaiah 6 may be the beginning of a larger insert into an earlier draft of the book, and, if so, we may wonder whether the extraordinarily moving experience it relates was actually Isaiah's own. We have noted also that Amos 3.7 is perhaps a prose addition to the poem beginning in 3.3. However, there is an important issue of content as well. Amos proclaims what *anyone* who would can see. He is not, as it were, an official press secretary giving occasional briefings from the otherwise strictly confidential minutes of Yahweh's privy council. When the books of Jeremiah and Ezekiel present their heroes as prophets called to their role in a specific inaugural commission they provide us with two big exceptions, but not a rule.

The Future of the People of God

It is here that we finally broach the largest group of questions posed and answered in the prophetic books. Would Yahweh reward or punish his people? What would be the nature of the 'day of the Lord'? If, after the disaster, there should be a 'return' of a 'remnant', how should that be defined? Would an 'anointed' king (Messiah) play a role in such a restoration? In short, what was the future of the people of God? What were they to make of the successive disasters that threatened and then fell on them, destroying Israel in 722 and Judah in 587/6 BCE?

Just because these questions are so prominent in the Latter Prophets, we must be careful not to read all prophetic writings in the light of them. First, the nation's future is not the dominant topic in every book: Nahum thunders single-mindedly against Nineveh, capital city of the Assyrian Empire. Secondly, the concerns of the books do not always correspond to the interests of the original speakers. And, thirdly, there is a range of different emphases even when aspects of the topic are being treated – not least because these prophets span several centuries.

Looking at the shifts in the meaning of some key terms offers an opportunity to get matters in historical perspective. The remnant idea is a good example. Amos's irony is all too bitter when he describes salvaging a few bones and bits of skin as 'rescuing' a sheep (3.12). Such savage protest against any false optimism is in perfect keeping with the bleak culmination of his series of five visions (7.1–9; 8.1–3; 9.1–4), with the divine sword stalking even the uprooted exiles. Jeremiah's poetry too foreshadows a 'mopping up' (15.9) of Israel's 'remnant' quite as thorough as the gleaning-process in an orchard or harvest field (6.9).

These devastatingly clear warnings before and after Isaiah give us a context for considering what he may have meant by calling one of his sons 'Shearjashub' (7.3): *she'ar* means a remnant; and *yashub* means 'will (re-) turn'. To an English speaker these components seem to add up to a promise, but in Hebrew they are naturally read as a threat: 'Only a remnant will (re-) turn' – for Hebrew emphasizes the subject of a clause by putting it before its verb, instead of after. When we remember that little Shearjashub has his mute, walk-on part after Isaiah's terrifying vision with its climax in the root-ing-out and burning of the final remaining tenth (6.13), and before 7.18–25 with its sequence of grim pictures of the disaster to come, it be-comes clear that his presence at Isaiah's side can hardly be a sign of hope. All of these remarks set the context for us to understand the original meaning of the 'sign' offered King Ahaz by an exasperated Isaiah on behalf of an exasperated Yahweh: 'God is with us' (Immanuel) is a threat rather than a promise when God is angry (7.14).

Yet in time the word 'remnant' was revalued and became a term of hope and even of honour. Haggai links together governor, high priest, and all the remnant of the people (1.12, 14; 2.2) in a single breath. In Zechariah 8, the picture of the repopulation of Jerusalem is followed by this promise: 'But now I will not deal with the remnant of this people as in the former days, says the LORD of hosts. For there shall be a sowing of peace . . . ' (8.11–12a)

The second element in Shearjashub's name supplies our next yardstick: the idea of *return*. The verb in question (*shub*) is often used with reference to a turning or return to God, in acknowledgement of repentance:

> All the ends of the earth shall remember
> and turn to the LORD;
> and all the families of the nations
> shall worship before him.
> For dominion belongs to the LORD,
> and he rules over the nations. (Ps 22.27–8)

After his dread locust visions, Joel reports the divine offer,

> 'Yet even now', says the LORD,
> 'return to me with all your heart,
> with fasting, with weeping, and with mourning;
> and rend your hearts and not your garments. (2.12–13a)

More sadly, we read in Amos 4.6–11 the five fold refrain after repeated divine hammer-blows, 'Yet they did not return to me'.

'Turning' in this earlier biblical sense may in fact always have had a literal, physical component. We should not think in merely mental and spiritual terms of 'turning to Yahweh'. For the action of turning had involved going to the shrine and prostrating oneself before the central sanctuary, where Yahweh was believed to be invisibly present. After the exile '(re)turning to Zion' acquired a new sense: that of returning home from exile to resettle and rebuild the 'old country'.

We look finally at the passages that talk of the day of Yahweh: 'the day of the Lord' or simply 'that day'. It is often said that Amos and Isaiah protest against popular optimism amongst their hearers who are looking forward to Yahweh's 'day' when all will be put right. Amos is typically direct on this matter:

> Woe to you who desire the day of the LORD!
> Why would you have the day of the LORD?
> It is darkness, and not light;
>   as if a man fled from a lion,
>   and a bear met him;
> or went into the house and leaned with his hand against the wall,
>   and a serpent bit him.
> Is not the day of the LORD darkness, and not light,
>   and gloom with no brightness in it? (5.18–20)

Isaiah too talks of a 'day' in which the Lord will be 'against':

> For the LORD of hosts has a day
>   against all that is proud and lofty
>   against all that is lifted up and high . . .
>   and the LORD alone will be exalted in that day. (2.12–17)

It is clear from the whole context in Isaiah 2–3 that it is the entire establishment in Judah which Yahweh is 'against'.

The phrase 'day of the Lord' is never used in the Bible before the time of Amos and Isaiah in the eighth century; but the way it is used in Joel, referring this time to a plague of locusts (1.15; 2.1, 11), suggests that menace had always been properly associated with this language in the pre-exilic period:

> The earth quakes before them,
>   the heavens tremble.
> The sun and the moon are darkened,
>   and the stars withdraw their shining.

The LORD utters his voice
  before his army,
for his host is exceedingly great;
  he that executes his word is powerful.
For the day of the LORD is great and very terrible;
  who can endure it? (2.10–11)

Amos and Isaiah may have been bringing into the national political arena an idea originally linked with what we would now call natural disasters.

Much commoner is the phrase 'in that day'. Most often it seems to have been used as a linking-device by the editors of the prophetic books, when they add further perspectives to what has already been said about the Lord's 'day'. There are good examples within Isaiah 2–4 at 3.18 and 4.1. Yet not infrequently 'in that day' introduces a sudden change of fortune: a promise of rich hope – at least for some. This is what we find immediately following 3.18–4.1: 'In that day the branch of the LORD shall be beautiful and glorious, and the fruit of the land shall be the pride and glory of the survivors of Israel' (4.2). We switch suddenly from threat to promise.

Another classic example ends the book of Amos. After the prophet's macabre picture (3.12) of the shepherd 'rescuing' some bits of a sheep from a lion, and his very cautious statement (5.15) that divine grace for such a 'remnant' of Joseph was a mere 'possibility', it is perplexing to find at the end of the book and introduced by 'in that day', rich promises of restoration, fertility and rebuilding (9.11–15) – quite a different 'day' from the one Amos has been threatening throughout.

As a rule, many more positive notes are sounded by the later, post-exilic prophets. Malachi certainly expects the coming day to be difficult to endure – because it will involve a purging, refining process (3.2). Yet the end of his dream is happier: 'For behold, the day comes, burning like an oven, when all the arrogant and all evildoers will be stubble . . . But for you who fear my name the sun of righteousness shall rise . . . you shall go forth leaping like calves from the stall.'

Figures such as Micah, Amos, Isaiah and Jeremiah were honoured, and their words remembered, because they prophesied the devastation of their land and capital city – and it happened. They had been right, and more optimistic spirits had been wrong. However, some of their words and phrases and promises could be heard again in a new way on the far side of the catastrophe. Once it was clear that exile and uprooting were not the end for God's people, 'remnant', which had once meant simply 'broken remains' (as in Isaiah's picture of a piece of shattered pottery – 30.14) became interpreted as 'survivors'; the old command to 'turn' to Yahweh became a new 'Zionist' imperative to 'return' and rebuild; and that terrible final 'day of the Lord' became a refining-process from which a purified nation would emerge. The old words from before the overthrow were still used – but they were now heard in a new sense. This revaluation of the earlier pre-exilic voices was a response to an event, but an event which required and received its own novel interpretation. Spared when they expected to perish, the survivors of disaster came to believe that they had been given back their lives for a purpose.

The most sustained poetic rhetoric in all the prophetic books is from *Second Isaiah* or *Deutero-Isaiah* – Isaiah 40–55. Much of this poetry is laconic: hard to pin down with any precision, yet important elements of movement and structure can be detected. The opening summons with its voices (40.3, 5) reminds us of the divine court in Isaiah 6. The sixteen chapters, though they are almost completely lacking in much of the distinctive language of the prophetic books, are 'bracketed' by the only two mentions in this material of 'the word' of God (40.8; 55.11). The democratization of the old royal Davidic covenant, spelled out at the end (55.3–5), only makes explicit a series of surprising hints and anticipations throughout the text.

The message of 'comfort' is made plain at the start in a series of alternative images: pardon, full punishment already received, conscripted army service complete (40.1–2). The whole introduction (40.1–11) is undergirded by a lengthy argument designed to prove Yahweh's power to act as he pleases (40.12–31), repeated briefly each time a novel point is introduced – as in 44.24–8 and 45.9–13, before and after styling the Persian emperor Cyrus as God's 'shepherd' (44.28) and 'anointed' or 'Messiah' (45.1), terms normally applied to members of the Davidic royal house.

It should hardly surprise us, therefore, that 'new' (42.9; 43.19; 48.6) and 'create' are keywords. 'Create' (*bara'*) is a remarkably rare term in the Hebrew scriptures. Our poet uses it many times of the creation of the world at the beginning – following the usage of the opening chapters of Genesis; but he also uses it with reference to Yahweh's new creative act of releasing the exiles for the rebuilding of Jerusalem.

We have no evidence that all later prophecy knew these powerful chapters, or that they directly influenced the reworking of the earlier prophetic message. However, Isaiah 40–55 does represent a high-water mark in biblical literature as a whole. 'Second Isaiah' is our most articulate witness to the potential in the return from exile – a 'novel' event 'creatively' interpreted.

Such dreams of restoration and programmes for reconstruction are the most detailed and substantial literary compositions in the prophetic books. Within the book of Isaiah we have Second Isaiah and dependent daughter compositions in chapters 56–66 ('Third Isaiah') and 34–5. Similar hopes are to the fore in the final third of Ezekiel: most memorably in the vision of the valley of dry bones (Ezek 37), and most extensively in the restoration programme of chapters 40–8. Inevitably such themes are developed more briefly in the minor prophets. We find, for example, a fundamental shift within Joel at 2.18; Amos's message of doom is, as we have already seen, capped by a surprisingly positive conclusion (9.11–15); and there are rich images of restoration in Zephaniah from 3.9.

Admittedly, not all of Second Isaiah's dreams actually came to pass as he stated them, or as soon as he expected; and this was recognized as a problem then as now. We can see this as we read the final eleven chapters of Isaiah. Several of the issues addressed by those who wrestled with the legacy of Second Isaiah are provided by the gap between prediction and reality in the work of the master. His 'now' (40.1–2) becomes their 'soon' (56.1). They are at pains to assure their people that Yahweh is not unequal to the promised taks, but it is the people's continuing sinful deeds that are getting in the way (59.1–2). The richness of the promise coupled with short-term disappointment led several of the supplementers of the prophetic books to expect a delay in the realization of the divine promises. More than a dozen times, for example, in the prose traditions of Jeremiah we read expectations introduced by the vague phrase 'days are coming'. 'Days are coming' when Yahweh will be known as the god who brought exiles back from Babylon, rather than Israel out of Egypt (16.14); when a righteous branch will be raised up for David (23.5); when a new covenant will be made (31.31). These things will all happen in times that are coming!

Conclusion

This chapter has included a mention, however tantalizingly brief, of all the books of the Latter Prophets. Unfortunately it has been impossible here to discuss them all in detail; but enough has been said to demonstrate the lack of neat, consistent patterns in biblical prophecy.

The latest books and parts of books were interested in reforming the organized religion of their times. Some of them also show no reserve about calling the spokesmen for reform 'prophets'. Their predecessors, who would not have called themselves 'prophet' at all, had a broader, more radical, vision. Their impatience with the title, and with those in their time who were prophets, is just a symptom of their impatience with the wider religious structures. And so, when we now use the term 'prophetic' to describe the radicalism of a Micah (read 3.5–12) or a Jeremiah (read 23.9–32), we use with renewed respect a word they would have shied away from.

The trouble with the word 'prophet' is that it belongs in the sphere of religion, the numinous, divination and the official oracle – which many of the so-called 'prophets' did not. We can with better conscience make more use of the terms 'dream' and 'vision', which are also scattered through the books we have been reviewing, ambiguous though these words are. Our spokesmen were not 'dreamers', but they had a 'dream' – of the sort Martin Luther King had in that most famous of his speeches of the 1960s. Few of them appear to have received their inspiration by paranormal means – but they could all imagine and seek to make their world other than it was. They all had vision, though not all experienced visions. Yet even the visions of an Ezekiel or a Zechariah are less opaque than the revelatory visions attributed to Daniel – which themselves required expert interpretation!

FURTHER READING

Barton, J. 1986: *Oracles of God: Perceptions of Ancient Prophecy in Israel after the Exile.*

Blenkinsopp, J. 1984: *A History of Prophecy in Israel, from the Settlement in the Land to the Hellenistic Period.*

Coggins, R. J., Phillips, A. and Knibb, M. (eds.) 1982: *Israel's Prophetic Tradition: Essays in Honour of Peter Ackroyd.*

Koch, K. 1982–3: *The Prophets*, 2 vols.

Petersen, D. L. (ed.) 1987: *Prophecy in Israel.*

Sawyer, J. F. A. 1987: *Prophecy and the Prophets of the Old Testament.*

Very useful as guides to individual prophetic books are the Old Testament Guides:

Auld, A. G. 1986b: *Amos.*

Carroll, R. P. 1989: *Jeremiah.*

Coggins, R. J. 1987: *Haggai, Zechariah, Malachi.*

Whybray, R. N. 1983: *The Second Isaiah.*

Part IV

Kethubim: the Writings

11

After the Exile

Richard J. Coggins

Preliminary Reading   Ezra; Nehemiah.

Post-Exilic History

The information available when we attempt to reconstruct an historical outline for the monarchical period in the history of Israel and Judah is remarkably detailed; for the period from *c.* 925 to 587 BCE the main national events can be set out with a fair measure of confidence that dates are accurate to within a decade, and that it is very unlikely that any major national crises have passed unnoticed. Of course, there is room for disagreement as to the interpretation of particular episodes, and as to the evaluation of the work of particular individuals, but that is of the stuff of history of any period.

When we turn to the period from 587 to 170 BCE, however, the situation is very different. For long stretches we simply have no information at all; the material that is available is episodic – that is to say, it is impossible to agree on any precise relationship of one piece of evidence to another, and there is almost no relevant extra-biblical information to help our reconstruction. It is worth asking why there should be this dramatic change, and various causes can be noted. The following sections will explore some of these reasons.

Before we consider the difficulties, however, it may be helpful to set out briefly a broad outline that emerges from ancient sources, so as to provide a framework for our discussion.

(1)   *Cyrus.* In about 550 BCE Cyrus of Anshan, a remote area of Media, first appeared in a larger historical context. During the following decade he pursued a successful career of military conquest, which reached its climax with the capture of Babylon in 539. Under his reign and that of his successor Cambyses, the Persian Empire was established in control of the whole area known as Mesopotamia, the land of the Two Rivers, and gradually also of

Syria and Palestine. Jerusalem and the surrounding area thus came under Persian control, though the exact date and circumstances of this are not known.

(2) *The Temple Rebuilt.* The Jerusalem Temple had been destroyed in 587/6, and as far as is known had remained in ruins for the following half-century. Eventually, however, the decision to rebuild it was taken, and this work was completed around 516. It is not clear how far this was a matter of rebuilding a structure that had fallen into complete ruin, or rather a matter of extensive repair; certainly from that time on the Temple (the Second Temple as it is often called in Jewish writings) played an important part as the focus of the religious life of the community.

(3) *Persian Rule.* Judah remained under Persian rule for nearly 200 years, until the Persian Empire collapsed, but we know nothing of it from Persian sources, and the only Jewish material available is the books of Ezra and Nehemiah. Here some Jews are depicted in positions of influence under the Persian rulers, entrusted with important commissions by them. In Daniel 1–6 and Esther, the stories assume that Jews such as Daniel and his companions or Mordecai could have an important position in the royal court.

(4) *Alexander the Great.* His career has been very variously assessed, but in terms of military conquest it is one of the most remarkable in the history of the world. During his reign (336–323 BCE) he led his conquering army to the borders of modern India, and overthrew the Persian Empire, till then the most powerful and extensive which the ancient world had known. During this triumphant progress he passed through Palestine. Yet of this the Hebrew Bible says nothing. Attempts have been made to find allusions to Alexander in various Old Testament books, but all of them are dubious and certainly none comes into the category of facts beyond serious dispute which we are currently seeking out. All we can say, then, is that Palestine, including the Jerusalem community, passed under Greek rule from the time of Alexander.

(5) *The Ptolemies.* Alexander's successors, the Diadochi, engaged in bitter disputes after his death, and the area of his conquests was eventually apportioned out between them. Through the third century Palestine was under the control of the Ptolemies, based at Alexandria in Egypt. So much we know, but additional detail is still very hard to come by. Daniel 11 is widely thought to refer to this period, but it is in a cryptic form, presented as the visions of a seer from an earlier time, and can be used as a primary source only with great caution. 1 Maccabees becomes an important historical source for the period from 175 onwards, but the earlier period is dismissed in one verse (1.9) as a time of great evils, with no further elaboration. The Jewish historian Josephus elaborates (*Antiquities*, XXI, 1–3) but gives few details.

In short, the third century is a very obscure period in the life of Palestinian community.

(6) *The Seleucids.* The Jews of Jerusalem came under Seleucid domination following their victory over the Ptolemies at Paneas *c.* 200 BCE. At first this change of master seems to have been widely welcomed, but tensions soon arose, and reached a climax during the reign of Antiochus IV (175–163). His attempt to strengthen his empire by promoting religious unity produced sharply differing reactions among the Jews, and the later chapters of Daniel and the two books of Maccabees all reflect these reactions. (1 and 2 Maccabees are two independent accounts, not one continuous history divided into two books.) Our knowledge of this period is much greater and fuller than for the third century.

'Post-Exilic'?

It may be helpful to consider why the above outline has to be so sketchy and full of uncertainties. Even the term 'post-exilic', conventionally used to describe the period here outlined, can be misleading and can certainly give a false impression. We are liable to envisage 'the exile' as a clearly definable period affecting a specific group of people, who were transported away from their own land at the beginning of that time and returned there at the end. As to the beginning of the exile, that is in broad terms true enough, though we should note that the statements in the biblical text of the numbers involved vary greatly; from 4600 (Jer 52.30) to total depopulation (2 Chron 36.20f). But it is much less clearly appropriate to speak of an end of exile in the same way. It is worth considering the available evidence; we have already noted that it is of very modest dimensions.

Haggai and Zechariah   From the period of the beginning of the exile we know of two named prophets: Jeremiah and Ezekiel. According to the tradition Ezekiel was active among the exiles in Babylon at least as late as 571 BCE (Ezek 29.17). For the next half-century no prophets are mentioned in any of our traditions. It is difficult to know how far this was sheer coincidence, or whether we should legitimately deduce from this silence something about the prophetic role: that, for example, it was bound up with kingship and an ordered court and cult. It is certainly striking that the material in the book of Isaiah with a background suggesting the 540s (Isa 40–55, and possibly Isa 40–66) is anonymous. By 520, however, when the Jerusalem Temple was being rebuilt, we once again hear of prophetic activity. Haggai and Zechariah were, according to the superscriptions to their work (Hag 1.1; Zech 1.1), contemporaries. Both were concerned with strengthening the Jerusalem community; both had words of praise and admonition for the leaders Zerubbabel and Joshua – the former a member of the Davidic royal family, the latter the leading priest. In neither case, however, is there any obvious suggestion that they were addressing a community all, or a substantial part, of which had recently returned from exile in Babylon. This impression would only be gained if we read Haggai and Zechariah in the light of Ezra 1–6 – an unwise procedure, since we should be reading the earlier evidence in the light of the later. Haggai in particular seems to know nothing of exile. The community he is addressing has the opportunity to restore its temple, which was not only a place of worship but also the very focus of the people's corporate existence – and they were very reluctant to commit themselves to what should have been a great opportunity. Haggai therefore sees his mission as essentially a matter of exhorting the people to prepare themselves for God's intervention by restoring his temple, and holding out great hopes for Zerubbabel when the time of restoration finally came.

Zechariah (only chapters 1–8 have their origin in this period) betrays more Babylonian links and does in fact refer to returning exiles (6.10–14), but the main thrust of his message is again addressed to the Jerusalem community, with only a few former exiled Jews mentioned. In short, the evidence of these two books suggests that there was a greater amount of movement between Babylon and Palestine than had once been possible, but nothing in terms of a mass return is hinted at.

Isaiah 56–66   The last chapters of the book of Isaiah are often dated in this period, but with very little specific evidence. It would certainly be possible to suppose that chapters 40–55 were composed in Babylon and chapters 56–66 in Palestine at a slightly later date, when the vivid expectations of the earlier chapters had been replaced by the prosaic reality of the life of a struggling Palestine community. The evidence is, however, at best circumstantial, and neither a mass return nor any suggestion of the precise location of these chapters can be established without ambiguity.

Ezra 1–6   The picture of an 'end of exile' is overwhelmingly a picture based on the early chapters of Ezra. Whatever the relations between the books of Chronicles and Ezra, the book of Ezra appears to be a sequel to the last chapters of 2 Chronicles. In 2 Chronicles 36 the exile is pictured as a total devastation of the land; all the inhabitants are taken into exile and the land is left 'fallow' for seventy years to keep Sabbath (2 Chron 36:20f). A picture of this kind owes more to theology than to history; the picture that the Chronicler wishes to portray is of a period of punishment and purgation to be undergone by people and holy land alike. When that punishment has been completed, then both people and land might be restored.

The early chapters of Ezra describe that restoration. In chapter 1 the decree of the Persian ruler is presented in a form which emphasizes (vv. 2–4) both that the sanctuary should be rebuilt and that the exiled people should return. Chapter 2 describes the return, at the earliest possible opportunity, of more than 42,000 exiles; chapters 3–6 picture the rebuilding of the holy place. The details cannot be easily accepted at face value. Many argue that chapter 2 incorporates a census account from some later period and that chapters 3–6 embody traditions relating to Haggai and Zechariah, and explain the delay in completing the Temple by picturing the problems that the community faced at the hands of its opponents (Ezra 4). In short, almost all the material in this section poses acute problems for any historical reconstruction; as with the end of 2 Chronicles, it looks as if a particular theological purpose was being pursued. There seems to be no clear evidence of 'the exile' as an historical phenomenon with an identifiable end.

A Dispersed Community

A more satisfactory way of picturing the Jewish community in our period would be to recognize from the outset that it was now dispersed very widely. No doubt during the Persian period movement between different communities was possible (the stories of Ezra and Nehemiah illustrate this), but there is no certain evidence of mass return to Palestine. From that period until our own century the idea of the Jews as a dispersed community has been an important aspect of their identity.

The Beginnings of Judaism

There is a further reason why it is difficult to construct a continuous history of Israel during the Second Temple period. Before the Assyrian and Babylonian conquest Israel and Judah had been states among other states, engaged in trade, diplomacy, warfare and the like. As such we naturally expect to find intermittent references to these states in the surviving records of their neighbours. From the sixth century on, a subtle change came over the community, a shift from a national identity to that of a religious community. Phrases such as 'Israel went into exile a nation and came back a church' are scarcely appropriate, not least because, as we have seen, it is difficult to speak of an 'end' of exile; but change there undoubtedly was. Indeed the very name Israel itself, formerly a description of a political identity, came increasingly to be used to designate the religious community. This change has reached its logical conclusion by the time of the New Testament, when Paul claims for the Galatians the status of 'the Israel of God' (6.16), but it can be seen already in the Hebrew Bible.

Much of the latest material in the Pentateuch, especially in Leviticus and Numbers, describes the community, presented as still in the wilderness, in terms of a religious gathering. It is not difficult to see in this the writer's hopes for the widely dispersed community of the Second Temple period – that when they were loyal to the commands given by Moses, they would be able to return to the Promised Land as the faithful people of God. The history of a religious community will be perceived differently from that of a nation-state, both by its own adherents and by those outside. The change did not come about suddenly, or without hopes for a restoration of former national glories. Messianic hopes are often linked with these aspirations; and it is at least arguable that one of the purposes of the Chronicler, in setting out the story of David and his successors in great detail, was to voice the hope that such glories might one day be restored.

The Chronicler

Although Jewish groups were to be found in widely scattered parts of the Levantine world in the Persian period, the Hebrew Bible is very much a Jerusalem collection, and so it is of the Jerusalem community that we know most. In particular this period is illuminated for us by the work of the Chronicler.

The books 1 and 2 Chronicles, Ezra and Nehemiah are found next to one another in all versions of the Bible. In modern translations Ezra and Nehemiah follow Chronicles, but in the Hebrew Bible they precede Chronicles, which is the last book in the Hebrew Bible. It has been a widely held view that Chronicles–Ezra–Nehemiah should be regarded as one continuous presentation of the people's experience, and this continuity appears to be strengthened by the way in which the end of 2 Chronicles is repeated at the beginning of Ezra. There have, however, been scholars in recent years who have challenged this view and have maintained that Chronicles stands apart from Ezra and Nehemiah. In part this differentiation is based on detailed linguistic study, in part on theological considerations. The attitude to those outside the community is more welcoming in Chronicles than in Ezra and Nehemiah, each of which regards mixed marriages as an unmitigated disaster for the community's standing before God. The attitude towards the continuing inhabitants of the northern kingdom is much more open in Chronicles (e.g. 2 Chron 30) than in Ezra 3–4. In Chronicles they still bear the name 'Israel'; in Ezra they are the 'adversaries of Judah and Benjamin'.

Over against this, there are undeniable similarities of viewpoint between Chronicles and Ezra–Nehemiah, in that all of them represent the Jerusalem community, probably of the fifth–fourth century, proclaiming that there alone the true people of God was to be found. We may perhaps speak of a 'Chronistic milieu' from which all of these works emerged (together, possibly, with the final form of Haggai and Zechariah 1–8); we may leave open the question of the exact relation between the different books.

1 and 2 Chronicles

These books have often been neglected, even among keen students of the Bible, and two immediate reasons suggest themselves; the daunting beginning (the first nine chapters consist almost exclusively of lists of names); and the fact that the greater part of Chronicles is a variant on themes already treated in Samuel and Kings. Nevertheless this unpromising basis affords important insight into the purpose and method of the Chronicler.

The genealogies play an important part in the Chronicler's work, emphasizing the identity of the community. In 1 Chronicles 1–9 by far the greatest amount of attention is paid to Judah (2.3–4.23) and to Levi (ch. 6). The national and religious aspects of the community were thereby given their identity at a time when that question – what constituted the true people of God? – was a pressing one. In the Judahite genealogies the family of David was prominent; and David was the true founder of the community, with a much more prominent role than that of Moses. The Levite genealogies were important as bringing out the unique role not only of the priesthood in general but also of the Levites in particular. Whereas earlier the Levites had claimed full priestly status (e.g. in the traditions represented by Deuteronomy) in the time of the Chronicler they had a subsidiary, though still important, role in the cultic hierarchy; and the Chronicler loses no opportunity to emphasize the faithfulness of the Levites in carrying out their duties (e.g. 2 Chron 29.34). In the last centuries BCE there were bitter disputes within the community as to who might legitimately exercise priestly functions; both the Dead Sea Scrolls and the Samaritan traditions illustrate this, and it may well be that such tensions were already beginning to emerge in the writings of the Chronicler.

The earlier books of Samuel and Kings consistently present a more accurate picture of the events described: not surprisingly, therefore, Chronicles has been neglected. There is, however, another important aspect of this. In many cases it appears as if the Chronicler deliberately interprets the earlier traditions, which were coming to be regarded as sacred texts, to make them applicable to the life of the contemporary community. Sometimes this was a matter of explaining apparent discrepancies in the earlier texts. In Samuel the death of the Philistine giant Goliath was credited both to David in the famous story in 1 Samuel 17, and to Elhanan in 2 Samuel 21.19; the Chronicler resolves this by having Elhanan kill Goliath's brother (1 Chron 20.5). Or there might be theological difficulties which needed to be resolved. In 2 Samuel 24 it is stated that Yahweh incited David to take a census, and was then angry that he did so. The Chronicler would not have wished to raise any doubts concerning Yahweh's ultimate control of events, but by this time the idea of subsidiary agents, some of whom might attempt to challenge the divine will, had become common. Among these was 'the Satan', who is pictured in Job 1 and Zechariah 3 as questioning God's description of the disposition of earthly affairs. So the Chronicler regards Satan's intervention as leading to the divine displeasure, and begins his version of the story. 'Satan stood up against Israel, and incited David . . . ' (1 Chron 21.1).

Exegesis can be as revealing in what it omits as in what it includes. Kings spends much time chronicling the wickedness of the northern kingdom, Israel. A major purpose of this is to warn Judah of the consequences of turning from true worship, and so save it from a fate like that of Israel (if a first edition of Kings was written before the exile), or simply to explain why a disaster had befallen Judah (if Kings is itself an exilic composition). That purpose was no longer relevant to the Chronicler, for whom the true community was the Jerusalem community. It was their story which he wished to set out, and references to the north could be omitted, save where they formed a necessary background to the story of Jerusalem.

Finally in this consideration of the use of earlier material, the Chronicler's explanation of the last years of the southern kingdom and of the exile is particularly revealing. For the Chronicler the ideal king was Hezekiah, and so we find a greatly expanded account of his reign as compared with 2 Kings. He, like David, had been the only true ruler of his day, for the apostate northern kingdom had been overthrown, and he gave opportunity for its former subjects to rejoin the faithful Jerusalem community. In the Chronicler we see the beginnings of the idealization of Hezekiah which led some groups in later Judaism to regard him as the prototype of the Messiah. His son Manasseh had the longest reign of any king of Judah; for 2 Kings 21 his reign was a time of unmitigated evil, but the Chronicler depicts him as repentant, acknowledging his former sins. (The length of his reign as a sign of God's favour may have been a contributory cause in this reversal of earlier judgements.) By contrast, Josiah, the ideal ruler of 2 Kings, who was killed prematurely in battle, is seen as failing to acknowledge God's word – coming through the unexpected medium of Pharaoh Neco (2 Chron 35.22).

The Exile

In his account of the events which led up to the exile, the Chronicler is still using earlier sources, but he is able to look back on the sending of some of the community into exile as an event in the past in a way which was impossible for the author of Kings, who was almost certainly writing during the exile itself. Although misleading historically, the idea of a national exile is an important part of the Chronicler's presentation and must be recognized as such. For him it was a time when the land lay fallow: 'it kept Sabbath to fulfil seventy years' (2 Chron 36.21). This exile was a disaster, as for Kings, but it was also a period of testing; only those who had gone through the exile had the right to regard themselves as part of the true community in the Chronicler's own day. So for the Chronicler *all* the true community were taken into exile, and *all* were eager to return at the first opportunity.

Ezra and Nehemiah

These two books are regularly considered together and this is not simply a matter of helpful convention. For a long time they were regarded as *one* book, so that, for example, in the Hebrew Bible the concluding editorial notes supplied for each book by the Masoretes (who preserved the text) are provided only at the end of Nehemiah. This may help to lessen the strangeness of the way in which Ezra's own ministry is described partly in Ezra (chs. 7–10) and partly in Nehemiah (ch. 8).

Ezra 1–6

Before Ezra himself is introduced, the first six chapters of the book present a picture of the restoration of the community. Chapter 1 pictures the return from Babylon as a movement of the whole exiled community undertaken with willing obedience and understood as the fulfilment of a prophetic word of Jeremiah. Cyrus himself is presented as permitting not only the rebuilding of the Jerusalem Temple but also the return of the exiles. The list of returning exiles in chapter 2 is found also in Nehemiah 7, and probably comes from a later list, possibly a census. The faithful group begin rebuilding in chapter 3, but face opposition in chapter 4, in a section which departs from chronological order and draws together sources from a variety of different periods, down to the reign of Xerxes (Ahasuerus) and Artaxerxes in the fifth century, returning to the sixth century only at v. 24. From v. 8 the text is in Aramaic, the language of the Persian Empire. This may indicate that genuine official sources have been included, but it is noteworthy that the story continues in Aramaic even when sources are no longer quoted. In chapters 5–6 the Temple is rebuilt, thanks also to the benevolent approval of the Persian emperor.

Ezra 7–10

These chapters describe events from a different period (*which* period is keenly debated). The story is presented as a unity with Ezra introduced by a simple 'after this' (7.1). The prior reference to Artaxerxes (in chapter 4) will have helped to strengthen this sense of unity. (It is difficult to know whether the author of Ezra knew that these events took place much later but did not think the time-lag important, or whether he was ignorant of Persian chronology.)

Ezra is presented as a learned priest and scribe (7.6, 12 – the latter verse being the beginning of another short Aramaic section, vv. 12–26), but it is not clear whether this is a *Jewish* viewpoint, emphasizing the leader's piety (and this was certainly the understanding of later tradition) or whether it is an allusion to Ezra's position in the Persian court, as a kind of secretary of state for Jewish affairs. This ambiguity is important, for it is possible to understand Ezra's mission in mainly religious terms, a revival of strict traditions in a community which had fallen into lax customs; or to understand his work as political, a task carried out on behalf of the Persian ruler in an area of his empire where peace and security were of particular importance. In these chapters, the former view is to the fore, since the main point of Ezra's mission is to impose stricter rules upon the community with regard to marriage. As a religious community they should be limited to endogamy, (marriage within the community of believers). From chapter 8 Ezra's mission is described in the first person – probably a stylistic technique to suggest dramatic immediacy rather than a sign that this section derives from Ezra himself.

Nehemiah 1–6

The book of Ezra ends in an unexpectedly abrupt way, but it is clear that Nehemiah 1 represents a new beginning. Nehemiah's circumstances in the Persian court under Artaxerxes 1 in 445 BCE are described. He is commissioned to go to Jerusalem to oversee the rebuilding of the ruined city. The destruction referred to in Nehemiah 1.3 might be the result of some otherwise unknown conflict in Nehemiah's own time; more probably, it is parallel to the account of the restoration of Jerusalem already given in Ezra, but with the chief credit given to Nehemiah. Chapters 1–2, 4–6 contain extensive sections in the first person singular, and so are sometimes referred to as the 'Nehemiah memoir'. This gives a misleading impression, for there is no ground for supposing that this was some kind of personal diary. Much more likely it was a story written in his honour, by a group which regarded him as the true restorer of Jerusalem. (A similar story connecting Nehemiah with the Second Temple is found in 2 Maccabees 1.18–22, written in the first century BCE.)

Nehemiah 7–13

7.1–5 completes the first section of first-person material and leads into a list almost identical with that already found in Ezra 2. Quite unexpectedly, the story of Nehemiah is set aside and in 8.1 Ezra reappears. Nehemiah is mentioned in v. 9 (perhaps a later gloss to link the two men together) but he plays no significant part in the story. Nehemiah 8 is not a direct continuation of Ezra 10, though it is so placed in the Apocryphal book 1

Esdras. It describes the climax of Ezra's work: the proclamation of the law of God to the faithful assembly, who understand what is read to them and keep a solemn festival as the law prescribed.

The prayers and ceremonies in Nehemiah 9–10 seem to have little connection with either Ezra or Nehemiah, though the former's name appears in the Greek translation at 9.1 (and in some English translations), and the latter's name in the Hebrew at 10.1. Both references appear to be later additions to give a context to anonymous material of a devotional kind.

The final chapters (11–13) consist of very varied material: lists of officials, genealogies, an account of the dedication of the wall of Jerusalem, and various reforms carried out by Nehemiah, with special emphasis on his concern for the right keeping of the Sabbath. This last section gives the impression that the final compilers were anxious to include all relevant material, rather than that a particular lesson is intended.

The Problem of Dating

This must be mentioned, since it has been so much discussed, but it would be wrong to give the impression (as has sometimes been done) that this is the main issue with regard to the ministry of Ezra and Nehemiah.

The Traditional Order   Since Ezra's work is said to have begun in the seventh year of Artaxerxes (Ezra 7.7) and Nehemiah's in the twentieth (Neh 1.1; 2.1) it might seem as if the only problem would be to identify which of the three kings named Artaxerxes is here intended. The emphasis on the continuity of the restoration process would support an earlier rather than a later date, so it has usually been assumed that Artaxerxes 1 is the king in question. He ruled 465–424 BCE, which would imply a date of 458 for Ezra and 445 for Nehemiah. (There is a slight complication in the case of Nehemiah, since the month mentioned in 1.1 is later than that mentioned in 2.1; but, since there were different calendars which began the year at different times, probably not too much should be made of this.) These traditional dates raise problems: the lack of cross-reference between the two men; the similarity of their role (or at least of the way in which it is presented); and the curious delay of Ezra, who did not carry out his main task, the proclamation of the law, for thirteen years. There are also detailed references which, in the view of some, are scarcely compatible with this traditional understanding, but these points are bound to be subsidiary. With regard to the three main points we may note that the Hebrew Bible provides frequent examples of independent traditions, with no cross-reference between important contemporaries (e.g. Jeremiah and Ezekiel), and that it is not at all clear whether Ezra and Nehemiah did indeed play a similar role, or whether we should look on Nehemiah as a political and Ezra as a religious figure.

The last difficulty remains; but it may be artificial in the sense that it is a deliberate part of the editorial process to link the two men together, and therefore to have Ezra's work reach its climax when Nehemiah was also present.

Ezra in 428 BC?   Some scholars have supposed that the difficulties would be eased by supposing that both men served the same Persian ruler, but that Nehemiah came first. To arrive at this result they have to suppose that a number has been omitted in Ezra 7; most commonly it is supposed that his commission took place in the thirty-seventh year of Artaxerxes, i.e. 428. This view, once popular, is now widely questioned: it rests upon a gratuitous emendation of the text which is quite unsupported by manuscript evidence; though it allows the retention of the texts which refer to Ezra and Nehemiah together (Neh 8.9; 12.36), it does nothing to solve the more basic matter of the lack of cross-reference from one to the other.

Ezra in 398 BC?   The most widely canvassed way of resolving the problem apparently caused by the traditional view is to suppose that Ezra's mission occurred during the reign of Artaxerxes II (404–358). This would obviate any emendation of the text, and would account for the lack of cross-reference; the verses which refer to the two men together would then be glosses added by later editors who failed to realize that they had worked in the time of two different Persian kings and who could not understand why each had seemed to ignore the other.

There are certain details of the text which have been widely held to give additional support to this solution. The late H. H. Rowley listed eleven such details, but many are of little importance. The point that has most commonly been used to support the argument relates to the presumed succession of high priests. Nehemiah's contemporary was Eliashib (Neh 3.1, etc.); in Ezra's time there was a Johanan, the son or grandson of Eliashib (Ezra 10.6), the relationship being established by a cross-reference to Nehemiah 12.11. In fact this identification is far from secure; both were common names; Johanan is never referred to as 'high-priest' in the Hebrew Bible, but only in a papyrus from Elephantine (Egypt). Other arguments are mainly of a 'psychological' kind: would Nehemiah have pursued a less stringent policy against mixed marriages after Ezra's more rigid requirements of their instant dissolution? Would Nehemiah have needed to repopulate Jerusalem if a few years earlier there had been a 'very great assembly' there (Ezra 10.1)? Arguments of this type are very subjective, and should not be allowed to carry much weight.

Increased Uncertainty   Dispute concerning the order of Ezra and Nehemiah provides a particularly revealing illustration of our lack of precise knowledge of the history of the Second Temple period. There is now a willingness to admit to gaps in our knowledge which will not be resolved without additional information from extra-biblical sources and a recognition that precise historical reconstruction is not all-important. There may be value in seeing the way in which the two leaders are presented as doing closely comparable jobs, apparently quite independently of each other; in noting the way in which later redactors have felt it necessary to link their work; more generally, in recognizing the way in which our interests in a text are not always the same as those of its first authors.

This uncertainty should certainly be admitted in any attempt to answer the question of who came first. Of the three proposals widely put forward, the emendation of the text to provide a date of 428 for Ezra seems the least likely. Of the others, the traditional dating, with Ezra earlier, is perhaps to be preferred in the present state of our knowledge; evidence that Nehemiah was earlier is are not strong enough to justify a historical reconstruction. This question should not blind us to the other important issues raised by the stories of Ezra and Nehemiah. The first of these is the nature of their mission.

Ezra as Religious and Nehemiah as Lay?

One common way of differentiating the two is to emphasize the role of Ezra as the priest, and Nehemiah as layman. Ezra's status is certainly emphasized in his genealogy (Ezra 7.1–5) and in the way in which he is subsequently referred to as 'Ezra the priest' (7.11, 12; etc.). By contrast, our picture of Nehemiah is very much that of a high officer at the royal court.

When we read the stories of the two men, however, a somewhat different picture emerges. What is remarkable is how similar their stories are. Each is the emissary of the Persian king Artaxerxes; each is a faithful servant of God and of the Persian ruler (for the editors of these books this was not an incompatible demand); each has as a main task the building-up of the Jerusalem community as *the* true community over against rival claims; each is faced with opposition from among the religious establishment – prophets and the priest Eliashib in the case of Nehemiah (Neh 6.13), Levites in the case of Ezra (Ezra 10.15); each opposes mixed marriages, which are regarded as debasing the purity of the community; in each case prayers of repentance play a prominent part, both acknowledging the guilt of the community and providing a measure of self-justification. Any one of these points might be explained by supposing that each was faced with similar historical circumstances and problems; such an extensive list of similarities suggests a greater measure of stylization, a setting-out of the role which an ideal hero of the community must have played.

Relevant also to this detail of presentation is the fact that the two are presented in almost total independence of each other. This is evident too in later works. Ezra plays an important part in the (later) Apocryphal book 1 Esdras, which is clearly dependent on some form of our books Ezra – Nehemiah, yet breaks off just at the point where Nehemiah would be introduced. The way in which this is presented in some modern translations, such as the NEB, makes it looks as if this break is accidental and some part of the original text has been lost; but, if this is so, it is a striking coincidence that the break should have occurred just at the point where we expect a reference to Nehemiah. By contrast to this, the list of famous men in Ecclesiasticus 44–9 refers to Nehemiah (49.13) but makes no mention of Ezra; and the same is true of another book from the Apocrypha, 2 Maccabees, where Nehemiah's role is presented in greatly exaggerated terms (1.18–36), but no mention is made of Ezra. Our knowledge of Second Temple Judaism is too incomplete for confident conclusions to be drawn about this curious disparity. Nevertheless, it does seem as if different groups each held one of these leaders in high esteem, as the *true* restorer of the community. The presentation of Nehemiah in 2 Maccabees as the one 'who built the temple and the altar' and 'offered sacrifices' is especially revealing. If an argument along these lines is correct, then it would be proper to see the present form of the books of Ezra and Nehemiah as the result of a deliberate drawing-together of previously separate, and possible rival, traditions.

Divisions within the Community?

The above survey will have demonstrated how partial our knowledge of this period must be. A question that has been frequently raised in recent discussions is: are there other sources of knowledge which would enable us to reconstruct the history in a fuller way, even if precise knowledge is not available? In particular, the suggestion has often been put forward that some of the biblical material, though not directly 'historical' in character, may still yield historical knowledge by virtue of its underlying assumptions and implications. More specifically, we may see from the divisions within the community which are implicit in many writings from this period something of the structure which underlay it. We shall look briefly at three proposed reconstructions along these lines.

Attitudes to Prophets

With the exception of Haggai and Zechariah, all those prophets whom we can date with any confidence were active in the pre-exilic period. Yet in no case is it likely that the books named after them were completed at that date. Prophets were essentially *speakers* rather than writers, and, whilst some may have committed teaching to writing (Isa 8.16; Jer 36) there is no clear evidence that they were themselves responsible for arranging their words into their final written form. Instead it seems that one way in which reverence for a prophet could be expressed was by adding fresh words to the collection handed down.

It seems likely, then, that among the religious community of our period were those who revered the memory of the prophets and treasured their words. This is best illustrated by the very fact that the great prophetic collections – Isaiah, Jeremiah, Ezekiel, the Twelve – have come down to us, but is also specifically illustrated by the reference to the 'former prophets' in Zechariah 1.4–6. For some the absence of prophets was a sign of God's displeasure with his people (Ps 74.9); but this was not the only attitude to be found. Zechariah's view is curious. It is almost universally agreed on internal evidence that Zechariah 9–14 comes from a milieu different from that of chapters 1–8, though there is no agreement at all about the nature of this milieu, the date of the material, or whether chapters 9—14 are themselves a unity. However that may be, we find in 13.2–6 a fierce attack on prophets and prophetism; 'prophets' and 'unclean spirits' are identified; to wear the special prophetic clothing is itself an indication of an intent to deceive; and anyone who prophesies can legitimately be disowned by his own family.

There were clearly bitter disputes between different groups within the community, each claiming true inspiration from God. There are striking similarities with the equally harsh condemnation of prophets to be found in Jeremiah 23.9–40. Some parts of that material may go back to the time of Jeremiah himself and reflect disputes between him and his adversaries in the Jerusalem community in the last days of the monarchy, but most commentators are agreed that the conflicts mirror the situation in the time of the editors of the book of Jeremiah, who read their own concerns into the material and expanded Jeremiah's words. This reveals disputes between those who claimed to be maintainers of the prophetic tradition, offering God's word to the community, and those who rejected such claims, or at least that particular manifestation of it. It is possible that Nehemiah's appeal to God against 'the prophetess Noadiah and the rest of the prophets' (Neh 6.14) is another illustration of this division. Despite these clear indications of a division within the community, it is unfortunately not possible to go further and make any confident suggestions as to the locale in which these groups were active.

'Theocracy and Eschatology'

This phrase is the title of a book published in 1959 by O. Ploger. Theocracy is rule by God; eschatology is concerned with the 'last things', the end of the age. Here too the decline of prophecy played an important part in leading to the discussion, but the main thrust lay with the different party groupings which could be discerned at a somewhat later period. There were some for whom God's overall rule was the essential fact to be retained; external political circumstances were of less importance, provided that it remained possible for the community to maintain the observances handed down in the Torah as binding upon God's people; the proper worship of the Jerusalem Temple was the touchstone of the well-being of the community, secure under a theocratic form of government.

Other groups within the community, however, felt that this was not the whole story. The great promises enshrined in the tradition handed down from their forefathers must, it was felt, lead to some more dramatic *dénouement* than the rather limited degree of freedom experienced first under Persian and then under Hellenistic rule. For such groups eschatological forms of expectation emerged, sometimes looking forward to dramatic changes in the life of the community in this world, sometimes expressing themselves in terms, strange to Judaism for most of its earlier history, of belief in a blessed future life in which the miseries and injustices of this present existence would be remedied. Such texts as Isaiah 26.19 from the so-called 'Isaiah Apocalypse' (Isa 24–7: apocalypse means 'unveiling' or 'revelation'), generally seen as a late addition to the book of Isaiah, and Daniel 12.2 (seen as a second-century-BCE text) embodied such a belief. It is also possible that beliefs in a coming 'anointed one', a Messiah, who would act as God's instrument in bringing about a more glorious future for the people, took root in such circles.

Such an approach has certainly focused attention upon some of the rich variety to be found within the Judaism of this period, but it still has obvious limitations. It is inevitably confined to the books which express particular views, and is not able to make any significant progress towards isolating the groups from whom these different views arose. It is not even entirely satisfactory to speak of one biblical book as embodying one point of view and another a different one. The books of Chronicles, for example, have often been taken as *the* characteristic expressions of the theocratic viewpoint, but it has also been widely held that the concern for kingship in general and that of David in particular found in Chronicles is best understood as an expression of a Messianic hope.

The Background of the Apocalypses

The last two sections should have made it clear that we cannot classify the divisions within the Jewish community simply by setting one book over against another; yet these books are all that we have by way of evidence. It might seem that an impasse has been reached. To break out of such an impasse, an attempt has been made to consider the books commonly held to date from this period not merely as literature, or even as sacred literature, but in terms of the social groupings which they betray.

On such an approach it has seemed possible to some scholars to distinguish between the *priestly 'establishment'*, who controlled the Jerusalem Temple, who were in favour with the ruling imperial power, and who were thus able to interpret the traditions of the people in terms that pointed to the dominance of the priestly class as the fulfilment of God's promises; and the *outsiders*, visionaries who were excluded from the positions of power, but looked for a better future, in which God would break into the established world order and fulfil his ancient promises.

Already in the period of the exile, it could be maintained, the difference between the detailed Temple blueprint of Ezekiel 40–8 and the visionary hopes of Isaiah 40–55 could be explained in this way. When the Temple was rebuilt, a similar contrast could be discerned between Haggai and Zechariah, who enjoyed official status and were able to control the Jerusalem Temple with its considerable political and financial resources, and the author of Isaiah 56–66, who expressed the bitterness of the excluded. These chapters contain some of the harshest religious polemic in the whole of the Hebrew Bible (e.g. chapter 58, condemning the fasts of the official cultus, and 66.1–4, where the very existence of the Temple and all its practices are regarded as hateful to God), and it is easy to envisage that this might have arisen from disputes over rights in the religious practice of the community. One view of the emergence of the apocalypses in the later period regards them as a product of this fact of exclusion: those with no immediate hope in the present order of affairs pinned their hope to a vision of God in which that order would be overthrown and their deepest hopes fulfilled. On such an understanding chapters 9–14 of Zechariah should be sharply differentiated from chapters 1–8: whereas the earlier chapters represented the voice of the establishment, 9–14 represent one stage in the development of an apocalyptic eschatology which looked forward to the overthrow of all such established ways.

It will be seen that a reconstruction of this kind has the advantage that it tries to take seriously the fact that books do not simply emerge from nowhere; they have a cultural and social background which has shaped them. There are, nevertheless, considerable problems about such reconstructions. While it is indeed true that Zechariah 9–14 does not appear to come from the same setting as chapters 1–8, that is a very different thing from claiming that they are so different as to represent completely opposed viewpoints. The hopes for Jerusalem as a universal centre of worship are found in both parts of the book (8.20–3; 14.16–19), and each part has also been claimed to furnish vital clues as to the development from prophecy to the apocalypses. Indeed, the very fact that the two sections are now bound together as one book suggests very strongly that in some quarters at least they were not perceived as being in opposition to each other.

There is, however, a more fundamental difficulty about reconstructions of this kind. They attempt a sociological analysis of the community and its constituent elements on dangerously inadequate data. Assessments of the political or economic or religious views of different groups in modern societies can often be extremely revealing, but they are based on plentiful evidence. In ancient Israel in general, and in this poorly documented period in particular, there is no such evidence available. We are thus reduced to arguing in a circle, assuming the conclusion felt to be inherently most likely, and then arranging the evidence so as to support that conclusion. Put thus, the procedure might seem almost fraudulent; it is not so, but simply an attempt to set out hypothetical reconstructions, which should never be regarded as anything more than that.

The Diaspora or Dispersion

The Hebrew Bible as we have it is essentially the product of the Jerusalem community. Some traditions (e.g. the words of Hosea) almost certainly originated elsewhere, but in the form in which they have come down to us they have passed through a Jerusalem edition. In so far, therefore, as our concern is simply with the Hebrew Bible, it might be legitimate to confine our attention to the Jerusalem community. But increasingly from the seventh century onward there were groups found elsewhere who claimed kinship with the Jerusalem Jews, who worshipped the same God, and some of whose traditions are reflected in our present Hebrew Bible.

'Ten Lost Tribes'?

One tradition relating to such groups must be mentioned even if only in order to dismiss it. In 722 BCE the Assyrians captured Samaria, the capital of the northern kingdom, Israel, and brought that country's independent existence to an effective conclusion. From then on it became part of the provincial system of first the Assyrian, then the Babylonian, and then the Persian Empire. In the Hebrew Bible this is pictured as if there was a complete deportation of the existing inhabitants and the substitution for them of alien settlers. From this there arose the later legend of the 'ten lost tribes', to which the first reference seems to have been preserved in the Apocryphal book 2 Esdras (13.40), which may date from the first century CE; the Jewish historian Josephus, writing at about the same time, preserves similar traditions. The book of Mormon, which emerged in the nineteenth century, details a landfall in the New World. In fact the Hebrew Bible lends no historical support to this picture of mass deportation, and neither do Assyrian records. The Assyrian king Sargon, whose inscriptions do not err on the side of modesty, claims to have deported some 27,000

Israelites-a small proportion of the total population. The picture of the two kingdoms as each composed of so many 'tribes' is itself a later idealization. In short, the great majority of the inhabitants of the land continued to live there, and so did their descendants. Of the fate of those who were deported, we know nothing; Ezekiel 37.15ff expresses a hope for their restoration to the ancestral homeland, but whether this hope is based on actual knowledge of a contemporary community still in existence we cannot say.

Jews in Babylon

Just as the idea that all the members of ten tribes were deported by the Assyrians lacks historical basis, so also must the supposition of a complete deportation of the southern tribes by the Babylonians be regarded as a later idealization (compare 2 Chronicles 36.20, which implies total depopulation, with Jeremiah 52.28–30, which lists a total of 4600 deportees). But we need not doubt that there was a substantial deportation, and, as we have seen already, many remained in Babylon even when Persian policy allowed greater freedom of movement. The stories of Ezra and Nehemiah each imply that there were Jewish groups from whom 'volunteers' might originate for a pilgrimage to the ancestral homeland. Ezra 8.1–20 makes it clear that it was necessary to exert some persuasion to obtain the requisite number of volunteers; Nehemiah 5.14–19 is less clear as to which groups came from which areas.

The Murashu Documents One substantial piece of evidence bears witness to the continued presence of Jews in Babylonia during the Persian period. Excavations carried out at Nippur, nearly 100 miles south-east of Babylon, brought to light a substantial archive of business documents from the house of Murashu dating from the second half of the fifth century BCE. Among the personal names listed there are many of clearly Jewish origin. It would seem that several strata of society were represented there. If this was the case in Nippur, which is not referred to in the Bible as a place of Jewish settlement, it is at least likely that there were comparable groups elsewhere. In short, the picture given in Jeremiah 29.6 of a community which was to 'multiply there [in Babylon] and not decrease' represents the true situation, whether this is a genuine Jeremiah saying or a later addition with knowledge of what took place.

Literary References The Murashu documents provide the only clear reference to Jews in Babylonia, but it is widely held that some of the texts which have found their way into the Hebrew writings also originate from this area: the stories of Daniel and his friends in Daniel 1–6 and the book of Esther in the Hebrew Bible; the stories of Susanna and of Tobit in the Apocrypha. All of these books probably reached their final form at a rather later date, but the traditions enshrined in them may well go back to the fourth or third century and say something of life in a Jewish Diaspora community.

Jews in Egypt

There was also a substantial Jewish community in Egypt. The book of Jeremiah gives some indication of this. The prophet Uriah unsuccessfully tried to take refuge there (26.20–3), and a group took Jeremiah with them to Egypt to escape reprisals from the Babylonian forces (43–4). There was, of course, no 'official' exile into Egypt, and so references to Jewish groups there are inevitably more spasmodic; there need, however, be no doubt that there was a significant Jewish presence there right down to the period when the Hebrew scriptures came to be translated into Greek and the Apocryphal books Ecclesiasticus and Wisdom of Solomon came to be translated or composed.

Elephantine The most important reference to Jews in Egypt comes from the extensive collection of papyri discovered early this century in Syene (Aswan) and the nearby island of Elephantine, near the first cataract of the river Nile. These make it clear that in the late fifth century BCE there was a large Jewish group in the district, mainly a military settlement, about whose life we are remarkably well-informed. Their religious practices have attracted particular attention, especially since it has been widely held that they worshipped Yahweh alongside the Canaanite goddess Anath.

Not all scholars accept this reading of the evidence, but, if it is a proper understanding, it remains much disputed whether this should be taken as a syncretistic debasement of the true Israelite cult, or whether it had been common in earlier times to worship Yahweh alongside a consort (the 'queen of heaven' of Jeremiah 44.15?), and that it was the Jerusalem community which had introduced changes, by imposing a stricter view of what the true worship of the one God entailed.

Conclusions

There can be no doubt that this whole period was a most creative one for the whole Jewish community, in Palestine or scattered abroad. It was the period during which Judaism was establishing itself as a religious community, no longer possessing political power, but giving religious explanations to its earlier history, including the disasters it had undergone, and seeking to ensure, through loyal service of its god, that such disasters could never recur.

Regrettably our knowledge of the history of the period is extremely fragmentary, and such information as we do have can nearly always be interpreted in more than one way. Nevertheless, it was a formative time which gave rise first to the essential concerns of Judaism and subsequently to the distinctive self-understanding of Christianity.

FURTHER READING

Ackroyd, P. R. 1968: *Exile and Restoration.*
Ackroyd, P. R. 1973: *1 and 2 Chronicles, Ezra, Nehemiah.*
Coggins, R. J. 1987: *Haggai, Zechariah, Malachi.*
Hanson, P. D. 1979: *The Dawn of Apocalyptic: the Historical and Sociological Roots of Jewish Apocalyptic Eschatology*, 2nd edn.
Smith, M. 1987: *Palestinian Parties and Politics that Shaped the Old Testament*, 2nd edn.
Williamson, H. G. M. 1977: *Israel in the Books of Chronicles.*
Williamson, H. G. M. 1987: *Ezra and Nehemiah.*

12

The Psalms

Roger Tomes

Preliminary Reading Psalms 2, 19, 22–4, 50, 51, 78, 96–104, 110, 118, 137, 139.

The Psalms in Jewish Worship

A cursory look through the *Authorised Daily Prayer Book* used by Orthodox Jewish congregations in the United Kingdom will show that the Psalms have a prominent place in Jewish worship. About half of them are used at some point in synagogue services (Simpson, 1965, 60–2). Particular psalms are said or sung at fixed points in the liturgy: there is nothing corresponding to the regular cycle of psalms in Anglican Matins and Evensong. The psalms used on Sabbath days are often different from those used on weekdays: for example, Psalm 24 is used after the reading of the lesson on weekdays, Psalm 29 on Sabbaths. There are also variations for particular seasons and festivals: Psalms 104 and 120–34 are used in the Sabbath afternoon service in winter, and Psalms 113–18 (known as the 'Hallel') are used during all the festivals.

The use of the Psalms in the Jewish liturgy is thus traditional, and yet they have only gradually acquired their position. It is clear from rabbinic writings that Jewish prayer after the biblical period has always centred around the recitation of the *Shema* and the *Amidah* or *Shemoneh Esreh* (Eighteen Benedictions; see Alexander, 1984, 68–74). The earliest plasms to be used in the Sabbath and weekday services were Psalms 145 (the Talmud specified that it should precede the Amidah) and 100; the Hallel psalms were used at festivals. At some time after 500 CE, following the practice of the Levites in the Second Temple (Mishnah Tamid, 7.4), a rota of daily psalms was introduced by popular demand; the use of Psalms 104 and 120–34 in the Sabbath afternoon service dates from the twelfth century, and Psalms 95–9 and 20 were introduced for the inauguration of the Sabbath by the Kabbalists (mystics) of Safed in Galilee from the sixteenth century (see Posner, Kaploun and Cohen, 1975, 18ff).

251

The Psalms in Jewish worship are sung to simple melodies flexible enough to accommodate a varying number of words. At special occasions, such as festivals or weddings, there may be more elaborate renderings by the *hazzan* or cantor. In Reform Judaism the text has been paraphrased so that the psalms can be sung to hymn-like tunes in regular metre, and in Israel verses from the psalms are sung to lively tunes, some of which (e.g. 'Jubilate') are now beginning to be used in Christian worship.

Jewish attitudes to the Psalms have changed over the centuries. In the tenth century CE the Karaites, a sect which rejected the oral law of the rabbis, maintained that the Psalms provided the only prayers which Jews might lawfully pray. Saadya Gaon (882–942 CE) defended the rabbinic tradition of prayer by insisting that the Psalms were not prayers at all, but rather a 'second Torah' cast in the form of prayers. Yefet ben Eli (*c*.920–1005) thought that the Psalms were 'prophetic', describing future events–in particular, the conflicts between the Karaites and rabbinists of his own day. In the eleventh century, Moses ben Samuel Gikatilla anticipated modern scholarship by saying that the Psalms must be interpreted in terms of the historical situation when they were written.

In many Jewish communities, reciting the Psalms has been regarded as an act of piety. People have come to synagogue before the service or stayed afterwards to recite them (Abrahams, 1922, 29, 114), and two groups recite the whole book daily at the Western Wall in Jerusalem. The Psalms have taken on new relevance for Jews since the foundation of the State of Israel, since they can now use them in the land in which they were composed. At the same time they have continued to sustain Jews in time of persecution: Anatoly Sharansky had the text of the Psalms with him throughout his internal exile in the Soviet Union, and was particularly helped by Psalm 27.

The Psalms in Christian Worship

Christians probably used the Psalms in preaching before they used them in worship. The chief references to the Psalms in the New Testament are to passages which seemed to predict events in the gospel story, such as the sharing-out of Jesus's clothes at the crucifixion (John 19.24, cf. Ps 22.18) or the resurrection (Acts 2.25–31, cf. Ps 16.8–11), or which seemed to speak of the Messiah (Acts 2.34f, cf. Ps 110.1; Hebrews 1.5, cf. Ps 2.7).

Psalms were used in Christian worship in New Testament times (1 Corinthians 14.26; Ephesians 5.19; Colossians 3.16; James 5.13), but it was not until the fourth century that they acquired a regular place between the lessons at the Eucharist (Dugmore, 1944, 96ff; Jungmann, 1960, 167f). Psalms were also used in daily prayer: at Antioch in the fourth century, Psalm 63 was regularly used every morning and Psalm 141 every evening (Bradshaw, 1981, 74). There were various ways of singing the Psalms: as a solo, the congregation responding with an antiphon; or the two halves of the congregation singing alternate verses; or the whole congregation joining together in a well-known psalm (Lamb, 1962, 38ff). With the emergence of monastic communities, greater use was made of the Psalter, used in its entirety to feed the prayers of individuals as well as to express the sentiments of the congregation. The monk was expected to make the thoughts of the psalmists his own and to use them as the subject matter of his meditation. There were proper (fixed) psalms for each of the hours of prayer, and also a cycle for saying or singing the complete Psalter once a week (although, as time went on, this cycle was increasingly interrupted for holy days and saints' days, when psalms appropriate to the occasion were said). In the Roman Catholic Church, and in the Church of England, it has been the duty of the clergy to say at least the main daily offices. Until the Second Vatican Council, Roman Catholic priests would say a large number of psalms each week, though they are now distributed over a longer period. Anglican clergymen used to work their way through the Psalter every month; now the cycle is spread over ten weeks. Lay people became familiar with the Psalms through Matins and Evensong. It is not surprising that many people came to know much of the Psalter by heart; the use of different translations in recent years has, however, made this more difficult.

In the sixteenth century, when the Reformers introduced services in the vernacular, congregational singing became one of the chief elements. In Germany Luther and others wrote hymns based on psalms ('Ein feste Burg', for example, is based on Psalm 46). The church in Geneva confined itself to psalm-singing, and the Psalms were translated into metrical form. Metrical psalms were the staple of congregational singing in England from the sixteenth to the eighteenth century, and in Scotland until late in the nineteenth century. With the Oxford Movement, the chanting of the Prayer Book version of the Psalms spread from the cathedrals to parish churches, and it had a vogue in the Free Churches for a time as well. In the twentieth century new ways of singing the Psalms have been introduced: a simpler method of chanting them was invented in France by Joseph Gélineau; freer metrical versions may be found in *Psalm Praise*; and parts of psalms have been used freely in the songs and choruses of the charismatic movement.

Since the Psalms originated in Israel before the time of Jesus, they do not express Christian sentiments directly. How then have Christians been able to use them as vehicles for Christian devotion? There have been five main ways in which the Psalms have been accommodated to Christianity.

1   They have been understood as the prayers of Jesus, which only attained their full meaning as he prayed them. When Christians pray

the Psalms, they are uniting themselves with the prayers of Christ (Benson, 1901)

2   They have been spiritualized. The sicknesses have been understood as sins, the enemies as spiritual enemies, the sacrifices as acts of devotion (Lewis, 1958).

3   They have been Christianized. Isaac Watts, the eighteenth-century nonconformist hymn-writer, rewrote the Psalms as Christian hymns, by removing all reference to events and institutions in the life of Israel and introducing references to Jesus and the Church. 'In all places I have kept my grand design in view, and that is, to teach my author to speak like a Christian' (Watts, 1719, Preface).

4   They have been anthologized. Free Church hymn books have printed only a selection of psalms most suitable for Christian worship, and have edited even these.

5   Modern versions of the Psalms have been produced: for example, Cardenal's rewriting of the Psalms as poems of the struggle for liberation in Latin America (Cardenal, 1981).

The History and Composition of the Psalms

There is no biblical account of how the Psalter was compiled, so the process has to be deduced from internal evidence.

The Psalter is divided into five books (Pss 1–41; 42–72; 73–89; 90–106; 107–150). These are clearly separated by the doxologies at the end of each book (e.g. 'Blessed be the LORD, the God of Israel, from everlasting to everlasting! Amen and amen' – 41.13), which are unrelated to the particular psalms to which they are attached. This division is fairly ancient, since the doxologies appear in the Septuagint, the Greek translation from the second century BCE. To some extent the books as we have them may represent earlier collections of psalms. Most of the psalms in book I are ascribed to David and are personal in character; books II and III contain the psalms attributed to Asaph and the sons of Korah and most of the psalms which are national in character; books IV and V have many psalms which are not assigned to any author and contain most of the hymns of praise. Psalms 42–83, most of books II and III, are also distinguished by mostly referring to God as Elohim. Opinion is divided about whether this is a sign that they come from a distinct 'Elohist' collection and had always used 'Elohim' or a sign of editorial alteration (compare Pss 14; 40.13–17; 108 with Pss 53; 70.1–5; 57.7–11; 60.5–12). An argument for the latter is that phrases which use 'Elohim' in these psalms read more naturally with 'Yahweh' elsewhere: compare, for example 'I am God, your God' in Psalm 50.7 with 'I am Yahweh, [RSV "the LORD"] your God' in Exodus 20.2. On the other hand, if the editor thought it necessary to change most of the occurrences of 'Yahweh' why did he leave it unchanged forty-three times?

The Psalm Titles

Most of the psalms have titles, which are counted as verses of the psalm in the Hebrew Bible but not in the English versions (so that if a reference is given to a verse in the Hebrew Bible it is often necessary to deduct one or two verses to find it in the English translation). The psalm titles (which have unfortunately been omitted in the New English Bible and relegated to footnotes in the Good News Bible) appear to offer five kinds of information (A.A. Anderson, 1972, 43–51).

(1) *The type of composition.* While the Hebrew title of the book of Psalms is *Tehillim* ('praises'), other terms are used in the psalm titles. The most frequent is *mizmor*, translated 'psalm' (Ps 3, etc.; 57 times), which probably means a song sung to instrumental accompaniment. Other terms, such as *maskil* (Ps 32, etc.; 12 times) and *miktam* (Ps 16, etc.; 6 times) have no generally accepted interpretation and therefore are usually left un-translated. The term translated 'Songs of Ascents' (Pss 120–34) may indicate that these psalms were sung by pilgrims on their way up to Jerusalem or in processions at festival times. There is nothing in the content of the psalms to indicate why the terms are distributed as they are.

(2) *Authors, compilers or collectors.* Many psalms are attributed to David, and significant series to Asaph (Pss 50, 73–83) and the sons of Korah (42–9, 84–5, 87–8). The Hebrew preposition used, however, does not necessarily mean 'by': more often elsewhere it means 'for' or 'belonging to'. Hence the title 'a psalm of David' need not mean 'a psalm composed by David' but could mean 'a psalm composed for David (or the Davidic king)' or 'a psalm from the Davidic collection'. The Asaphites were a guild of Temple singers in the post-exilic period (Ezra 2.41; 3.10), and the names Asaph, Korah, Heman (Ps 88) and Ethan (Ps 89) also figure among the Temple singers or their ancestors in the account of David's reign written in the post-exilic period (1 Chron 6.33, 37, 39, 42). The natural conclusion to draw would be that the psalms associated with these names were composed or handed down by particular groups of Temple singers, though a case has recently been made that the psalms in question were earlier associated with the northern sanctuaries of Dan and Bethel (Goulder, 1982).

(3) *Liturgical usage.* Certain psalms are designated for use on specific liturgical occasions; for example, 'at the dedication of the Temple' (Ps 30); 'for the memorial offering' (38, 70); 'for the thank offering' (100); and 'for the Sabbath' (92). According to the Mishnah (Tamid, 7.4), Psalm 92 was the psalm for the Sabbath in the weekly cycle in the Second Temple. The

Septuagint titles assign psalms to other days in agreement with the Mishnah list: Psalm 24 to the first day of the week, 48 to the second, 94 to the fourth, and 93 to the sixth (the connection of Psalm 82 with the third day and 81 with the fifth goes unnoticed). The Septuagint also assigns Psalm 29 to the last day of the feast of Tabernacles. These notices indicate the occasions on which the psalms were *used* at certain periods, but they do not necessarily tell us that the psalms in question were *composed* for these occasions.

(4)   *Technical musical expressions.* The significance of the term 'To the choirmaster' (Ps 4, etc.; 55 times) is unknown. It may indicate that the psalms to which it is attached come from an earlier collection. Some psalms are to be sung 'with stringed instruments' (Ps 4, etc.; 7 times), but it is not clear why these particular psalms should be singled out for this. Some other terms – 'according to the Sheminith' (Pss 6, 12), 'according to the Gittith' (Pss 8, 81, 84) – are probably best interpreted as the names of tunes. The term 'according to Do Not Destroy' (Pss 57, 58, 59, 75) prompts the speculation that a composer's anxiety that his work should not be lost has been interpreted as the name of a tune! Or Isaiah 65.8 may suggest that these psalms were to be sung to the tune of a well-known drinking-song!

(5)   *The historical circumstances of composition.* A number of the psalms (3, 18, 34, 51, 52, 54, 56, 57, 59, 60, 63, 142; and in the Septuagint also 143 and 144) are assigned to known situations in the life of David. But the psalms do not make any precise reference to the people or events concerned, whereas other poems attributed to David are very specific in their references (2 Sam 1.19–27; 23.1–7). The Septuagint has other suggestions to make, connecting psalms with later periods in Israel's history: Psalm 71 is attributed to 'those who were first carried captive' and 96 to the time 'when the house was being built after the captivity'. These are almost certainly later guesses about the circumstances of composition rather than authentic traditions.

Thus the psalm titles suggest to us that there were earlier collections underlying the Psalter and that certain psalms in the course of time became associated with particular cultic occasions. But they also suggest that the circumstances of their composition have been forgotten. Therefore we must turn to the text of the Psalms themselves to see if any further light can be shed on their history.

The Dating of the Psalms

The Psalms offer four kinds of evidence (Ackroyd, 1953) which may help us to decide what period in Israel's history they come from.

(1)   *Historical allusions.* Psalm 137 refers to the exile in Babylon in the early sixth century BCE as an experience which is still going on, and there-

fore was almost certainly composed during the exile. Psalm 126, on the other hand, presupposes the return in 538 BCE. Psalms 74 and 79 both refer to the desecration of the Temple and its destruction, and therefore could well refer to the events of 587/6 BCE. There was however a desecration of the Temple in 167 BCE (1 Macc 1.54; 2 Macc 6.1f), and for a long time many scholars favoured the Maccabaean period as the time of composition of these psalms, pointing out that Psalm 74.8 refers to the burning of 'all the meeting places of God in the land', which might imply the existence of synagogues, and that v. 9 mentions the absence of prophets, which echoes a favourite idea of the Maccabaean period (1 Macc 4.46; 9.27; 14.41). The argument that many other psalms are also Maccabaean, on the ground that the 'righteous' and the 'wicked' so frequently mentioned in the Psalter must be the Hasidim and Hellenists of that period, is less convincing, since we know of other periods in which there were deep divisions and party strife: the returning exiles were at odds with 'the people of the land' in the sixth century (Ezra 4.1–5); Nehemiah's rebuilding of the walls of Jerusalem was opposed in the fifth century (Neh 4, 6; cf. Ezra 4.6ff).

Another argument of this kind is that psalms which mention the king (see 'Royal psalms' below) must have been composed between the time of David and the fall of Jerusalem in 587/6 BCE. The idea that such psalms referred to the foreign ruler to whom the Jews were subject in the post-exilic period or to one of the Maccabaean leaders was an attempt to explain away evidence inconvenient to the theory that most psalms were Maccabaean or at least post-exilic.

Very few psalms contain allusions which allow them to be dated to any particular period. The situations they presuppose are the kind which can occur at any time, such as sickness and the plots and assaults of enemies. Some psalms (e.g. the hymns of praise) may indeed have been composed for use on repeated occasions. However, the above evidence makes it likely that psalms from widely separated periods are to be found in the Psalter.

(2) *Language*. It is possible to say about certain biblical writings that they must be post-exilic, because they contain Persian words, or that they must come after the conquests of Alexander the Great, because they contain Greek words. There are no such clear linguistic indicators in the Psalter. Some psalms (29, 68) have been thought to be early, because of stylistic affinities with Ugaritic texts of the fourteenth century BCE. On the whole, however, linguistic and stylistic criteria offer little help with dating.

(3) *Quotations*. Psalm 79.2 is quoted in 1 Maccabees 7.17. This need not, of course, mean that Psalm 79 was *written* in the Maccabaean period: it need only mean that it was found relevant at that time. All that can be said for certain is that it must have been written before 1 Maccabees. Psalm 18 is included in full in 2 Samuel 22, which means that it must have been in

existence when the books of Samuel or the Deuteronomic History were completed, and therefore it is probably pre-exilic. 1 Chronicles 16 includes parts of Psalms 96, 105 and 106, and so these must have been written before the early fourth century BCE; 2 Chronicles 6.41f quotes Psalm 132.8–10. Other alleged quotations are less certain: is 'The LORD reigns' (Pss 47.8; 93.1; 96.10; 97.1; 99.1) a reminiscence of Isaiah 52.7, or is the latter a reminiscence of the Psalms, or are both drawing on a traditional exultant shout?

(4) *Religious ideas.* Certain psalms (1, 19, 119) express passionate devotion to the law: it is likely that they were composed after the discovery of a law book in 621 BCE (1 Kings 22) and possibly after the work of Ezra in the fifth or early fourth century (Ezra 7ff; Neh 8ff). Psalms which dismiss the worship of other peoples as idolatry (96.5; 97.7; 115.4–8 = 135.15–18) may reflect or anticipate the teaching of the prophets. Psalm 73, which questions the orthodox view that the righteous prosper and that the wicked are punished, may belong to the reflective period after the exile when the book of Job was being written.

It is clear from the above discussion that the dating of most psalms has to be very tentative. It is also clear that psalms were used at times other than their period of composition. Hence interest in the types of psalms and the occasions on which they were probably used has dominated much of the discussion of the Psalms this century.

Psalm Types and the Occasions of their Use

The classification of the Psalms which is adopted in nearly all commentaries today is basically H. Gunkel's, admirably summarized by Aubrey Johnson (Gunkel, 1967; Johnson, 1951). Ignoring the psalm titles for the most part, Gunkel demonstrated that five main categories of psalm could be distinguished by style and content.

(1) *The hymn.* About twenty-five psalms (Johnson, 1951, 166) contain no petition but are devoted entirely to the objective worship of God. God is often referred to in the third person rather than addressed directly: the psalms begin with exhortations such as 'Sing to the LORD' (95.1; 96.1), 'Bless the LORD' (103.1; 104.1), 'Praise the LORD' (111.1; 112.1), 'Give thanks to the LORD' (105.1; 136.1). Praise thus has the character of testimony before others. God is praised for his attributes (145), for his creation of the world (136.4–9), for his self-revelation in the phenomena of nature (29, 104), for his faithful care for Israel (33, 105, 136) or for the individual (103.2–5) and for his expected deeds in the future (96, 98).

The quotation of and references to some of these psalms in Chronicles (1 Chron 16; 2 Chron 5.13; 7.3; cf. Ezra 3.11) suggest that in the post-exilic period at least these psalms were used on important festival occasions and were sung by Levites to instrumental accompaniment. Whether the Chronicler is right in asserting that this way of using them goes back to the time of David is less certain, since he is dependent for the main outline of his account of David and Solomon on the earlier history in Samuel and Kings, which makes no mention of the Levites as Temple singers. Internal evidence confirms the use of musical instruments (33.2f; 68.24f; 149.3; 150).

In 1922 S. Mowinckel (Johnson, 1951, 190–7) proposed that certain of the hymns, together with other psalms which contain the acclamation 'The LORD reigns' (47, 93, 95–9), had been used in the pre-exilic period during a New Year festival to celebrate the enthronement of Yahweh as King. Mowinckel was led in this direction by the fact that in the Babylonian New Year festival Marduk was enthroned. The idea of such a festival provides an imaginative context into which many psalms can be fitted with greater or lesser plausibility (Johnson, 1967), but, in the absence of any direct evidence that the pre-exilic autumn festival in Jerusalem had this character, the case for regarding the psalms as having been used in this way remains hypothetical.

(2) *The communal lament.* We have already seen that certain psalms presuppose diasters which have overtaken the whole community (44, 74, 79, 80, 83). These Gunkel classified as communal laments. The psalm is designed to be spoken either by Israel as a whole ('We') or by the king or other representative of the community ('I': 44.4, 6; 74.12). It consists chiefly of petition and God is addressed directly. The chief interest lies in the arguments which are used to move God to action. The distress of the community is described (e.g. 74.4ff); God's memorable deeds in the past are recalled (e.g. vv.12ff); he is reproved for being inactive (e.g. v.10ff) and he is reminded that his own interests are at stake (e.g. v.10).

How and when were such psalms used? During the exile in the sixth century BCE there were at least four fast days held in Jerusalem each year to mark the stages in the fall of the city (Zech 7.5, 8.19; 2 Kgs 25.1, 3, 8, 25) and these laments may well have been used then (unless, of course, they are Maccabaean psalms: the fact that a convincing context for their use is better attested for the exilic period than for the Maccabaean period provides an additional argument against a Maccabaean date).

(3) *Royal psalms.* The psalms in this group are varied in form and content, but they are related by the fact that they are all prayers by or for a king. Two of the psalms (2, 110) would be most appropriate on his accession; another on his marriage (45); two more before and after battle (20, 21). Psalm 72 is a general prayer for the success of the king's reign. Psalm 132

is a celebration both of the covenant with David and of God's choice of Jerusalem. It has been suggested (Johnson, 1967, 102ff) that Psalms 2 and 110 were also used at a re-enthronement of the king at the New Year festival, and preceded by psalms marking a humiliation of the king (89.38ff), a confession on his part (101) and his thanksgiving after (ritual) deliverance (18, 118), similar to the experience of the king in the Babylonian New Year festival.

It has already been shown that these psalms most probably come from the time when there was a native monarchy in Israel, between the time of David and the exile.

The category of royal psalms may of course be much larger than this. It may be entirely fortuitous that the king is mentioned only in some nine psalms. In particular, many of the psalms in which an individual is speaking may originally have been prayers of the king (see below on the 'individual lament'), and some commentators (e.g. Eaton, 1967; 1986) treat nearly all psalms as royal psalms.

(4) *The individual lament.* About thirty-eight psalms come into this category (Johnson, 1951, 169). There was once a vogue for regarding the 'I' who speaks in these psalms as a personification of the community, but it is much more likely that he is an individual. As in the communal laments, the psalmist describes his distress in order to excite God's pity. The reference is generally to sickness or the assaults of enemies or both, but it is described in highly figurative language, so that it is difficult to determine the precise nature of the psalmist's sufferings. He will sometimes confess his sin (51, 130), but is just as likely to protest his innocence (7, 17, 26).

There have been a number of attempts to identify the psalmists' enemies (Johnson, 1951, 197ff). Gunkel pointed out that in some psalms (41, 55, 69) they are neighbours and erstwhile friends who perhaps see in the psalmist's sufferings evidence that he has committed some sin, while in others (e.g. 12, 17, 26, 28) they are the rich and powerful as a class, who scorn the piety of the humble believer. Mowinckel, armed with the knowledge that other societies attributed sickness to sorcery, suggested that the phrase translated 'workers of iniquity' (6.8; 14.4; 28.3; etc.) identified the enemies as sorcerers and that the psalms in question were counter-spells devised by priests to accompany some purificatory rite (51.7). H. Schmidt pointed out that 1 Kings 8.31f provides for a case against an individual which cannot be decided in a local court being settled at the Temple by his swearing an oath that he is innocent, and argued that certain psalms which contain such a protestation of innocence (7, 17, 26, etc.) are prayers which the accused man can use in this situation. H. Birkeland drew attention to psalms in which the psalmist has many enemies (56, 57, 59, etc.) who are at war with him, and held that these are the (foreign) enemies of the king. L. Delekat has interpreted the many prayers for protection and the claims that one is taking refuge in Yahweh or under the shadow of his wings (e.g. 57.1) as meaning that the psalmist is seeking asylum, perhaps from creditors or landlord, at a sanctuary; and he further takes the Septuagint translation of the term *miktam* in the title of Psalm 57 and other psalms with the refuge theme as *stelographia*, 'inscription on a tablet', as meaning that the psalms in question were written inscriptions rather than spoken prayers (Eaton, 1979, 256f). All these suggestions are helpful in so far as they draw attention to features of the psalms which would otherwise be overlooked, but dangerous if they are taken to offer total and exclusive interpretations.

(5) *The individual song of thanksgiving.* Certain psalms (30, 41, 138) are thanksgivings which presuppose that a situation of distress has passed, that God has answered a prayer for deliverance. The thanksgiving may even quote the earlier lament (30.8–10; 41.4), and sometimes the thanksgiving may be the second half of the individual lament (22.22ff; 31.21ff; 69.30ff). This suggests that what may have intervened is not actual recovery or deliverance but a reassuring oracle or sign, such as the psalmist sometimes asks for (86.27). The Psalms contain a number of passages which are oracles addressed by God to the worshipper rather than prayers addressed by the worshipper to God (12.5; 91; 75.2–5). This fact has prompted the suggestion that both these oracles and the prayers to which they were the response were composed by cultic prophets, who thus fulfilled their dual role as spokesmen for God and intercessors for the people (Johnson, 1979). One important feature of the thanksgivings is that they are sung or uttered before a congregation (22.22, 25; 32.11; 116.14, 18).

Not all the psalms fall into one or other of these main types, and some share the characteristics of more than one type. Indeed, some of the most familiar are exceptions. Psalm 23 is the psalm of an individual, but neither a lament nor a thanksgiving: it is best described as 'a psalm of confidence'. Psalm 139 is similar. Psalms 1, 19 and 119 are linked by their interest in the law; 15 and 24 contain statements of the conduct God requires in his worshippers; 1, 37, 49 and 73 share an interest in the respective fates of the righteous and the wicked; 50, 81 and 95 are all intended for use on an important festival occasion, but are dominated by a prophetic appeal to obey God.

If the suggestion that series of psalms were used at festivals is correct, then it is likely that varieties of psalm types would be used in the series (Johnson, 1967; Goulder, 1982).

The Psalms as Poetry

The Psalms share in the general characteristics of biblical Hebrew poetry. The most important element in its structure is *parallelism*, the construction of short sentences divided into two brief clauses (each sentence usually corresponding to a verse). The clauses often have some element in common, such as the same syntactic structure (e.g. subject + verb + object or adverbial phrase) or the repetition of a word. Sometimes the second clause virtually restates the first in different words, as in Psalm 146.2 ('I will praise the LORD as long as I live; / I will sing praises to my God while I have being'); but more frequently only part of the first clause is repeated, as in Psalms 24.1 ('The earth is the LORD's and the fullness thereof, / the world and those who dwell therein' – the attribution to 'the LORD' is not repeated) and 9.9 ('The LORD is a stronghold for the oppressed, / a stronghold in times of trouble' – the word 'stronghold' is the only common element). The second clause may complete the sense of the first clause, as in Psalm 3.2 ('Many are saying of me, / there is no help for him in God'), or give a reason, as in Psalm 25.15 ('My eyes are ever toward the LORD, / for he will pluck my feet out of the net'), or describe the result, as in Psalm 40.12 ('My iniquities have overtaken me, / till I cannot see'), or describe someone mentioned in the first clause, as in Psalm 35.19 ('Let not those rejoice over me/who are wrongfully my foes'). One clause may provide a simile for a statement in the other, as in Psalm 103.13 ('As a father pities his children, / so the LORD pities those who fear him'), or may turn a statement into a question, as in Psalm 6.5 ('For in death there is no remembrance of thee; / in Sheol who can give thee praise?'), or may make a contrasting statement, as in Psalm 1.6 ('For the LORD knows the way of the righteous, / but the way of the wicked will perish'). Thus the relation between the two clauses is very varied, but the effect is nearly always to give emphasis to what is being said (Kugel, 1981, 1–58).

Hebrew poetry does not have rhyme or strict metre, though the clauses which make up the line or verse often balance each other in sound as well, by having the same number of stressed syllables (two, three or four). The New English Bible in its translation of poetry has indicated the varying length of lines by its typographical arrangement: it can easily be seen that the metrical pattern in the Psalms is much less regular than that in Job or Proverbs. Psalms can rarely be divided into stanzas on any ground but the sense, though occasionally there is a refrain which serves this function, as in Psalms 42–3, 46, 80 and 107.

Another interesting device is the *acrostic*, in which the lines begin with the twenty-two letters of the Hebrew alphabet in sequence. Psalms 9–10, 25, 34, 37, 111, 112, 119 and 145 are acrostics; the same device is used outside the Psalter in Proverbs 31.10–31, in Lamentations and in Nahum 1.1–10. Various reasons for the arrangement have been suggested (Gottwald, 1954, 23ff), the most likely being that it was 'either a mnemonic aid or, perhaps, another way of saying that the subject matter has been dealt with from A to Z' (Anderson, 1972, 106).

Attempts have been made (e.g. Auffret, 1977; Magonet, 1982) to show
that some psalms at least have a very carefully composed overall structure.
For example, Psalm 145, in addition to being an acrostic, also seems to be
arranged concentrically. The Psalm opens and closes with the theme of
blessing God's name for ever and ever, while the centre of the psalm
(vv.11–13) is about God's kingdom and is sandwiched between two
passages of praise (vv.4–10, 14–20), both of which include lists of the divine attributes.

The way in which Hebrew poetry is constructed – out of brief sentences
divided into two clauses – means that the style of the Psalms is relatively
simple and straightforward. Adjectives and adverbs are sparingly used, and
subordinate clauses are few. Stock metaphors are used again and again: God
is a rock (18.2; 28.1; 31.3; 71.3; 144.1), a shield (3.3; 18.2; 28.7; 33.20),
a king (5.2; 10.16; 24.7; 29.10; 47.2; 95.3; 145.1), a shepherd (23.1;
28.9; 80.1). The psalmists' enemies are wild animals (10.9; 17.12; 22.12,
16, 20f; 58.4; 59.6); they dig pits and set traps for the righteous (9.15;
10.9; 31.4; 35.7; 57.6; 91.3), but they will be blown away like chaff (1.4;
35.5; 83.13). The psalmists' physical sufferings are like drowning (18.16;
32.6; 40.2; 42.7; 69.1f); human life is as short as a few handbreadths (39.5;
89.47), as insubstantial as a shadow (39.6; 102.11; 144.4), a dream
(73.20; 90.5) or a single crop of grass (37.2; 90.5; 102.11; 103.15). The
righteous flourish like a tree (1.3; 52.8; 128.3; 144.12). Occasionally a
more distinctive image is used: unity in a family is as fragrant as the priest's
anointing-oil and as refreshing as the dew on the mountains (133); a man
with sons is like a warrior with a quiver full of arrows (127.4f) – but generally the Psalter keeps to well-tried metaphors as a means of 'expressing and
reinforcing the accepted system of order or belief' (Caird, 1980, 153).

It is sometimes difficult to know whether the psalmists are using
language literally or metaphorically. Sometimes, when they describe their
enemies as using weapons against them, they are clearly referring to their
slanders and insults (55.21; 57.4; 64.3f; cf. God's weapons in 7.12f and
35.3), but in other cases they may have literal attack in mind (11.2; 22.20;
37.14). Again, the language of the law court may sometimes be used
metaphorically, but, as we have seen in the discussion of the individual
lament, it has more than once been suggested that the psalmist was accused
of a crime and was seeking the verdict of a court (7, 17, 26, 35). Whether
references to God's or the king's victories over all the nations are to literal
victories or dramatized ones depends on the likelihood or otherwise of there
being a New Year festival in which ritual drama played a part (2, 18, 21,
46, 48, 89, 110; Johnson, 1967).

One of the obstacles to the universal use of the Psalms is the fact that they
bear the marks of a particular time and place. When enemies are identified,
they are Israel's historical enemies: Edom, Moab, Amalek, Ammon,

Philistia and Assyria (60.8; 83.6–8; 108.9f; 137.7) and Babylon (137). The historical events in which God's hand is seen are those of the exodus from Egypt (78, 80, 81, 105, 106, 114, 135, 136), some victories described in Judges (83.9–12; cf. Judg 4f; 6–8), the covenant with David and the choice of Zion as the Temple site (78.70f; 89.3f, 19–37; 132.11f and 76.2; 78.68; 132.13ff). A number of psalms show a deep affection for Jerusalem (48, 76, 87, 122, 125, 137, 147) and for the Temple (23, 27, 42–43, 63, 65, 84), although some of these psalms may originally have referred to other sanctuaries (Goulder, 1982). Attachment to the land of Israel is also expressed, though perhaps not as frequently or as explicitly as one might expect (67, 85).

It is also important to recognize that the psalmists shared a picture of the world which differs from our own in a number of respects (Keel, 1978). It is not an entirely consistent picture. Thus the earth is constructed above the waters (24.2; 136.6), but also appeared when the waters receded (104.5–9). There are waters above the heavens (148.4), but the waters have been firmly assigned to their own sphere (33.7; 65.7; 89.9; 104.8f). The heavens have been stretched out like a tent (104.2). The sun of course travels daily across the heavens (19.4–6). The sun, the moon and the stars are there to mark off day and night respectively (104.19f; 136.7–9). Earthquakes and storms are God's messengers (148.8), manifestations of his anger (18.7–15; 50.3; 77.16–18) and glory (29, 97). The order of creation has been established for ever (119.90f; 148.5f). Along with the familiar features of the natural world, however, creation also contains God's supernatural messengers (103.20f; 148.2) and sea monsters, which once stood for hostile forces which God had to overcome in order to create the world (74.13f; 89.10; 104.24–6; 148.7). Human beings are both made in their mother's womb and 'intricately wrought in the depths of the earth' (139.13,15). When they die, they go down to the underworld, variously called Sheol (16.10; 18.5; 30.3; 88.3), Abaddon (88.11), the Pit (28.1; 30.3,9; 88.4) and 'the land of forgetfulness' (88.12).

Theological Themes

If the Psalms were composed, as seems likely, by many different people, at many different times, in a variety of national or personal circumstances, and for a variety of cultic purposes, it is unlikely that one unified theology will be expressed in the Psalter. Nevertheless, the Psalter will not simply reflect the various emphases and interests which are found outside it, elsewhere in the Bible. Praise and complaint and thanksgiving create theology as well as express it and mirror it. Hence there is some justification for viewing the Psalms as 'an integrated system' with 'something to say quite independent of the intentions of the authors of individual psalms, the collectors of groups of psalms or the editors of the psalter' and as a book with 'an identity, a character and a voice of its own' (Collins, 1987, 41,56).

One theme which is constantly being rehearsed in the Psalter is that of God's memorable deeds in the past. This is a feature of many of the hymns, of course, but also of the communal laments and some of the royal psalms. 'We have heard with our ears, O God, / our fathers have told us, / what deeds thou didst perform in their days, / in the days of old' (44.1). These past deeds include creation (8; 24.1f; 33.6f; 74.12–17; 95.5; 104.1–9; 124.8; 136.4–9; 146.5f; 148.5f), but it is obvious that the events which created Israel as a nation are much more important to the psalmists. It was God who brought Israel out of Egypt, drove out the nations and secured the land for them (44.2f; 114; 135.8–12; 136.10–22). He planted Israel in its land like a vine (80). All this was in fulfilment of the promises to the patriarchs (105) and despite Israel's sins (106). He fought off the Canaanites and the Midianites in the period of the Judges (83.9–12), and eventually chose David as his anointed king (89.19–37; 132.11–18) and Jerusalem as his holy city (87; 132.13–16). A latter psalmist celebrates God's restoration of the fortunes of Zion after the exile (126). On a more personal level a psalmist recalls the way God has 'ransomed, healed, restored, forgiven' him (103.1–5; cf. 143.5): others give thanks for particular deliverances (30, 41, 116, 138).

These past experiences have helped to shape the psalmists' faith in God in the present. There is no comparison between Israel's god and the gods of other nations (77.13; 86.8; 89.6–8; 95.3; 96.4; 97.9), whether those gods are regarded as subordinate divine beings responsible to Israel's god for maintaining justice in the nations (58.1; 82) or dismissed contemptuously as the work of human hands (96.5; 97.7; 115.4–8 = 135.15–18). God is responsible for maintaining the life of all creatures (104.10ff; 145.15f; 147.8f) and for making his people prosperous (65, 67, 144, 147). He maintains justice, whether this is conceived as vindicating the righteous and punishing the wicked (1.6; 5.4–6; 7.9–11; 9.7f; 34.15–17; 58.11) or as being the champion of the poor and the oppressed (9.18; 10.14; 68.5f; 69.33; 103.6; 113.7; 146.7, 9). He rescues people from all manner of critical situations (107). He alone is the security both of the nation (20.7f; 33.16f; 115.9–11; 146.3f) and of the individual (23; 27; 91; 118.5–9). Jerusalem (46, 48, 76, 87, 132) and the Davidic king (2; 20; 21; 45; 89.19–37; 132) are the objects of his special care and protection.

These beliefs, however, are threatened by adverse circumstances. How can the Jews continue to sing these songs of confidence and praise when they are in exile in Babylon (137)? How can they continue to believe in God's willingness or ability to protect Jerusalem when the city lies in ruins (79) and the Temple has been burned to the ground (74)? How can the king believe in the promises to David when he is ending his days in defeat and shame (89.38–51)? The problems can be no less acute for the individual. He may begin by thinking that properity is the normal state of affairs (30.6), and therefore may interpret adversity as a sign of God's anger (6, 38, 39, 77, 88) or as a sign that God has forgotten him (13, 42–3, 77), or he may be perplexed that God is taking so long to come to his rescue (35, 69). Particularly unsettling for faith are the denials of other people that God can or will intervene (14 = 53; 42–3, 74, 94), which is sometimes echoed in the psalmist's own reflections on the way the wicked seem to prosper (73.1–14). And some psalmists are haunted by the thought of oblivion in the grave (6, 88).

How are these problems resolved? In some cases, the psalmist does not get beyond calling for God's vengeance on his or the nation's enemies (35, 55, 58, 69, 79, 83, 109) or puzzled or angry outbursts against God himself (38; 44; 88; 89.46–51). Confession that the psalmist has been at fault is relatively rare (32, 38, 51), and that the nation has been at fault even rarer (106.7; 130), though the people of Judah are quite willing to agree that the people of Israel (the northern kingdom) have got what they deserved (78.67–72). Most psalmists, however, include a reaffirmation of trust in God's eventual intervention (31, 56, 57, 62). Where there is a sharp break between complaint and expression of confidence (6, 13, 22, 28, 54, 59, 64, 69), it is possible that we should assume that the psalmist has received some renewal of God's promises, in the form of an oracle (12.5; 91), a dream (3.5; 17.15) or some other visible sign (86.17). It is also possible that ritual drama enacting the victory of God or his anointed king over the nation's enemies in a New Year festival provided reassurance (2, 18, 20, 21, 46, 48, 76, 110). Elsewhere the resolution is reached in a more reflective way. Psalm 34 (an alphabetical psalm) admits that the righteous experience many afflictions but insists that God always delivers them. Psalm 37 faces the problem of the prosperity of the wicked, and concludes that it is short-lived; the righteous have only to wait patiently. Psalm 49 is a reminder that the wicked must die and leave their possessions to others. Psalm 94 represents the view that the persecution of the righteous is intended by God as chastening and does not permanently invalidate God's just rule of the earth. Psalm 73 is the most explicit about the threat to faith posed by the prosperity of the wicked: the psalmist is ultimately consoled when he considers their end, but is also sustained by his own communion with God.

Does this last psalm envisage a communion with God which continues after death? The 'honour' or 'glory' in v. 24 does not necessarily refer to an afterlife, and probably means no more than a return to an honoured place in society. Similarly, those passages in which the psalmist says that God will not give him up to Sheol (16.10) or will redeem him from Sheol (49.15) or has delivered him from Sheol (30.3; 86.13) probably refer to no more than rescue from a near-fatal illness and premature death. There is therefore no certainty that any psalmist could find a resolution of the theological problems in the thought of judgement after death.

There is no real eschatology in the Psalms. The psalmists do not speak about what God will do 'in the latter days'; judgements are immediate and continuous (7.6f, 11; 58.11; 67.4; 96.13; 98.9). The deliverances celebrated and looked for are this worldly ones: victory over enemies (20, 60), return from exile (126), recovery from sickness (88). The nation looks to be able to live in its land in peace and prosperity (67, 85, 144, 147); the king to enjoy a long and successful reign (72), the individual a life under God's protection and blessing (23, 27, 91). However, for a number of psalmists the good life is not complete unless they can be near God (23, 27, 42–3, 84), observant of his law (1, 19, 119), prizing God above all things (16, 36, 63, 131, 139).

FURTHER READING

Anderson, A. A. 1972: *Psalms.*
Anderson, G. W. 1962: 'The Psalms', in *Peake's Commentary on the Bible.*
Rogerson, J. W. and Mackay, J.W. 1977: *Psalms 1–50; Psalms 51–100; Psalms 101–150.*

13

The Wisdom Books

David J. A. Clines

Preliminary Reading   Job; Proverbs; Ecclesiastes.

Identification of the Wisdom Books

This chapter limits its scope to the Hebrew Bible, and so considers only the three 'wisdom' books that are found there: Proverbs, Ecclesiastes and Job. If we took into account the Old Testament as a whole – that is to say, all those books which have been acknowledged by Christians at one time or another to be part of the Old Testament – we should have to add two other wisdom books appearing only in the Greek Old Testament and now included in the Apocrypha or among the deutero-canonical books: Wisdom (or the Wisdom of Solomon) and Ecclesiasticus (or the Wisdom of Jesus ben Sirach). All the wisdom books are so called because of their didactic contents; among the books of the Old Testament they are distinctive in that they deliberately set out to be instructional about right living or right thinking.

The Category of 'Wisdom'

It has been customary in biblical study, since the beginning of modern criticism, to approach the texts of the Bible from the standpoint of their historical setting. So we are often told that the only way, certainly the only correct way, of understanding books such as Proverbs, Job and Ecclesiastes is to begin by reconstructing their social and historical background. Not only do we need to know the dates at which they were written; we also need to know how they themselves as books evolved into existence. In this way we can trace the development of the ideas they contain, noting what is more primitive and what is more advanced, and, in particular, drawing lines of connection between the books we are studying and other works of the same

period, in order to establish influences and pinpoint the purpose for which
the books were composed. It is especially important, according to this
approach, to identify the social background of the works, to discover what
group each work speaks for, what the circles or schools of thought were that
gave rise to the work.

Now, it would be foolish to adopt any approach to anything that
consisted of shutting one's eyes to facts, although it might be allowed that
there are times when the mind cannot take in all the conceivably relevant
facts and it might be valuable to limit – if only temporarily – one's field of
concentration. But the question in the present case is, not whether it might
be desirable to leave aside for the time being questions of historical and
social background for our books, but whether there are indeed any facts in
that realm that will illuminate these books for us.

The common view has been that these books, Proverbs, Job and
Ecclesiastes, are the products of a school of thought called 'wisdom',
promulgated by a recognizable social group of the 'wise'. These are thought
to have been professional wise men (males, that is), earning their living
either in the bureaucracy of the court or in the educational system, or in
both. They will have applied the principles of wisdom to their everyday
tasks, and, in turn, have developed the wisdom ideas through their own
experience of life. Such groups of the 'wise' may well have existed, it is
thought, from as early as the time of Solomon and down to the Persian
period. For Proverbs contains a collection (chs 10–24) entitled 'Proverbs of
Solomon' (10.1) and another called 'proverbs of Solomon which the men of
Hezekiah king of Judah copied' (25.1, in reference to chs 25–29); and
Ecclesiastes, with its various evidences of a quite late date of origin, would
show that the 'wise' remained in existence well into post-exilic times.

A further refinement of this view has been that the earliest forms of
'wisdom' in Israel – what has been called 'old wisdom' – were essentially
secular and prudential in nature, and that a later layer in the wisdom
literature comes from the injection into wisdom of religious ideals, especially
from the prophetic sphere. By this criterion, the central section of Proverbs,
for example, will be evidence largely of 'old wisdom', since the religious note
is relatively subdued, and God appears mostly as nothing more that the
guarantor of the moral order that these proverbs affirm; whereas the first
section, chapters 1–9, with its heavy insistence on wisdom as a divine gift
and indeed, as a divine attribute, witness to the later view of wisdom. Such
views became the critical orthodoxy in the 1960s with the publication of W.
McKane's *Prophets and Wise Men* and R. N. Whybray's *Wisdom in Proverbs*.

The question that must be asked today, however, is whether our evidence
truly enables us to make such reconstructions. It can reasonably be doubted
that there was ever a period in which wisdom was either purely religious or
purely secular, and, more to the point, whether there was a professional class

of the wise at all. R. N. Whybray's second book on the subject, *The Intellectual Tradition in Israel* (1974), justifiably argues that wisdom was not regarded in Israel as the preserve of any social class, and that what we are in the habit of calling the wisdom literature could perhaps more accurately be called the more intellectual literature of the nation. Perhaps even 'intellectual' is too strong a term for some of the wisdom literature, such as Proverbs, which claims to be little more than practical ethical instruction. There must have been very few responsible adults in Israel, whether male or female, who could not have been regarded as purveyors of wisdom. For, inasmuch as wisdom means the traditional knowledge of life that children learn in the home from their parents, any well-brought-up child had learnt wisdom.

A further reason against the strongly historical approach is that, in the last twenty years, we have lost confidence in our ability to date the literature of the Old Testament, especially books such as these which contain no references to historical events. Nowadays it seems impossible that we should imagine a social group of the professional wise men enduring for six or seven centuries, through the vicissitudes of Israel's political life, from the time of the monarchy, through the exile, to the period of foreign rule in the post-exilic period. No such group can be postulated as the home of wisdom, and we must simply take a more agnostic position than most of our current textbooks prescribe.

It is also probably a mistake to suppose that literature inevitably reflects the views of a particular class or circle. On the one hand, much of Proverbs seems to be drawn from the folk wisdom of the people generally; and, on the other, everything about the book of Job, as also about Ecclesiastes, suggests that the author was writing as a unique and somewhat unorthodox individual. The book of Job, especially, is such an intensely intellectual work that it is hard to imagine that it had a very much wider appeal to its ancient readers than it has to readers of the present day; its presence in the canon of the Hebrew Bible may be due as much to happy accidents as to any deliberate preservation of the book by a class of intellectuals or administrators for whom it spoke.

Of course, we are not entirely in the dark about life and thought in ancient Israel, and our general knowledge about the ancient world, about the Hebrew language, about the customs and intellectual ideas of the ancient Near East still need to be brought into play whenever we open one of these texts. However, an agnostic position on historical background leads us to a more determined concentration on the books themselves. Even if we cannot reconstruct chains of historical influence, it is still worthwhile to compare and contrast literary works, and to ask what their relation to one another – in terms of their ideas, though not of the circumstances of their composition – may be.

The Wisdom Books Compared and Contrasted

Even though there may be no common social background for the books of
Proverbs, Job and Ecclesiastes, it is instructive to compare them theologically, since intellectually they are closer to one another than to any other
books of the Hebrew Bible.

Proverbs is, next to Deuteronomy, the most stalwart defender in the
Hebrew Bible of the doctrine of retribution. In it the underlying principle is
that wisdom – which means the knowledge of how to live rightly – leads to
life and folly leads to death (e.g. Prov. 1.32; 3.1–2,13–18; 8.36).
Everywhere it is asserted – or else taken for granted – that righteousness is
rewarded and sin is punished (e.g. 11.5–6). The world of humans is divided
into two groups: the righteous (or wise) and the wicked (or foolish). Which
group a particular individual belongs to seems to be determined by
upbringing and education, and there is little hope or fear that a person may
move from one category to the other. Thus there is a determinism about the
outlook of Proverbs, and a rather rigid notion of cause and effect, which
would be reasonable enough if we could be sure that it was designed for the
education of the young, but is in any case lacking in intellectual
sophistication and, to be frank, in realism.

Job and Ecclesiastes introduce that needed element of sophistication and
realism into the philosophy of wisdom, calling into question as they do so
the universal validity of the tenets of Proverbs.

Ecclesiastes does not doubt the value of the quest for wisdom: 'wisdom
excels folly as light excels darkness' (2.13). Yet the author insists on raising
the question, what happens to one's wisdom at death? Since death cancels
out all values, not excepting wisdom, life cannot be meaningful if it is made
to consist of gaining something that is inevitably going to be lost. However
valuable the pursuit of wisdom is, it is even better for a human being to
regard life as an opportunity for enjoyment: 'There is nothing better for a
man than that he should eat and drink, and find enjoyment in all his toil'
(2.24). For enjoyment is not a cumulative possession or a process leading to
a goal which can then subsequently be destroyed; enjoyment exists in the
course of living along with the activity that produces it, and so it cannot be
lost. Ecclesiastes thus inscribes a challenging question-mark in the margin of
Proverbs.

Job confronts the ideology of Proverbs at a different point. The book of
Job is an assault on the general validity of the doctrine of retribution. In the
framework of the thought of Proverbs, the man Job is an impossibility. If he
is truly righteous, he finds life, and wealth, and health. If, on the contrary,
he is in pain, he is one of the wicked and the foolish. In the end, the book of
Job does not completely undermine the principle of retribution, for Job ends

up both pious and prosperous; but, once the principle is successfully challenged, as it is in the book of Job (even in a single case), its moral force is desperately weakened. For, once the case of Job becomes known, if a person who has a reputation for right living is found to be suffering (the fate Proverbs predicts for wrongdoers), no one can point a finger of criticism; the story of Job establishes that the proper criterion for determining whether people are pious or not is the moral quality of their life and not the accidental circumstances of their material existence. At the same time, the book maintains that a truly religious attitude does not consist of passive resignation to misfortune, but includes a courage to enter into confrontation with God.

Even though both Job and Ecclesiastes dissent, in their own way, from the leading theological statement of Proverbs on retribution, all three works may appropriately be labelled 'wisdom' literature; for, whether explicitly or implicitly, they are all concerned with instruction on how to live rightly.

Proverbs

Structure

As is so often the case, the structure of the book is the most important clue to its meaning. In Proverbs, there is a clear disjunction between chapters 1–9 and chapters 10–31. While 1–9 are extended and coherent discourses on the theme of wisdom, its origins, desirability and effects, 10–39 are for the most part collections of single-sentence proverbs arranged in random order.

It is often thought, because the sentence proverbs of chapters 10–31 are the most easily accessible, down to earth, and intelligible, that they are the most characteristic element of the book, and in fact some descriptions of the book proceed as if they were all there is to Proverbs. However, to appreciate the book as a whole, it is essential to read it from beginning to end – which is to say, to accept that chapters 1–9 are intended to be read as a preface to the sentence proverbs and to dictate how they are to be understood.

To be concrete: it is sometimes asked whether Proverbs is essentially pragmatic or essentially religious. Are its readers to follow its advice because they will profit from doing so, or because it is God's will that they do so? So long as we focus on the sentence proverbs, it is easy to think that their ethics are more or less simply prudential; for God is rather seldom mentioned, and there is very little sense that right behaviour is regarded as a religious duty. Yet, if we approach the sentence proverbs from the perspective of chapters 1–9, we find that the advice being given in chapters 10–31 is conceived of as a divine gift, as sharing in some degree in God's own wisdom, and is regarded as the path to life. None of these perceptions is visible in chapters 10–31 themselves.

The second most significant feature of the structure of the book is provided by its last chapter. 31.10–31 is a depiction of the ideal wife, and quite different in form from almost everything else in the book. In some ways it is like the brief depictions of the ideal son (e.g. 10.1) or the generous person (e.g. 11.24–5), but it is different in that it is very much more elaborated than those thumbnail sketches, *and* it is about a woman, not a man. What it most resembles elsewhere in the book is the description of the figure of Wisdom in chapters 8–9, personifying as a woman the virtue which the book as a whole praises (compare especially Wisdom's activities in 9.1–6). There is more than a hint that the idealized figure of Wisdom is incarnated, or at least, brought to reality, in the figure of the ideal woman of chapter 31. The flow of the book would then be from the general to the particular to a concrete worked example, with chapter 31 the climax or conclusion of the entire book.This need not be a particularly feminist view, since the point about the ideal woman is not so much that she is a woman but that she is an ideal practitioner of wisdom, applying to the round of everyday life all the principles inculcated by the book. In any case, since the book is very probably a male creation, all we are being proffered is a male perspective on the woman, with the inevitable misapprehensions, idealizations and prejudices that come when one sex tries to depict the other. Nevertheless, the fact remains that it is the capable housewife who appeals to the author as the most convincing exponent of practical wisdom, and the linkage between Lady Wisdom of chapters 8–9 and the woman of chapter 31 is impressive.

The Prologue (Chs 1–9)

The primary emphasis of the prologue is that wisdom, meaning knowledge of the right way to live, is something that can be learned – and must be learned (1.5, 8; 2.1–5; etc.). This may seem a rather obvious and unnecessary point to make; but in fact it is not difficult to think of alternative attitudes: for example, that ethical behaviour is a matter of instinct, personality or temperament, or that it is purely a matter of divine enablement, or that it is justifiable or meaningful only within a religious context. This belief in the possibility of acquiring wisdom by study is the fundamental datum of the book, for on it is built the very existence of the book itself, as a manual of wisdom instruction.

It is an extension of this view that the wisdom that is worth having is not very difficult to attain; as the figure of Lady Wisdom says, 'Whoever looks for me can find me' (8.17). It is accessible to the young (note the typical address to 'my son', in 5.1 for instance). It can be acquired by effort (2.2; 6.6), though generally it is thought of as surrounding people and constantly being offered to them; they need only pay attention and take care not to ignore or forget it (3.1; 4.2, 21). There is no question about what is and what is not wisdom; it is not open to debate.

The prologue also handles the issue of the origin of wisdom, but it does not take up an unequivocal position. On the one hand, wisdom is what is learned as a child from one's parents, father and mother both (1.8; 4.3–4; etc.); though, admittedly, as far as the prologue goes, the teaching of the parents seems to be largely about the desirability of acquiring wisdom rather than about the content of wisdom itself. On the other hand, the prologue is at pains to point out that the wisdom so acquired is divine in its origin: this means that the wisdom one learns is in fact largely (or fundamentally; interpretations of 1.7 differ) religious reverence, the 'fear of Yahweh' (1.7; 2.1–5; 3.7). These two statements on the origin of wisdom are of course not logically incompatible, but neither are they obviously connected.

An extension of the idea that wisdom comes from God is that the wisdom one learns is in some sense *his* wisdom. Hence the portrait of the figure of Wisdom as God's female assistant at creation, an 'executive' (if that is how the word at 8.30 should be translated) devising plans for the structures of the universe. The thought is not particularly subtle: if God created the world 'by wisdom' or 'in his wisdom' – which is to say, wisely – then we may regard God's wisdom as an adjunct to God himself, even to the extent of personifying it (as one might say, 'My courage let me down'). What does call for an imaginative leap, or, shall we say, nerve, is to allege that the kind of humdrum wisdom that Proverbs recommends, enabling its clients to scrape by in everyday affairs more agreeably, is somehow the same kind of thing that brought the universe to completion.

That is to say, there is an unmistakable mystical quality about the figure of Wisdom which attempts to persuade readers that its contents are not just piecemeal snippets of advice about laziness or envy but a whole, coherent worldview. It is perhaps not surprising that at this point the language of the emotions comes into play, especially the emotions of joy and love. Previously in the book, the getting of wisdom had been depicted as an essentially intellectual activity and as the performance of right ethical behaviour. Now there is the idea of calling Wisdom one's 'sister' (7.4) – or 'girlfriend' rather, since the term seems to be used in the more erotic sense; of Wisdom at creation delighting in the work of the Almighty and enjoying an affectionate relationship with him (8.30–1); and of her 'loving' those who love her (8.17).

As a foil to the figure of Wisdom is that of her opposite number, Dame Folly, represented as equally eager for the attentions of young men, but as a 'foreign woman' or prostitute (7.5–27; 9.13–18). The gaining of wisdom is hereby portrayed not as a simple matter of the gradual accumulation of life skills, but as a life-and-death, hearts-and-minds struggle between two opposing principles, wisdom and folly, for the allegiance of humans. In this way also the wisdom enterprise is given some kind of cosmic dimension.

The Sentence Proverbs (Chs 10–31)

A fundamental perspective on these chapters of the book is that they are instantiations of what is said of Wisdom in the prologue. This means that the sentences do not stand alone as individual examples of Israelite ethics, but only have meaning within the framework given them by the book. So, for example, none of these proverbs can be claiming to be 'truth' or even 'commandment', at least not in any absolute sense; rather, they are examples of what one must know if one is to live wisely. They are directed to a practical end, and they stand under the sign of the conditional: *if* you want length of days and years of life, then these are the things you must know (3.2).

The most prominent theological theme of the sentence proverbs is the doctrine of retribution. This is the basic element in Hebrew ethics, that rightdoing and wrongdoing incur reward or punishment. However crude such a doctrine may be, it should perhaps be seen as a way of emphasizing the practicality and seriousness of ethical decisions. Doing the right thing is a matter not just of conforming to a rule, but of acting with a view to consequences. Given a choice between an ethical theory that simply maintains that one should do good because that is the right thing to do, and one that argues that one should do good because the outcome is better if one does, it is hard not to prefer the second. The fact that there is a lot of evidence against the *truth* of the second theory is not a great criticism of it, for such theories are more a matter of positioning oneself before the onrush of events rather than of drawing logical inferences in patient hindsight.

An important function of the proverb is to persuade us that there are underlying patterns in life, patterns which are not obvious before they are pointed out. The first time that we see pride leading to a fall, for instance, it does not occur to us that this may be an *example* of anything: it is just a one-off event. Without the proverb it may take many such episodes for us to see a common theme; indeed we may never analyse a string of events as pride going before a fall unless we have the formulation of the proverb to structure our thoughts. We might have been thrown off the track by noticing cases where this did not seem to happen. The proverb filters out contrary data in the interests of manageable generalities. Once the proverb exists, it becomes a resource for living, in the following way: we know that it will not always be true, for proverbs are not infallible *truths*, but we do know that it is an observable tendency. Once we have the proverb, we cannot help asking, when we observe what we would call pride, Is that person heading for a fall? And we cannot help feeling that a fall is somehow fitting. We have taken on board, quite often unreflectingly, the moral outlook of the proverb.

Proverbs, it can be seen, stands on the side of tradition against experimentation. It sets itself forth as the teaching of a parent to a child, as the wisdom of a former generation, itself learned from a yet earlier generation. Thus the father's instruction is explicitly said to be the very instruction he received from his father (4.1–5). Putting this positively, we can say that wisdom stands for not having to find everything out for yourself by making all your own mistakes. Putting it more negatively, we could say that wisdom stands for submission to authorities and against flexibility, critical reflection, or novelty.

There is a certain rationalism in wisdom as presented in Proverbs. The work sets itself up as a testimony to order and reason, as a monument to a belief that the world, and especially the world of humans, is patient of explanation. There is optimism in its confidence that by observation, application and study wisdom may be acquired and the world's secrets unlocked. There is a confidence that the ways of God follow due and reasonable processes, and that therefore the person trained in wisdom will be able to predict how and when God will act, whether with reward or punishment. Ecclesiastes and Job, in their different ways, take issue with this central element in the outlook of Proverbs.

Ecclesiastes

While Proverbs affirms that wisdom is the path to life, Ecclesiastes asks, in effect, 'And what is life the path to?' Answer: 'Death.' Everything, therefore, that wisdom stands for has to be rethought from the vantage point of the inevitability of death.

This does not amount to any kind of refutation of Proverbs. Ecclesiastes has no doubt that 'wisdom excels folly as light excels darkness' (2.13); but it does constitute a certain relativizing of Proverbs' commitment to wisdom. How can the one important thing in life be to gain what is inevitably going to be, in the end, lost?

The only way of coping with the problem is to adopt an view of life that does not see it as the pursuit of acquisition, whether wisdom, wealth or whatever. Hence Ecclesiastes' proposal of the category of 'enjoyment': 'There is nothing better for a man than that he should eat and drink, and find enjoyment in his toil' (2.24). For enjoyment is not a cumulative possession or a process leading to a goal which can then be annihilated; enjoyment comes into being in the course of living, along with the activity that produces it, and so it cannot be lost; it has already been created and it has already been used up.

It is not easy to come to grips with the book of Ecclesiastes by examining its structure. The argument of the book weaves about so delicately that no simple outline can be presented. But one way of analysing the thought of the book is to study its distinctive terminology.

Vanity

This term (*hebel*, literally 'breath') is a fundamental concept for Ecclesiastes. It signifies primarily that things are empty, light – as is breath; but sometimes also that they are transitory – as, again, breath is.

In what does the 'emptiness' of vanity consist? Some have thought that the term refers to the meaninglessness of existence, but perhaps it is a little more precise than that. It is most illuminating to see this as a term for the 'absurd', in the sense that, in human affairs, actions do not lead to reasonable and predictable consequences. If it is the case that what befalls the fool, namely death, befalls the wise also (2.15), this is an instance of the 'absurd' as expressed in this century by Beckett or Camus. The common fate of the fool and the wise leads the 'Preacher' immediately to the question, 'Why then have I been so very wise?' That is to say, recognition of the absurd inevitably calls into question the presuppositions of the wisdom teaching. It is not the wisdom teaching itself that is challenged, for wisdom is without question better than folly; but its presupposition, that one should strive for what is better. Ecclesiastes can hardly support *striving* for wisdom if the final outcome is to be the loss of what one has striven for.

Ecclesiastes' first example of the absurd appears early in the book: 'What does man gain by all the toil with which he toils under the sun?' (1.3) It is *absurd* that a whole lifetime of activity should leave nothing to show, no residual 'gain' once the person is dead. The natural order of the world is perpetually renewed, loss in one place being compensated for by gain somewhere else, rivers running into the sea and being fed again by the same waters, winds blowing from one quarter and then shifting around to blow from the other (1.5–7). The point here is not the aimlessness of nature, but the contrast with the human experience, in which loss cannot be compensated for but is permanent; among humans, there is in the end 'no remembrance', nothing surviving out of a whole life.

The second parade example of 'vanity' is the famous depiction of the 'times' in 3.1–9. This is not, as is often thought, a recommendation of the appropriate times for various activities, as if it meant 'a *right* time' to weep or laugh; rather, it is that, despite the huge variety of human activities, from which one might think that something at least would survive, the question has to be asked at the end, 'What gain has the worker from his toil?' (3.9). The reality is that no surplus remains after death; the sum of everything is zero. Life is therefore *absurd*.

It is often thought that the analysis of everything as 'vanity' is the essence of Ecclesiastes' position, and indeed the appearance of the phrase 'vanity of vanities' (i.e. 'extreme vanity') as a key phrase both at the very beginning of the text (1.2) and as what appears to be a summarizing conclusion (12.8) suggests that strongly. If that were indeed the case, Ecclesiastes would be nothing but the utter pessimist he is sometimes said to be. It is, however, a grave misunderstanding of him not to see that 'vanity' is just his starting-point, and that his finishing-point, the recommendation of 'enjoyment', is very far distant from that.

'Portion' or 'Lot'

To recognize that there is no 'gain' to show from life, and that therefore life is 'absurd' or 'vanity', is not in itself to affirm that life is depressing or unbearable. Ecclesiastes makes the surprising move of not bemoaning the fact that life adds to zero or death but of affirming that this is how it is meant to be. What we have, this existence that adds to nothing, bounded by birth and death, is no accident but what we have been given. It is the package or 'portion' that each individual has been given by God. Life consists of the 'days of your vain life [i.e. the days from which no lasting gain results] which he [God] has given you under the sun [i.e. so long as you live], because that is your portion [*heleq*] in life [i.e. consisting of life]' (9.9; cf. also 5.18–19). This means to say that life, however 'absurd' in this technical sense, is not be reckoned as cruel fate or a savage joke, but as God's gift. Though life is *absurd*, it is *given* to humans.

One does not have to be religious to see this stance as a possible option, even if one has decided on the 'vanity' of life. For, as surely as life ends in death, so surely is death preceded by life. The question is, what is to be done about these two facts? Is one to bewail the fact that everything one does leads in the end to the grave, or to rejoice in the fact that up to the very moment of death there is the opportunity to experience the multifariousness of life?

'Work'

This term ('*amal*), often translated 'toil', does indeed sometimes refer to hard labour as distinct from pleasure (4.7), but much more frequently it means simply 'activity'; so in 1.3 the question can be translated, 'What does a human gain from all the activity in which that human is occupied throughout life?' In that sense '*amal* is not antithetic to pleasure, and pleasure can actually be found in '*amal*. Thus in 3.13, 'it is God's gift to man that every one should eat and drink and take pleasure in all his toil [activity]', or in 5.18, 'what I have seen to be good and fitting is to eat and drink and find enjoyment in all the toil with which one toils [activity with which one is active] under the sun the few days of his life which God has given him, for this is his lot'.

This means to say that, though life is *absurd*, it is *given* to humans for the sake of *activity*.

'Enjoyment'

'Enjoyment' in Ecclesiastes has no negative connotation, as if it meant feckless laughter. Rather it is viewed as the appropriate behaviour in the circumstances about life which the book has uncovered. Pleasure in activity is in fact the reward for the activity (2.10). Unlike Proverbs, where reward is envisaged as something that follows after an act, Ecclesiastes sees the reward as the experiencing of the act, or, rather, the experiencing of it to the full, the appreciation of it. Enjoyment is of no use (2.2), indeed, for to think of it as useful would be to fall prey to the idea of 'gain' or 'profit' as the significance of life.

Ecclesiastes sees this 'enjoyment' of activity as itself a divine gift: 'Every man also to whom God has given wealth and possessions and power to enjoy them, and to accept his lot and find enjoyment in his toil – this is the gift of God' (5.19; cf. 9.9). Humans should 'eat . . . bread with enjoyment, and drink . . . wine with a merry heart; for God has already approved what you do' (9.7). How could he not approve, when the ability to experience, and to savour the experience, is what is implanted in humans by their creator? Even more fundamental than the ethics of right and wrong – which is Proverbs' concern – is the understanding of the meaning of life.

It perhaps needs to be said that the repeated references to eating and drinking should not be taken as signifying some gluttonous or self-indulgent hedonism on Ecclesiastes' part; these are just conventional examples of human activity, and stand for the whole range of legitimate behaviour.

Ecclesiastes should be seen therefore as a critic of the moral simplism of the doctrine of retribution as expounded in the Proverbs. He criticizes it not so much because he thinks it is false but because he thinks its horizons are too constricted: it concerns itself entirely with the lifetime of the individual and does not bring into its reckoning the fact of death. When the reality of death is taken into account (and Ecclesiastes is one of the few books of the Hebrew Bible that takes death truly seriously), life cannot any longer be regarded as a quest for wisdom. Neither need one suppose that the reality of death must cast a shadow over the whole of life, for no other biblical author can offer such a vigorous recommendation of pleasure or so weighty a theological defence of it. (For further discussion of Ecclesiastes, see chapter 14.)

Job

Job confronts the doctrine of retribution much more directly than does Ecclesiastes. It is true that the book is about the problem of suffering, especially if we define the problem of suffering not as the question of its cause or origin but as the more existential question of how one is to behave when one is suffering. But to cast the problem of the book as essentially concerned with the issue of suffering distracts attention somewhat from its critique of the wisdom theology; for Job may even more properly be said to focus on the question of moral order in the universe, of which the question of suffering is perhaps no more than an instance.

The question of moral order is the question of whether the doctrine of retribution is true – whether, that is to say, there is any rule whereby goodness is rewarded and wickedness is punished, whether there is an exact correspondence between one's behaviour and one's destiny. In one form or another this doctrine is shared by most human beings, not just religious people, since it is the foundation of most people's childhood upbringing: certain behaviour will earn rewards, while certain other behaviour will bring pain or disaster. There is indeed a mismatch between this principle, which we seem to require in some form or other for the world to have coherence, and the realities that contradict the principle; and to this mismatch both the narrator and the characters of Job turn their attention. Each of them has a distinctive standpoint on this question of retribution or the moral order.

Being nothing but an extended discussion of this theological issue, Job is the most consistently theological work in the Old Testament. Its chief literary feature is that it does not expound or defend a dogma from one point of view, but portrays a debate in which conflicting points of view are put forward, none of them being unambiguously presented as preferable to the others. This makes it perhaps the most intellectually demanding book of the Hebrew Bible, requiring of its readers a mental flexibility and even a willingness, in the end, to be left with no unequivocal message.

But it is not only a work of intellectual vigour: it is also a literary master-piece that belongs with the classics of world literature, with the *Iliad*, the *Divine Comedy* and *Paradise Lost*. In design it has both the form of an un-sophisticated prose narrative, which none the less contains intriguing surprises, and that of a series of subtle speeches in poetry of great delicacy and power. The interplay between prose and poetry, between naïveté and rhetorical finesse, mirrors the interplay among the six characters in the book: Job, the four friends, God – and the narrator.

The Starting Point

The narrator in fact founds the whole story upon the doctrine of retribution. Job, the wealthiest of all orientals, is equally the most pious; there is no coincidence here, the narrator means to say. Job 'was blameless and upright, one who feared God and turned away from evil' (1.1). That is 'deed'; and here is consequence: 'There were born to him seven sons and three daughters [the perfect family]. He had seven thousand sheep, three thousand camels', and so on (vv. 2–3). There is the doctrine of retribution in the first two sentences, wearing its more acceptable face: piety brings prosperity. Into that prosperity there then breaks on one day the most terrible of calamities: Job loses all he has – which is not only his children and his wealth, but, worse than that, his social significance and, worse still, his reputation as a righteous man. For the other, and more unlovely, side of this principle of world order is that suffering is caused by sin.

Up to this moment Job has believed in retribution, but now, unshakably convinced that he has done nothing to deserve his misery, he is launched on a quest for another moral order. The doctrine has failed the test of reality – reality, that is, as he experiences it. Job's three friends, too, find their dogma challenged by Job's experience, for they have always taken Job at face value, as a pious man.

What the friends have in common is their unquestioning belief that suffering is the result of sin. Their doctrine of retribution, that sin produces punishment, is also reversible: see a man suffering and you can be sure he has deserved it. There is no doubt in their minds of the order: Job's misery is by the book. But there is room for difference of opinion over what precisely Job's sufferings signify.

Eliphaz

Eliphaz, the first friend, starts from the assumption that the innocent never suffer permanently: 'Who that was innocent ever perished? Or where were the upright ever cut off?' (4.7). For him Job is essentially one of the innocent, so whatever wrong Job has done must be comparatively trivial, and so too his suffering is bound to be soon over (v. 6). Job is blameless on the whole, pious in general. Even the most innocent of humans, such as Job, must expect to suffer deservedly on occasion.

Bildad

The second friend, Bildad, is if anything even more convinced of the doctrine of retribution, for he has just now seen a compelling exemplification of it. Job's children have died, cut off in their prime; it is the classical picture of the fate of the wicked: 'your children have sinned against him, he has delivered them into the power of their transgression' (8.4). The very fact that Job still lives is proof that he is no gross sinner, like his children. However serious his suffering, it is not as bad as it might be; therefore his sin is not as serious as he may fear.

Zophar

Now, whereas Eliphaz has set Job's suffering in the context of his whole life (his suffering is just a temporary pinprick), and Bildad has set it in the context of the fate of his family (the children are dead, Job is not), Zophar, the third friend, perceives no such context for Job's pain. The fact is, he would say, that Job is suffering, and suffering is inevitably the product of sin. To contextualize Job's suffering and try to set it in proportion is ultimately to trivialize it. Zophar is for principle rather than proportion; and the bottom line is that Job is a sinner suffering hard at this moment for his sin. Since Job refuses to acknowledge his sin, claiming that his 'doctrine is pure' and that he is 'clean in God's eyes' (11.4), it follows that he is a secret sinner. In fact, if only the truth were known, it would no doubt transpire that Job is a worse sinner than anyone suspects (vv. 5–6). For all his talk about divine secrets, 'higher than heaven – what can you do? Deeper than Sheol – what can you know?' (v. 8), Zophar holds a theology of the essential knowability of God. God's wisdom is not of a different kind from human wisdom; it only means that he knows more about humankind than anyone realizes, and that means more about their sins. Where there is suffering but no visible reason, we can be sure, says Zophar, that God's wisdom holds the reason. What is more, it will not be some mysterious, ineffable, transcendental reason, but a reason that could easily be comprehended by a human being if only God would 'open his lips'. So, while we cannot always be sure why God is punishing people, we can be sure that when they are suffering he is punishing them for some reason or another, never without cause or gratuitously.

Zophar has in addition a more distinctive contribution to make: it concerns the role of God's mercy in the outworking of the principle of retribution. Job might be tempted to think that, even though there is doubtless no escape from the working of the law of retribution, perhaps he could appeal for mercy to soften its blows. But what you must know, says Zophar, is that 'God exacts of you less than your guilt deserves' (11.6). Any mercy that God is going to allow to temper justice has already been taken into account when the law of retribution comes into play. Discounts for mercy's sake are included in the price you pay.

Elihu

Another participant in the dialogue enters only after the first three friends have completed all they have to say, Elihu, the young man, at first 'timid and afraid to declare [his] opinion' (32.6), in the end intervenes, realizing that 'It is not the old that are wise' but rather 'it is the spirit in a man, the breath of the Almighty, that makes him understand' (vv. 8–9). His point about retribution is that it is not some universal balancing-mechanism that operates ruthlessly and inescapably, but rather a channel by which God speaks to humans. Suffering is not so much a mystery, more a revelation.

Sometimes, for example, God speaks in visions of the night, in terrifying nightmares, to warn people against committing sins they are contemplating. At other times, a person may be 'chastened with pain upon his bed' (33.19), as Job is. The purpose of such suffering is not retribution, but to lead the sinner to confess, to be restored to favour with God, and to praise God publicly (vv. 26–7). The other friends, and Job, have been narrow-minded in their view of retribution as a tit-for-tat process. Look to its design, says Elihu, and you will find that it is an instrument of divine communication.

For Elihu as for the three other theologians, the retribution principle stands unshaken by Job's experience. Eliphaz has allowed a redefinition of 'innocent' to mean 'well, hardly ever wicked', Bildad has stressed that the law of retribution has a certain sensitivity (if you are not extemely wicked, you don't actually die), while Zophar has declared that the principle of retribution is not at all a rigorous *quid pro quo*, for a percentage of the punishment that should light upon you has already been deducted for mercy's sake. Even Elihu, while recognizing that there are more important theological truths than strict retribution, still affirms its validity.

Job

By contrast with the friends' single-minded and static positions, Job's mind in confused, flexible and experimental. In every one of his eleven speeches he adopts a different posture, psychologically and theologically. In the end he admits that he has nothing to rely upon, not even God – nothing except his conviction of his own innocence.

His first, religious instinct, is to accept what has happened to him as God's doing, and to bless God even for calamity: 'the LORD gave, and the LORD has taken away; blessed be the name of the LORD' (1.21; cf. 2.10). His second thoughts are more reflective and theological, because he realizes that order has collapsed about him. When in chapter 3 he wishes he had never been born, it is not mainly because he is suffering from his physical illness and from the grief of bereavement; he is expressing a psychic reaction to disorder. Since it is too late now to strike his birthdate out of the calendar, which is the first thought that occurs to him (3.6), in his second speech he cries out for God to kill him and so put an end to his disorientation: 'O . . . that it would please God to crush me, that he would let loose his hand and cut me off!' (6.8–9).

When nothing makes sense any longer, and especially when the most fundamental moral order of all – the principle of retribution – is subverted, and disproportion reigns, there is nothing to live for (7.11–16).

Even so, to have nothing to live for, and to live without order, does not mean for Job that he can have no desire. In his third speech he openly desires what he lacks: a declaration that he is innocent. It is a desire impossible of fulfillment, but it his desire all the same. The problem with

God is not just that he is super-wise and super-powerful (9.19); it is rather that he is by settled design hostile to his creation. As Job puts it, sardonically, 'Being God, he never withdraws his anger' (v. 13). The ancient myths were right, thinks Job, when they recounted that the first thing God ever did was to create the world by slaying the chaos monster, in a primeval act of aggression (v. 13). Not only toward creation at large but towards Job in particular God's attitude has been, since Job's conception, one of perpetual hostility and cruelty, masked indeed by an apparent tender concern (v. 8). It is hopeless to seek vindication, he says; so he will not do it. Yet in the very act of saying to God, 'It is hopeless to ask you for what I deserve', Job is in reality demanding what he believes he is entitled to.

Something has happened to Job in expressing his hopelessness. For in his next speech (chs 12–14) he has moved to a decision that, come what may, he will present his case to God. 'No doubt he will slay me; I have no hope; yet I will defend my ways to his face' (13.15). His decision is more startling than that, however. He cannot literally defend himself against the pain which God is inflicting on him; he can only defend himself *verbally*. Since God is not *saying* anything, Job can only defend himself verbally by creating a scenario where both he and God are obliged to speak, each in his own defence. In short, Job summons God to a lawsuit! He challenges God to give an account of himself – to explain what Job has done wrong to deserve such suffering. Since Job believes he has done nothing wrong, implicitly he challenges God to confess that he and not Job is the criminal.

This is a case that must be heard promptly, for Job does not believe he can have much longer to live, considering how God is buffeting him. If Job's name is not cleared now it never will be, and certainly not in any afterlife.

What is now certain, in all the uncertainty that surrounds him, is that his word of challenge to God has been uttered – and cannot be unsaid. It is written into the heavenly record, and stands as his witness to himself in heaven. It is his own assertion of his innocence that he is referring to when he says in his fifth speech (chs 16–17), 'Even now, behold, my witness is in heaven, my advocate [RSV "he that vouches for me"] is on high . . . my eyes pour out tears to God, that he would maintain the right of a man with God . . .' (16.19–21). It is the same affirmation of innocence that in his sixth speech (ch 19) he speaks of as his 'advocate': 'I know that my advocate [RSV "Redeemer"] lives' (19.25). He has in mind here no heavenly figure who will defend his cause before God, since there is none – and least of all God himself, who has proved to be nothing but his enemy. He is compelled to undertake his own defence, and leave his own affidavit to speak in his behalf.

The climax to Job's defence of his own innocence and his demand to God that he explain why he has been tormenting Job comes in the last of Job's speeches (chs 29–31). Here Job reviews his past life in a final attempt to discover whether there can be any cause in himself for the suffering he has been enduring. Whatever area of his life he considers, he can judge himself blameless. He brings his speeches to a conclusion with a mighty oath affirming his righteousness. Still working within the metaphorical scenario of the lawsuit, he imagines himself signing a declaration: '(Here is my signature [to my oath of exculpation]! let the Almighty answer me!) Oh, that I had the indictment written by my adversary!' (31.35). So brief would any bill of charges against Job be, and so trivial would be the faults that could be levelled against him, that Job would be proud for all the world to see how little he had offended against God and how greatly he had fulfilled the ideal of human piety: 'Surely I would carry [the indictment] on my shoulders; I would bind it on me as a crown; I would give him an account of all my steps; like a prince I would approach him' (vv. 36–7).

Job's impressive and convincing protestation of innocence poses a desperate problem for the moral order of the universe, however. For, if Job is innocent, the doctrine of retribution is false; and there is no other principle available to replace it.

God

Only God can address the problem. He is compelled, by Job's metaphor of the lawsuit and by the logic of the author's narrative, to enter the conversation. But what divine word can both defend Job's innocence – to which God committed himself in chapter 1 – and at the same time affirm the working of a moral law in the world?

In reality, God's speeches (chs 38–41) are remarkable as much for what they omit as for what they contain. There is, in the first place, not a word of the retributive principle here. This must mean that it is not so fundamental to understanding the world as all the previous characters of the book have thought. It must also mean that it is not entirely wrong, either. If God were passionately in favour of it or violently against it, would he not have had to mention it?

In the second place, the divine speeches are notorious for their insistence on asking questions rather than giving answers, quite apart from the seeming irrelevance of the questions themselves to the fundamental issues of the book. Such questions as these are the substance of God's words: 'Where were you when I laid the foundation of the earth? . . . Have you entered into the springs of the sea . . . ? . . . Do you know when the mountain goats bring forth?' (38.4, 16; 39.1). Those – and suchlike excursions into cosmology and natural history – are, amazingly enough, the substance of the divine speeches. The purpose of God's parade of unknown and unknowable features of the natural world can hardly be to browbeat Job with dazzling displays of his power and intelligence – for Job has not for a minute doubted that God is wise and strong, too wise and strong indeed for human comfort and for his own good. Rather, God invites Job to reconsider the mystery and complexity – and, often, sheer unfathomableness – of the world that God has created.

God's questions to Job are arranged in three distinct sequences. First there is the series that focuses on Job's non-participation in creation, with questions such as 'who shut in the sea with doors?' (38.8). These mean that Job is not qualified to hold views on the nature of the universe. Secondly, there is the series on the management of the world, among which we find, 'Have you commanded the morning since your days began? . . . Can you bind the chains of the Pleiades, or loose the cords of Orion?' (38.12, 31). Job has never organized the appearance of a new day; how can he speak then about the governance of the universe? Thirdly, there is the sequence of questions about the animals, lion and raven, goat and hind, wild ass, ostrich, war horse, hawk and eagle. Through these questions Job's gaze is deliberately fastened upon animals that serve no purpose in the human economy but are, instead, useless to humans, their habits mysterious to us. In these chapters there is no mention of those domesticated animals, sheep, ass and camel, that Job possessed in abundance and knew the ways of. The subject here is wild animals, the purpose of whose existence is unintelligible to humans. By the end of the second divine speech (40.7–41.34) the focus has come to rest upon two animals, Behemoth and Leviathan, hippopotamus and crocodile, symbols of primeval chaos, who of all the animal creation are supremely wild and terrible.

The point must be that hippopotamus and crocodile, however alarming, are part of God's creation. God expects Job to realize, and Job is not slow at grasping the point, that the natural order – the principles on which the world was created – is analogous to the moral order, the principles according to which it is governed. In both these orders, there is much that is incomprehensible to humans, even threatening their existence, but all of it is the work of a wise God who has made the world the way it is for his own inscrutable purposes. Innocent suffering is a hippopotamus. The only sense it makes, it makes to God, for it is not amenable to human rationality.

Job has no right to an explanation for his suffering, any more than he has a right to have the purpose of crocodiles explained to him. He is not even entitled to be told whether he is being punished for some fault he has committed, or whether he is indeed the innocent sufferer he believes himself to be. The order of creation sets the standard for the moral order of the universe; and that is, that God must be allowed to know what he is doing, and lies under no obligation to give any account of himself.

What does this viewpoint expressed by the character God do to the doctrine of retribution? It neither affirms nor denies it; but it marginalizes it. In Job's case, at least, the doctrine of retribution is beside the point. We, the readers, have known from the beginning of the book that Job is innocent, for the narrator and God have both affirmed it (1.1, 8; 2.3); and Job himself, though suffering as if he were a wicked man, is unshakably convinced of his innocence. We and Job, therefore, know that the doctrine of retribution is not wholly true. Yet God never tells Job that he accepts Job's innocence; so Job never learns what God's view of the doctrine is. All that Job learns from God is that the issue is not retribution, but whether God can be trusted to run his world.

Job capitulates. His religious instinct for reverence which prompted his initial acceptance of his misfortune (1.21; 2.10) had become overwhelmed by his more intellectual and theological search for meaning. His religion and his theology are suddenly able to cohere. He replies to God, '"Who is this that hides counsel [darkens the divine design by words] without knowledge?" [So you have rightly said, Yahweh.] Therefore I have uttered what I did not understand, things too wonderful for me, which I did not know . . . I had heard of thee by the hearing of the ear, but now my eye sees thee' (42.3, 5). In other words: I knew you, but did not know you; what I knew of your workings (through the principle of retribution) was real knowledge, but it was not the whole truth about you; the whole truth is that you are ultimately unknowable, and your reasons are in the last analysis incomprehensible. In v. 6, as it should probably be translated, Job melts in reverence before God and receives his comfort, even while sitting in dust and ashes.

Religiously Job finds this position acceptable, even actually comforting: to bow in awe before a mysterious God he cannot grasp, perceiving only the outskirts of his ways' (26.14).This is the Job of the prologue, but with a difference: the religious instinct is now supported by a theological realignment. Now he not only feels, but also has come to believe, that it makes sense that God should not be wholly amenable to human reason. It was the theology of wild animals that convinced him, the inexplicability of whole tracts of the natural order, the apparent meaninglessness of creatures useless to humankind but unquestionably created by God nevertheless. Now he knows that that was a paradigm for all knowledge of God.

The Finishing-Point

The book does not conclude at this point, however. The narrator has yet to tell us of the reversal of Job's fortunes. There is more to this happy ending of the book than at first appears, for the issues of the moral governance of the world and the doctrine of retribution are still on the agenda. What this concluding episode does for these issues is, surprisingly, to reinstate the dogma of retribution as the principle according to which the world operates. For the story shows at its end that the righteous man Job is also the most prosperous, just as he was at the beginning. Job is here described as the 'servant' of the Lord, who has spoken of God 'what is right', unlike the friends (42.7–8); and when he has prayed for forgiveness of the friends' 'folly' he is rewarded with twice the possessions he had to begin with (v. 10).

It must be admitted that the ending of the book undercuts to some extent the divine speeches of chapters 38–41; for, although God has implied that questions of justice and retribution are not the central ones, the narrator's concluding word is that, after all, the principle of retribution stands almost unscathed by the experience of Job. By rights, according to the principle, the innocent Job should never have suffered at all; so the principle was partially defective. Yet in the end the principle becomes enshrined in the history of Job, and he functions as a prime witness to its general validity. Even if it does not explain human fates in every instance, in the main it is affirmed by the book of Job as the truth about the moral universe.

What, finally, of the disclosure in the opening chapters that the suffering of Job has nothing whatsoever to do with Job's own character and behaviour – except, paradoxically of course, that he of all humans least deserves what happens to him? Job suffers in fact because of some conflict in heaven, which can only be resolved by an experiment upon a human being to see whether humans are ever pious disinterestedly, without regard to the consequences. The sole possible means of testing whether piety depends on prior prosperity, or whether a human might possibly continue in reverence for God even if there was no reward to be gained from it, is to find a pious and prosperous person who can then be deprived of that prosperity. And Job fits the bill admirably on both counts.

So what is being tested in Job is the universal validity of the principle of retribution. Given that right behaviour leads to reward, and that piety leads to prosperity, can right behaviour lead to anything else? Even if it is true that suffering is the consequence of wickedness, can it ever be the consequence of anything else? Piety, for instance? The doctrine as formulated by the friends, as also no doubt by the majority of teachers of wisdom, never considered such questions, but rashly transformed undoubted truths into universal generalizations. So the book of Job can be seen as bringing into the spotlight logical fallacies that have attached themselves to the doctrine. Its aim is not merely the systematization of thought; it seeks primarily for the right standards for the estimation of individuals, and perhaps also for the release of the socially ostracized from unjust criticism.

Conclusion

The collection of wisdom books is especially interesting for their dialectical relations. That is to say, it is as if they were engaged in a dialogue with one another. They all speak a common language, the language of proverb, speech and argument; and they share a common concern, for making sense of human behaviour and destiny and for justifying the ways of God to humans. They represent the intellectual tradition in Israel, appealing neither to divine revelation not to religious interpretations of Israel's history nor to the experience of the divine in cult, but to everyday experience, observation and logic.

Nevertheless, though they can communicate, they do not agree. Proverbs is obviously the norm from which the other two books deviate; and Proverbs is also the most uncritical. The stance of the other two books is much more self-aware; they give the sense of having a programme that needs to be presented and argued for, whereas Proverbs takes for granted that all right-minded people automatically assent to its theological position.

Neither Ecclesiastes nor Job subverts the principle of retribution so central to Proverbs. Ecclesiastes deflects attention from it, to be sure, by arguing that the quest for wisdom, however valuable, cannot explain the meaning of life; and, if the quest for wisdom is not the principal thing, then the truth about retribution, which is in large measure what wisdom wants to inculcate, cannot be a truly fundamental issue. There is an important sense, according to Ecclesiastes, in which the doctrine of retribution is actually untrue: since the righteous and the wicked come to the same end, in the long run there is no such thing as appropriate reward and punishment. The Preacher does not want to deny that there is often within human life a reasonable connection between act and consequence (e.g. 2.26); he only wants to say that it is not predictable and reliable, and that in the end it fails to operate at all.

Job seems, for the greater part of its course, to be a very much more frontal attack on the doctrine. The case of the man Job in his suffering shows how gravely wrong the doctrine can be: a man who even bears God's certificate as righteous, more upright indeed than any other human, is by the doctrine made out to be a dreadful sinner. Without the divine speeches or the epilogue, the book would be an implacable enemy of Proverbs. Yet the divine speeches signal to us that, rightly to evaluate the doctrine of retribution, there must be more on the agenda than that single item. God turns the attention away altogether from the question of correspondence between act and consequence, insisting that the moral order of the universe is a matter of divine design which is by its very nature not accessible to human comprehension. The epilogue to the book, taking yet another tack, affirms that the righteous man Job is in the end rewarded, with blessings far beyond those he had enjoyed at the beginning. So the book could be seen, from one angle, as a stout defence of the principle of retribution and, from another, as a drastic modification of it that denies its general validity. To deny the general validity of the doctrine comes perilously near to denying any validity to it at all; for, unless it may be relied upon to explain all particular acts of behaviour, it ceases to be a law, a statement of order, a plan, a design, and becomes no more than a statistical probability.

None of the wisdom books says as much, or so deeply, taken alone as when it is read as part of a collection. Even if no one unequivocal truth emerges from the welter of argument, no serious reader is able to escape from these texts without having been personally interrogated.

FURTHER READING

Crenshaw, J. L. 1981: *Old Testament Wisdom. An Introduction.*
Eaton, J. H. 1985: *Job.*
Fontaine, C. 1982: *Traditional Sayings in the Old Testament.*
Habel, N. C. 1985: *The Book of Job: a Commentary.*
Williams, J. G. 1981: *Those Who Ponder Proverbs: Aphoristic Thinking and Biblical Literature.*

For further reading on Ecclesiastes, see the list at the end of chapter 14.

14

The Five Megilloth

Sybil Sheridan

Preliminary Reading   *The Song of Songs; Ruth; Lamentations; Qoheleth (Ecclesiastes); Esther.*

The title Five Megilloth ('five scrolls') designates the books Song of Songs (Song of Solomon), Ruth, Lamentations, Qoheleth (Ecclesiastes) and Esther. Originally these books were found in chronological order among the other books of the Writings (Talmud, Baba Bathra, 14b) though the Septuagint places Ruth and Lamentations among the Prophets. Later manuscripts and modern Hebrew Bibles put the Five Megilloth together in the order indicated above, reflecting their liturgical use during the festival year.

The Song of Songs is read on the Sabbath during Passover because of the association of love with springtime. Ruth is read at Shavuoth (the feast of Weeks) since 1.22 refers to the beginning of the barley harvest, which also features in this festival. Lamentations has a clear connection with *Tishah Be-Ab*, the ninth of the month of Ab – the fast that remembers with deep mourning the destruction of the Temple – traditionally the saddest day in the Jewish year. The association of Qoheleth with the Sabbath during Sukkoth (Tabernacles or Booths) is less evident. Some see the charge to 'rejoice' during Sukkoth as paralleled in the phrase 'eat, drink and take pleasure'. Others observe that autumn, the decline of the year, echoes Qoheleth's sad and regretful mood. Sukkoth combines solemnity with rejoicing, just as Qoheleth combines reflection with enjoyment. Finally, Purim (14 Adar) is closely linked with the story of Esther. The reading of the Esther scroll is the main item of the day. *Ta'anith Ester*, the Fast of Esther, is kept of 13 Adar, but does not date from biblical or even Talmudic times.

The Song of Songs

The first statement, 'O that you would kiss me with the kisses of your mouth' (1.2), shocks our senses and we know at once we are encountering something different. As we read on, our suspicions are confirmed: from that first invitation to the final request, this book is about sex. So what is it doing in the Bible?

To answer this question, scholars over 2000 years have given conflicting interpretations. For commentators, both ancient and modern, the Song has provoked an exegetical free-for-all. Unique in the Bible, it has no nationalistic emphasis, and no reference to God. As profane poetry, the Song has countless parallels. In particular, songs from the ancient Indus valley civilization, and others from nineteenth-century Syria and Palestine, have provided interesting comparisons; but the poetry is not unusual. It is its place in the Bible that has created the furore.

Authorship and Date

Scholars cannot agree over an early or late date. If we examine the references to Solomon, varying conclusions can be reached:

(1)   that Solomon wrote the book himself (1.1; cf. 1 Kgs 4.32), the traditional Jewish and Christian view;
(2)   that court poets wrote it for his wedding (3.7–11; 8.11–12), around 960 BCE (Segal, 1962, 470–490);
(3)   that the book was written by critics of the king focusing either on his moral conduct (6.8; cf. 1 Kgs 11.3) or his political strategy which resulted in the division of the northern and southern kingdoms after his death.

On the other hand, all these references could be later glosses. The reference to Solomon could have been introduced to give the book some authority. Other descriptions may have been intended to create a setting in a romantic bygone age. There are interesting linguistic elements with constructions reminiscent of Aramaic and Mishnaic Hebrew, which may suggest a late date in the fourth or third century BCE. Alternatively, we may wish to argue that Aramaic was in use considerably earlier than is usually assumed; or that the Aramaisms were introduced by a late redactor. *Pardes* (garden) is a Persian word, anglicized as 'paradise'. This would suggest a date no earlier than the sixth century BCE. However, references to Tirzah, the capital of the northern kingdom before Shechem, suggest a time between 928 and 876 BCE (Gordis, 1974, 23–4). Or do we take *pardes* to be a late addition, and Tirzah as an anachronistic reference back to a bygone age?

Comparisons with other biblical books have suggested linguistic similarities with Judges, Isaiah, Job and Qoheleth (Ecclesiastes): comparison with other cultures have suggested links with Ugaritic, Egyptian, Aramaic and Greek. So, it seems we can set the book in any period from the tenth to the third century BCE.

Structure

There is one aspect upon which all scholars seem to be in agreement: namely, the high quality and consistency of the book as it now appears. The editor – or was it an *author?* – has done a good job. The traditional view assumes the book to be a single song; yet it has also been explained as a collection – fifty-four separate songs, according to a fifteenth-century German. It has been also been analysed as seven songs for the seven days of wedding-festivities; as twenty-three folksongs from different places and different periods in Israelite history, joined by the editor through refrains; as twenty-five songs arranged on a catchword principle; as an anthology of thirty-one songs with no connection between them; and as six carefully worked poems in a series of interlocking parallels (see Pope 1976, 39–54).

Mysticism and Allegory

Interpretations of the Song have on the whole been coloured by a need to justify its place in the canon. Doubt was already cast on its suitability at the council of Jamnia (*c.* 95 CE), but Rabbi Aqiba (50–135 CE), no stranger to mystical insights, jumped to its defence: 'Heaven forbid that any man in Israel ever disputed the Song of Songs . . . for the whole world is not worth the day upon which the Song of Songs was given to Israel, for all the Writings are holy but the Song of Songs is the Holy of Holies' (Mishnah Yadaim, 3.5). This final play on words became understood mystically. The Holy of Holies, the centre of the Temple and of Jewish worship, was impenetrable except by the high priest after elaborate preparations one day a year (the Day of Atonement). The Song is equally impenetrable except by one who is prepared and able to understand its secrets. The first commandment of the Bible, 'Be fruitful and multiply' (Gen 1.28), brought procreation under the jurisdiction of God and sexual intercourse became a divine act which later mystics saw as symbolic of the union of God and the worshipper. The mystical view resulted in the custom observed in Sephardi synagogues of reading the Song every Sabbath evening.

Within Christianity this interpretation ran counter to the distinction normally drawn between the sinful flesh and the spirit. Some Jewish elements were unhappy with it too and so they turned instead to allegory. The Song was seen as a description of the nature of God's love for Israel/the Church, or as a veiled history starting from the patriarchs, or as a prophecy of Jesus, from his advent to his second coming. For some time the two faiths waged war with the Song as ammunition, each using it to show how they represented the true love of God. This view of the Song as allegory is still held today, but with enormous variations of interpretation. An example of Jewish allegory is provided by the Mishnah (Ta'anith, 5.8), which interprets

> Go forth O daughters of Zion,
>   and behold King Solomon
> with the crown which his mother crowned him
>   on the day of his wedding,
>   on the day of his gladness of heart (3.11)

thus: 'on the day of his wedding – this is the giving of the law'; 'on the day of his gladness – this is the building of the Temple'.

Cultic Theories

The association of sex and religion in ancient fertility cults has suggested to some that the Song is related to the myths of Tammuz and Ishtar (Mesopotamia), or Osiris and Isis (Egypt). In these, the lovers are brother and sister (cf. 4.9f; 5.1). The myth follows the cycle of the year, culminating in the god's death and spring resurrection. The link between the Song and such myths has been conceived in terms of the following theories:

(1)   that the Song is a complete re-enactment of the Osiris myth;
(2)   that the original litany was translated into a hymn to God;
(3)   that the original was carefully demythologized and specifically national elements added;
(4)   that the context was forgotten and the author knew it only as a love song;
(5)   that it was a specifically Israelite composition, but using images that were once part of the pagan cult, much as we use Greek mythology today (see Pope, 1977, 145–53).

Literary Criticism

In opposition to cultic theories about the Song stand those that take a more literal and literary view of it. There range from the view of the Song as a play to current theories that relate it to the development of wisdom. The Song may be intended to depict a scene where Solomon tries to seduce a country girl who nevertheless remains faithful to her lover. Annotations in some fourth- and fifth-century Christian manuscripts indicate that it was then viewed as a play: the view has persisted and can be found today in the New English Bible. The Song has been seen as the story of two lovers, their wooing, the consummation and their death, or their flight from the city. It could describe Solomon's marriage culminating in the crowning of the Shulammite as his queen (Goulder, 1986). It can also be viewed as secular poetry on the theme of love (Falk, 1982). Some passages (4, 5.10–16, 6.4–9, 7.1–9) are reminiscent of modern Arabic love songs. Similarities have also been seen between the Song and ancient texts from India, Egypt and Sumeria. We could take the view that erotic literature is appropriate in a religious context and that it is only our Western minds that finds this peculiar (so Rowley, 1952). Others have concluded that the Song is totally secular, with no specific religious symbolism or explicit references to God. Considering that the love song is so international a genre, we may legitimately doubt the need for theories of direct borrowing.

Biblical Comparisons

Attempts to find a religious context are made by comparisons with other biblical literature, and again the conclusions vary greatly. The Song has been seen as an inversion of the story of Eden: the garden is central to both. Adam and Eve eat the forbidden fruit, and shame, expulsion, fear and exploitation follow; in the Song, the garden becomes a refuge from the world and the apple tree (8.5) restores the relationship between man and woman to one of equality, harmony and trust (Trible, 1973, 30–48).

Thus the Song could be a midrash or exposition of the first creation story, with its abundant descriptions of animals and vegetation and command to be fruitful. Love thus stemmed from creation and was declared to be good. Parallels to Qoheleth have also been claimed. It has been argued that both books were written in the third century BCE and react against the disillusionment of Palestinian society at that time: Qoheleth with a recommendation of 'enjoyment' (Eccles 2.24) and the Song with an escape into fantasy 8.6–7 could be a direct answer to Qoheleth's preoccupation with death – to the Song of Songs 'all is vanity except love' (Landy, 1983, 15). Similarities to Ruth and to Hosea 13–14 have been noted. There are in the book hints that it is late spring (6.11–12; 7.12–13), which may suggest a liturgical connection with Shavuoth before the current link with Passover (Goulder, 1986, 82–5). The book may be, like Ruth, a condemnation of the laws on intermarriage instituted by Ezra – the Shulammite is not only foreign, but black. The book was early connected with the ancient festival of 15 Ab, when the 'daughters of Jerusalem' would go into the vineyards and the young men followed them to find a wife (see Ta'anith 5.8). The book has also been described as an antidote to the story of David and Bathsheba (2 Sam 11), with Solomon 'atoning' for the sin of his father, David. All of these comparisons attempt to demonstrate a *religious* dimension to the book.

A Feminist View

If we look at the Song purely as literature, we find that it was written from the female point of view. The women's thoughts and desires are recorded, and generally speaking the lovemaking shows a mutuality out of keeping with a male-dominated society. Men, with the exception of Solomon, are absent from the scene. Two mothers are mentioned but no fathers. The woman speaks only to the daughters of Jerusalem. 8.6–7 suggests a stand for romantic love as against marriage for money or power – a peculiarly female view in a polygynous society where the man could have both. The love lyrics of 5.10–16 describing a man is unusual. Certain words, usually feminine, are here in the masculine; and the imagery used and its meaning in the Song corresponds with Freudian dream symbols – but symbols that occur only in the dreams of women, in the view of Dr Max Pusin (Pope, 1977, 133–4).

It could be that the Song was written by a woman for a female audience – conversations in the harem were likely to be far more explicit than those in the rare encounters between the sexes in oriental society. However, this would make its position in the Bible even more extraordinary.

There is a possible explanation in early Jewish mysticism. At the heart of mysticism is the desire for union with God – often expressed in sexual imagery. In a society where heterosexual love is the ideal, and mysticism the prerogative of the male, a problem arises. Either God must be described in female terms – such as actually happened in the case of the Shekinah, the divine presence – or man must play the female role. The latter is preferable in view of the dominant masculine language for God, encouraging the worshipper to utilize female erotic literature.

The Song is open to many such interpretations. The moral clearly is: read it for yourself, enjoy it, and reach your own conclusions.

Ruth

At first glance, the book of Ruth is no more than a 'pastorale', a gentle tale of simple folk set long ago – of Naomi, left penniless in Moab on the death of her husband and her sons; of the loyalty of her daughter-in-law Ruth; of their return to Bethlehem; of Boaz's kindness to them; and of how, on the birth of Obed, all their problems are resolved. However, there is more to the story than this.

Literary Appreciation

The book is a short story in the genre of Jonah and Tobit – short, but linguistically rich. It is complete, in that all characters fulfil their purpose, and every situation is resolved. The language presents problems – some words are in the wrong gender or person – but is lively and imaginative. The story may seem simple, but its construction is highly sophisticated.

There are six scenes, mostly of conversation. Boaz's language stands out as different (a local dialect?) from that of Ruth (classical Hebrew learnt by a foreigner?). Each scene ends with a hint of what is to come (2.22; 3.13; etc.), creating a sense of suspense that carries the narrative swiftly forward. The 'unknown kinsman', and references to David, are introduced at points of climax in the story and add to the tension and quality of the work. The book has a symmetrical plan (Bertman, 1965) through which we see a smooth progression from desire to fulfilment, from emptiness to completion.

The Stranger

Ruth is throughout the 'stranger' (1.22; 2.6, 10, 19; 4.5, 10). Leviticus 19.33 states, 'When a stranger sojourns with you in your land, you shall not do to him wrong. The stranger who sojourns with you shall be as the native among you and you shall love him as yourself: for you were strangers in the land of Egypt.' This law was not always observed, but Boaz follows it to the letter.

Ruth is more than a stranger; she is a Moabitess – a race despised in biblical literature: 'No Ammonite or Moabite shall enter the assembly of the LORD; even to the tenth generation, none belonging to them shall enter the assembly of the LORD forever' (Deut 23.3; cf. Gen 19.37, Num 25.1–9; Judg 3.12). The justification was the Moabites' ancient opposition to Israel. Yet Ruth does enter. Her speech in 1.16–17 ('your people shall be my people, and your God my God') is a recognition of the God of Israel and of her desire for the life of an Israelite; and her own acceptance into the community is shown by her marriage to Boaz and by their illustrious offspring. In asking to be covered by Boaz's skirt (or 'wing', *kanaph* – 3.9) she is seeking shelter under Yahweh's wings (*kanaph* – 2.12).

Patriarchal Elements

The story deliberately brings in elements closely associated with the patriarchal narratives. For example, some names, such as Mahlon ('sweet'? 'weak'?) and Chilion ('completeness'? 'failing'?), have *recognizable* meanings – indeed, the name seems to play on the range of meanings. The change of the name Naomi ('my pleasantness') to Mara ('bitter') mimics Sarah's and Jacob's significant name-changes. The story of Naomi, like those of Sarah, Rebecca and Rachel, uses the theme of barrenness and childbirth (1.11–12; 4.16–17). The theme of famine and leaving the land similarly has parallels with Abraham and Isaac stories. Ruth's departure (1.16; 2.11) may be a conscious reminder of Abraham's call (Gen 12.1) and the water (Ruth 2.9) serves the same function of meeting and marrying as do the wells of Genesis and Exodus. The book may be viewed as a *reversal* of patriarchal type scenes: Ruth initiates and controls the action, playing a heroine's role (Williams, 1982, 84–8). The heroine comes from a foreign land to find a husband; she is offered water by Boaz, and the young men draw it for her; she heroically refuses to leave and marry a young husband; she goes to him on his home ground; instead of negotiating, she engineers an implied consummation. This reverses the typical betrothal scene (see Alter, 1981, 58–60). The book also gives a revolutionary twist to the creation story and to traditional ideas of relationships between the sexes. Ruth 'clings' to Naomi, her mother-in-law (*not* to a new husband – Gen 2.24) and will not abandon her. In Genesis, the man *leaves* his parents and *clings* (same verbs) to his wife.

One story in particular is echoed – that of Judah and Tamar (Gen 38). Both heroines are foreigners, two brothers die in each, and the plot revolves around the continuation of the deceased's line. In both, the women take the initiative in rather unorthodox ways; yet they are praised for it (Ruth 4.10; Gen 38.26) and both are responsible for ensuring that the male line continues. The significant difference is that Judah tries to avoid his obligations while Boaz does much more than his position as distant kinsman requires. The connection between the two stories is made explicit in Ruth 4.12, and the genealogy suggests that Boaz, as a direct descendant of Judah, was putting right the wrongs of his ancestor.

Legal Issues

The connection with Tamar raises the question of levirate marriage. According to Deuteronomy 25.5–6,

If brothers dwell together, and one of them dies and has no son, the wife of the dead shall not be married outside the family to a stranger; her husband's brother shall go in to her, and take her as his wife, and perform the duty of a husband's brother to her. And the first son whom she bears shall succeed to the name of his brother who is dead, that his name may not be blotted out of Israel.

If the brother did not wish to marry her, the woman was empowered to 'pull his sandal off his foot, and spit in his face' (v. 9). The man would be reviled for failing in his obligation. Some elements in the book of Ruth appear to echo this (1.11; 4.5, 8, 9) and the verb *'agan*, used only here (1.13), is the root of the Talmudic *'agunah*, describing the status of a woman so bound to her brother-in-law. Yet the story also shows marked divergences from this model, perhaps continuing the reversal theme. There are no surviving brothers, Ruth is free to marry anyone (3.10), and Boaz is only distantly related. The shoe (4.8) involves not Ruth but Boaz and the unknown kinsman, and may be part of the legal transaction relating to the transfer of property. Finally, the son born does not preserve the name of Ruth's first husband, at least in the genealogy.

There is also a connection with the office of redeemer (*go'el*): 'If your brother becomes poor and sells part of his property, then his next of kin shall come and redeem what his brother has sold' (Lev 25.25). One object of this law is to help out an impoverished relative, but its main function is to ensure that the land remains within the clan. In Ruth the impoverished vendor is Naomi: Ruth, in 3.6-13, is acting as agent. The redeemer can add the family property to his own estate; but the news that a levirate marriage is part of the deal makes the unknown kinsman think again. Should Ruth have a son in her first husband's name, that son would have a right to the property. In refusing to act as redeemer (*go'el*), the unknown kinsman is putting his personal interest before the clan's interest and before the principle of preserving the land for the family. Boaz yet again does the right thing – not only protecting Naomi's future, but also preserving the inheritance of Elimelech for future generations.

Love

Boaz's reference to 'acquiring' (RSV 'buying') Ruth (4.5) complicates the issue. *Qanah* (acquire) is used of marriage in the Mishnah, possibly echoing Ruth. No legal situation within the Hebrew Bible covers such a matter, so interpretations abound. Is the reference to a real sale, or is it a metaphor, or is it ironic? Another theme in the book affects our view of such a sale: *hesed* (lovingkindness). This is not love in a general sense but love expressed within the framework of *covenant*. It suggests loyalty and obligation, a love that transcends death (cf. 1 Sam 20).

The word is found in the text three times, at three important points: 1.8, 2.20 and 3.10, spoken by Naomi and Boaz, of Boaz and Ruth. Ruth, like Boaz, does more than legally required in her loyalty to Naomi (1.15-18; 2.23; 3.10), spurning opportunities to improve her own lot: the loving-kindness ultimately turns to love. The adoption of Obed (4.14-17) also has no legal basis in the Torah. It could be an older unrecorded practice but it might simply praise a doting grandmother, without further legal implications.

God

Whenever *hesed* is mentioned, it is in a formula which compares human deeds with those of God (1.8; 2.20; 3.10). God is cited with great frequency throughout the book, though in the main he does not participate. We do have, however, in 2.3 an example of divine providence – a providence which accompanies the characters through their whole story. Two other passages must be considered. 1.6 is reminiscent of the Deuteronomic view of God acting in history: God restores his bounty by providing food. 4.13, however, echoes the Yahwist, for whom God is personally involved in the lives of individuals. This is not to suggest a variety of sources for the book of Ruth; rather we should think of an author consciously applying different styles and making the work fit into a particular historical context.

Date and Purpose

Dating Ruth with certainty is probably impossible. The book has alternative positions in early texts: in the Masoretic Hebrew, among the Writings (confirmed by the Talmud; Baba Bathra, 14a); and, in the Greek Septuagint, among the Prophets (next to Judges, with which it is chronologically tied). The writer may have intended the book to be an appendix to Judges, but the extent of Judges may have been already fixed; or Ruth may have been detached through its association with Shavuoth. The story could have been written at the time of the judges and have had an oral prehistory. It could have been considerably adapted at a later period, perhaps to provide a link to King David; or it could be a very late work, deliberately archaized to fit in with the period of the judges. We have to ask whether its references to the Torah can be explained by common traditions, or whether they show that the Torah was already authoritative. It is interesting that the Torah is not slavishly followed. The Jewish interpretative tradition was very open and flexible, in seeking meaning from every detail and every inflexion.

The purpose of the book is equally a game of inspired guesswork. It could be a polemic against the stringent marriage laws of Ezra, an example of how to rebuild the post-exilic community. It could be a message of hope, showing how God's providence acts in the world. Thus a midrash notes, 'This megillah has nothing of impurity and purity, or forbidden and permitted – so why was it written? To teach how great is the reward of those who do deeds of lovingkindness' (Ruth Rabba, 1.1). Others see the book's purpose as bound up with King David.

David

4.17 introduces David for the first time, and we are presented with a genealogical tree of ten generations from Perez to David in which Boaz takes a significant seventh place. There are hints earlier in the book. The first verse of Ruth recalls the last verse of Judges, which in the Christian Bible precedes it: 'In those days there was no king in Israel; every man did what was right in his own eyes' (Judg 21.25). This verse looks to a time when a king will arise, and the book of Ruth brings him closer. When Boaz rights the wrongs of Judah he is symbolically cleaning up the family tree for the arrival of David. The barrenness – childbearing motif offers parallels not only to the matriarchs (Sarah, Rachel), but also to Hannah in 1 Samuel, which follows (again, in the Christian Bible). Ruth 4.15 ('more to you than seven sons') is a clear hint for 1 Samuel 1.8: 'Am I not more to you than ten sons?' The stage is being set for the anointing of the king.

The question arises whether the Davidic material is integral to the book. Several scholars see a deliberate break in the text in 4.17 (see Eissfeldt, 1976, 479f). A later editor may have altered the ending to link the story with David, encouraged by the story's setting in Bethlehem. The typical name-explanation formula has been broken (the word 'name' appears where the proper name ought to) and the explanation 'A son has been born to Naomi' (4.17) bears little relationship to the name Obed ('servant [of God]'). We would have expected a name such as Ben-noam ('son of pleasantness'). If the text has been altered here, the reason may have been to bolster David's or Solomon's claim to the throne; to create an apologetic for David's Moabite ancestry or for Solomon's Ammonite wife; to romanticize a golden age of a single monarch in a unified country at a later, fraught and fragmented period; or to look to a future restoration of those good old days and of David's line. The change may even have been the work of the original author, adapting the folktale to suit his own political purposes. The Davidic genealogy in Ruth forms the basis of 1 Chronicles 2.4-15 (although it could be argued that Ruth borrowed from Chronicles). Of course, a genealogy tracing Boaz back to Perez may have existed before references to Obed and David were inserted.

Ruth was accepted because of its connection with David, in a period when Messianic kingship was associated with the return of David's line and the role of the redeemer (*go'el*) took on a new significance. The return of each tribe to its apportioned land was one of the expectations of the Messianic age–an age prefigured every fiftieth (jubilee) year, when land was restored and slaves went free (Lev 25). In Christianity the Messianic association developed along different lines, but for both faiths this small book with its themes of providence, redemption and love became one of undoubted significance.

Whatever its origins, Ruth is no longer a simple folktale. Its seemingly artless exterior reveals a sophistication of thought and a complicated theology that in four short chapters challenges the very best in the Bible.

Lamentations

Forty years before the destruction of Jerusalem, Josiah, king of Judah, shook off Assyrian domination, and with newfound strength and confidence, set about the religious and political reform of his country. The battle against idolatry seemed finally won, and rule and worship were concentrated in Jerusalem. The importance of the Temple, its priests and its cult was absolute.

The national revival was short-lived. In 609 BCE Josiah was killed in the battle of Megiddo and Judah again became subject to foreign powers. However, belief in the inviolability of Jerusalem remained strong. The view, found in Deuteronomic law, that God would reward faithfulness supported a confidence that was ill-judged in the circumstances. Jehoiakim's rebellion in 601 precipitated the Babylonian siege and capture of Jerusalem. Zedekiah's revolt brought about the longer and eventually catastrophic siege that eventuated, after months of intolerable suffering, in the fall of Jerusalem in 587/6. The leaders were deported; the Temple was razed (2 Kgs 22-5).

What religious effect did these events have on the people left behind? There were several responses. Some continued as if nothing had changed, to have faith that eventually Judah would win. Some returned to the old idolatry – either in desperation (Ezek 8) or from convinced theological motives (Jer 44) – or accepted the gods of the conquering nation, since they had proved stronger than the God of Israel. Others believed that God had himself willed the catastrophe (Pss 44, 74, 79): the people had been judged, but this need not be the end of the covenant. Finally, there were those who interpreted the future in light of the destruction. The 'day of the Lord' had come about. God had acted in history with a significance equalled only by the exodus. Such a judgement was, however, necessary for the future salvation of the people (Second Isaiah, Zephaniah).

Between the view that God had abandoned his people and that of God acting out of love lies the book of Lamentations.

What is Lamentations?

If 2 Kings provides the details of the destruction, Lamentations interprets the meaning. There are no historical references, or specific people or places mentioned. Instead, we have a continuous outpouring – as of grief – in an attempt to grasp the significance of the event. Jerusalem is the subject, personalized in the feminine.

Biblical scholars have recognized the 'lament' as a distinct literary form (see for example Isa 14.4; Jer 9.17-22; 2 Sam 1.17-27). H. Gunkel identified three specific types in Lamentations: funeral songs (chs. 1, 2, 4), individual laments (ch. 3); and communal or national laments (ch. 5) (Hillers, 1972, xxvii f). Sometimes these types are mixed – proof, Gunkel suggests, that Lamentations is a late example of the genre. On the other hand, this feature may be a sign of poetic creativity. The book could even be the work of several authors, for the style varies.

Dating is also uncertain: the poems could have been written at any time between the first siege and the end of the exile in Babylon. The language is lively and vivid, quite in line with the supposition that much is based on direct observation. W. Rudolf dates the first chapter just after the first siege (598 BCE), as it talks of capture and not of destruction. He finds in chapters 2 and 4 eyewitness accounts of the second siege (587 BCE), and assumes that the remainder, lacking the artistry of the earlier chapters, was completed shortly afterwards.

The Septuagint links Lamentations with Jeremiah, but this is not usually accepted as proof of authorship today. 2 Chronicles 35.25, written much later, attributes a lament on Josiah to Jeremiah, but there are major differences in style and teaching between Lamentations and Jeremiah. The ascription is easily explained as a popular tradition, and itself explains why Lamentations is placed among the prophetic books in the Christian Bible. In the Hebrew Bible it is placed in the Writings, and takes its name from its first word, *Ekah* ('How'). There are also early references to the book as *Qinoth*, Hebrew for 'Lamentations' (Baba Bathra, 15a).

Four out of five of the poems are alphabetic acrostics, the initial letters of each line being consecutive letters of the Hebrew alphabet (although chapters 2, 3 and 4 reverse the usual order of *ayin* and *pe*). This deliberate structure can be viewed as an exercise in style, an aid to memory, a framework in which to concentrate one's thoughts, or a symbol of completion such as noted in the Talmud (Shabbath 55a): 'The people have fulfilled my Torah from *aleph* to *taw*' – or, as we might say, from A to Z (*taw* is the final letter of the Hebrew alphabet). The last chapter is not an acrostic, but has twenty-two lines just as the Hebrew alphabet has twenty-two letters. Is this coincidence, or is there some other reason?

The Form

The five poems are arranged in a chiastic pattern, with the central chapter as the core and the outer chapters paired symmetrically. This arrangement is often found in the Hebrew Bible (see Gordis, 1974) and here gives the structure shown in table 14.1.

Table 14.1 Structure of Lamentations.

Chapter	Structural layer	Contents
1	*Outer layer*	The indignities of national subjection
2	*Inner layer*	Contemporary lament on the catastrophe
3	*CORE*	Personal reflection
4	*Inner layer*	Contemporary lament on the catastrophe
5	*Outer layer*	The indignities of national subjection

B. Johnson (1985) sees the combination of chiastic form and acrostic as akin
to 'atbash' – a ciphering-device whereby the first and last letters of the
alphabet (*aleph* and *taw*) are interchanged, then the second and second last
(*beth* and *shin*), and so on. For example, Jeremiah 25.26 has *Sheshak* instead
of *Babel* (Babylon), and 51.1 uses *Leb qamay* for *Casdim* (Chaldeans). Each
chapter divides into two halves, a 'fact' half and an 'interpretation' half –
often distinguishable by a change in voice. In each half, the same themes
occur in chiastic sequences focused on the central verses.

Chapter 2 is the most perfect example. It begins by taking up the theme
of the central and therefore most crucial theme of chapter 1: the day of
God's anger (1.11) (table 14.2).

Table 14.2

Verses	Contents
1–5	The day of God's anger
6–8	The destruction of the sanctuary
9–10	The rejection by the city
11–12	The hungry children
13–14	The rejection by the city
15–17	The destruction of the sanctuary
18–22	The day of God's anger

Chapter 3 is not so consistent. It falls clearly into five parts, but the parallels
are not so close (table 14.3).

Table 14.3

Verses	Contents
1–18	An individual lament
19–20	Transition to middle section
21–41	The theological answer
42–51	In the style of chapters 1 and 2
52–66	An individual lament

It is the central verses of this chapter (and, incidentally, of the book) that are
most important, because here we have the meaning and purpose of the
entire book.

The Meaning

For those who maintained a belief in God after the destruction of the
Temple, vital questions remained. Did the destruction mean the covenant

was broken? Did it mean that God was powerless? Interestingly, Lamentations shows no conc⌐rn for the sacrificial cult. The suffering of the Jerusalemites is described in great detail, but the desolation of the Temple only cursorily (1.4; 2.6, 9). The destruction has a symbolic significance – not a practical one. Further, there is no interest in which sins were responsible for the catastrophe. The classical prophets blamed idolatory, social injustice, the folly of Israel's leaders. 2.14 simply notes that 'Your [Jerusalem's] prophets have seen for you false and deceptive visions; they have not exposed your inquity to restore your fortunes . . . '

Further, God does not speak. God is the source of destruction and his day of anger brought it about; yet there is no dialogue, no questioning or challenging as there is in Job or Jeremiah, and no protest over the suffering of the innocent as in Psalm 44.17–22.

The author is dealing with a totally new situation, and the answer he finds is unique. He finds it by speaking personally. In chapters 1 and 2 we have the image of Zion as an abandoned woman – one not entirely guiltless but still an object of pity. The image may appeal to the emotions, but it does not help in finding meaning. In chapter 3, an individual lament, the suffering is personalized: 'I am the man who has seen affliction under the rod of his wrath' (v. 1); yet the author is speaking on behalf of all Israel. Communal guilt has brought about communal suffering – so he offers communal hope.

In vv. 1–18, God is the aggressor. He is harsh and unrelenting – and not mentioned once by name until v. 18. After a transitional passage, v. 21 comes as a complete contrast. God is the subject and the other side of his nature is expressed. All hope resides in him: he offers unlimited love, unlimited mercy. The emphasis on waiting suggests that the destruction is not the end, and that, the punishment over, there is hope for the future. Israel's present task is to repent and return to God (v. 41). The author has combined two opposing sets of facts. On the one hand, the destruction has taken place; on the other, God is good, his love unending. The one is past; the other is present and future. What we have here is essentially a Deuteronomic view of history, but one expressed as direct response to crisis, without the benefit of hindsight. The rest of the chapter returns to the suffering and anger of God, balancing the first part; but now there is a difference. The writer speaks directly to Israel, for his answer is the people's answer. God has not abandoned them and in future the wrath of God will be unleashed on their enemies.

Conclusion

We do not know what other works may have been written in response to the events of 587/6 BCE; but that Lamentations became the accepted response to the disaster is evident from its presence in the Hebrew Bible and from the many compositions that have emulated it – such as the medieval *qinah* (lament) read at the Jewish fast of Ab. We are so accustomed to these thoughts that the message may appear banal. Our reading of the text *as if prose* obscures the poetry and the chiastic structure: it may seem in English dull and repetitive. Yet, as writers and theologians today grapple to find meaning in the Holocaust, one can can appreciate the contribution of Lamentations as though for the first time.

We can see, too, greatness amid the constraints of a rigid structure – a power of expression intensified by the short, simple sentences, with profound ideas simply put. Behind all this, we can see a faith unshakable in the midst of immeasurable suffering.

Qoheleth (Ecclesiastes)

The book Qoheleth is an enigma. Although the subject it broaches is found in other biblical books, its conclusions are very different. The style often appears confused, the contents contradictory. It has been called 'boring', 'repetitious', 'aimless', 'disorganized', 'blasphemous', 'wrong-headed', 'heretical' (*Encyclopaedia Judaica*, VI, 349). Yet its message, as the discussion in chapter 13 shows, is consistent and logical, a reappraisal of life from the standpoint of the certain knowledge that we shall all die.

Qoheleth has always troubled people. At the council of Jamnia in about 95 CE, rabbis discussed which books should be included in the canon. 'Rabbi Judah said, "Song of Songs defiles the hands [i.e. is holy], but concerning Qoheleth, there is a dispute"' (Mishnah Yadaim, 3.5). Later Jewish writers complained that it contains contradictory statements, and has no religious content; that, moreover, it contradicts the conclusions of other biblical books and appears to deny the doctrine of life after death – important to Pharisaic Judaism in its struggle with the Sadducees.

Two factors secured the book canonical status: recognition that its concluding statement echoes the traditional teaching about God; and attribution of the work to King Solomon. For those who wished it, the contradictions could be resolved, the difficult passages reinterpreted. Hence, in rabbinic tradition, the phrase 'eat, drink and take pleasure' (Eccles 3.13) became a metaphor for the study of Torah; medieval Christian commentators in contrast saw in it a reference to the Eucharist.

Origins and Background

The superscription (1.1) has been taken to mean that King Solomon wrote Qoheleth: 'The words of the Preacher [Qoheleth], the son of David, king in Jerusalem.' This is supported by a strong extra-biblical tradition. Some early versions even introduce Solomon's name into the text. According to a midrash, 'Solomon wrote Song of Songs in his youth, Proverbs in middle age, and Qoheleth when he was old and weary of life' (Song of Songs Rabba, 1.1).

The reign of King Solomon introduced a period of peace and prosperity for Israel – and with it cultural and intellectual contact with other nations. 1 Kings stresses Solomon's wisdom and oratory (3.16–28; 5.9–14; 10.1–10, 24) giving a clear hint that, in the historian's view, Hebrew wisdom literature began here. Proverbs includes several superscriptions attributing authorship to Solomon: for example, 'These also are proverbs of Solomon which the men of Hezekiah king of Judah copied' (25.1). However, these could be later additions. It was common practice to attribute books to famous characters in order to get them taken seriously: the works known as 'The Wisdom of Solomon', 'Enoch' and 'The Testament of the Twelve Patriarchs' are excellent examples from the intertestamental period, and the book of 'Daniel' is, in the view of most scholars, a prime biblical instance of the same practice. Solomon's legendary wisdom may have given rise to the tradition that he wrote the three canonical books associated with him.

Ecclesiastes 1.12 claims that Qoheleth was a king in Israel. No king of that name is known: the word *qoheleth* is a present participle from the root *qhl*, 'assemble' – that is, 'one who assembles the people'. It is in the feminine, which suggests not a name but an official title, and it is twice preceded by the definite article. A *qoheleth* gathered an audience to teach words of wisdom: hence the English rendering of the term as 'the Preacher' and the equivalent Greek title 'Ecclesiastes'.

Was there one *qoheleth* or several behind this book? The disjointedness could suggest a work by many hands, but equally it could be the work of a single writer, perhaps with editorial additions. The book is in the first person, 'I', but the third person ('says the Preacher') occasionally appears (as in 7.27; 12.8). If the compiler was a pupil, this would make excellent sense – with some words quoted and others reported. This could also account for the structuring of the book like an anthology. The introduction (1.1–2) and conclusion (12.9–14) in particular use the third person; the conclusion helps to make the work theologically acceptable (Gordis, 1968).

The language of the book is different from the Hebrew of other biblical books and closer to the Hebrew of the Mishnah (*c*.200 CE). It contains Persian and possibly Greek loan words, Egyptian parallels and Aramaisms: this puts the date at the earliest after the return from Babylonian exile in 458 BCE. The Apocryphal book Ben Sirach (Ecclesiasticus) was written in response to Qoheleth and is generally dated about 190–180 BCE. Fragments of Qoheleth from Qumran cave 4 date from the same time. The problem of dating is complicated by the possibility that the book is a translation from Aramaic or Greek. 'Missing' original texts could still be discovered, but until then we have to assume that we are dealing with a

Hebrew original – and date it somewhere around 250 BCE. In this period of Greek influence, oratory was highly regarded. We cannot be dogmatic about where the book was written – Alexandria, Egypt and Palestine are all possible.

What is certain in Qoheleth?

One certainty is that life goes on. Chapters 1 and 3 speak of the eternal cycle of time. People, set in this framework, live, labour and die just like animals – 'all are from the dust, and all turn to dust again' (3.20). Anything else is mere speculation. The world is neither better nor worse for our existence – it just continues.

Equally certain is that God is in control (3.4; 7.13–14; etc.) and humanity is powerless. Qoheleth gives no thought to ritual or prayer, and without it there is no relationship between man and God. God does not act act specifically anyway. What God does endures for ever, without late changes or additions. God has created the process of time and eternity (3.14–15). The appropriate human response is reverence, a combination of dependence and appreciation. 'Remember also your creator in the days of your youth' (12.1): rejoice in the time you have, but do not forget that there will be days of darkness (11.8). Enjoy your life, but remember God's ultimate judgement (v. 9). Do not be vexed, for the problems of youth are 'vanity' (v. 10).

The same fate comes to all (2.14–16; 6.1–6). If God no longer acts for man, then the assumption 'do good and you will prosper' is wrong. What happens to a man has no bearing on what he does. What is the point of anything (3.9)?

Humanity cannot begin to understand. In 3.11, God is said to have put '*olam* in man's heart. This is translated variously as 'the world' – God makes man's heart finite so he cannot understand the infinite; and 'eternity', or the striving for eternity – people will always desire what they cannot attain. If they can never 'understand or know', (6.12, 8.7) what are they to do?

They can enjoy what life has to offer (2.24; 3.12–13; 9.7–9). This is not a hopeless hedonism (or desire for pleasure), but an appreciation of life *as it is* rather than as we would wish it to be. As the Jerusalem Talmud says much later, 'On Judgement Day man will be called to give account for all the things in life he could have enjoyed and did not.'

Qoheleth expresses the doubts and fears of many an agnostic today. The issues he raises are still real. There is no miraculous or mystical side to his analysis – no talk of a future life. Such realism should appeal. The book's place in the canon confirms that the Bible is an anthology: the Hebrew Bible expresses the thoughts and experience of different people in different periods. Yet, Qoheleth remains firmly rooted within the biblical tradition.

The certainty of God remains and the Preacher's concentration on this life is wholly Hebrew in character. He faces the same dilemma as Job and Jeremiah, that nothing happens as it should. Since there is injustice and oppression, no merit to be gained in being virtuous – so what is life's purpose? Qoheleth rejects traditional answers. Two theories emerged in Babylon and were supported by Persian and Greek thought: dualism (stressing competition between the forces of good and evil) and a future judgement. Neither of these ideas impinges on Qoheleth, which suggests they were not yet being taken seriously within Judaism. Dualism was always officially opposed in Judaism, but did find its way into apocalyptic literature. Judgement and life after death became central to Pharisaic thought. What we have in Qoheleth is something very exciting – a voice speaking at a crossroads of development in Hebrew thought.

Esther

There have been immense prejudices against Esther for centuries. In Martin Luther's view, the book 'Judaized too greatly' and was full of 'pagan impropriety' (see Eissfeldt, 1976, 512). The book has been declared to be unhistorical, excessively nationalistic and vengeful. Eissfeldt calls it a 'grotesque fantasy' justifying a festival 'shot through with hatred' (507, 510). God is not mentioned. These objections are not new: they were raised as arguments against canonization and refused to go away. Jewish and Christian scholars over the ages have been hard-pressed to defend the book as scripture. One approach to the difficulties has been to disregard the detail and view Esther as an heroine in the mould of Judith and Susanna, or to emphasize the Jews' miraculous deliverance. A Christian approach has been to allegorize Esther as the Church, Vashti as the synagogue and the villain Haman as (ironically) the Jews. There have also been attempts to 'improve' the story: hence the versions found in the Septuagint (and, following this, in Catholic Bibles) and the later Targums (see Grossfeld, 1973). None of these approaches is really satisfactory. Consequently it is easy for Christian commentators to appear anti-semitic, and for Jews to seem excessively apologetic.

Background

When Cyrus decreed that the Jews in exile could return to Jerusalem (538 BCE), the majority opted to stay behind. Life was good in Babylon. They had adapted well, developing into the thriving community that is later reflected in the Babylonian Talmud.

Here begins the story of the Jewish Diaspora, and the tension between the Jews living within the ancient homeland and those abroad. The latter did not 'need' the Temple, though they supported it. They were indifferent to the priestly cult and lost the yearnings for Zion so beautifully expressed in the Psalms. Yet as an 'ethnic minority' they became more conscious of their identity as Jews and, unlike their Palestinian brethren, acted as one body, spoke with one voice. Things were either 'good' or 'bad' for the Jews. Persian rule on the whole was good. It resulted in religious tolerance, but this proved to be precarious. The vast empire was threatened with rival factions, with a ruler whose position was never totally secure. This explains the nationalism in Esther, the unethical behaviour of those at the top, the disregard for Jerusalem and the covenant – but it does not explain the book's omission of God.

God

It has been suggested that references to God have been edited out of Esther because excessive drinking at Purim threatened profanation of the divine name (Paton, 1908, 94). Others have argued that the story conveys a strong sense of *providence*, and that this sufficiently witnesses to God's presence. Through the lots cast, through the chance happenings upon which the plot hinges, God is so immanent and obvious it is unnecessary to mention him directly. In wisdom literature, God is often an accepted presence who does not interfere. God may be indicated in 4.14 – 'deliverance will rise for the Jews from another quarter' – although this interpretation is contestable. In rabbinic Judaism, the omission of God's name is itself seen as indicative of a detailed theology. Deuteronomy warns Israel that apostasy will lead God to withdraw from the world, bringing disaster: 'I will surely hide my face in that day on account of all the evil they have done, because they have turned to other gods' (Deut 31.18). In Hebrew 'I will hide' is *astir*; the name Esther (*Ester*) uses the same consonants. Thus, in traditional Judaism, God is considered to be 'hiding' within the written text. Moreover, 5.4 supplies a case in point: the initial letters of *Yabo' Hammelek Wehaman Hayyom* ('let the King and Haman come today') spell out the divine name YHWH.

Esther as Story

Whatever its deficiencies, the book of Esther is a 'good read'. It has great style and is cleverly constructed with parallels throughout. The two halves of the book (1.1–4.14; 4.15–8.17) are perfectly balanced. We begin with feasting (1.1) and end with feasting (8.17). Haman's decree (3.12–13) is word for word echoed in Mordecai's decree (8.11). Mordecai rises to power as Haman falls.

The opening (1.1–2.23) sets the scene satirically, with royal banquets, Queen Vashti's refusal to attend, King Ahasuerus's search for a new queen, Esther's preparation and accession, and Mordecai's discovery of a plot against the king. These scenes reveal a Persian world full of rivalries, insecurities and obsessions. It was a multi-racial world in which Jews could not feel safe. Law was a matter of whim, and even the king could be caught out by the effects of his irreversible decrees. In a legalistic society, a call for wine becomes an edict (1.8), and a solemn decree, promulgated in every language, is needed to ensure that wives honour their husbands (1.20–2). The comedy almost becomes farce. Mordecai's loyal act is entered into the chronicles, raising in the reader's mind the question – and the certainty – of its future significance.

The main action (3.1–9.19) revolves around the four main characters: Haman, Mordecai, Ahasuerus and Esther. The major themes are court conflicts and the inviolable royal will (Clines, 1984, 12–25). The story moves from individual conflict (between Mordecai and Haman) to corporate conflict (Agagites against the Jews – an age-old rivalry) and the story's tensions receive a sharp dual focus. When Haman persuades Ahasuerus to sign an edict allowing an armed rising against the Jews on a day selected by lot (*pur*), this introduces race as an important theme: deep prejudice lies under the surface of institutional harmony.

The terms 'Haman the Agagite' and 'Mordecai the Jew' alert the reader of potential conflict to come. Esther's victory is not won easily: her unbidden visit to the king could lead to her death (4.16); the king's choice between his prime minister and his queen could go either way (he has to go into the garden to think it over) and his final decision is based on a total misunderstanding – Haman trips and falls against Esther and is finally condemned for assault! The Jews win their victory in spite of their refusal to observe the king's laws. The book is cynical about both the propriety and the effectiveness of Persian law. 'This wicked Haman' (7.6) acts within the law. The evil is legal, but it is still crushed. Haman's death does not remove the institutional evil: the decree cannot be revoked. The most Esther can win is the concession that Mordecai can send any order concerning the Jews throughout the empire – remembering, of course, that the first, anti-semitic edict must stand. Mordecai's new edict permits the Jews to defend themselves. This does not wipe out the original decree: it makes it appear ludicrous and unworkable. In the end there is no opposition to speak of: rather the Jews are held in honour. There follows a jarring note. This temporary freedom to take arms encourages the Jews to strike against their enemies. Institutional racism causes the civil conflict: the tensions for which it is responsible are not easily eliminated, for the threat of violence encourages a bloody requital.

The characters have been criticized as one-dimensional, but this may be underestimating the subtlety of the writer, who is a master of understatement. Ahasuerus seems a fool, but in a world of intrigue and assassination it may be wiser to appear so. He carefully sets up Mordecai and Haman, for after the discovery of the plot (2.21) it is Mordecai who should promoted, not Haman. Mordecai's refusal to bow down may well indicate his feelings on the matter. Only after Haman dines with the queen does the king honour Mordecai: 'when the queen takes an undue interest in the number two man, it is time for the king to get worried. And, thus it is no coincidence that he cannot sleep' (Magonet, 1980, 173). Whilst two powerful men, both foreigners, hate each other, the king is safe. Esther is no dumb beauty; she procrastinates over her request till she has flattered and spoilt the king with two banquets.

There is great humour too – often missed by over-zealous commentators. Ahasuerus, the powerful emperor, cannot command the obedience of either wife: Vashti refuses to enter (1.12); Esther enters unbidden (5.2). His attempt to suppress his first wife's disobedience serves only to publicize it further (1.18–19). The king's insomnia is downright comic, and at the climax of the story (7.6) Haman trips and falls over. Yet behind the humour is menace. The fate of thousands depends on a whim (3.6, 11) and, had Haman not fallen onto the queen's couch, the king might not have granted Esther her request. The ridiculous pomposity of the Persians as portrayed by the writer is a foil for the seriousness of his message. The comedy raises tension, and resolves it. The trivial is taken seriously; the serious in understated. The story is vivid and well-crafted, an impressive success on a literary level.

Origins and Historicity

In the early twentieth century, much effort was expended on establishing whether the events of Esther really happened. Historicity was considered to be closely linked to authenticity, whereas today it is recognized that matters are not that simple: for example, history may be fictionalized and still give an 'authentic' picture of the time. Esther contains a number of Aramaic features, but no signs of Greek influence, suggesting a Diaspora setting in the fourth century BCE before the Hellenistic period. However, the theme of mass destruction may suggest a date after Antiochus IV Epiphanes (175–163). Esther was therefore written at some time between the fourth and second centuries BCE, but it is impossible to be more precise.

Source critics have argued that Esther is not an integral whole. The concluding section, 9.1–10.4, which sets out details of Purim, contradicts earlier chapters in that the defensive action there envisaged is turned into an offensive. Clines (1984, 26–30) argues cogently that 8.17 provides an appropriate ending to the story, with the edict neutralized. It is clear that no massacre will take place, and all will live happily ever after. There is no preparation for what follows in chapters 9 and 10, and the plot here is not linked artistically with what precedes. These chapters establish Purim as an annual festival, justified by ferocious and unexpected bloodletting, and can therefore be regarded as a later addition. If this is right, then Esther is not a story about the origin of Purim, but an oriental court tale hinging on the cleverness of cancelling out one irrevocable law with another (Clines, 1984). Chapter 1 has also, less convincingly, been seen as an independent tale. In the remainder, small joins and discrepancies have been noted, apparent evidence for two different sources: one describing the rivalry of Mordecai and Haman (2; 3; 5.9–14); the other to do with Esther's hatred of Haman (4; 5.1–9; 7; 8). The first would be a story of court intrigue, the second a tale of harem intrigue; neither need originally have been Jewish. This view cannot be accepted as established, since one scholar's 'editorial seams' can be another scholar's 'rhetorical skill'. This is why it is important to use a range of interpretative methods together, as they can illuminate each other, and cancel out individual bias.

On an alternative view, the origins of Esther were cultic. The names Mordecai and Esther have been seen as versions of the names Marduk and Ishtar (Babylonian deities), Haman and Vashti as equivalents of Humman and Mashti (Elamite deities). On this view we have, in Esther, a demythologized account of the victory of the Babylonian gods over their Elamite rivals. The Septuagint calls Haman not an Agagite, but a Buggite, a name associated with the Elamite pantheon. Purim, originally called 'Mordecai's Day' (Marduk's day?) could derive from the Persian Farvardigan – a New Year festival of the dead (see Moore, 1971; Eissfeldt, 1976, 509). However, there is insufficient evidence to prove any of these hypotheses conclusively.

Purpose

Whatever its origins, Esther became popular and was accepted into the canon. One reason for this was that the book explains the origins of Purim. This, as we have seen, may not have been its earliest function. The word *Purim* itself presents a problem. A Hebrew plural of a Babylonian word for a Persian festival sounds odd – particularly as the story mentions only one *pur* (lot), which plays a very minor role. Moreover, the festival is celebrated on the day *after* the anniversary of the events. It is thus probable that the story of Esther originally had an independent life, and only later became associated with Mordecai's Day (2 Macc 15:36).

Like Daniel, the book gives hope to persecuted people. Daniel relates to the Maccabaean revolt, and possibly Esther had a similar reference. The strident militarism of the end of the story, as enemies are wiped out, could have struck a popular chord in the Maccabaean struggle. However, the story's Diaspora setting and indifference to Jerusalem makes an *origin* in this period unlikely. Its failure to condemn Esther's assimilating lifestyle suggests, if anything, a Hellenizing author. The book recommends the Jewish people to a non-Jewish ruler. The Septuagint version shifts the emphasis onto God's providence and the Jews' fighting-skills. It appears to say that Jews are loyal people, strong fighters, who with God on their side overcome their enemies. The substantial reworking of the story in the Septuagint made the story more reminiscent of Ezra, Nehemiah and Daniel – and so helped it to win acceptance as scripture (Clines, 1984, 168-74).

The book also has an eschatological dimension, depicting the ultimate victory over evil. Haman is an Agagite, descendant of the king of the Amalekites, the Israelite enemy *par excellence* (Exod 17.16; Deut 25.18f). Even the Egyptians are forgiven, but Israel took upon itself a divine mission to 'blot out the rememberance of Amalek from under heaven' (Deut 25.19). The opportunity comes when Saul meets Agag (1 Sam 15) and destroys his army. Saul spares Agag, but an angry Samuel 'hewed Agag in pieces before the LORD in Gilgal' (v. 33). Mordecai is a descendant of Saul (Esth 2.5) and the scene is set for a replay of the ancient battle. This explains the savagery of the vengeance (9.5), why Haman's sons were killed, and why the battle takes on the features of the ancient *herem*, ban (9.10, 15, 16), in which the taking of plunder was forbidden.

Each of these perspectives helped to establish the book in mainstream Hebrew literature and scripture. The first eight chapters presents a powerful story of persecution and its resolution. Victory is won by diplomacy, not by force or violence. The last two chapters have a harder edge. The threat is eradicated by military action and bloodshed. God clearly helps those who help themselves. In Jewish tradition, the battle against Agag continues. He has become a symbol for absolute evil. In the post-Holocaust era, it is surprising that more notice is not taken of this book. Such evil raises important issues involving survival, ethics and providence.

FURTHER READING

Song of Songs
Falk, M. 1982: *Love Lyrics from the Bible: a Translation and Literary Study of the Song of Songs.*
Goulder, M. D. 1986: *The Song of Fourteen Songs.*
Landy, F. 1983: *Paradoxes of Paradise: Identity and Difference in the Song of Songs.*

Ruth
Beattie, O. R. G. 1977: *Jewish Exegesis of the Book of Ruth.*
Sasson, M. 1979: *Ruth.*

Lamentations

Gordis, R. 1974: *Song of Songs and Lamentations: a Shidy, Modern Translation and Commentary*, 2nd edn.

Gottwald, N. K. 1954: *Studies in the Book of Lamentations*.

Harrison, R. K. 1973: *Jeremiah and Lamentations*.

Qoheleth (Ecclesiastes)

Crenshaw, J. L. 1988: *Ecclesiastes*.

Fox, M. V. 1989: *Meanings and Values in Qoheleth*.

Ogden, G. 1987: *Qoheleth*.

Esther

Childs, B. S. 1979: *Introduction to the Old Testament as Scripture*, 598–607.

Clines, D. J. A. 1984: *The Esther Scroll: the Story of a Story*.

Moore, C. A. 1982: *Studies in the Book of Esther*.

15

The Other Books

Margaret Barker

It is all too easy for those who read the Protestant version of the Bible to turn from Malachi to Matthew as if there were nothing in between. This chapter will deal with what came in between, the intertestamental period. It will soon become apparent that this period cannot be isolated from what preceded it, or from what followed, whether our subsequent studies be of Jewish or of Christian materials. The writings of this period provide a wealth of information about the world in which the Old Testament books were first transmitted and interpreted. When we think about this period, we must always have in mind the fact that the Hebrew (and Greek) writings were by no means fixed, or already designated as canonical and uncanonical. These are later labels, and show us a very different attitude towards Scripture. In this so-called intertestamental period the older traditions were freely interpreted to serve the needs of new situations, using methods which to us may seem bizarre. If scholars, especially Christian scholars, work without this information, the bare texts of the Old Testament, read as we read them now, come to be used, without reserve, as background to later texts such as those of the New Testament, and this inevitably distorts. There were four centuries between Malachi and Matthew, and as much happened in that period as happened in England between the time of the first Queen Elizabeth and the accession of the second. The Hebrew Bible must not to be treated as some great fixture, which, in the form we now know, was the background to all later developments and disputes. It is all too easy to allow the wisdom of our own hindsight to condition the way we imagine all others read, or should have read, those texts which became scriptural. If this period shows us nothing else, it shows us that every generation has believed its own interpretation of sacred traditions to be, at last, the correct one.

We often work as though the Bible (whichever version of it our tradition chooses to use) contains everything that the Israelite people wrote on the subject of religion, but this is far from correct. By choosing our canon we choose our religion. We, or rather our ancestors in the faith, chose what books should be canonical, and then declared that this divinely given canon defined the nature of all true religion. Protestants have rejected the Apocryphal books of the Greek Septuagint (see ch 2). Jews have rejected the New Testament, which, we must remember, is a Jewish book, written almost entirely by Jews about events in a Jewish context. Nobody even considers admitting the Qumran scrolls to Holy Writ, even though the people who wrote them believed they were the inspired word of God to their generation. For us these do no more than provide interesting historical information about the state of religion at that time. Protestants, Catholics and Jews have all rejected the Pseudepigrapha, but the ancient church of Ethiopia has the book of Enoch in its Bible. If we want to read it, we consult a volume labelled 'Pseudepigrapha'.

All the books which were eventually rejected by various groups for their various reasons had something important to say. When we try to read biblical books in context, we must understand them against their background, remembering the rich debates about religious issues which were by no means settled by the time the canonical books were written. We should do better, perhaps, to think of the intertestamental writings not as 'between the testaments' but rather as 'around the testaments', informing us of their situation, and warning us of ours.

Diaspora Communities

The period of the Second Temple begins with the returned exiles re-established in Jerusalem, and the law of God made the basis of the new community. Later tradition in the Sayings of the Fathers (Pirke Aboth, the earliest section of the Mishnah) describes the unbroken chain of teaching from Moses, through Joshua, the elders, the prophets and finally the men of the Great Synagogue – i.e. Ezra and the scribes who followed him. Purity of teaching was all important in a world where everything was changing. There had to be certainties. The Christians developed something similar in the idea of the apostolic succession.

Not all the heirs of ancient Israel, however, were included in this new community. In Palestine were the people who later became known as the Samaritans. We do not know exactly what caused the division between them and Jerusalem, or when it happened. Some Jews, the Covenanters of Qumran, sought to cut themselves off from the impurities of others by settling in the desert. Others tried to come to terms with foreign ways and were condemned for their pains. Finally, there were those who actually chose to live, or to stay, outside their homeland.

Some did not return from the exile in Babylon, but stayed to form the community which we meet later in the tales of Bel and the Dragon, Tobit, and Susanna. We know surprisingly little about the eastern communities in this period. We know that they had their own calendar, dating from the origin of the Seleucid kings in 312 BCE, and that they paid taxes to the Temple in Jerusalem. The historian Josephus (first century CE) wrote his *Jewish War* for these brothers 'across the Euphrates' to show them that it was not the Romans who were responsible for the terrible destruction of 70 CE. The Jews of Babylon had not supported the Jewish revolt. Josephus also tells us that Jewish soldiers in the time of Alexander the Great were excused from working in the temple of Bel in Babylon (*Against Apion*, I, 192) and that a Babylonian Jewish nobleman visited Jerusalem in the time of Herod the Great (*Antiquities*, XVII, 23ff). From Babylon came Hillel, the great leader of the Pharisees, and centuries later this community was to produce the great Targum of Onkelos, which became the official commentary on the Pentateuch.

Not all dispersed Jews lived in Babylon; many had migrated south and settled in Egypt. Jeremiah 42–3 reports one group's flight there, and there was a Jewish military colony at Elephantine (near Aswan), whose surviving letters are invaluable. There were Jewish settlements in the north, especially in Alexandria, and a Jewish temple at Leontopolis built by Onias IV, the son of a murdered high priest (see 2 Macc 4.33ff). Because the community of Alexandria produced many religious writings, we are able to learn rather more about it. Legend has it that the Septuagint was translated there in the time of Ptolemy II Philadelphus (285–47 BCE). The Letter of Aristeas, which tells the story, gives a picture of peaceful coexistence, but 3 Maccabees describes persecution and insensitivity. It tells how Ptolemy IV insisted on entering, and therefore violating, the Holy of Holies in Jerusalem. When thwarted, he planned a terrible revenge on the Jews of Egypt, ordering them to be trampled by drunken elephants, but again he was thwarted. The great wisdom books of the Apocrypha also come from Egypt: the Wisdom of Solomon was written there, and Ecclesiasticus was translated and preserved there. The most famous Egyptian Jewish writer was Philo of Alexandria, a contemporary of Jesus who wrote expositions of the Law to help Jews living in the Greek environment of Egypt.

The problems of living in a pagan environment are reflected in tales from both Babylon and Egypt. From the east we have the persecution of Daniel (set in the east, although probably not actually written there) and the heroic story of Esther. From Egypt we have 3 Maccabees and the Elephantine letters, which tell us that the temple in the south had been destroyed by hostile local people. The letters also show us a side of the problem which other Jewish writers do not mention. Jews complained about idolatry, and the violation of their holy place, but Egyptians were disgusted by the animal sacrifices which were part of Jewish worship. The temple at Elephantine was only rebuilt on the condition that there would be no more sacrifices.

The Palestinian Community

The Jewish community in Palestine, because of its geographical situation at the meeting-point of the great powers of the day, was deeply affected by the upheavals of the fourth century. For over a hundred years the empire of Persia, whose king Cyrus had been the instrument of the return from Babylon, had ruled the area, but from the time of Ezra and Nehemiah this rule had been far from secure. A new super-power emerged to alter the old patterns. No longer was it a choice of Egypt or the Mesopotamian empires. Alexander the Great, whose father Philip of Macedon had conquered and united all Greece, crossed into Asia and confronted the Persian Empire. Darius II was routed at the battle of Issus in 333 BCE. Alexander marched south through Syria-Palestine and Egypt, securing them before turning his attention eastwards to the rest of the empire. He died in 323 BCE, the European master of the Persian Empire. But he left no heir. His death was followed by forty years of struggles, known as the Wars of the Diadochi (Greek for 'successors'). The decisive battle was at Ipsus in central Asia Minor in 302 BCE. The exact details of the result are not clear, but two centres of power emerged in the eastern Mediterranean: Egypt, ruled by Ptolemy, the first of many of that name; and Babylon–North Syria, ruled by Seleucus, who gave his name to a dynasty. Palestine and Coele-Syria were between the two and were disputed, although for nearly a century they were in fact under the rule of Egypt, and enjoyed relative peace. Disputes arose again, culminating in the battle of Panion in northern Palestine in 198 BCE. Antiochus III the Great became the Seleucid master of Palestine.

The change of rule in Palestine would not have been so significant had it not also brought a change of culture and settlements. Greek ways followed in Alexander's wake, and his successors established many Greek cities in Palestine. Judah itself was not colonized, but there were cities built in Samaria–Galilee, on the coast, and east of the Jordan, in the area later known as the Decapolis (Greek for 'ten cities'). The first section of the book of Enoch could well come from this period; it deals with the devastation wrought by the fallen angels, but the apocalyptists often described earthly rulers as wicked angels. Ecclesiasticus is also from this period, before Greek ways became a threat to the Jewish lifestyle. The writer looks back to the time of Onias IV, the great high priest who died in 198 BCE, and there is a certain nostalgia in his writing when he describes himself as the last one to glean in the vineyard of the sages.

Under the first Seleucid ruler there was no direct attack upon the Jews. There were Greek influences all around them in everyday life, but Antiochus recognized their right to live under their own ancient law, and to be governed by their high priest in Jerusalem. The next ruler had grave financial problems, and attempted to rob the Temple treasury (2 Macc 3).

After him came Antiochus IV, who thought himself divine. Many troubles followed, in the course of which the legitimate high priest Onias III was murdered. His son fled, and established a Jewish temple in Egypt, at Leontopolis. Enoch probably comments on this; the priests regarded themselves as servants of the heavenly sanctuary, and 1 Enoch has plenty to say about the defilement of such beings. In Kislev (December) 167 BCE the Temple was defiled with a pagan structure on the altar. Resistance then began in earnest. 1 and 2 Maccabees – two *separate* accounts of the Maccabaean revolt – describe these years.

The Hasmonaeans

Antiochus V succeeded his father in 164 BCE, and restored religious freedom to the Jews, but the troubles continued. The struggles for supremacy within the Seleucid dynasty were reflected in their appointed high priests in Jerusalem. When Alcimus was high priest he had sixty Hasidim put to death. Who the Hasidim were is not certain; they had joined Mattathias at the beginning of the revolt, and were described as an assembly of pious ones (*hasid* means 'pious' in Hebrew), mighty warriors of Israel (1 Macc 2.42). They are often connected with the Essenes, as we shall see later. Judas Maccabaeus continued to oppose the puppet high priest, and, when Demetrius I sent help against him, Judas was finally killed and his army crushed. He was succeeded by his brother Jonathan, who, by careful manoeuvring and supporting the eventual winner in the dynastic struggles, became both high priest and governor of Judaea. He was assassinated in 143, as the result of further intrigue. Another brother, Simon, took over, and, after more manoeuvres, found himself high priest, ethnarch and commander of the Jews. Gentiles were removed from Jerusalem (1 Macc 13.41), and the Hasmonaean priest–kings established. Simon was assassinated in 135, and succeeded by his son John Hyrcanus. After initial setbacks, Hyrcanus was able to take advantage of the decline in Seleucid influence and expand. He captured Shechem and destroyed the Samaritan temple nearby, and he forced the Idumaeans (Edomites) in the south to accept Judaism. His son reigned only one year, and was succeeded by his widow Salome Alexandra. She then married his eldest surviving brother, Alexander Jannaeus, who became the high priest Jonathan, and ruled as king. He expanded his territory to include Galilee and Transjordan, but he was a man of great cruelty, on one occasion crucifying 800 enemies. After his death in 76 BCE, his widow Salome reigned, but strife between her sons after her death in 67 soon involved Pompey and the power of Rome.

The Romans

Jerusalem was besieged by Pompey in 63 BCE, and defeated. Many Jews were taken to Rome as captives; Jerusalem and Judaea had to pay tribute, and all the territories acquired by the Hasmonaeans were given over to the Roman governor of Syria. Those vying for power in Judaea then had to play the Roman power games, as their predecessors had played the Seleucid one. The eventual winner was Herod, an Idumaean who had supported Antony and the future emperor Augustus. He entered Jerusalem in 37 BCE as king. History remembers him as Herod the Great. His reign was marred by domestic strife and intrigue. He was responsible for many impressive buildings in Palestine. Some of his projects, such as the harbour city at Caesarea, were intended to honour his Roman masters; others, such as the extension and rebuilding of the Temple, sought to win the favour of his Jewish subjects, in whose eyes he remained an Idumaean, a foreigner. When he died in 4 BCE few of his sons were still alive. The kingdom was divided between Herod Antipas (Galilee and Peraea), Herod Archelaus (Judaea, Idumaea and Samaria) and Herod Philip (the lands east of the Jordan). Archelaus was deposed, and replaced by direct Roman rule.

There followed the years of rebellion described by Josephus in his *Jewish War*. Several popular leaders emerged who were quickly removed; this is the context in which we must read the War Scroll and the Habakkuk Commentary. This is the world of John the Baptist and Jesus. We can easily understand why Messianic claims were thought a threat to national security. Eventually the threat was too great, and Rome came to suppress and destroy. Palestine was left in ruins and Jerusalem was no more. Masada, the last stronghold, fell. Many writings record the despair of this time after the revolt of 70 CE. The writers of apocalypses such as 2 Baruch and 4 Ezra asked why God allowed Gentiles to triumph. Others set about the business of survival. The centre of religious affairs moved to Jamnia, where there was an academy established by Rabbi Johanan ben Zakkai. Here scholars collected and reflected. They brought together the holy books and their interpretations, especially the books of the Torah. A new era in Judaism began. There was soon a new translation of the Hebrew Bible into Greek. The Septuagint had become too closely associated with Christianity, and the needs of Greek-speaking Jews were met by Aquila's version. Christianity and Judaism, once they had left their Palestinian homeland, drew further and further apart.

Deutero-canonical Writings: the Apocrypha

The term *Apocrypha* (Greek for 'hidden' [writings]) was used by St Jerome to describe the writings which were in the Greek 'Old Testament' but not in the Hebrew Bible. The Greek Church calls them *Anaginoskomena* ('books to be read'). When Jerome made his Latin translation of the Old Testament at the end of the fourth century CE (the Vulgate) he included these

Apocryphal books, but scholars generally think that he spent less time and trouble on them. The Roman Catholic Church has kept all the books of the Greek Bible as its Old Testament, whereas Protestant versions use only those of the Hebrew Bible, though arranged in the same order as in the Catholic versions. Luther retained the Apocrypha, but Calvin did not. Article 6 in the Anglican Book of Common Prayer says that 'the Church doth read [the Apocrypha] for example of life and instruction of manners, but yet doth not apply them to establish any doctrine'. In the Common Bible the same books are in both Catholic and Protestant versions, but they are in different places. The Catholic version has the Old Testament with the deutero-canonical writings in their original position, dispersed as in the Greek Bible, whereas the Protestant has them collected together and printed between the two Testaments.

These books are an important source of information for the period of the Second Temple, when the world of Judaism was no longer confined to Palestine. The tales of Bel and Tobit are set in the eastern Dispersion, and may seem to us little better than tall stories, but Bel shows us the Jewish contempt for pagan ways, and Tobit that a pious Jew lived in a world peopled with angels, demons and magic. Both are vitally important for our understanding of the times. Before we speak too freely about Jewish monotheism in this period, we have to be sure that we understand the outlook of the Jews who lived then. They were only too well aware of the work of other heavenly powers, and this must influence our picture of their world. This was also the world of the first Christians, with their stories of miracles and exorcisms. In Palestine itself there had been devastating changes in the wake of Alexander the Great, a new world of contact with Europe. The books of Maccabees give us the first known stories of Jewish martyrs. Deuteronomy had long taught that faithfulness to the Torah would be rewarded with long life and prosperity; suddenly Jews found themselves martyred because of their faithfulness. We cannot begin to understand what this meant for them, or how it affected their devotion to the Torah. Some people, it is true, had already begun to question the link between religion and prosperity, as in Job, but widespread persecution in their own land was a new thing.

The Wisdom of Solomon

There are two 'wisdom' books in the Apocrypha. Wisdom literature is not an easy category to define (see above, ch 13), but this is no justification for the frequent neglect of these works. The Wisdom of Solomon (or Wisdom) is a thoroughly Jewish work in every respect, though written in Greek. This in itself is an important sign of change. The book is attributed to Solomon because Solomon was the great wise man. Wisdom had an ancient

association with the kings in Jerusalem, something to be kept in mind when
we look at the figure of Jesus, who was proclaimed as Messiah, or king. The
book of Wisdom is thought to come from the last decades BCE, or maybe a
little later, and presents wisdom as something which pervades the natural
order, an aspect of God which is visible in creation. We must beware of
trying to force these ideas into our own moulds in order to label or to cate-
gorize them neatly. The Stoic concept of the spirit was somewhat similar to
the idea of wisdom, and may have influenced the way Wisdom was written,
but we cannot be certain.

Wisdom was personified as female, a feminine aspect of God. In some
respects it was like the spirit of God in the Hebrew Bible. ('Spirit' is a
feminine noun in Hebrew, and so the spirit of God, or of Wisdom, was
described in feminine terms.) The best way to begin to understand what was
meant by wisdom is to read a wisdom text. In Wisdom 7–9 Solomon
describes how he was born an ordinary child like any other (7.1–6), but
prayed for and was given wisdom (v. 7), which sat by the throne of God
(8.4). Wisdom was the most precious of all things (7.8ff) and eventually
helped Solomon to became rich (v. 11). Wisdom gave Solomon insight into
the ways of creation, enabling him to live in harmony with it and showing
him how to correct imbalances and thus restore justice. The most famous
definition of wisdom is 7.17ff:

> unerring knowledge of what exists,
> to know the structure of the world and the activity of the elements;
> the beginning and end and middle of times,
> the alternations of the solstices and the changes of the seasons,
> the cycles of the year and the constellations of the stars,
> the natures of animals and the tempers of wild beasts,
> the powers of spirits and the reasonings of men,
> the varieties of plants and the virtues of roots . . .

which indicates that Solomon's wisdom encompasses astrology, astronomy,
the natural sciences, medicine and 'secrets'. Wisdom could teach him all
these things because wisdom had shaped the creation (v. 22). Wisdom in
creation showed God at work. It was the image of God, enabling human
beings to glimpse the ways of God. Wisdom made Solomon immortal
(8.13).

These descriptions reveal how wisdom writings still drew upon the old
royal imagery, but we cannot know how much this was believed to be
literally true, and how much was figurative. In the days of the ancient kings,
wisdom was God's gift to them (as in Isa 11.2) which enabled them to rule
wisely and to heal. (Josephus tells us that Solomon was also remembered as a
great healer and exorcist – *Antiquities*, VIII, 45.) Psalm 2 shows us that 'son

of God' was a royal title; in Wisdom, a wise man is numbered among the sons of God, among the saints (4.5). Both 'son of God' and 'saint' meant an angelic, heavenly being. Wisdom transformed people into godlike beings, immortals (8.13). What we do not know is how this was understood.

The first part of the book is addressed to the rulers of this world, and all others who despise wisdom. Again the pattern comes from the old royal cult. Psalm 2 describes hostile rulers coming against the exalted son of God. The 'servant songs' in Isaiah describe the exaltation of one who suffers, who is vindicated and rises above his persecutors. Both themes appear here. 2.1–24 describes the godless, and how the wise are mocked by them (vv. 12, 13); and 3.10ff describes the fate of the wicked. They will be speechless before the Lord at the great judgement (4.18ff), but the righteous will be rewarded and receive a crown (5.15ff). All creation will fight against the enemies of God (5.17ff). The third section of the book is complicated; its framework is the history of Israel from creation to the exodus, when God released his people from the horrors of Egypt. This history, which shows how wisdom has always worked for the good of God's people, is broken by two lengthy digressions (11.15–12.27; 13–15) showing us the attitude of this 'Solomon' to the pagan world in which he was living. Those who worship snakes and animals, he says, as do the Egyptians, are punished by them – hence the plagues; and those who worship idols will live a life of violence and make a bad end.

No Jewish writer in the earlier centuries CE quotes from the book of Wisdom; it owes its survival to Christian hands, and it is not hard to see why this is so, with its themes of an afterlife for the wise, and a judgement upon idolaters. Similar ideas are not far below the surface in Paul's letter to the Romans.

If we had to find an equivalent word for 'wisdom' it would not be easy, but even this fleeting glimpse of what it meant shows that it is an idea worth exploring in a modern context. We are today increasingly aware of the relationship of the moral and natural orders. We can see all too clearly how those who lack insight into the ways of creation make bad rulers. It may be possible to formulate a new version of this ancient insight, a new wisdom to enable humankind to see the ways of God in the complexities of the natural order.

Ecclesiasticus

Ecclesiasticus is a very different type of wisdom book. It is not a single integrated composition like Wisdom, but rather a collection of proverbs and sayings. It has been described as a teacher's scrapbook. There were many such wisdom books in the ancient world, both inside and outside Israel, and scholars have found several points of contact between Ecclesiasticus and

Egyptian texts. The Greek version of the book does actually come from Egypt, although it had been translated from a Hebrew original. Some of the Hebrew was rediscovered during the last century, when fragments of an eleventh-century copy were found in the ruins of an old Cairo synagogue. Pieces have also been found amongst the scrolls at Qumran and at Masada, and are about a thousand years older.

The writer was Jesus ben (son of) Sirach (or Sira), who lived in Jerusalem (50.27). His grandson settled in Egypt about 130 BCE, and translated the work into Greek. For several centuries there had been a flow of population from Palestine to the more prosperous land of Egypt; with Ben Sirach's grandson we see not only this movement, but also firm evidence that the Jewish community in Egypt wanted its books written not in Hebrew but in Greek. This was a major cultural change. Those who lived in a Greek world and spoke Greek, but could no longer read Hebrew, must have found themselves cut off from a large part of their heritage. They will, perhaps unconsciously, have assimilated Greek ways.

In his preface the writer gives an important warning about the problems of a translator. He knew that there was far more to translating than just finding equivalent words: 'For what was originally expressed in Hebrew does not have exactly the same sense when translated into another language. Not only this work, but even the Law itself, the prophecies and the rest of the books, differ not a little as originally expressed.' We must remember this warning for all translations.

Ecclesiasticus contains advice on many matters: how to treat old people, how to raise children, good manners, money matters, and so on. But it also has hymns and psalms which show the distinctively Jewish beliefs of its author. 16.24ff describes the mighty works of God in creation, and his plan for all things (cf. 42, 15ff). 33.7ff explains how good and evil came to exist side by side; God created all things in pairs, each with its opposite, and we all are what we are. Ben Sirach seems to know that he comes at the end of a long tradition; he follows others and gleans what is left in the vineyard (3.16). In his time the wise man is the student of the Law – thus 1.26, 6.37, and especially, 39.1–11:

> On the other hand he who devotes himself
>   to the study of the Law of the Most High
> will seek out the wisdom of all the ancients,
>   and will be concerned with prophecies;
> he will preserve the discourse of notable men
>   and penetrate the subtleties of parables . . . (vv. 1–2)

The whole of chapter 24 describes how wisdom came to be established in Jerusalem, ministering in the tabernacle, growing like a mighty tree, and irrigating a barren world with water from the rivers of Eden (24.25ff). The young are advised to seek wisdom, which is 'the fear of the Lord', to lead a blameless life and regard this as a religious duty, yet not to shun pleasure, since the good things in life are to be enjoyed (14.11ff).

The final section of the book, as in Wisdom, is a review of Israel's history, cast in the form of a hymn of praise extolling Israel's heroes. The opening verses are one of the best-known passages in the book, often read at memorial services today:

> Let us now praise famous men,
>   and our fathers in their generations
>   . . .
>
> And there are some who have no memorial,
>   who have perished as though they had not lived;
> they have become as though they had not been born,
>   and so have their children after them. (44.1, 9)

This section also contains the great poem in honour of the high priest Simon (50.1–24). If we want a glimpse of the rituals and glories of the Second Temple, we find it here, and perhaps, too, begin to understand what the Temple meant to people of that time. The horrors of desecration by Greek, Roman or impure Jew, the joy of repossession in the time of Judas Maccabaeus, the disgust at a high-priesthood which could be bartered and given to the highest bidder, the fury of Jesus of Nazareth when he turned out the money-changers – all these must be seen against the background of these great expressions of love and awe. The high priest Simon is the great leader and protector of his people, repairing the Temple and fortifying the city against siege. Decked in his glorious robes he leads the worship and pronounces the blessing of the Lord:

> How glorious he was when the people gathered round him,
>   as he came out of the inner sanctuary!
> Like the morning star among the clouds,
>   like the moon when it is full
>   . . .
>
> Then Simon came down, and lifted up his hands
>   over the whole congregation of the sons of Israel,
> to pronounce the blessing of the Lord with his lips,
>   and to glory in his name. (50.5–6, 20)

This account can profitably be read alongside others from around the same time. Particularly important is the description of Temple worship in the Letter of Aristeas (83ff), where the writer concludes, 'I am convinced that anyone who takes part in the spectacle which I have described will be filled with astonishment and indescribable wonder, and be profoundly affected in his mind at the thought of the sanctity which is attached to each detail of the service' (83ff). The Testament of Levi (8.2) indicates the splendour of the priestly vestments:

> Put on the robe of the priesthood, the crown of righteousness
> the breastplate of understanding, the garment of truth,
> the plate of faith, the turban, and the ephod of prophecy.

And the Blessing of the Priests in a Qumran text evokes the aura of sanctity of Temple worship, though from a different milieu:

> May you be as an Angel of the Presence in the Abode of Holiness
> to the glory of the God [of Hosts] . . .
> May you attend upon the service in the Temple of the Kingdom
> and decree destiny in company with the Angels of the Presence . . .

The characteristic mixture of piety and advice about daily living in Ecclesiasticus made it very popular in later times. It is often compared with the Sayings of the Fathers, which reached written form about the middle of the second century CE. In Ecclesiasticus we see Judaism two centuries before the beginning of the Christian era.

Pseudepigrapha

The word *pseudepigrapha* literally means 'false writings', meaning here works written under a false name. Until very recently such translations as existed were only to be found in large editions published at the beginning of the twentieth century, but, since these books are now the fastest growing area in biblical study, many modern editions are now available. There is no agreement as to what is to be classified as pseudepigrapha and what is not. As a rule of thumb, if the writing is neither canonical nor deutero-canonical, neither in the Bible nor in the Apocrypha, and is from roughly the intertestamental period, it may well be found in someone's edition of pseudepigrapha. The original English edition of these writings was compiled by R. H. Charles in 1913, and contains such unfamiliar works as the book of Jubilees, which is a rewriting of Genesis; the Ethiopic Enoch, a massive work containing visions of judgement, astronomical calculations, and social protests in the manner of the classical prophets; the Testaments of the Twelve Patriarchs, purporting to be the last speeches of the twelve sons of Jacob, each warning against a particular evil which was his own downfall; and the Sayings of the Fathers, a collection of sayings mostly on religious matters, attributed to the Jewish teachers of the two centuries before and after the birth of Christianity.

It is extremely hard to date works in the pseudepigrapha, and thus to know exactly which situation each addresses. We must not be misled into thinking that we need physical evidence of a book's existence before we can attempt to date it. This would give biblical and classical texts a very late date indeed. We must also resist the temptation to see the pseudepigrapha simply as a sort of postscript to the body of canonical works. Some of them may be very old, or contain very old materials. We may have to come to terms with the idea that among them have survived very ancient religious books from Israel which are not in the Hebrew Bible.

The most important type of writing represented in the pseudepigrapha is termed 'apocalyptic'. Apocalypses are visions (the name means 'revelations') and these visions usually reveal the secrets of the great judgement and the triumph of the elect. The best-known work of this kind is the Christian book of Revelation, or Apocalypse. These bizarre books have only been preserved by Christian hands, even though their roots lie deep in the traditions of Israel. The story of their recovery shows the dedication of generations of scholars. The great traditions of the Enoch apocalypses, have for example, been recovered from texts preserved in Ethiopic by the churches of Ethiopia, from Aramaic fragments found among the Dead Sea Scrolls, from Slavonic books preserved by the Russian Church, and many other sources. Now that we have access to these ancient works, we can begin to understand more clearly many of the incidents and sayings in the gospels.

Enoch

1 Enoch is an apocalypse, describing revelations to the wise man Enoch: it is often known as Ethiopic Enoch, since the most complete surviving text of the book is in Ethiopic. For the first three centuries, it was used by the Church, but then fell out of use except in Ethiopia, where it became a part of the canon. Other books about the seer Enoch, also called 'prophet Enoch', have survivied elsewhere. In the Russian Church there is a Slavonic text known as 2 Enoch, and a Hebrew Enoch (known as 3 Enoch) is one of the great Jewish mystical writings. R. H. Charles, whose translation of this book is still in use, thought it 'the most important Jewish work written between 200 BC and 100 AD', and, though there are those who would dispute this judgement, none would deny that it is a vital preliminary study to any reading of the New Testament, especially as knowledge of 1 Enoch has been much increased by the discovery of the remains of eleven manuscripts at Qumran. This Aramaic text is very similar to the Ethiopic, but in parts it is fuller.

We can best approach 1 Enoch by looking at its major themes. The most important is the myth of the fallen angels in chapters 6–10. 200 angels conspire in heaven against the Great Holy One, come to earth, and take human women to bear their demon children. Being angelic they are also wise, and they bring their knowledge to earth. Here they misuse their essentially practical wisdom for their own ends, and corrupt the creation. The writer of this ancient book recognized that such knowledge brought superhuman power which, when abused, could destroy creation:

And Azazel taught men to make swords and knives and shields and breastplates, ... Semjaza taught enchantments and root cuttings, Armaros the resolving of enchantments, Baraqijal taught astrology .... And as men perished they cried and their cry went up to heaven. (1 Enoch 8)

The demon children of the angels are left to infest the earth with disease and decay. These are the demons we meet in the gospel narratives, their exorcism being a sign that the kingdom of God has come (Luke 11.20). Eventually there is a great judgement; the evil angels are imprisoned for seventy generations until the End, when they are destined for the fire (1 Enoch 10).

Two points of importance emerge: first, this myth is clearly the background to much of the gospel material; and, second, it does not describe the origin of evil in terms of the Adam and Eve story. Evil is seen as the result of supernatural powers who had corrupted and bound the creation. It was angelic, not human, disobedience which had destroyed the world and which would bring the great judgement. This makes a considerable difference to the way we interpret New Testament passages such as Colossians 2.15 and Romans 8.18ff. It also helps us see why Enoch was quoted as a prophet by Jude (Jude 14) and kept as a Christian book by some churches.

Enoch the prophet, seer and wise man ascends in a vision and sees the throne of God, exactly as did the Jewish mystics several centuries later. This is the second important theme. Until the Enoch fragments in Aramaic were discovered at Qumran, nobody suspected that the roots of Jewish mysticism were so ancient. Later texts describe the mystics' contemplation of the great throne of God. (This was in the form of a chariot (Hebrew *merkabah*), hence the name Merkabah mysticism). In Revelation, John is caught up and sees the heavenly throne and the great judgement. Aramaic Enoch takes us back to the second or even the third century BCE, and we can begin tentatively to suggest where this mysticism originated. Much of the description in Enoch is based on the Temple layout: one house, a second house, and then the great throne. Isaiah saw the throne of God in the Temple; and Ezekiel too saw the chariot throne leaving the Temple. We may be reading in Enoch and the later mystics a meditation based on the cult of the ancient Temple which goes back to the biblical prophets.

The Similitudes or Parables of Enoch are important not only for their themes but also for their form. The Hebrew word for 'parable', *mashal*, is also translated 'proverb'. In 1 Enoch the 'parables' are visions; they are called 'the vision of wisdom' (37.1), and were equally the domain of the wise. One aspect of their wisdom was to find the correspondence between heaven and earth, the ways of God and how humankind could perceive them. The parables of Jesus may tell an earthly story, but in fact teach about the kingdom of God. Enoch's parables work in the other direction; they give a glimpse of the heavenly realities being worked out on earth. The vision of John in Revelation is also a parable in this sense, in that it refers to present realities, and is not only a prediction of the future.

There are two important themes in the Similitudes. Each of the three similitudes is a vision of the last judgement where the great agent of judgement is an angelic being called the 'Son of Man' or the 'Elect One'. He appears before the heavenly throne and judges the kings and the mighty. Much of the imagery used in these visions resembles that in Daniel 7, where one 'like a son of man' goes with clouds to the throne of God, and is given great power. We do not know if the Enochic material derived from Daniel, or if both were based on a pattern of ideas which was well-known and available to each of the visionaries. We make an assumption if we say that one text derives from another, unless one quotes the other. The same pattern of imagery also occurs in several gospel sayings, and has led scholars to wonder if some of these gospel sayings were put into the mouth of Jesus in order to link him to the figure of Daniel's vision. We have no proof either way. Nor, alas, do we have any proof that Enoch's Similitudes are pre-Christian: no part of them has been found at Qumran. If they were pre-Christian it could settle a lot of scholarly arguments as to what Jesus meant when he used the phrase 'son of man'. As it is, we can only say that the material in the Similitudes seems to be very old, that their themes seem to stem from the cult of the First Temple. No matter when they were actually written down, and by whom, it is unlikely that they were an original composition, entirely the creation of their author's imagination.

The second theme in the Similitudes is closely linked to the first. When the kings and the mighty of the earth are judged by the Son of Man, creation is restored to its original state. We find here a picture of the creation different from that in Genesis; the natural order is bound by a great covenant or oath, and this oath has been broken by the fallen angels. This 'cosmic covenant' can be restored once the evil sons of God have been judged. (See 1 Enoch 46, 62 and especially 69).

Through this oath the sea was created . . .
Through this oath the depths are made fast . . .
And through that oath the sun and the moon complete their course . . .
And the sum of judgement was given to the Son of Man

And he caused the sinners to pass away and be destroyed
from off the face of the earth,
And those who have led the world astray. (69.18, 19, 27)

The Son of Man is not only the agent of the judgement; he is also the means
of renewing the creation. Thus Enoch gives us another picture of the origin
of evil and also another account of the creation which presupposes a time
when the great natural powers were bound by God to serve him. Whenever
they break free there is chaos. This binding and conflict account of creation,
though hardly ever noticed, is also present in the canonical and deutero-
canonical books. Job 38.8 describes the sea shut in by God; 38.31 describes
the chains which bind the stars in their courses. Prayer of Manasseh 3 (in the
Apocrypha) addresses God as the one who shackled, confined and sealed the
sea. The Similitudes are important for understanding New Testament
imagery. Whatever their date, the ideas in them are very old, and can
illuminate Christian texts (e.g. Matthew 25.31ff; Roman 8.18ff; Jude).

The third part of 1 Enoch is a complex work on astronomy which we do
not yet fully understand. We know that there were several disputes about
calendar reckoning in the period of the Second Temple – should the cult be
governed by a solar or a lunar calendar? Enoch does not seem to relate to this,
however, and serves yet again to warn us how little we really do know about
the period. What is important is that we now have evidence to substantiate
what pagan writers said of the Jews – that they were astronomers. Porphyry,
a pagan writer of the third century CE, describes the Jews as philosophers
who converse about the deity and gaze at the stars.

The fourth section of 1 Enoch is a history of Israel told as an animal fable.
Israel's enemies are wild beasts, whereas her heroes are white bulls and rams.
The history culminates in a description of the Maccabaean period,
suggesting that it was written at this time, and that the writer thought those
struggles were the beginning of the Messianic age. The final section is
known as the Epistle of Enoch, and in many ways it resembles the writings
of the classical prophets, with its outcry against social injustice, and threat of
judgement. Some have thought that it was an early Essene work. Embedded
in it is another short history of Israel, which divides the whole period from
creation to the last judgement into ten 'weeks'; hence its name the
'Apocalypse of Weeks'. The age of this piece is not known, but it does show
us two important things about the people who wrote the Enochic books.
Just before the exile, it says, wisdom was abandoned, and the people who
restored Jerusalem in the sixth and fifth centuries BCE were impure and
untrue to the faith:

And in the sixth week . . . the hearts of all of them shall
godlessly forsake wisdom.

And after that in the seventh week shall an apostate generation arise
And many shall be its deeds, and all its deeds shall be apostate. (93.8–9)

1 Enoch is a bizarre book, yet it was important in the early Church and its imagery and ideas permeate the New Testament. The scribes who wrote it had an ancient quarrel with the Judaism of the Second Temple, and, although the book is deeply rooted in the imagery and ideals of Hebrew religion, it never quotes from any biblical text.

Jubilees

The book of Jubilees is attributed to Moses. (Other writings were also attributed to him: Deuteronomy is one, although we tend not to think of it as a pseudepigraphon; the Temple Scroll, the largest of the Qumran finds, is another.) Jubilees takes its name from the jubilee year in the sacred calendar. After seven years there was a sabbatical year, a year of rest. After seven sevens came a jubilee year. Jubilees reckons its history in jubilees (i.e. periods of fifty years). It too has survived in its entirety only in Ethiopic, although it was composed in Hebrew and also translated into Greek; but, unlike Enoch, it is closely related to a biblical text. Jubilees expands, revises and interprets Genesis 1 to Exodus 12, and is especially interested in *halakah* – a 'way' of life based on the interpretation of biblical texts and laws. Many of the ideas in Jubilees are similar to those in the writings of the Qumran community. It is quoted as an authority in their Damascus Document, and fragments of twelve manuscripts of Jubilees have been identified among the scrolls.

The writer of Jubilees sets out to show that the current customs and practices of his people were established from the most ancient times, even if this means rewriting Genesis. Their view of Scripture was different from ours (they had no concept of an authoritative canon of holy books) and such rewriting was not considered irreverent. Yet this practice does raise an important question. If expositors were free to rewrite scripture, then those who edited and 'wrote' scriptural books may also have done so. When we see the difference between Jubilees and Genesis, we are bound to ask what the difference might be between Genesis and whatever came before it. In Jubilees the events and festivals are dated by the old solar calendar, which our writer, like 'Enoch', considers a part of the created order. The patriarchs observed the calendar, just as they observed the Law. Thus Noah followed the correct procedure for a sacrifice (Jubilees 7.3–5), and he celebrated the feast of Weeks (6.18). Jacob kept the Day of Atonement when he heard the news of Joseph's 'death'. Our author roots the Day of Atonement in the grief of Jacob for his lost son. Abraham collects many more stories and attributes: he was a learned wise man who invented the plough (11.23), improved agriculture, spoke out against idolatry, and finally left Ur after setting fire to a pagan temple (12.12ff). He was an astronomer (12.16) and a student of Hebrew literature (13.28), although we are told that he only studied when it was raining! Above all, Abraham was tested and remained faithful. Abraham is a great hero and a figurehead. He is depicted as everything which the author of Jubilees admires. The question of historical accuracy, the 'real' Abraham, does not arise.

Like 1 Enoch, Jubilees knew a world full of demons and fallen angels. It was Mastema, the chief of the evil spirits, who provoked the sacrifice of Isaac, by testing Abraham's loyalty to God. This is not unlike the prose framework of Job, where the question raised is not 'Why is there evil?' but 'Is Job's loyalty to his God strong enough to withstand the tests of evil which, apparently, God permits?' The children of the fallen angels infested the earth and brought diseases, but the good angels taught Noah about medicine so that he could heal: 'And we explained to Noah all the medicines of their diseases . . . how he might heal them with the herbs of the earth' (10.12).

The dominant feature of Jubilees must be the idea that everything was predetermined, and ordained by God from the time of the creation. Everything was written on heavenly tablets, and Moses's forty days on Sinai were spent learning about these, as well as about the commandments: 'And he said to the Angel of the Presence: "Write for Moses from the beginning of creation until my sanctuary has been built among them for all eternity"' (1.27).

Despite this determinism, mankind was still thought to be free to keep the Law, and therefore to be responsible for its own actions in breaking the Law: 'And the judgement of all is ordained and written on the heavenly tablets in righteousness, even the judgement of all who depart from the path which is ordained for them to walk in' (5.13).

The book was probably written in the middle of the second century BCE, and shows how the interpretation of Scripture was becoming increasingly important. Exposition of a holy book was replacing the claim to direct revelation as the accepted means of expressing religious ideas. Later interpreters and expositors adhered more strictly to the text, as we see in the Qumran commentaries and the methods of the later rabbis.

The Pharisees

The Pharisees are the best-known and yet least understood of all Jewish sects. Their origin is obscure, and the New Testament, a major primary source, gives a very unfavourable picture of them. They are depicted as the main opponents of Jesus; as a result, the name Pharisee has passed into common usage as a term of abuse for one who is self-righteous and emphasizes the external aspects of religion at the expense of the spiritual. 'You tithe mint, rue and every herb, and neglect justice and the love of God' (Luke 11.42) sums up well the prevailing Christian perception not only of the Pharisees but of all Judaism in the early Christian period. It is a sad fact of history that the New Testament's picture of the Pharisees has coloured most later Christian descriptions and condemnations of Judaism. Since Judaism, as we know, it is actually rooted in the ways of the Pharisees (not least in the institution of the synagogue, with which they were so closely associated), it is important to see just how much truth we can recover from this legacy of bitterness. We have three sources of information: Josephus, Jewish historian and younger contemporary of Jesus; the rabbinic writings of the first and second centuries CE (Tannaitic literature); and the New Testament.

Josephus was himself a follower of the Pharisees, but his information is not always easy to evaluate since he wrote as an historian and dealt only with the public activities of the Pharisees and not with their internal affairs. He wrote for readers outside Palestine, for whom he may have expressed Palestinian ideas in Greek or pagan terms, and he wrote to make the point that Rome was not to blame for the disaster of 70 CE – the Jews of Palestine had, he argued, been misled by a minority. His material about the political role of the Pharisees at this time must therefore be read with care. The Pharisees first appear in his accounts (*Antiquities*, XIII, 171–3) in the time of the Hasmonaean Jonathan, and later playing a major role in the reign of John Hyrcanus. He began as one of their followers, but then quarrelled with them over his right to the high-priesthood, and gave his support instead to the Sadducees, a party with conservative political views. He abrogated the 'tradition of the fathers', the Pharisees' oral law, which had until then enjoyed considerable popular support. It was these laws which most clearly distinguished Pharisee from Sadducee. To quell the troubles, eight hundred Pharisees were crucified. When Alexander Jannaeus was king and high priest, Pharisees led a popular rebellion against him (*Antiquities*, XIII, 399–404), but Alexandra, his widow and successor, made peace with them and the oral law was restored to its former status.

When Judaea came under Roman rule, Josephus was at pains to show that there was a distinction between Pharisees and Zealots, whom he called 'the fourth philosophy' – the third being the Essenes, a monastic sect normally associated with Qumran and the Dead Sea Scrolls. Pharisees and Zealots, he said, agreed in all things except in their attitude to national liberty. The Zealots would accept no master but God (*Antiquities*, XVIII, 23–5), which implies that the Pharisees would accept Roman rule provided that it did not interfere with the religious laws. Josephus's other information about them is expressed in very un-Jewish terms, and was probably his attempt to put Jewish ideas into an equivalent Greek form. The Pharisees, he says, believed in Fate, even though each man had to make the choice between good and evil, and they believed in the survival of the soul. The good passed into another body, and the wicked suffered eternal punishment.

There is a major problem of discrepancy: our other two sources give a rather different picture. The rabbinic material is concerned very much with the internal affairs of the sect, and with the two great houses of Hillel and Shammai and their respective interpretations of the Torah. Here too there is a problem, since the followers of Hillel came to dominate in the transmission of traditions about the earlier Pharisees, and their rivals, the followers of Shammai, appear in a less than favourable light. Before Hillel and Shammai, approximate contemporaries of Jesus, there had been a chain of teachers stretching back in pairs to the time of Simon the Just, the last legitimate high priest. The Sayings of the Fathers makes him the link between the Pharisees and the men of the Great Synagogue, who were in their turn the heirs of the prophets. There seem to have been five pairs of teachers, who had the titles Nasi (prince) and Ab (father) of the Beth Din. The former led the majority party, the latter the minority. If we allow a generation, say thirty years, for each pair, we find that the first pair, Jose ben Joezer and Jose ben Johanan, flourished in the middle of the second century BCE, at exactly the time when Josephus first mentions the sect. Perhaps this is when they began. Very little survives of the teachings of these early Pharisees, but, since Josephus describes them as political figures who were savagely persecuted in the time of Alexander Jannaeus, it is not surprising that little of their teaching survived. Certainly, by the time we meet them in the gospels, the Pharisees resemble the figures of the later rabbinic writings, concerned with food laws and Sabbath observances, and Josephus specifically says that they were not politically involved. A change had come over them, but we do not know who was responsible for the transformation.

Most of our pre-70 materials come from the first century CE, and show us the Pharisees as a group concerned primarily with the observance of purity laws outside the Temple. (Inside everyone would have kept them.) They ate their food in a state of ritual purity, just like a priest in the Temple. The purity laws extended to the growing and preparation of the food: correct preparation included correct tithing, since untithed food was not pure. Groups of Pharisees shared a common meal and applied their rules of purity to all aspects of life, thus sanctifying even the most humble acts, and living out a faith divorced from specific rituals and holy places. About three-quarters of all the rabbinic materials which relate to the pre-70 Pharisees deal with the topics for which the gospels made them notorious: food laws, purity, Sabbath observance and vows. They tell us nothing of events outside the sect; there is no mention of the Hasmonaeans, the Romans, the Herods. We know nothing of their theology of history, or even if they had one. Only Josephus tells us of their relationship to the politics of the day, and for our other information we have to rely upon the very biased Christian sources.

Within the New Testament there are two types of reference to the Pharisees: those which show them as the opponents of Jesus, and those which show them as the model for the Paul's pre-conversion life. Paul reacted very violently against this past when he was converted to Christianity, even though he never really rid himself of its values. He describes himself 'as to the Law a Pharisee, as to zeal a persecutor of the church, as to righteousness under the Law, blameless' (Philippians 3.5–6); and zealous for the traditions of the fathers (Galatians 1.14). Luke's account of Paul is similar: he had been a pupil of Gamaliel, educated according to the strict manner of the law of the fathers (Acts 22.3). When he was on trial before the Sanhedrin, he could plead that his belief in the resurrection – a belief he brought to his Christianity from his upbringing as a Pharisee – had been the reason for his arrest. Thus, says Luke, the Sanhedrin was divided, the Pharisees supporting Paul, the Sadducees not. Yet this same upbringing as a Pharisee had led Paul to become the most bitter persecutor of the infant Church. It is clear that there is great deal about Paul, the Pharisees and the early Christians that we just do not know.

The synoptic gospels (Matthew, Mark, Luke) give an ambivalent picture of the Pharisees. Jesus says that the scribes and Pharisees sit in the seat of Moses; their teachings are correct (Matthew 23.2–3). The righteousness of his followers must exceed that of the Pharisees, since he had not come to abolish the Law but to fulfil it (Matthew 5.17–20). But these same Pharisees are blind guides, emphasizing tradition at the expense of the spirit of the Law. By the time Matthew's gospel was written, they were persecuting the Christians (Matthew 23.29ff), perhaps because Christian teaching was undermining the supreme authority of the Law. The minutest details of their practices were ridiculed – their attitude to oaths, their fastidious care in tithing, their ritual washings (Matthew 23.16ff; Mark 7.1–23; Luke 18.10ff). These concerns are all represented in the Tannaitic accounts, showing that the synoptic picture is accurate as to their practices, even if it is bitter in its attitude. Throughout there is emphasis on the tradition of the fathers, the oral law (e.g. Mark 7.3).

In some aspects, the synoptic picture goes beyond the evidence of the later Jewish sources. They were concerned with fasting (Mark 2.18ff; Matthew 6.16–18), with the recognition of the Messiah and his Davidic descent (Matthew 22.41ff), with the forgiveness of sins (Luke 5.17ff), with baptism (Matthew 3.7), with divorce (Mark 10.2ff), with relations to their

Roman rulers (Mark 12.13ff), with observance of the Sabbath (Mark 3.1ff). They believed in resurrection (Matthew 22.23ff), and that some commandments were more important than others (vv. 34ff).

The picture in the Fourth Gospel is different again, possibly because it reflects the situation of a later period. The Pharisees are the general rulers of the Jews, who challenge only the authority of Jesus and his origins (John 7.45ff; 8.12ff). Their law, or perhaps their power, is at stake, and they fear the consequences for political stability (11.45ff). They have power to expel from the synagogue (12.42–3). Nowhere do we find the issues of the oral law or their differences from the Sadducees. Perhaps by the time the Fourth Gospel was written the Pharisees were Judaism as it was then known, since so much of the older religion had been destroyed in the war against Rome.

This destruction may well account for the very limited information which we have about the Pharisees. From their own accounts we can reconstruct only the picture of a group concerned with table fellowship, and the correct procedures for sanctifying the everyday things of life, based upon the unwritten law. They do not tell us what was their canon of scripture, what they believed of the afterlife, what was their attitude to Messianic claims, and the apocalyptic teachings associated with them. Their strength lay in this very concern for the santification of all life. When the cultic centre had been destroyed, it was this emphasis which formed the basis of the ongoing faith. And it was this emphasis which, perhaps misunderstood or distorted in New Testament times, has led to their being misrepresented ever since.

The Dead Sea Scrolls

In 1947 the oldest known fragments of Hebrew literature were discovered in caves near the Dead Sea. Archaeologists linked the find with a monastic settlement whose ruins lay nearby: this monastery at Qumran had been occupied for about 200 years. The first period was from the time of Simon (142–134 BCE) until the time of the earthquake in 31 BCE; the second from about 4 BCE until the war against Rome, about 68 CE. Nearby was a cemetery with skeletons of men, women and children. The writings are now designated by the number of the cave in which they were found. Thus 4QEn means a text of Enoch found in cave 4; 11QMelch means a text about Melchizedek found in cave 11. Some of the first books on the scrolls invented their own names to describe the texts since none had been generally agreed, but names have now become standardized. It can cause confusion to discover that the Damascus Document, the Zadokite Document and the Damascus Rule are all the same text! Other scrolls also have several names, although their numerical designation has always been consistent.

It is now generally agreed that the Qumran monastery was an Essene settlement, even though there are some discrepancies between ancient accounts of the Essenes and the evidence supplied by archaeology, not least the evidence of the female skeletons. Ancient writers describe the sect as celibate. In the appendix to his *Jewish War*, Josephus says that the Essenes scorned wedlock; and the Elder Pliny in his *Natural History* (V, 73) tells of a solitary tribe of Essenes which was remarkable because it had no women. Josephus also tells us that the Essenes lived in the towns and villages of Judaea, whereas the community's own Rule does not mention these other settlements. Other possible places of settlement have been found, but, in general, the ancient writers and the archaeologists give a similar picture. The settlement was north of En-gedi, as Pliny said, and they lived a communal life, sharing property and food, just as Josephus described them. They had elaborate admission procedures, a complex hierarchy, and gave great atttention to ritual purity. They have been linked to the Hasidim, the pious warriors who supported the Maccabees in their early struggles; the Aramaic equivalent of *hasid* (pious) is *hasen*, which could give us the name Essene.

The writings which have been found are of two types: some are fragments of known texts – the oldest known manuscripts of biblical books (all except Esther are represented) or fragments of books only previously known in translation (e.g. 1 Enoch, 4QEn); others were books written by the community to describe their own life and origins, and to interpret the scripture in their own characteristic way. We learn of their history in the Damascus Document, so called because the sect describe their founders as members of the New Covenant in the land of Damascus. (A copy of this text had already been found in the ruined synagogue in Cairo in 1896, and several guesses had been made as to who wrote it. Because the fullest text was found in Cairo, it is designated CD, whilst the fragments from Qumran are 4Qfrg.) Much of the text is cryptic, and obviously refers to people and events in the troubled years of the Hasmonaean kings. God had visited his people 390 years after Nebuchadnezzar took Jerusalem, and had caused a root to grow from Israel and Aaron. Those who repented of the evil ways of their people entered into a New Covenant, and were given, after twenty years of 'blindness', a Teacher of Righteousness, one who could reveal hidden truths about the times they were living in. These teachings concerned the true calendar (which must have stood for the true pattern of religious observances), and possibly also the true interpretation of holy writings, since the sect developed its own way of expounding both Law and Prophets. The sectarians had to live apart, avoiding those who lived in sin and error, those who followed the 'Spouter of Lies' and the Temple establishment in Jerusalem. If we take the sect's own figure of 390 years from the capture of Jerusalem, we find ourselves in the early years of the Seleucid domination of Palestine, with the high priesthood being sold to the highest bidder, and Greek ways in holy places. Withdrawal to a life of purity is entirely understandable. Members of the sect believed, as did the earliest Christians, that they were living in the last days; from them the New Age would come, and so they searched the holy writings for new guidance.

The sect had several ways of interpreting and using Scripture. These are seen most clearly in the texts known as *pesharim* (solutions, interpretations), which look for historical events and signs of the End in biblical prophecies. The sectarians believed that their interpretation of Scripture was inspired like Scripture itself, and in this they differ markedly from other Jewish interpreters. The longest *pesher* found is a commentary on Habakkuk (1QpHab), which comes from the end of the first century BCE. It seems to be dealing, however, with events in the middle of the second century BCE, and uses the prophecies to describe the conflict between the Teacher of Righteousness and his two enemies, the Man of Lies and the Wicked Priest. The latter was probably Jonathan the Maccabee, since the sect thought him a good man until he was corrupted by wealth and power. The *pesher* also tells of Kittim, taken from the prophecy of Balaam (Num 24.24), who represent the foreign enemies of God's people. In Daniel 11.30 the Kittim were the Greeks; in this *pesher* they are the Romans. This gives us a clear example of the way one biblical text was reused in new situations. There are also *pesharim* on Nahum (4QpNah) and on the Psalms (4QpPs), as well as several small fragments expounding other texts, such as Isaiah, Micah, Zephaniah and Hosea. The Genesis Apocryphon (1QapGen) rewrites Genesis, introducing many new stories, such as one in which Noah, as a baby, was suspected of being an angel child.

Many of the sect's writings deal with the time of the End. The War Scroll (1QM) describes the final battle between the Sons of Light and the Sons of Darkness. The Scroll is based on descriptions in the Hebrew Bible of the war before the great judgement, but adapts these to suit the community's own times. The final battle would soon come, and, when it did, there would be a coalition of earthly and heavenly forces. The Sons of Light were the community and the host of good angels commanded by Michael, the archangel of Israel; and the Sons of Darkness were a coalition of Kittim, earthly rulers, renegade Jews, and the hosts of evil led by Belial. This was to be a real war, in which the Sons of Darkness would win some of the battles. There are detailed descriptions of weapons and tactics, as well as the expected emphasis on ritual purity at all times. This was holy war. There was no question in the minds of the sectarians as to whether or not religion and politics should mix! The great war against evil was real, earthly and imminent.

The day-to-day life of the sectarians whilst they awaited the final battle is vividly described in their writings. The picture given in the Damascus

Document is filled out by the Rule of the Community (1QS), a text which has survived almost in its entirety. In all, twelve copies have been found, stressing its importance. The regulations in the Damascus text and the Rule are not identical in every detail; perhaps they come from different stages in the history of the community. The Master of the community has to instruct in the Law of Moses; priests and Levites have to fulfil their allotted duties as long as the dominion of Satan endures. The Sons of Light believed that there were two spirits battling for the control of man: the spirit of truth and the spirit of falsehood. It was from this struggle that good and evil came (not from any taint or tendency inherited from Adam).

A number of liturgical texts have also been found. From the first century BCE comes a collection of hymns (1QH) and psalms (11QPs), some resembling the biblical psalms, but others with different themes. Several speak of exile and persecution, and of the gift of knowledge given by God to the psalmist and his community. From the beginning of the first century CE comes the Angelic Liturgy (4QShirShabb), of which there are four surviving manuscripts. The Liturgy contains the prayer for every Sabbath of the Essene year, and shows us how the angels not only shared the sectarians' warfare but also their worship. The liturgy of the heavenly temple corresponds to that of the earthly. There are several heavens, possibly seven, and many ranks of angels, some of whom are called ruling princes.

From cave 11 have come two remarkable texts. One concerns Melchizedek, the mysterious priest-king who appears in Genesis 14 and Psalm 110, and reappears in the epistle to the Hebrews as prefiguring Jesus in the role of high priest. Nobody knows the real significance of the Melchizedek figure, but this text (11QMelch) may illuminate the problem. The Sons of Light are Melchizedek's men, and on the Day of Judgement Melchizedek will judge even the holy ones of God. Texts which in the Hebrew Bible describe God here describe Melchizedek (Ps 82.1; Isa 52.7). He is God's representative, even his manifestation. Also found in cave 11 was the Temple Scroll (11QT), the longest of the scrolls and the last to be published, because it has had a very chequered history since its discovery. The scroll is from the end of the second century BCE, and is a rewriting of much of the Law, depicted as a new revelation to Moses. The city of Jerusalem is seen as equivalent to the camp in the wilderness, and all laws applying to the purity of the camp and the Tabernacle are applied to the whole city and its temple. No impure person is even allowed into the holy city. No women can live there and all defecation has to be outside the city. These rules are very like those for the war camp of the Sons of Light in the War Scroll. The temple itself is a strange building, square, as in the temple of Ezekiel's vision (Ezek 40–8), and designed as a series of concentric areas with the holiest in the centre. The Temple Scroll has its own characteristic calendar, based upon the solar calendar of the sect, and it has additional festivals unknown in biblical accounts of Temple practice: a festival of New Wine (fifty days after the feast of Weeks), and a festival of New oil (fifty days after that). There are several additions to the laws about the king: he may not marry a foreign woman, and he may have only one wife, whom he may not divorce.

The discovery of the Dead Sea Scrolls has revolutionized our picture of Judaism in the second and first centuries BCE. We now know far more about the period in which Judaism and Christianity went their separate ways; but at the same time we have been made aware how much we have still to learn.

FURTHER READING

Charlesworth, J. H. 1983: *The Old Testament Pseudepigrapha*.
Gowan, D. E. 1976: *The Bridge between the Testaments*.
Neusner, J. 1984: *Judaism in the Beginning of Christianity*.
Nickelsburg, G. W. 1981: *Jewish Literature between the Bible and the Mishnah*.
Nickelsburg, G. W and Stone, M. E., 1983: *Faith and Piety in Early Judaism*.
Stone, M. E. 1982: *Scriptures, Sects and Visions*.
Vermes, G. 1987: *The Dead Sea Scrolls in English*, 3rd edn.

There is also a comprehensive series on the period and its literature: 'Cambridge Commentaries on the Writings of the Jewish and Christian World, 200 BC to 200 AD', general editors P. R. Ackroyd, A. R. C. Leaney, J. W. Packer.

1 (i)   J. R. Bartlett, *Jews in the Hellenistic World: Josephus, Aristeas, the Sibylline Oracles, Eupolemus*.
1 (ii)   R. Williamson, *Jews in the Hellenistic World: Philo*.
2   M. A. Knibb, *The Qumran Community*.
3   H. Maccoby, *Early Rabbinic Writings*.
4   M. de Jonge, *Outside the Old Testament*.
5   G. N. Stanton, *Outside the New Testament*.
6   M. Whittaker, *Jews and Christians: Graeco-Roman Views*.
7   A. R. C. Leaney, *The Jewish and Christian World 200 BC to 200 AD*.

Glossary

This glossary is intended to assist in the reading both of this book and of the works recommended as further reading. Words appearing in bold in the definitions have their own entries. For a fuller discussion, the reader should consult the main index, where page references in bold type denote the major discussion of the subject. The index also provides access to items not included in the glossary.

acrostic (alphabetic)   A poem the successive lines of verses of which begin with each of the letters of the alphabet in turn.

aetiology   A story giving an explanation of the origin of a name, a place or a custom.

aggadah, haggadah   'Telling', and therefore 'narrative', 'story', often with a theological purpose. *The* Haggadah is the story retold during **Pesach** (Passover) about the exodus from Egypt in the time of Moses.

Amoraim   Jewish teachers from the period between 200 and 500 CE, whose work culminated in the **Talmud**.

amphictyony   A tribal confederation centred around a Greek temple, once used as an illustrative model for ancient Israel's political structure.

anamnesis   A process of symbolism in which people remember and re-enact past events, for example, in festivals.

aniconic   Pertaining to worship in which images or icons are deliberately not used. See **iconography**.

apocalypse   Literally an 'unveiling' of something hidden. Apocalyptic literature claims to reveal the future and to show how the divine plan will be worked through in history.

Apocrypha   Deutero-canonical   books found in the **Septuagint** but not in the Hebrew Bible.

Aramaic   A language in the same family as Hebrew, used in Daniel 2.4–7.28; Ezra 4.8–6.18 and 7.12–26; and Jeremiah 10.11. Its square script replaced the Old ('Palaeo') Hebrew script in Hebrew manuscripts before the Christian Era.

charismatic   Filled with the divine, or with God's spirit. This state may be linked with ecstasy or trance, which is reported to have been experienced by the early prophets and by Saul, the first king.

cherubim   (singular **cherub**) Mythical celestial winged creatures prominent in Temple decoration, perhaps representing the storm winds.

chiasmus   (adj. **chiastic**) A literary device in which, for emphasis, the second part of a text is parallel to the first, but in reverse – e.g. ABBA, ABCBA.

Chronicler   Writer of the books of Chronicles; generally considered to be a later interpreter of the history of Judah.

345

covenant An agreement between two parties, used as a metaphor of God's relationship with his people. The Hebrew term is *berith*.

cubit A unit of measurement, the distance from elbow to fingertip – around 0.5m.

Dead Sea Scrolls A range of scrolls dating back to the first century BCE found in caves near the Dead Sea from 1947 onwards. They are generally thought to be linked with the 'monastery' at Qumran, and with the **Essenes**.

decalogue Laws collected into a group of ten: *The* Decalogue is the Ten Commandments.

demythologize The process of interpreting a myth in non-mythic language to express its meaning without clinging to its mythic form.

deutero-canonical Pertains to writings regarded as Scripture by some (particularly by Christian groups) but not contained in the Hebrew Bible. See **Apocrypha** and **pseudopigrapha**.

Deuteronomic History The history of Israel and Judah which comprises Joshua, Judges, Samuel and Kings, the authors of which are often thought to have been greatly influenced by Deuteronomy.

Diaspora The technical term for the dispersion of the Jewish people, a process which began after defeats in 722 and 587/6 BCE and resulted in the growth of sizable Jewish communities outside Palestine.

Elohist The name given to a reconstructed source underlying **Pentateuchal** narratives. It is said to be characterized by the use of the divine name **Elohim**, 'God'. See also **Yahwist**.

eponym A supposed ancestor whose name is the same as, or related to, the name of a later group, tribe or nation.

eschatology The doctrine of the last things; speculation and teaching about the end-time.

Essenes A Jewish group who lived in retreat in the wilderness of Judaea between the first century BCE and the first CE, according to Josephus, the elder Pliny, and Philo. See also **Dead Sea Scrolls**.

exegesis The process of drawing out meaning from a text.

form criticism The analysis of the Hebrew Bible to discover traditional formal structures behind the present text.

Former Prophets The technical name for the books of Joshua, Judges, Samuel and Kings – possibly as it was assumed that prophets had written them.

Gemara Commentary on the **Mishnah**, together with which it comprises the *Talmud*. The teachers underlying the Gemara are called **Amoraim**.

genre A type of literary text; for example, a story, saga, novel or history.

halakah Meaning literally 'going' (i.e. how we go about our daily lives), halakah deals with practical guidance, rules and expectations in Judaism.

Hanukkah The festival of 'Dedication', recalling the re-dedication of the temple after its desecration in the time of the **Seleucid** king Antiochus IV Epiphanes (second century BCE).

Hasmonaean Hasmon is said to be the family name of the Maccabees, so the **Maccabaean** rulers are often referred to as Hasmonaean.

Hellenistic Pertaining to Greek culture as disseminated by the conquests of Alexander the Great, and the rule of his successors.

hermeneutics   The strategy of interpreting texts to enable them to be applied to circumstances contemporary with the interpreter.

Hexateuch   The first six books of the Hebrew Bible. There may be an underlying assumption that these belong together historically.

iconography   The expression of religious principles or doctrines using pictorial or symbolic images or icons. These may serve as visual metaphors. A faith which favours this type of expression is called 'iconic'.

Israel   A secondary name for Jacob; the name of the ten northern tribes who formed the 'kingdom of Israel' (alternatives are 'Ephraim' and 'Samaria'), destroyed in 722 BCE; also used as the name for the whole territory ('Palestine') occupied by the Israelites/Jews.

jubilee   The name is derived from a ram's-horn trumpet. Every fiftieth year was a jubilee (the year following seven times seven years, or seven weeks of years). Special arrangements during this year were designed to aid the poor and dispossessed.

Kabbalah   Jewish mystical writings.

Kethib (that which is written)   Usually a word or phrase difficult to interpret and replaced in public reading by a **qere**, an alternative noted in the margin.

Kethubim   (Writings) The last of the three main divisions of the Hebrew Bible, including Psalms, Proverbs, Job, the five Megilloth or 'Scrolls' (Song of Songs, Ruth, Lamentations, Ecclesiastes, Esther), Daniel, Ezra, Nehemiah and Chronicles.

Latter Prophets   The technical name for the collection of prophetic writings, comprising the books of the three 'major' prophets (Isaiah, Jeremiah, Ezekiel) and those of the twelve 'minor' (or shorter) prophets, sometimes collectively called 'the Book of the Twelve'.

Levites   Temple officials who traced their ancestry from the patriarch Levi. They were distinct from the priests (who traced their ancestry to Aaron) and could not serve as priests.

literary criticism   The analysis of the Hebrew Bible on the basis of literary structure, devices and strategies. (In older books, it may mean **source criticism**).

Maccabaean   From the period of Judas Maccabaeus (Judah Maccabee) and his brothers, second century BCE.

Masoretes, Massoretes ('transmitters'; adj. **Masoretic**)   Transmitters of the text of the Hebrew Bible, active from 500 CE. They introduced vowel signs, accents (**pointing**) and marginal notes (*masora*).

midrash   The process of interpreting and expounding scriptural texts in Judaism. Midrash **halakah** focuses on expounding rules; and midrash **aggadah** deals with the interpretation of stories.

mimesis   The reporting of events or incidents in such a way as to convey a sense of reality – for example, by using the sort of language believed to have been used at the time.

Mishnah ('Repetition')   A thematic compilation of legal material; in particular a compilation by Rabbi Judah Hannasi ('the Prince', i.e. president), of laws based ultimately on principles laid down in the **Torah**. Produced aound 200 CE, it became the most authoritative collection of **oral Torah**.

monolatry   The worship of one god whilst recognizing the existence of others.

Nebi'im   ('Prophets') The second main division of the Hebrew Bible, comprising the **Former** and the **Latter Prophets**.

oral Torah   Applications for contemporary situations, found in the oral tradition before the completion of the **Mishnah**, of **Torah** texts and principles. The Jewish belief in both a written (*torah she-bi-ketab*, 'teaching that is by writing') and an oral (*torah she-be-'al peh*, 'teaching that is by mouth') Torah is known as 'the dual Torah'.

Orthodox Jews   Jews who base their lives on the **Torah** as expounded through the **Talmud**, and maintain traditional customs and values.

paradigm   An intellectual framework consisting of a set of assumptions.

Pentateuch   (adj. **Pentateuchal**) The first five books of the Hebrew Bible, which together comprise the **Torah**.

Pesach   The Hebrew term for Passover, a festival recalling the escape from Egypt in the exodus.

Pharisees   A Jewish religious group which is first reported in the time of the **Hasmonaean** priest-kings in the second century BCE. Their political influence fluctuated, but their religious influence survived the Jewish defeat at the hands of Rome, giving them a major role in the reconstruction of Judaism.

pointing   The vowel signs and accents introduced into the consonantal Hebrew text by the **Masoretes**.

Progressive (or Liberal) Jews   Jews who seek to adapt and update traditional customs, rules and beliefs.

pseudepigrapha   Writings purporting to be by somebody (usually a famous historical or legendary figure) who is not the author; used generically for **deutero-canonical** writings not in the **Apocrypha**.

Purim   The festival of 'lots', celebrating deliverance as described in the story of Esther.

qere' 'that which is to be read'   A **Masoretic** marginal note replacing something difficult that is written (**kethib**).

recension   A revised edition.

redaction criticism   The analysis of the Hebrew Bible to determine the contribution of the editor, author or **redactor**.

redactor   The editor of a composite work.

rhetorical criticism   The analysis of a text on the basis of its rhetorical devices. It is therefore very similar to **literary criticism**.

Samaritan   Samaria was built as capital of Israel, the northern kingdom, in the ninth century BCE and fell in 722 BCE when leading members were deported. Probably, exiles from elsewhere were settled here and mixed with the Israelites who remained. Their descendants are known as Samaritans.

Sanhedrin   The highest court and council, with seventy-one members. The name comes from the Greek synhedrion.

Seleucid   The dynasty of Seleucus, a general of Alexander the Great, which ruled Syria and Asia Minor after Alexander's death. Seleucid rule in Palestine was ended by the Maccabees in the second century BCE.

Semitic   Pertaining to a race, language or culture linked to the line of Shem (see Gen 10). Among Semitic languages are Hebrew, Aramaic and Arabic.

Septuagint   The Greek translation of the Old Testament, consisting of the books of the Hebrew Bible and some **deutero-canonical** books, now know as the **Apocrypha**.

Shavuoth   Often known as the feast of 'weeks' or Pentecost, it occurs fifty days after **Pesach** (Passover) and celebrates harvest, and the giving of the **Torah**.

Shema   The Jewish prayer, based on Deuteronomy 6.4–9, which begins 'Hear, O Israel'. *Shema* 'Hear' is the first word in Hebrew.

Simchat Torah   ('Rejoicing in Torah') An annual celebration during the feast of **Sukkoth** at which the reading of the **Torah** is completed and recommenced, from Genesis 1.

Sitz im Leben   A German phrase meaning 'setting in life', generally referring to the context of a tradition or ritual.

source criticism   The analysis of the Hebrew Bible to determine its underlying sources.

Sukkoth   Often known as the feast of 'Booths' or 'Tabernacles', it commemorates the wilderness wanderings and gives thanks for the vintage.

Talmud   Commentary to the **Mishnah** (see also **Gemara**). Two Talmuds have been preserved – the Jerusalem (*c*.400 CE) and the Babylonian (*c*.600 CE).

Tannaim   Jewish religious authorities and teachers during the first and second centuries CE who contributed to works such as the **Mishnah**. *Tanna* means 'one who repeats' – that is, one who passes on traditions by word of mouth.

Targum   Aramaic translation of sections from the Hebrew Bible.

tell   A mound which contains the ruined remains of a town. Each layer (or level, stratum) represents a particular historical period.

Tenakh, Tanakh   The Jewish term for the Hebrew Bible, made up of the initial letters of **Torah, Nebi'im** and **Kethubim**.

Tetrateuch   The first four books of the Hebrew Bible. There may be an underlying assumption that these belong together historically.

theocracy   (adj. **theocratic**) A constitution in which God is regarded as ruler or sovereign.

theophoric   An element in a proper name which derives from a name for God.

Torah   ('Instruction, Direction') The first main division of the Hebrew Bible, comprising the first five books or **Pentateuch**; the 'instruction' it contains. See also **oral Torah**.

tradition criticism   Sometimes called the 'traditio-historical method'. The analysis of the Hebrew Bible to uncover possible oral strands underlying the final form of the text.

type-scene   A typical conventionally structured story.

wisdom literature   In the Hebrew Bible, those books of a predominantly didactic (Proverbs) or philosophical (Job, Ecclesiastes) cast. In the **Apocrypha**, Ecclesiasticus and the Wisdom of Solomon belong to the didactic tradition of wisdom literature.

Yahwist   The suggested author of narrative, in the **Pentateuch** particularly, which favours the use of the divine name Yahweh. A reconstructed source suggested to lie behind early Hebrew history. See also **Elohist**.

Yom Kippur   The Day of Atonement, a solemn day of penitence and fasting. This is 'the day' (*Yoma*) of the **Mishnah** – the most significant day in the calendar.

Zealot   Someone zealous for the **Torah**; and in particular a member of a Jewish group, founded perhaps by Judas the Galilean in 6 CE, made up of dedicated political activists who opposed Roman rule.

References and Bibliography

Abrahams, I. 1922: *A Companion to the Authorised Daily Prayer Book*. London: Eyre and Spottiswoode.

Ackroyd, P. R. 1953: 'Criteria for the Maccabean Dating of Old Testament Literature'. *Vetus Testamentum*, 3, 113–32.

Ackroyd, P. R. 1968: *Exile and Restoration*, London: SCM.

Ackroyd, P. R. 1973: *1 and 2 Chronicles, Ezra, Nehemiah*. London: SCM.

Aharoni, Y. 1979: *The Land of the Bible: a Historical Geography*, rev. edn, ed. A. F. Rainey. Philadelphia: Westminster Press.

Aharoni, Y. 1982: *The Archaeology of the Land of Israel*. Philadelphia: Westminster Press.

Alexander, P. S. 1984: *Textual Sources for the Study of Judaism*. Manchester: Manchester University Press.

Alt, A. 1966: 'The Settlement of the Israelites in Palestine'. In *Essays on Old Testament History and Religion*, Oxford: Basil Blackwell.

Alter, R. 1981: *The Art of Biblical Narrative*. London: Allen and Unwin.

Anderson, A. A. 1972: *Psalms*, New Century Bible. Grand Rapids, Mich.: Eerdmans; London: Marshalls.

Anderson, G. W. 1962: 'The Psalms'. In M. Black and H. H. Rowley (eds), *Peake's Commentary on the Bible*, London: Nelson, 409–43.

ANET: J. B. Pritchard (ed.), *Ancient Near Eastern Texts Relating to the Old Testament*; 3rd edn (1969). Princeton, N. J.: Princeton University Press.

Auffret, P. 1977: *The Literary Structure of Psalm 2*. Sheffield: JSOT Press.

Auld, A. G. 1986a *Kings, Daily Study Bible*. Edinburgh: St Andrew; Philadelphia: Westminster Press.

Auld, A. G. 1986b: *Amos*, Old Testament Guides. Sheffield: JSOT Press.

Avigad, N. 1983: *Discovering Jerusalem*. Oxford: Basil Blackwell.

Bar Efrat, S. 1988: *Narrative Art in the Bible*. Sheffield: JSOT Press.

Barr, J. 1961: *The Semantics of Biblical Language*. Oxford: Clarendon Press.

Barr, J. 1968: *Comparative Philology and the Text of the Old Testament*. Oxford: Clarendon Press.

Barr, J. 1983: *Holy Scripture: Canon, Authority, Criticism*. Oxford: Clarendon Press.

Barton, J. 1984: *Reading the Old Testament: Method in Biblical Study*. London: Darton, Longman and Todd.

Barton, J. 1986: *Oracles of God: Perceptions of Ancient Prophecy in Israel after the Exile.* London: Darton, Longman and Todd.

Barton, J. 1988: *People of the Book? The Authority of the Bible in Christianity.* London: SPCK.

Beattie, O. R. G. 1977: *Jewish Exegesis of the Book of Ruth.* Sheffield: JSOT Press.

Benson, R. M. 1901: *The War Songs of the Prince of Peace.* London: John Murray.

Berlin, A. 1983: *Poetics and Interpretation of Biblical Narrative.* Sheffield: Almond Press.

Bermant, C. and Weitzman, M. 1979: *Ebla: an Archaeological Enigma.* London: Weidenfeld and Nicolson.

Bertman, S. 1965: 'Symmetrical Design in the Book of Ruth'. *Journal of Biblical Literature*, 84, 165–8.

Beyerlin, W. 1965: *Origins and History of the Oldest Sinaitic Traditions.* Oxford: Basil Blackwell.

Beyerlin, W. 1978. *Near Eastern Religious Texts Relating to the Old Testament.* London: SCM.

Birkeland, H. 1938: *Zum hebräischen Traditionswesen: die Komposition der prophetischen Bücher des alten Testaments.* Avhandlinger utgitt av det Norske Videnskaps-Akademi i Oslo.

Blenkinsopp, J. 1984: *A History of Prophecy in Israel.* London: SPCK.

Boadt, L. 1984: *Reading the Old Testament: an Introduction.* New York and Mahwah, NJ: Paulist Press.

Bokser, B. M. 1984: *The Origins of the Seder: the Passover Rite and Early Rabbinic Judaism.* Berkeley, Calif.: University of California Press.

Bradshaw, P. F. 1981: *Daily Prayer in the Early Church.* London: SPCK.

Bright, J. 1981: *A History of Israel*, 3rd edn. London: SCM

Brueggemann, W. 1977: *The Land: Place as Gift, Promise, and Challenge in Biblical Faith.* London: SPCK.

Caird, G. B. 1980: *The Language and Imagery of the Bible.* London: Duckworth.

Callaway, J. A. 1985: 'Response'. In A. Biran (ed.), *Biblical Archaeology Today*, Jerusalem: Israel Exploration Society, 72–8.

Camp, C. V. 1985: *Wisdom and the Feminine in the Book of Proverbs.* Sheffield: Almond Press.

Cardenal, E. 1981: *Psalms.* London: Sheed and Ward.

Chaney, M. 1983: 'Ancient Palestinian Peasant Movements and the Formation of Premonarchic Israel'. In D. N. Freedman and D. F. Graf (eds), *Palestine in Transition: the Emergence of Ancient Israel*, Sheffield: Almond Press, 39–90.

Charlesworth, J. H. 1983: *The Old Testament Pseudepigrapha* London: Darton, Longman and Todd.

Childs, B. S. 1974: *The Book of Exodus: a Critical, Theological Commentary*, Old Testament Library. London: SCM.

Childs, B. S. 1979: *Introduction to the Old Testament as Scripture.* London: SCM.

Clements, R.E. 1975: *Prophecy and Tradition.* Oxford: Basil Blackwell.

Clines, D. J. A. 1982: *The Theme of the Pentateuch*, 2nd edn. Sheffield: JSOT Press.

Clines, D. J. A. 1984: *The Esther Scroll: the Story of a Story.* Sheffield: JSOT Press.

Coats, G. W. 1983: *Genesis with an Introduction to Narrative Literature: the Forms of Old Testament Literature*, vol. I. Grand Rapids, Mich: Eerdmans.

Coats, G. W. (ed.) 1985: *Saga, Legend, Tale, Novella, Fable: Narrative Forms in Old Testament Literature.* Sheffield: JSOT Press.

Coats, G. W. 1988: *Moses: Heroic Man, Man of God* (Sheffield: JSOT)

Coggins, R. J. 1987: *Haggai, Zechariah, Malachi,* Old Testament Guides. Sheffield: JSOT Press.

Coggins, R., Phillips, A. and Knibb, M. (eds) 1982: *Israel's Prophetic Tradition: Essays in Honour of Peter Ackroyd.* Cambridge: Cambridge University Press.

Cohn-Sherbok, D. 1988: *The Jewish Heritage.* Oxford: Basil Blackwell.

Collins, T. 1987: 'Decoding the Psalms: A Structuralist Approach to the Psalter'. *Journal for the Study of the Old Testament,* 37, 41–60.

Coote, R. B. and Whitelam, K. W. 1987: *The Emergence of Early Israel in Historical Perspective.* Sheffield: Almond Press.

Cragg, K. 1988: *Readings in the Qur'an.* London: Collins.

Crenshaw, J. L. 1981: *Old Testament Wisdom: an Introduction.* Atlanta: John Knox Press.

Crenshaw, J. L. 1988: *Ecclesiastes,* Old Testament Library. London: SCM.

Croft, S. L. 1987: *The Identity of the Individual in the Psalms.* Sheffield: JSOT Press.

Cross, F. M. 1973: 'The Themes of the Book of Kings and the Structure of the Deuteronomic History'. In *Canaanite Myth and Hebrew Epic.* Cambridge, Mass.: Harvard University Press, 247–89.

Davies, P. R. 1985: *Daniel,* Old Testament Guides. Sheffield: JSOT Press.

Dugmore, C. W. 1944: *The Influence of the Synagogue on the Daily Office.* London: Oxford University Press.

Eaton, J. H. 1967: *The Psalms,* Torch Commentaries. London: SCM.

Eaton, J. H. 1979: 'The Psalms in Israelite Worship'. In G. W. Anderson (ed.), *Tradition and Interpretation,* Oxford: Clarendon Press.

Eaton, J. H. 1985: *Job,* Old Testament Guides. Sheffield: JSOT Press.

Eaton, J. H. 1986: *Kingship and the Psalms,* 2nd edn. Sheffield: JSOT Press.

Eissfeldt, O. 1976: *The Old Testament: an Introduction,* rev. edn. Oxford: Basil Blackwell.

Eslinger, L. 1985: *Kingship of God in Crisis: a Close Reading of 1 Samuel 1–12.* Sheffield: Almond Press.

Falk, M. 1982: *Love Lyrics from the Bible: a Translation and Literary Study of the Song of Songs.* Sheffield: Almond Press.

Ferguson, D. S. 1987: *Biblical Hermeneutics: an Introduction.* London: SCM.

Fiensy, D. 1987: 'Using the Nuer Culture of Africa in Understanding the Old Testament: an Evaluation'. *Journal for the Study of the Old Testament.* 38, 73–83.

Finkelstein, I. 1988: *The Archaeology of the Israelite Settlement.* Jerusalem: Israel Exploration Society.

Finley, M. I. 1964–5: 'Myth, Memory and History'. *History and Theory,* 4, 281–301.

Fontaine, C. 1982: *Traditional Sayings in the Old Testament.* Sheffield: Almond Press.

Fortes, M. and Evans-Pritchard, E. E. 1940: *African Political Systems.* Oxford: Oxford University Press.

Fox, M. V. 1989: *Meanings and Values in Qohelet.* Sheffield: JSOT Press.

Goldingay, J. 1981: *Approaches to Old Testament Interpretation.* Leicester: IVP.

Gordis, R. 1968: *Koheleth: The Man and his World,* 3rd edn. New York: Schocken Books.

Gordis, R. 1974: *The Song of Songs and Lamentations: a Study, Modern Translation and Commentary,* 2nd edn. New York: Ktav.

Gordon, R. P. 1984: *1 and 2 Samuel,* Old Testament Guides. Sheffield: JSOT Press.

Gottwald, N. K. 1954: *Studies in the Book of Lamentations.* London: SCM.

Gottwald, N. K. 1979: *The Tribes of Yahweh: a Sociology of Liberated Israel, 1250–1050 BCE.* London: SCM.

Gottwald, N. K. 1985: *The Hebrew Bible: a Socio-Literary Introduction.* Philadelphia: Fortress Press.

Goulder, M. D. 1982: *The Psalms of the Sons of Korah.* Sheffield: JSOT Press.

Goulder, M. D. 1986: *The Song of Fourteen Songs.* Sheffield: JSOT Press.

Gowan, D. E. 1976: *The Bridge between the Testaments.* Edinburgh: T. & T. Clark.

Grant, R. M. 1984: *A Short History of the Interpretation of the Bible,* 2nd edn, rev. D. Tracy. London: SCM.

Gray, J. 1986: *Joshua, Judges, Ruth,* New Century Bible. Basingstoke: Marshalls.

Grossfeld, B. (ed.) 1973: *The Targums to the Five Megilloth.* New York: Ktav.

Gunkel, H. 1967: *The Psalms: a Form-Critical Introduction.* Philadelphia: Fortress Press.

Gunkel, H. 1987: *The Folktale in the Old Testament.* Sheffield: Almond Press.

Gunn, D. M. 1978: *The Story of King David.* Sheffield: JSOT Press.

Gunn, D. M. 1980: *The Fate of King Saul.* Sheffield: JSOT Press.

Gunn, D. M. 1982: 'The Hardening of Pharaoh's Heart: Plot, Character and Theology in Exodus 1–14'. In D. J. A. Clines, D. M. Gunn and A. J. Hauser (eds), *Art and Meaning: Rhetoric in Biblical Literature,* Sheffield: JSOT Press.

Habel, N. C. 1985: *The Book of Job: a Commentary,* Old Testament Library. London: SCM.

Hanson, P. D. 1979: *The Dawn of Apocalyptic: the Historical and Sociological Roots of Jewish Apocalyptic Eschatology,* 2nd edn. Philadelphia: Fortress Press.

Harrison, R. K. 1973: *Jeremiah and Lamentations.* Leicester: IVP.

Hayes, J. H. 1979: *An Introduction to Old Testament Study.* London: SCM.

Hayes, J. H. and Miller, J. M. 1977: *Israelite and Judaean History.* London: SCM.

Heaton, E. W. 1977: *The Old Testament Prophets,* 2nd edn. London: Darton, Longman and Todd.

Herrmann, S. 1973: *Israel in Egypt.* London: SCM.

Herrmann, S. 1975: *A History of Israel in Old Testament Times.* London: SCM.

Hillers, D. R. 1972: *Lamentations,* Anchor Bible. New York: Doubleday.

Hopkins, D. C. 1985: *The Highlands of Canaan: Agricultural Life in the Early Iron Age.* Sheffield: Almond Press.

Hornung, E. 1983: *Conceptions of God in Ancient Egypt: the One and the Many.* London: Routledge and Kegan Paul.

Huizinga, J. 1963: 'A Definition of the Concept of History'. In R. Klibansky and H. J. Paton (eds), *Philosophy and History,* New York: Peter Smith.

Irving, T. B., Ahmad, K. and Ahsan, M. M. (eds) 1979: *The Qur'an: Basic Teachings*. Leicester: Islamic Foundation.

Isbell, C. 1982: 'Exodus 1–2 in the Context of Exodus 1–14: Story Lines and Key Words'. In D. J. A. Clines, D. M. Gunn and A. J. Hauser (eds), *Art and Meaning: Rhetoric in Biblical Literature*, Sheffield: JSOT Press, 37–61.

Jeremias, J. 1969: *Jerusalem in the Time of Jesus*. London: SCM.

Johnson, A. R. 1951: 'The Psalms'. In H. H. Rowley (ed.), *The Old Testament and Modern Study*, Oxford: Clarendon Press.

Johnson, A. R. 1967: *Sacral Kingship in Ancient Israel*. Cardiff: University of Wales Press.

Johnson, A. R, 1979: *The Cultic Prophet and Israel's Psalmody*. Cardiff: University of Wales Press.

Johnson, B. 1985: 'Form and Message in Lamentations'. *Zeitschrift fur die alttestamentliche Wissenschaft*, 97, 58–73.

Jungmann, J. A. 1960: *The Early Liturgy to the Time of Gregory the Great* London: Darton, Longman and Todd.

Kaniel, M. 1979: *The Art of World Religions: Judaism*. Poole: Blandford Press.

Keel, O. 1978: *The Symbolism of the Biblical World*. London: SPCK.

Keller, W. 1980: *The Bible as History*, rev. J. Rehork. London: Hodder and Stoughton.

Kenyon, K. M. 1974: *Digging up Jerusalem*. London: Ernest Benn.

Kirkpatrick, P. G. 1988: *The Old Testament and Folklore Study*. Sheffield: JSOT Press.

Klein, L. R. 1988: *The Triumph of Irony in the Book of Judges*. Sheffield: Almond Press.

Knight, D. A. and Tucker, G. M. (eds) 1985: *The Hebrew Bible and its Modern Interpreters*. Philadelphia: Fortress Press; Chico, Calif.: Scholars' Press.

Koch, K. 1982–3: *The Prophets*. 2 vols. London: SCM.

Kort, W. A. 1988: *Story, Text and Scripture: Literatary Interests in Biblical Narratives*. University Park: Pennsyslvania State University Press.

Kugel, J. L. 1981: *The Idea of Biblical Poetry*. New Haven, Conn.: Yale University Press.

Lamb, J. A. 1962: *The Psalms in Christian Worship*. London: Faith Press.

Landy, F. 1983: *Paradoxes of Paradise: Identity and Difference in the Song of Songs*. Sheffield: Almond Press.

Lemche, N. P. 1985: *Early Israel: Anthropological and Historical Studies on the Israelite Society before the Monarchy*. Leiden: E. J. Brill.

Lemche, N. P. 1988: *Ancient Israel: a New History of Israelite Society*. Sheffield: JSOT Press.

Lewis, C. S. 1958: *Reflections on the Psalms*. London: Geoffrey Bles.

Licht, J. 1978: *Storytelling in the Bible*. Jerusalem: Magnes Press.

Luce, J. V. 1969: *The End of Atlantis*. London: Thames and Hudson.

McCarthy, D. J. 1963: *Treaty and Covenant: a Study in Form in the Ancient Oriental Documents and the Old Testament*. Analecta Biblica 21.

McCarthy, D. J. 1972: *Old Testament Covenant: a Survey of Current Opinions*.

Oxford: Basil Blackwell.

McFague, S. 1982: *Metaphorical Theology: Models of God in Religious Language*. London: SCM.

McKane, W. 1965: *Prophets and Wise Men*. Studies in Biblical Theology. London: SCM.

Magonet, J. 1980: 'The Liberal and the Lady: Esther Revisited'. *Judaism*, 29, 167–76.

Magonet, J. 1982: 'Some Concentric Structures in Psalms'. *Heythrop Journal*, 23, 363–76.

Malamat, A. 1973: 'Tribal Societies: Biblical Genealogies and African Lineage Systems'. *Archives Européennes de Sociologie*, 14, 126–36.

Mayes, A. D. H. 1985: *Judges*, Old Testament Guides. Sheffield: JSOT Press.

Mellor, E. B. 1972: *The Making of the Old Testament*. Cambridge: Cambridge University Press.

Mendenhall, G. E. 1954: 'Covenant Forms in Israelite Tradition'. *Biblical Archaeologist*, 17, 50–76.

Mendenhall, G. E. 1962: 'The Hebrew Conquest of Palestine'. *Biblical Archaeologist*, 25, 66–87.

Miller, J. M. and Hayes, J. H. 1986: *A History of Ancient Israel and Judah*. London: SCM.

Miscall, P. D. 1983: *The Workings of Old Testament Narrative*. Philadelphia: Fortress Press; Chico, Calif.: Scholars' Press.

Montefiore, C. G. and Loewe, H. 1974: *A Rabbinic Anthology*. New York: Schocken Books.

Moore, C. A. 1971: *Esther*, Anchor Bible. New York: Doubleday.

Moore, C. A. 1982: *Studies in the Book of Esther*. New York: Ktav.

Musaph-Andriesse, R. C. 1981: *From Torah to Kabbalah: a Basic Introduction to the Writings of Judaism*. London: SCM.

Nelson, R. D. 1981: *The Double Redaction of the Deuteronomic History*. Sheffield: JSOT Press.

Neusner, J. 1984: *Judaism in the Beginning of Christianity*. London: SPCK.

Neusner, J. 1987: *What is Midrash?* Philadelphia: Fortress Press.

Nicholson, E. W. 1967: *Deuteronomy and Tradition*. Oxford: Basil Blackwell.

Nicholson, E. W. 1973: *Exodus and Sinai in History and Tradition*. Oxford: Basil Blackwell.

Nicholson, E. W. 1986: *God and his People. Covenant and Theology in the Old Testament*. Oxford: Clarendon Press.

Nickelsburg, G. W. 1981: *Jewish Literature between the Bible and the Mishnah*. London: SCM.

Nickelsburg, G. W. and Stone, M. E. 1983: *Faith and Piety in Early Judaism*, Philadelphia: Westminster Press.

Nineham, D. 1976: *The Use and Abuse of the Bible: a Study of the Bible in an Age of Rapid Cultural Change*. London: Macmillan.

Nohrnberg, J. 1981: 'Moses'. In B. O. Long (ed.), *Images of Man and God: Old Testament Short Stories in Literary Focus*. Sheffield: Almond Press.

Noth, M. 1930: *Das System der zwölf Stämme Israels*. Stuttgart: Kohlhammer.

Noth, M. 1960: *The History of Israel*. London: A. & C. Black.

Noth, M. 1981: *The Deuteronomic History*. Sheffield: JSOT Press.
Noth, M. 1987: *The Chronicler's History*. Sheffield: JSOT Press.
Nyberg, H. S. 1935: *Studien zum Hoseabuch*. Uppsala Universitets Årsskrift.
O'Brien, J. and Major, W. 1982: *In the Beginning: Creation Myths from Ancient Mesopotamia, Israel and Greece*. Chico, Calif.: Scholars' Press.
Ogden, G. 1987: *Qoheleth*. Sheffield: JSOT Press.
Otto, R. 1917: *The Idea of the Holy*. Harmondsworth: Penguin.
Paton, A. 1908: *Esther*. International Critical Commentary. Edinburgh: T. & T. Clark.
Paul, S. M. 1970: *Studies in the Book of the Covenant in the Light of Cuneiform and Biblical Law*. Supplements to *Vetus Testamentum* 18.
Petersen D. L. (ed.) 1987: *Prophecy in Israel*. London: SPCK.
Phillips, A. 1970: *Ancient Israel's Criminal Law: a New Approach to the Decalogue*. Oxford: Basil Blackwell.
Polzin, R. 1980 *Moses and the Deuteronomist: a Literary Study of the Deuteronomic History*, pt 1. New York: Seabury Press.
Pope, M. H. 1976: *The Song of Songs*, Anchor Bible. New York: Doubleday.
Posner, R., Kaploun, U. and Cohen, S. 1975: *Jewish Liturgy*. Jerusalem: Keter.
Prag, K. 1988: *Jerusalem*, Blue Guide. London: A. & C. Black.
Rad, G. von 1953: *Studies in Deuteronomy*. London: SCM.
Ramsey, G. W. 1981: *The Quest for the Historical Israel: Reconstructing Israel's Early History*. London: SCM.
Ramsey, I. 1957: *Religious Language: an Empirical Placing of Theological Phrases*. London: SCM.
Robertson, D. 1977: *The Old Testament and the Literary Critic*. Philadelphia: Fortress Press.
Rogerson, J. W. (ed.) 1983: *Beginning Old Testament Study*. London: SPCK.
Rogerson, J. W. 1986: 'Was Early Israel a Segmentary Society?' *Journal for the Study of the Old Testament*, 36, 17–26.
Rogerson, J. W. and Mackay, J. W. 1977: *Psalms 1–50; Psalms 51–100; Psalms 101–150*. Cambridge: Cambridge University Press.
Rowley, H. H. 1952: 'The Interpretation of the Song of Songs'. In *The Servant of the Lord and Other Essays*, Oxford: Basil Blackwell.
Rowley, H. H. 1976: *Worship in Ancient Israel: its Forms and Meaning*, rev. edn. London: SPCK.
Russell, L. M. (ed.) 1976: *The Liberating Word: a Guide to Non-Sexist Interpretation of the Bible*. Philadelphia: Westminster Press.
Russell, L. M. (ed.) 1985: *Feminist Interpretation of the Bible*. Philadelphia: Westminster Press.
Salibi, K. 1985: *The Bible Came from Arabia*. London: Jonathan Cape.
Sandars, N. K. (tr.) 1972: *The Epic of Gilgamesh*. Harmondsworth; Penguin.
Sasson, M. 1979: *Ruth*. Baltimore: John Hopkins University Press.
Sawyer, J. F. A. 1987: *Prophecy and the Prophets of the Old Testament*. Oxford: Oxford University Press.
Schimmel, A. and Fallaturi, A. D. (eds.) 1979: *We Believe in One God: the Experience of God in Christianity and Islam*. London: Burns and Oates.
Schmidt, W. H. 1983: *The Faith of the Old Testament*. Oxford: Basil Blackwell.

Segal, M. H. 1962: 'The Song of Songs'. *Vetus Testamentum*, 12, 470–90.

Seltzer, R. M. 1980: *Jewish People, Jewish Thought: the Jewish Experience in History.* London: Macmillan.

Seters, J. van 1975: *Abraham in History and Tradition.* New Haven, Conn.: Yale University Press.

Seters, J. van 1983: *In Search of History.* New Haven, Conn.: Yale University Press.

Simpson, W. W. 1965: *Jewish Prayer and Worship.* London: SCM.

Singer, S. 1890: *The Authorised Daily Prayer Book.* London: Eyre and Spottiswoode.

Smith, M. 1987: *Palestinian Parties and Politics that Shaped the Old Testament,* 2nd edn. London: SCM.

Soskice, J. M. 1985: *Metaphor and Religious Language.* Oxford: Clarendon Press.

Sternberg, M. 1978: *Expositional Modes and Temporal Ordering in Fiction.* Baltimore: Johns Hopkins University Press.

Sternberg, M. 1985: *The Poetics of Biblical Narrative: Ideological Literature and the Drama of Reading.* Bloomington: Indiana University Press.

Stone, M. E. 1982: *Scriptures, Sects and Visions.* Oxford: Basil Blackwell.

Thompson, T. L. 1974: *The Historicity of the Patriarchal Narratives: the Quest for the Historical Abraham.* Berlin and New York: Walter de Gruyter.

Thompson, T. L. 1987: *The Origin Tradition of Ancient Israel,* vol. I: *The Literary Formation of Genesis-Exodus 1–23.* Sheffield: JSOT Press.

Trible, P. 1973: 'Depatriarchalizing in Biblical Interpretation'. *Journal of the American Academy of Religion,* 41, 30–48.

Unterman, A. 1981: *Jews: their Religious Beliefs and Practices.* London: Routledge and Kegan Paul.

Vater, A. M. 1982: 'A Plague on Both our Houses: Form- and Rhetorical-Critical Observations on Exodus 7–11', in D. J. A. Clines, D. M. Gunn and A. J. Hauser (eds), *Art and Meaning: Rhetoric in Biblical Literature,* Sheffield: JSOT Press.

Vermes, G. 1987: *The Dead Sea Scrolls in English,* 3rd edn. Harmondsworth: Penguin.

Watson, W. G. E. 1984: *Classical Hebrew Poetry.* Sheffield: JSOT Press.

Watts, I. 1719: *The Psalms of David Imitated.* London: J. Clark.

Webb, B. G. 1987: *The Book of Judges: an Integrated Reading.* Sheffield: JSOT Press.

Weippert, M. 1971: *The Settlement of the Israelite Tribes in Palestine: a Critical Survey of Recent Scholarly Debate.* London: SCM.

Westermann, C. 1984: *Genesis 1–11.* London: SPCK.

Whybray, R. N. 1965: *Wisdom in Proverbs: the Concept of Wisdom in Proverbs 1–9,* Studies in Biblical Theology. London: SCM.

Whybray, R. N. 1983: *The Second Isaiah,* Old Testament Guides. Sheffield: JSOT Press.

Whybray, R. N. 1987: *The Making of the Pentateuch,* Sheffield: JSOT Press.

Wilkinson, J. 1978: *The Jerusalem Jesus Knew.* London: Thames and Hudson.

Williams, J. G. 1981: *Those Who Ponder Proverbs: Aphoristic Thinking and Biblical Literature,* Bible Literature Series. Sheffield: Almond Press.

Williams, J. G. 1982: *Women Recounted: Narrative Thinking and the God of Israel*, Bible and Literature Series. Sheffield: Almond Press.

Williamson, H. G. M. 1977: *Israel in the Books of Chronicles*. Cambridge: Cambridge University Press.

Williamson, H. G. M. 1987: *Ezra and Nehemiah*. Old Testament Guides. Sheffield: JSOT Press.

Wilson, R. R. 1977: *Genealogy and History in the Biblical World*. New Haven, Conn: Yale University Press.

Wolff, H. W. 1975; 'The Kerygma of the Deuteronomistic Historical Work'. In W. Brueggemann and H. W. Wolff (eds), *The Vitality of Old Testament Traditions*. Atlanta: John Knox Press, 83–100.

Würthwein, E. 1980: *The Text of the Old Testament*. London: SCM.

Index

Page references in bold type denote key discussions on the subject.

ablutions, 60–1
Abraham, 45–6, 55, 57, **87–8,**
    91–171, 335–6
acrostic, **262,** 305–6
Adam, 45
adultery, 67
aetiology, **84, 86, 88**
aggadah, 147–8
Ahijah, **190–1**
Alexander the Great, 19, **230,**
    321–2, 325
Allah, 43
allegory, 39, **70,** 145–6
alphabet, 11
Amalek, 128
Amidah (prayer), 251
Ammonites, 105
Amoraim, **147**
Amos, 207–8, **211–12,** 218–19
amphicyonic hypothesis, 161, **165–7**
analogy, **69–70**
anamnesis, **64**
Anath, Canaanite goddess, 248
aniconic, **52–3**
anthropomorphism, **73–4**
Antiochus IV Epiphanes, **19–20,** 62,
    202, 231, 314, 323
apocalypse, -ptic, 244, 324, **331,**
    334
Apocrypha, 23, 30, 320–1, **324–30**
Aquila, 28

Arabah, 6
Aramaic, **25,** 202
archaeology, **8–12,** 92–4
Aristeas, letter of, 24, **27,** 321, 329
Ark
    Holy, 33, 56
    of the Covenant, **54–5,** 78,
        172–3, 178. *See also* temple
art, Hebrew, **55–6**
Atonement, Day of, 64, 385

Baal, 132, 176, **193–4,** 198
Babel, Tower of, **113**
Balaam, 67, **132**
Bible, unity of, **38–9**
blessings, **66–7**
buildings, **9–10**
bull, ceremonial, 52, 175, 191. *See
    also* golden calf

Canaan, 5
canon, **29–30**
census, 235
charismatic, **189**
cherubim, **54,** 56, 178
chiastic, 199, **305–6,** 308
Christianity, **37–43,** 182, 252–4,
    324
Chronicler, **234–7**
circumcision, **62,** 136–7
climate, **7–8**

codex, 24
conquest, **162–3**
covenant, xiii, 12, 57, 62–3, 87,
  113, 117, 124–5, 130, **135–8,**
  117, 190, 260, 333
covenant, book of the **139–40**
creation, 41–2, 49, 56, 72, 107,
  111–12, 114, 333–4
cuneiform, 11
curses, **66**
Cyrus, **229–30,** 237

Daniel, 25, **201–2**
David, 15, 46, **170–3,** 189–90,
  302–3
day of Yahweh, **222–4**
Dead Sea, 6
Dead Sea Scrolls, xv, 12, 23, 25–6,
  30, 235, **340–4**
death, **277–80**
Deborah, Song of, 25
Decalogue (ten commandments) 42,
  52, 55, 63, 129, **138–9**
demons, **331–2,** 336
deutero-canonical, **30,** 324
Deuteronomic history, **155–9,** 174,
  176, 185–7
Deuteronomy, **141,** 185, 258
Diadochi, **230,** 322
Diaspora (Dispersion), 180, 233,
  246–8, 311, 314, 320–1
documentary hypothesis, **97**
dualism, 311

Ecclesiastes, 30, 48, **277–80,** 297,
  308–11
Ecclesiasticus, 30, 309, 322,
  327–30
ecology, 106 (see also creation)
Egypt, 11, 16–18, 248
Elephantine, 180, **248,** 321
Elijah, 47, 176, **193–6**
Elisha, 47, **196–8**
Elohist, **83**
English versions, 29
Enoch, **331–5**

ephod, **52–3,** 173
eponym, **88–9,** 104–5,
eschatology, **243–4,** 267, 316
Essenes, 337, **340–1**
Esther, 30, 48, **311–16**
ethics, **35–6, 42–3,** 273–6, 280
euphemism, 69
exegesis, **xv**
exile 18–19, 180, **236–7**
exodus, 14, **124–8**
eye for an eye, **143–4**
Ezekiel, 30
Ezra, 232–3, **237–42,** 247

fables, 74, 86
festivals, 63–4
figures of speech, 68–70
flood, **112–13**
food, 62
form criticism, xvi, 84 **94–6**
Former Prophets, **210**

Gad, **189–90**
Gemara, 32, **147–8**
genealogies, 235
Genesis 14, **94–102, 107–10,**
  170–1, 343
genre, **85–6**
geography of Palestine **5–7**
Gilgamesh, 112
God, 39, 69, **77–9, 286–8**
golden calf, 55, **130–1,** 175

Hagar, 46
Haggai, 207, 221, **231–2,** 245
halakah, **32–3,** 147, 335
Hammurabi, Code of, 12
Hanukkah, 54, **64**
Hasidim, 341
Hasmoneans, **323**
Hebrew (language), 24
Hellenism, **19–20,** 322
hermeneutics, **39**
Herod the Great, 324
Hexateuch, **85**
Hillel, **146,** 321, 338

Holiness Code, 141
Hosea, 207, 216
Huldah, prophetess, 186, **200–1**
hypotheses, xiv, 21, **90–8**, 162–8

iconography, 52–3
idolatry, 52, 57, 65
images, **52–3**
inter–testamental, 319–20
irony, 68
Isaac, 45, 88, 171
Isaiah, **211–13, 219–20**
   'Second Isaiah', 209–10, 215, **224**
   'Third Isaiah', **224–5,** 232
Ishmael, 45
Islam, **43–7,** 182–3
Israel, 5

Jacob, 57, **89–90,** 335
Jamnia (Jabneh), **29,** 295, 308, 324
Jebusites, 170–1
Jehu, 192
Jeremiah, 208
Jeroboam, 191
Jerusalem, 15–20, 66, **169–83,**
   245–6, 260, 264–5, 303–4,
   321, 324
Jethro, 129
Job, 47, 8, **280–9**
Joel, 207
Jonah, 47, **198–200**
Joseph, **89–90**
Josephus, 29, 321, 324
Joshua, book of, 64, **151–3**
Josiah, 17–18, 65, 126, **141,**
   200–1, 236, 303–5
jubilee, **303,** 335
Jubilees, book of, 335–6
Judah, 89
Judaism, **31–6,** 181, 251–2, 293,
   324, 330, 335, 337, 344
Judges, 151, **153–4**
Jehu, 192

Ka'bah (Mecca), 45–6, 183
Kabbalah, 148
Kethib, 26

Kethubim, 23, 31
kingship, 174–7

Lamentations, **303–8**
land, 3–5, **64–6,** 154
language, religious, **66–77**
Latter Prophets, **203–6**
law, 40–1, **138–48**
   ancient Near Eastern, 144
   compensation, 143
   rabbinic, 145–8
legend, 86
leprosy, 61
Levites, **178–9**
literary criticism, **102–3**
lost tribes, 246–7
Lot, 45, 105

Maccabees, 20, **323,** 341
Malachi, 207
man of God, **191–2**
manuscripts, 26
Marcion, 37
Masada, 324
Masoretes, **26**
Mecca, see Ka'bah
Megilloth, Five, 34, **293–317**
Melchizedek, 171
menorah, **54,** 56
Messiah, **39–40,** 48–9, 71, 236,
   244, 252
metaphor, **69**
mezuzah, **55**
Micah, 216
Micaiah, **192–3,** 219–20
midrash, xv, 32
mimesis, 103–4
Miriam, 127–8, 131
Mishnah, 31, 32, **146–7**
Moabites, 105
models, **70–5**
monolatry, 77
Mormon, book of 246
Moses, 13–14, 46, **117–34**
Muhammad, 43, 46
Murashu documents, **247**
myth, **75–7,** 86, **110–16**

Nahum, 262
Nahushtan, 52
names, 56
Nathan, 190
Nebi'im, 23, 31
Nehemiah, 238–42, 247
Noah, 45, 335
novella, 85

offerings, 59, 207–8
Old Testament, xiii
Omri, house of, 16–17
oral Torah, 31, 146, 337, 339
oral tradition, 94–6
Origen, 28
Orthodox Judaism, 31

Palestine, 5, 322
papyrus, 12
parable, 68–9
paradox, 74
parchment, 12
Passover, 48, 56–7, 63, 119, 124–7,
    179, 293
pastiche, 70
patriarchs, 13, 87–90
Paul, 339
Pentateuch, 23.
    sources, 96–8
personification, 74
Pesach, *see* Passover
Pharisees, 336–40
Philo, 29, 70
poetry, 261–4
pointing, 26
polytheism, 78
prayer, *see* Amidah, Shema
Priestly Writer, 83, 114, 140–1
priests, 178–9
printed texts, 26–7
procession, 63
Progressive Judaism, 31
promise, 83–116, 117
prophecy, 42,
prophets, 185–202, 203–26, 242–3
    Latter Prophets, 203–6
    major and minor, 205–6

Muslim, 45–7
Proverbs, 30, 273–7
Psalms, 37, 251–67
    dates of psalms, 256–8
    Hallel psalms, 251
    imagery, 263–4
    psalm titles, 255–6
    royal psalms, 176, 257, 259–60
Pseudepigrapha, 30, 320, 330–6
Ptolemies, 19–20, 230, 231
purification, 60–2
purity, religious, 206–10
Purim, 64, 293, 312, 314–15

qere', 26
Qoheleth, *see* Ecclesiastes
Qumran, 12, 320, 330–2, 336
Qur'an, 43–7

rabbinic teaching, 34–6, 135, 336
redaction criticism, xv, 98
redactor, xv
red heifer, 61
remnant, 220–4
restoration, 224–5, 237
revelation, 31
rhetorical criticism, 103–4
roads, 4, 7
Romans, 323–4
roots (verbal), 24–5
Rosh Hashanah, 55
Ruth, 30, 48–9, 298–303

Sabbath, 146, 293
sacrifices, 56–60
Sadducees, 337
saga, 85
salvation history, 113–16
Samaria, fall of, 17
Samaritan Pentateuch, 27
Samaritans, 235
Samuel, 187–9
Sanhedrin, 146–7, 339
Saul, 15, 173–4, 187–9
scripts, 10–11
scrolls, 24, 37, 53
Sea of Reeds, 14, 121, 127–8

segmentary society model, 167–8
Seleucids, 19–20, **231**
semitic, 24
Septuagint (LXX), 19, **27–8,** 254,
    324
settlement, 14–15, **159–65**
    conquest model, **162–3**
    indiginous development model,
        164–5
    infiltration model, **160–2**
    peasant revolt model, **163–4**
Shammai, 338
Shavuoth, **48,** 293
Shema, **55,** 251
Shemaiah, 191
Sheol (underworld), 264, 267
Shephelah, 5, 6
Shiloh, 172–3
shophar (ram's horn), **55,** 56
Simchat Torah, 33
simile, **69–70**
Sinai, **129–30**
Sitz im Leben, 96
social justice, **214–17**
Solomon, 15–16, 46–7, 174
Song of Songs, 30, 48–9, 70–1,
    294–8
Son of Man, 333
sons of God, 71, **112–13,** 331–2
source criticism, **96–102**
spirit (*ruah*), 67–8
stele (*stela*), 11–12
story, **102–10**
suffering, 280–1
Sukkoth, 64, 293
symbol, xv, **51–80**
Symmachus, 28
synagogue, 37, **53–6,** 251–2, 320,
    337–8, 340–1
Syriac, **28–9**

tallith, 55
Talmud, **31–2,** 148.
Tannaim, 145–7
Targums, **28,** 321
Tell, **8–9**
temple, **173–80,** 190, 230, 232–4,

244–5, 251, 264, 266, 304,
    312, 320, 323, 332–3, 341,
    343–4.
Temple Scroll, 335
Tenakh, 4, **23**
tephillin (phylacteries), **55**
teraphim, 52
text, xiv–xv
Tetrateuch, **85**
theocracy, **243**
Theodotion, 28
theophoric, 119
Thummim, 53
tithes, 59
Torah, 23, 31–4, **83–6**
tradition criticism, **84**
transcendence, 75
tsitsith (tassles), **55**
type scene, **107,** 300
typology, **38,** 42, 70, 145

Ugarit, 9, 11, 12, 177
Urim, 53

values, 42–3
Vulgate, **29,** 324
water supply, 10
wilderness wanderings, **131–2**
wisdom, **269–91,** 325–9
    books, **272–3**
Wisdom of Solomon, **325–7**
writing (ancient), **10–12**
written documents, 11–12

Yahweh (YHWH), xvi, 26, **78–9,**
    123, 312
Yahwist, **78, 83**
Yom Kippur (Day of Atonement),
    34, 55, **58,** 60, 64

Zadok, 178
Zealots, 337
Zechariah, 209, 214–15, 231–2,
    245
Zerubbabel, 231–2
ziggurat, 122
Zion, 181